HQ 536 .M568 1994
More than kissing babies
194119

DATE DUE

MORE THAN KISSING BABIES?

MORE THAN KISSING BABIES?

Current Child and Family Policy in the United States

Edited by
Francine H. Jacobs and
Margery W. Davies

AUBURN HOUSE
Westport, Connecticut • London

Lines from "On the Pulse of Morning" by Maya Angelou. Copyright © 1993 by Maya Angelou. Reprinted by permission of Random House, Inc. and Virago Press.

Grace Abbott quote from Edith H. Grotberg, ed. (1977). *200 Years of Children.* Washington, D.C.: U.S. Department of Health, Education, and Welfare.

Library of Congress Cataloging-in-Publication Data

More than kissing babies? : Current child and family policy in the United
    States / edited by Francine H. Jacobs and Margery W. Davies.
        p. cm.
    Includes index.
    ISBN 0–86569–223–8 (alk. paper).—ISBN 0–86569–224–6 (pbk. :
alk. paper)
        1. Family policy—United States. 2. Child welfare—Government
policy—United States. 3. United States—Social policy—1993– .
I. Jacobs, Francine Helene. II. Davies, Margery W.
HQ536.C876 1994
362.82′0973—dc20   93–37492

British Library Cataloguing in Publication Data is available.

Library of Congress Catalog Card Number: 93–37492
ISBN: 0–86569–223–8 (hc)
      0–86569–224–6 (pbk)

First published in 1994

Auburn House, 88 Post Road West, Westport, CT 06881
An imprint of Greenwood Publishing Group, Inc.

Printed in the United States of America

The paper used in this book complies with the
Permanent Paper Standard issued by the National
Information Standards Organization (Z39.48–1984).

10 9 8 7 6 5 4 3 2 1

This book is dedicated to our families:

Barry Dym
Jessica and Gabriel Dym
Miriam and Albert Jacobs
Rhoda Kirsch

and

Arthur MacEwan
Karla Greenleaf-MacEwan
Anna, Peter, and Julia MacEwan
Philip W. and Ruth C. Davies
Mary G. MacEwan

Sometimes when I get home at night in Washington I feel as though I had been in a great traffic jam. The jam is moving toward the Hill where Congress sits in judgment on all the administrative agencies of the Government. In that traffic jam there are all kinds of vehicles moving up toward the Capitol. . . . There are all kinds of conveyances that the Army can put into the street—tanks, gun carriers, trucks. . . . There are the hayricks and the binders and the ploughs and all the other things that the Department of Agriculture manages to put into the streets. . . . the handsome limousines in which the Department of Commerce rides. . . . the barouches in which the Department of State rides in such dignity. It seems so to me as I stand on the sidewalk watching it become more congested and more difficult, and then because the responsibility is mine and I must, I take a very firm hold on the handles of the baby carriage and I wheel it into the traffic.

> Grace Abbott
> Chief, United States Children's Bureau
> 1921–1934

> Women, children, men,
> Take it into the palms of your hands,
> Mold it into the shape of your most
> Private need. Sculpt it into
> The image of your most public self.
> Lift up your hearts
> Each new hour holds new chances
> For a new beginning.
> Do not be wedded forever
> To fear, yoked eternally
> To brutishness.

> Maya Angelou
> from "On the Pulse of Morning"
> 1993

Contents

Acknowledgments

This volume results from the efforts and encouragement of many individuals, only some of whom appear here as authors. The idea for an edited casebook arose in the rather bleak days (for child and family policy advocates) of the mid- to late-1980s, during meetings of the newly-established Social Policy Interest Group in the Eliot-Pearson Department of Child Study at Tufts University. It was nurtured along by Social Policy Interest Group members, and by our other colleagues at Eliot-Pearson. We would particularly like to thank Donald Wertlieb who, as department Chair at Eliot-Pearson during most of this work, extended himself in every way—providing helpful feedback on substantive issues, administrative support to produce the manuscript, and a steady belief in its value. The late President Jean Mayer of Tufts shared this commitment to the project, a commitment that, in a small way, reflected his tireless dedication to the world's children.

More than a hundred experts were interviewed by chapter authors, providing countless hours and invaluable insights to the studies in this volume. The authors and editors gratefully acknowledge their contributions, without which this book could not have been produced.

At the casebook's mid-phase, Nancy Thomas, Editor of the Society for Research in Child Development's *Social Policy Report*, gave us an unexpected and much appreciated boost with her invitation to submit an article on this topic to the *Social Policy Report*. Barry Zuckerman, Professor and Chair of the Department of Pediatrics at the Boston University School of Medicine and Boston City Hospital, and Gerald Gill, Associate Professor of History at Tufts, generously reviewed and critiqued drafts of several chapters. Leanne Barrett, Anne Brady, Martha Crowe, Jessica Dym, and Kim Westheimer, graduate students in Child Study or Urban and Environmental Policy at Tufts, improved the manuscript considerably with their careful research and editing; Kristen Cota meticulously prepared the final document for publication.

Special acknowledgments are due to William Harris, the founder and treasurer of KIDSPAC, whose nifty turn of phrase ("not just kissing babies") inspired the title for our book, and Ann Rosewater, formerly the staff director of the Congressional Select Committee on Children, Youth, and Families, and currently Deputy Assistant Secretary of Policy and External Affairs, U.S. Department of Health and Human Services, for her enthusiasm for this project in its early stages. We also gratefully acknowledge the Graduate School and the College of Liberal Arts and Jackson at Tufts, and the Bergstrom Fund for Innovative Programs in Child Study, for supporting a portion of this research.

   As one might expect, our families have had a large hand in bringing this book—about families—to completion. My (Fran's) husband, Barry Dym, played every role imaginable: He was a receptive sounding board for ideas and worries, a gentle critic and editor, an astute problem-solver, and a constant source of support and good humor. Jessica and Gabriel Dym (our children), Miriam and Albert Jacobs (my parents), Marcia Jacobs and Steven Jacobs (my sister and brother), and Rhoda Kirsch (my mother-in-law) closely and sympathetically followed the progress of this work.

   My (Margery's) family has been a limitless source of support. My husband, Arthur MacEwan, has simply always been there, intellectually and emotionally, for me and our children. I could not have worked on this book without him. Our children, Karla, Anna, Peter, and Julia, have encouraged me from beginning to end. My parents, Philip and Ruth Davies, and my mother-in-law, Mary MacEwan, have cheered me on, for which I am grateful. I also appreciate the support I have received from all of my colleagues in the Community Health Program at Tufts.

   Just as our families have supported our work on this book, they have also helped to inspire our passionate interest in the welfare of all children and families. We hope that this book will encourage, in some small way, investment in "other people's children."

MORE THAN KISSING BABIES?

Introduction

Francine H. Jacobs and Margery W. Davies

Washington, D.C. had barely cleaned up from the inaugural hoopla when President Clinton stood in the White House Rose Garden, in early February, 1993, and proudly signed into law the Family and Medical Leave Act (FMLA), vetoed twice by former President Bush.[1] One could interpret this event in a number of ways. It could be the first bold step in a new era for governmental policies toward children and families in the United States—the signal that at long last the federal government is going to move beyond rhetoric and establish a strong network of programs and policies designed to support all children and families. Or it could be an acknowledgment of failure: calculating that the passage of stronger legislation granting families more weeks of leave, covering more workers, or even mandating paid leave was a political impossibility, Clinton and FMLA supporters settled for a law that was much weaker than the one initially proposed years earlier. Or it could be political opportunism pure and simple: rather than investing time and effort to forge a stronger, more comprehensive law, Clinton expediently used the enactment of this compromised legislation as a pulpit from which to announce the end of gridlock in Washington.

Is the Family and Medical Leave Act, then, a limited success or a limited failure? Is it "the doughnut or the hole"?[2] In a broader context, are we truly making progress towards comprehensive policies for children and families, or, to paraphrase folksingers of the 1960s, have we simply been down so long, "it looks like up to us"?

We are going to press at a fascinating moment in the development of policies for children and families in the United States. The federal government appears more interested in the well-being of children and families than it has been for over a decade. States and municipalities have diversified and strengthened their portfolios of public investments in children. In areas such as child care, education reform, and health care, public-private partnerships between corporate and governmental entities have formed and flourished. Political partisanship on children's issues has faded somewhat, as people across the political spectrum talk of increasing public and personal responsibility for children. Yet those of us who have observed society's treatment of children and families over decades wonder whether we have truly entered the dawn of a new day. Is this more than kissing babies? And if it is, will we move past superficial gestures to deeper expressions of public affection for children?

This book is meant to orient a broad audience to basic issues of child and family policy in the United States today. It includes an overview of the recent history of child and family policy in the United States, an exploration of several political economic conditions underlying changes in these policies, case studies of selected local, state, and federal policies, an analysis of key themes that emerge from the cases, and some predictions about the future course of child and family policy. We draw from disparate fields—developmental psychology, political science, social history, early childhood education, and public policy—to arrive at a common language for discussing children and families, and an integrated framework for analyzing policies to promote their well-being.[3]

We have chosen a case study approach to illustrate themes in child and family policy. Bonoma and Wong define the case study as "a description of a situation using interview, archival, naturalistic observation, and other data, constructed to be sensitive to the context in which the process takes place and to its temporal constraints."[4] Case study research is recommended in situations where the general phenomenon being studied is broad and complex, when studying it out of context will not yield valid data, when the researcher cannot manipulate the events under investigation, and when the research questions are of the "how and why" variety.[5] According to Cheryl Hayes, editor of a classic volume on the federal policy-making process, the case method is ideal for "testing and modifying existing models and developing new hypotheses concerning the policy process."[6] Telling "policy stories" has enabled us to discern patterns in successful and unsuccessful policies, clarify assumptions and values that underlie programs and policies, and develop criteria to evaluate them.[7]

Social policies comprise a distinct subset of public policy, which is the sum of governmental actions, or intended activities, taken on the state's behalf.[8] Social policies directly address the needs of individuals and groups in society; they are statements of social purpose meant to improve the quality of life of particular people, or of society as a whole. There are numerous mechanisms available to accomplish these goals: Some, for example, provide immediate or long-term material relief and support; others redistribute wealth or rebalance access and opportunity. Still others work to strengthen intergroup relations.[9]

Social policies reflect dominant cultural values. In the United States their primary purpose appears to be the promotion of individual responsibility and the prevention of public dependency. They have generally, though not always, been reserved for those individuals who have failed at the job of providing for themselves.[10] Therefore, American social welfare policy is primarily public charity. It is distributive rather than redistributive, having as its foremost goal improving the very worst conditions of the very few, rather than, for example, reducing structural inequities. The limits of such benevolence are clear.[11] Gifts of charity are voluntary; they can be withheld as well as bestowed. Philanthropic social policy maintains social stratification, clearly distinguishing between the givers and the takers, the powerful and powerless, "them and us."[12]

In the broadest sense, child and family policies are any actions or "strategic statements,"[13] taken by public (that is, extrafamilial and formal) entities, to promote the well-being of children and families.[14] The term is generally used, however, to denote *governmental* activities designed to change the circumstances, composition, or behavior either of family units, or of particular family members.[15] These are *explicit* family policies, according to Kamerman and Kahn; they "do things to and for the family" to achieve family-oriented goals.[16] There are also *implicit* family policies—those "not specifically or primarily addressed to the family, but which have indirect consequences [for it]."[17] While generally analysts in the field concentrate on the former genre, as do we in this volume, the Family Impact Seminar[18] has generated a set of family criteria to apply to any public policies or policy proposals.

AN OUTLINE OF THE VOLUME

There are many potentially useful frameworks available from which to draw themes, and, thus, to make sense of the policy stories in this volume. For example, one could identify patterns across the cases according to their stages in the policy process,[19] their substantive areas, the levels of government at which the policy activity takes place,[20] or the political cultures of the particular city or state.[21] In fact, we have compiled a varied set of cases to facilitate just these analyses: there are a couple each at the local, state, and federal levels of government; a few focus on the policy development stage, while the others focus on policy implementation and evaluation. Each draws a distinctive picture of the political culture that spawned the policy under discussion.

The primary analytic framework of the book, however, is a set of five characteristics, or dimensions, of child and family policy that have particular resonance for these issues at this time.[22] They can be expressed as questions: (1) Are policies child-centered or family-centered? (2) Do they provide families economic support or support for caregiving and nurturance? (3) Are they targeted or universal? (4) Do they promote treatment strategies or preventive strategies? (5) Do they suggest a preference for private solutions to family concerns or more public approaches? The authors tell their policy stories so as to highlight these characteristics.

The book begins with Francine Jacobs's overview of child and family policy in the United States since 1980, framing it within both historical and contemporary social contexts. It introduces the five policy dimensions described above, and situates policies of the 1980s along those dimensions. In chapter two, Margery Davies explores the political economic history of the work of caring for children and the implications that history has had for family policy. The framework she uses is a simultaneous analysis of both "productive" and "reproductive" work, with "productive" work meaning the making of things and other activities ancillary to that production, and "reproductive" work meaning the making of people. She concludes that after industrialization, reproductive work, and particularly the work of caring for children, was redefined, and over time, devalued, as part of a newly privatized "family life." In chapter three, Cherilyn Davidson surveys the various social policies that have been directed towards "dependent children"—those children whom society has deemed as improperly or inadequately cared for—and their families from the seventeenth century to the present. She draws an analytical distinction between "family preservation" and "family dissolution" policies, and chronicles the shift back and forth between the two.

These overview chapters are followed by six case studies. The first three focus on the formulation of policy. Katharine Karr Kaitin examines the Family and Medical Leave Act in chapter four. She traces the history and fate of federal family and medical leave legislation, focusing on the version of the Family and Medical Leave Act that progressed through several steps in the 100th Congress, though never passed.[23] A detailed story that focuses on the processes of policy initiation, the chapter provides a thorough-going explanation of why it took so long to pass the federal family and medical leave legislation.

In chapter five, Bonnie Hausman focuses on "policy entrepreneurship" as the primary vehicle for introducing family support programs in three states: Kentucky, Maryland, and Missouri. She examines each state's political culture as a context for tracing the rise to prominence of child and family issues in each state. She finds that parent education and family support programs have broad-based support across the political spectrum, but must be forwarded by small cadres of individuals, operating collaboratively both within state government and outside it, in order to place them on a state's political agenda.

Priscilla Little analyzes three municipal policy approaches to homeless families in chapter six. She focuses on the stage of policy formation in Atlanta, Seattle, and St. Louis, and examines how the political culture of each city—particularly local attitudes toward public intervention in the private, albeit homeless, family—influences the character of these policies. She also proposes a developmental course through which cities appear to progress in their services to homeless families.

These studies of policy formulation are followed by two case studies of policy implementation. In chapter seven, after reviewing the history of the enactment of federal "Baby Doe" regulations, Martha Pott examines the extent to which they were actually implemented. Baby Doe regulations mandate that, with certain exceptions, medical personnel must provide life-sustaining treatment to all infants, no matter how disabled, and regardless of parents' wishes. The author concludes that concerns about the violation of the private family's decision-making prerogatives have seriously compromised implementation of these regulations.

In chapter eight, Robert Griffith investigates the development and implementation of AIDS education policy in the Cambridge, Massachusetts, public schools. While the Cambridge school system has in some respects been touted as an innovator, it ran into controversy over this issue. Concerns about the schools taking over parental functions were never far from the surface. In addition to analyzing the array of competing interests and ideologies that affected the development process, Griffith examines the extent to which policies, once formulated, were actually implemented.

Lucy Hudson and Susan Vlodaver Latts's examination of the Massachusetts Day Care Partnership Project focuses on the third phase of policy analysis—policy evaluation. In chapter nine, they examine Massachusetts' innovative public-private partnership of the mid-1980s that addressed several of child care's structural problems: a lack of affordable slots for low- and moderate-income families; the low pay and high rate of turnover among child care teaching staffs; and the likely compromise of quality that results. From a current vantage point, the authors conclude that however progressive states may be in child policy arenas, they are ultimately constrained by local, state, and regional economies. Federal support, therefore, is critical.

In the two concluding chapters, Francine Jacobs and Margery Davies draw together some of the most important themes and issues found in the preceding chapters. First, they highlight the crucial importance of considering race, class, and gender in defining social problems, setting policy agendas, structuring policies and programs, and evaluating program and policy efforts. They then project the possibilities for U.S. child and family policy for the remainder of the decade. They emphasize the centrality of rethinking the public-private dichotomy in view of the importance of our country's taking responsibility for all of its children and families. Perhaps the policy stories told in this book will contribute to that goal.

NOTES

1. The Family and Medical Leave Act is parental leave legislation. It guarantees job security to certain workers for up to twelve weeks, should they need to leave their positions for the birth or adoption of a child, or to attend to a seriously ill family member. The leave is unpaid. Only workers in businesses with more than fifty employees, who work at least twenty-five hours a week and have done so for at least one year, are eligible. Family and Medical Leave Act becomes law (January/February, 1993). *CDF Reports, 14*(3), 17.

2. S. Moses-Zirkes (May, 1993). The family leave act—is it the doughnut or the hole? *APA Monitor*, 52–53.

3. It is our view that much policy-relevant research with potentially broad applicability to the practice and study of policy is lost because it remains too tightly tethered to the generating discipline. Economists have tended to talk to economists, educators to educators, historians to historians, epidemiologists to the public health community, and so on. This volume is, in part, a response to that situation. We are not alone in this diagnosis. See, for example, T. Skocpol (April, 1992). The narrow vision of today's experts on social policy, *Chronicle of Higher Education, 38*(32), B1-B2.

4. T. V. Bonoma & K. B. Wong (1985). A case study in case research: Marketing implementation. Unpublished paper. Cambridge, MA: Harvard University Graduate School of Business Administration, 7.

5. Bonoma & Wong (1985), A case study in case research; R. K. Yin (1989). *Case study research: Design and methods*. Newbury Park, CA: Sage Publications.

6. C. Hayes (Ed.) (1982). *Making policies for children: A case study of the federal process*. Washington, D.C.: National Academy Press, 8. These characteristics of case study research—the potential for external validity and for theory development, the use of multimethod data collections strategies, and the high degree of contextual relevance—make the case study method well-suited for this volume.

7. A uniform research protocol, developed and implemented for the seven case studies, facilitated cross-case comparisons.

8. D. A. Stone (1988). *Policy, paradox, and political reason*. Glenview, IL: Scott, Foresman.

9. There is an extensive literature on social policy in the United States with which any serious student of child and family policy must become familiar. See, for example, C. Jencks (1992). *Rethinking social policy: Race, poverty and the underclass*. Cambridge, MA: Harvard University Press; N. Glazer (1988). *The limits of social policy*. Cambridge, MA: Harvard University Press; W. J. Wilson (1987). *The truly disadvantaged: The inner city, the underclass, and public policy*. Chicago: University of Chicago Press; L. M. Mead (1986). *Beyond entitlement: The social obligations of citizenship*. New York: The Free Press; R. Morris (1985). *Social policy of the American welfare state: An introduction to policy analysis* (2nd Ed.). New York: Longman; C. Murray (1985). *Losing ground: American social policy, 1950–1980*. New York: Basic Books; T. Marmor (1983). Competing perspectives on social policy. In E. F. Zigler, S. L. Kagan, & E. Klugman (Eds.), *Children, families, and government: Perspectives on American social policy*, 35–56. Cambridge: Cambridge University Press; D. Gil (1981). *Unravelling social policy: Theory, analysis, and political action toward social equality* (3rd Ed.). Cambridge, MA: Schenkman Publishing Company.

10. J. K. Galbraith, in his 1992 volume, *The culture of contentment*, Boston: Houghton Mifflin, 14–15, notes that well-heeled citizens also have benefited from "social policies," with little concern in these instances about how their self-sufficiency might be undermined. "Where the impoverished are concerned . . . government support and subsidy are seriously suspect . . . because of their adverse effect on morals and working morale. This, however, is not true of government support to comparative well-being. By Social Security pensions or their prospect no one is thought damaged, nor, as a depositor, by being rescued from a failed bank. The comparatively affluent can withstand the adverse moral effect of being subsidized and supported by the government, not so the poor." Social historian S. Coontz (1992), in *The way we never were: American families and the nostalgia trap*, New York: Basic Books, makes a similar point.

11. L. Gordon (Ed). (1990). *Women, the state, and welfare*. Madison, WI: University of Wisconsin Press; I. Glasser (1981). Prisoners of benevolence: Power versus liberty in the welfare state. In W. Gaylin, I. Glasser, S. Marcus, & D. J. Rothman (1978), *Doing good: The limits of benevolence*, 99–168, New York: Pantheon; F. F. Piven & R. A. Cloward (1971). *Regulating the poor: The functions of public welfare*. New York: Pantheon.

12. M. Katz (1989). *The undeserving poor: From the War on Poverty to the war on welfare*. New York: Pantheon.

13. G. D. Brewer (1983). The policy process as a perspective for understanding. In Zigler et al., *Children, families, and government*, 57–76.

14. There is also an extensive literature on child and family policy. For broad discussions of the field, see, for example, E. A. Anderson & R. C. Hula (Eds.) (1991). *The reconstruction of family policy*. Westport, CT: Greenwood Press; A. J. Cherlin (Ed.) (1988).

The changing American family and public policy. Washington, D.C.: Urban Institute Press; S. Zimmerman (1988). *Understanding family policy: Theoretical approaches.* Newbury Park, CA: Sage Publications; R. Moroney (1986). *Shared responsibility: Families and social policy.* Hawthorne, NY: Aldine; Zigler et al. (1983), *Children, families, and government*; G. Y. Steiner (1981). *The futility of family policy.* Washington, D.C.: Brookings Institution; S. Kamerman & A. Kahn (Eds.) (1978). *Family policy: Government and families in fourteen countries.* New York: Columbia University Press; G. Y. Steiner (1976). *The children's cause.* Washington, D.C.: Brookings Institution.

15.   There are numerous definitions of family policy. Zimmerman defines it as "everything that governments do that affect families, directly or indirectly." S. Zimmerman (1992). *Family policies and family well-being: The role of political culture*, 3. Newbury Park, CA: Sage Publications. Aldous and Dumon propose a somewhat more limited definition, calling family policy "objectives concerning family well-being and the specific measures taken by governmental bodies to achieve them." J. Aldous & W. Dumon (November, 1990). Family policy in the 1980s: Controversy and consensus. *Journal of Marriage and the Family, 52*, 1136–1151, 1137. Kamerman and Kahn were among the first to grapple with a definition, proposing the notion that "'family policy' means everything that government does to and for the family." S. B. Kamerman & A. J. Kahn (1976). Explorations in family policy. *Social Work*, (21), 181–187, 183.

16.   Kamerman & Kahn (1978), *Family policy*, 3.

17.   Kamerman & Kahn (1978), *Family policy*, 3.

18.   T. Ooms & S. Preister (Eds.) (1988). *A strategy for strengthening families: Using family criteria in policymaking and program evaluation*, Washington, D.C.: The Family Impact Seminar.

19.   One popular view of the policy process is as a linear set of decisions beginning with vague proposals for change and concluding with empirically based evaluations of policy outcomes. The earlier steps include problem identification, agenda setting, the selection of a policy direction, and the development of programs. Latter phases include policy and program implementation, their evaluations, and then, when necessary, modifications. Policy scholarship historically has focused more heavily on policy development, assuming a rather straightforward process once the legislation is passed or an agreement reached on a policy direction. More recent scholarship has revealed a process more recursive than linear, and as responsive to "extraneous" influences (personalities, agency "turf" issues, random events) as to rational planning. For example, implementation does not always follow policy formulation; some "groping along"—figuring out the proper program components during implementation—appears fairly routine and even necessary in certain cases.

For general readings on the policy process, see, for example, Kelman (1987). *Making public policy: A hopeful view of American government.* New York: Basic Books; J. W. Kingdon (1984). *Agendas, alternatives, and public policies.* Boston: Little, Brown; Brewer (1983), The policy process as a perspective for understanding; R. Haskins & J. Gallagher (Eds.) (1981). *Models for analysis of social policy: An introduction.* Norwood, NJ: Ablex Publishing. Regarding "groping along," see O. Golden (1990). Innovations in public sector human services programs: The implications of innovation by "groping along." *Journal of Policy Analysis and Management, 9*(2), 219–248; R. Behn (1988). Management by groping along. *Journal of Policy Analysis and Management, 7*(4), 643–663.

20.   Differentiating roles and responsibilities for government at the local, state, and federal levels is as old as the republic itself; it is relatively new, as an area of scholarship, regarding children and families. E. F. Zigler, S. L. Kagan, & E. Klugman (Eds.) (1983),

Children, families, and government, provides a sound starting point. See also S. Wisensale (1991). State initiatives in family policy. In Anderson & Hula (Eds.), *The reconstruction of family policy*, 59–76; S. Zimmerman (1991). The policy functions of family policies in three states: A comparative analysis. In Anderson & Hula (Eds.), *The reconstruction of family policy*, 45–58; J. L. Fitzpatrick & R. E. Hero (March, 1988). Political culture and political characteristics of the American states: A consideration of some old and new questions. *Western Political Quarterly, 41*(1), 145–153.

21.   Political culture has been defined as: "The particular pattern of orientation to political action in which each political system is embedded," by D. J. Elazar (1984). *American federalism: A view from the states* (3rd Ed.). New York: Harper & Row, 109; "the values and attitudes that people hold toward government and toward each other," by Zimmerman (1992), *Family policies and family well-being*, 36; and "a set of values that are widely endorsed by politicians, educators, and other opinion leaders and that animate the principal institutions of a society," by S. Feldman & J. Zaller (February, 1992). The political culture of ambivalence: Ideological responses to the welfare state. *American Journal of Political Science, 36*(1), 268–307, 271. For an introduction to the central theory on state political culture, see Elazar (1984), *American federalism*. See also Zimmerman (1992), *Family policies and family well-being*; R. Erikson, J. P. McIver, G. C. Wright (1987). State political culture and public opinion. *American Political Science Review, 81*(3), 797–813. See C. Clark & B. Oliver Walter (September, 1991). Urban political cultures, financial stress, and city fiscal austerity strategies. *The Western Political Quarterly, 44*(3), 676–697, for an example of how political culture influences municipal behaviors.

22.   These dimensions were first discussed in F. Jacobs & M. Davies (Winter, 1991). Rhetoric or reality? Child and family policy in the United States. *Social Policy Report, 5*(4), 1–25.

23.   Further versions of this bill were passed by both the 101st and 102nd Congress, but were killed by presidential veto.

1

Child and Family Policy:
Framing the Issues

Francine H. Jacobs

After more than a decade of disregard, children and families are once again on the national agenda, a priority for the Clinton administration and Congress.[1] President Clinton was a member of the National Commission on Children, and as governor of Arkansas, was a driving force behind the National Governors' Association Education for the Year 2000 Task Force. Hillary Rodham Clinton is a children's advocate of long standing who served as chair of the board of directors of the Children's Defense Fund, as has the secretary of the Department of Health and Human Services, Donna Shalala.[2] The 103rd Congress is the most diverse in our history, with significantly more women and persons of color.[3] According to the president of the House of Representatives' freshman class, family and children's issues "will play well" there.[4] Or, to paraphrase a prominent children's lobbyist, "it's a great time for kissing babies."[5]

Yet President Clinton's 1992 election came on the heels of a heated debate on "family values"—a controversy with deep historical resonance.[6] It reflects our profound and enduring ambivalence about public attention to the private family.[7] Similar rhetoric about proper family constellation and functioning characterized the 1980 White House Conference on Families, setting the tone for an often contentious decade of child and family policy. So how are we to know whether or not we are making real progress towards a more accepting view of "good families," a more inclusive sense of public responsibility for children, and a more comprehensive, supportive set of policies?

This chapter offers a brief historical review of major policy initiatives and position papers in the 1980s and early 1990s, up to President Clinton's election, as the context for analyzing policy development during that period. I then propose four criteria critical to determining progress in child and family policy. These criteria may be profitably applied across the cases in this volume, and serve as the basis for our concluding analyses.[8]

THE BEST OF TIMES . . . THE WORST OF TIMES

The White House Conference on Families was the Carter administration's modification of the decennial White House Conferences on Children. With hindsight, this slight shift in focus seems to have been a mistake. While previous Conferences had established some common rhetoric supporting children,[9] there was no comparable consensus on families—their proper composition, their role in society, and the government's role in sustaining them. The 1980 conference saw the political Right preemptively claim the "profamily" title; and without an articulate, positive vision of their own, liberals and those to the Left were kept busy fending off the "anti-family" label. Ideologically polarized delegates argued their positions, apparently without resolve to arrive at a consensus.[10] Gilbert Steiner, in his analysis of the conference entitled *The Futility of Family Policy*, despaired of the United States ever achieving a coherent and comprehensive national family policy.[11]

This absence of consensus fit neatly into the domestic policy agenda of the first Reagan administration.[12] Reagan had campaigned and won the presidency on a conservative, New Federalist platform that reflected deep-seated skepticism about government's ability to solve social problems and a belief that social programs lead to lifelong public dependency.[13] He exhorted the nation to return to traditional family values and embrace a traditional family structure. Getting the government "off the backs of the people," then, would reinforce the privacy of the family and the primacy of parental rights and obligations in raising children.

Congress acknowledged the antigovernment mandate Reagan appeared to have won by passing the sweeping Omnibus Budget Reconciliation Act of 1981 (Public Law [P.L.] 97-35), which reduced federal spending in twenty-five major children's programs by 11%.[14] Child and family policy solutions favored by the new administration emphasized parental authority and called for changes in personal behavior. Adolescent pregnancy prevention programs, for example, were to focus on abstinence and not on dispensing contraceptive information; drug education meant teaching children to "just say no."

The Reagan administration's later efforts to curtail domestic spending on social programs were less successful.[15] Furthermore, the cost-saving effects of benefit reductions were largely offset by the impact of higher unemployment rates and the recession.[16] On the other hand, federal tax changes during the 1980s introduced regressive measures that taxed poor and middle-class families more heavily than in the past, and gave substantial cuts in taxes to the wealthiest.[17] On balance, the 1980s proved far kinder to the wealthy than to others.

While upper-income families, particularly those in the top one percent, "experienced significant income growth in the 1980s, the bottom 40% of families actually experienced a decline in income."[18] By the decade's end, increasing income inequality yielded the largest gap in income between rich and poor families since World War II.[19] Overall, the real median income for families with children fell by five percent between 1979 and 1990.[20] By 1991, the percentage of children living in poverty was 21.8%; this figure represents a 19% increase over the 1980 child poverty level of 18.3%.[21] Children in young families—those headed by someone younger than thirty—fared even worse: Poverty rates for these children were 40% by 1990, compared to a rate of 20.1% in 1973.[22]

Macroeconomic and demographic changes, in addition to public policy decisions, accounted for this predicament.[23] Stagnant wages through much of the 1970s and the 1980s hampered attempts by low-paid workers, many of them young and with children, to keep their families out of poverty.[24] Single-parent mother-headed families increased from 11% of all family households in 1970 to 17% in 1991.[25] Because women consistently earn less than men for comparable work and because they perform two jobs—caring for children and working in the paid labor market—these families are particularly vulnerable to "working poverty." And since Aid to Families with Dependent Children (AFDC) benefits are not indexed for inflation in most states, their real value has eroded substantially since the early 1970s, rendering government anti-poverty programs increasingly ineffectual in maintaining economically marginal families above the poverty line.[26] As Sandra and Sheldon Danziger conclude, "Children have fared badly because their fathers' real earnings have hardly kept pace with inflation, because an increasing percentage of fathers do not earn enough to support a family, because more children live in mother-only families, and because few receive sufficient government benefits."[27]

During the 1980s, the Reagan and Bush administrations provided little guidance or support for innovative planning and programming for children. This shifted responsibility to state and local governments. Some state governments moved in, attempting to "pick up" the slack; for example, many states contributed new state dollars to support necessary child care services in response to drastic Title XX cuts. But none could wholly compensate for the reduction in federal revenues. States added from their own coffers to extend existing federal programs such as WIC (Women, Infants, and Children—a supplemental nutrition program for income-eligible families) and Head Start. They served as laboratories by experimenting with and implementing new programs and policies. Among the numerous examples were the funding of public early childhood education; the provision of family preservation services to stabilize families in crisis and avoid out-of-home placements; the design of "workfare"—work and training—welfare programs; and the passage of parental leave legislation.[28] Models of public-private collaboration, such as Massachusetts's Governor's Day Care Partnership Project, and Maryland's Friends of the Family, also emerged.[29]

Although the White House appeared disinterested, the worsening plight of children during the first Reagan administration did capture the attention of a handful of members of Congress. In 1982, the U. S. House of Representatives' Select Committee on Children, Youth and Families was established. Representative George Miller (D-CA), instrumental in its creation, became the committee's first chairperson; he attracted and retained members from both parties and across the ideological spectrum. The committee collected information and held public hearings on issues ranging from child care to family homelessness, from pediatric AIDS to foster care.[30] In addition to educating Congress and keeping children visible, Congressman Miller succeeded in creating a "profamily" umbrella under which members from both sides of the aisle could sit.

By the mid-1980s, a shift in public sentiment about children and families—away from the extreme positions of the early Reagan days—seemed evident in several influential "position" documents of that time. The 1986 report by the White House Working Group on the Family, *The Family: Preserving America's Future*, is one example.[31] While this report was filled with conservative rhetoric about the primacy of parental rights and authority, and the damages wrought by "antifamily" forces (the media, certain child development experts, the family courts, and the public welfare system), it acknowledged that public action on behalf of groups of children—not only needy individuals—was warranted, and left room to negotiate specific remedies.

Marian Wright Edelman's 1986 W.E.B. Dubois Lectures at Harvard University, published in 1987 as *Families in Peril: An Agenda for Social Change*, argued for sustained, serious public investment in children.[32] While this was in no way a new message from Edelman or the Children's Defense Fund, the investment metaphor—that is, identifying children as social capital—suggested a strategy aimed at broadening the appeal of the issue to include not only "do-gooders," but also dollar-conscious Americans. Edelman acknowledged further that families and communities had responsibilities for helping secure promising futures for children.

Senator Daniel Patrick Moynihan (D-NY) explicitly strove to identify "common ground" between conservatives and liberals on family issues in his 1985–1986 Godkin Lectures at Harvard University, published later as *Family and Nation*.[33] An advocate for some universal family benefits since the 1960s,[34] Moynihan proposed a "credible family policy" that assigned responsibility hierarchically, beginning with the individual and family, but also including government when necessary. His major recommendations, reflected subsequently in changes to the federal tax code in 1986, and elements of P.L. 100–385, the Family Support Act of 1988, were aimed at achieving economic security for families.

Congress became more active on behalf of children and families in the mid-to-late 1980s and early 1990s. An unprecedented number of bills were introduced, though relatively few passed. Among the more noteworthy successes were P.L. 99–457 (in 1986) and P.L. 102–119 (in 1991), extensions of the Education for All Handicapped Children Act, to include infants, toddlers and their families; the Comprehensive Child Development Act of 1987, to establish demonstration child and family service centers in high-risk neighborhoods; P.L. 100–385, the Family Support Act of 1988, also known as the Welfare Reform Act; the Child Care and Development Block Grant (1990), introduced originally as the Act for Better Child Care; and the Family and Medical Leave Act of 1993, signed into law two weeks after President Clinton's inauguration. The Child Care and Development Block Grant was the first piece of comprehensive child care legislation ever signed into law; the last such attempt, in 1971, had been vetoed by President Nixon, who stated he was unwilling "to commit the vast moral authority of the National Government to the side of communal approaches to child rearing over and against the family-centered approach."[35] These federal legislative successes held symbolic, as well as actual, value: they attested to the existence of common ground and common language.

The Family Support Act was viewed as a major achievement of the 100th Congress. Over the decade, discussion about public welfare had gone from Charles Murray's[36] suggestion that it be defunded altogether ("cut the Gordian knot") to legislation requiring states to provide education and training to women on AFDC to enable them to work their way into economic self-sufficiency and off the public rolls. A report issued in 1987 by the privately funded Working Seminar on Family and American Welfare Policy, *A Community of Self-Reliance: A New Consensus on Family and Welfare*, offered a rationale for this approach.[37] It identified both individual (behavioral) and structural (societal) determinants to family poverty, and spoke of social obligations between welfare recipients and the taxpaying public. There are shortcomings to this report as there are to the legislation itself, which hardly reforms the public welfare system as some supporters had hoped it would.[38] Nonetheless, this legislation is noteworthy for the compromise reached on the central premises: that a publicly woven safety net for disadvantaged families was necessary, though to be used sparingly; that public welfare should provide temporary, rather than long-term, support to families in economic crisis; that recipients should have access to job-related training and education, and then employment, in order to attain financial independence; that this independence cannot be achieved, and is not likely to be sustained, without supports to family life such as child care and health care; and that noncustodial parents should contribute to their children's economic well-being. What emerged was a more balanced vision of public and private obligations for family economic stability than one might have thought possible in 1980.

The Progressive Policy Institute, a newly established private foundation, presented an agenda for family policy change toward the end of 1990. *Putting Children First: A Progressive Family Policy for the 1990s*,[39] moved past the "safe" ground of family economic security into a reasoned discussion of family values, family composition and parental functions, and the impact of family law (e.g., divorce law) on family stability. The National Commission on Children, a federal initiative chaired by Senator John D. Rockefeller IV (D-WV), already in its second year, addressed many of these issues at the same time. And a recent report of the conservative Family Research Council, *Free to Be Family*, notes with some surprise "an unprecedented left-right convergence on the importance of the traditional family and the need for economic relief to families."[40] It calls this development "promising and unusual."

Since 1980 the private sector has participated increasingly in child and family policy discussions. Employers are concerned about retaining their present work force which, in 1990, included 60% of all mothers of children under age six; the comparable figure in 1980 was 46%.[41] And demographic prediction of a dwindling labor force in need of greater technical skills raises equal concerns about the competitiveness of their future workforce. The Committee for Economic Development, a small but vocal group (250 members) of corporate executives and educators, has promoted greater private and public investment in children.[42] The committee's reports trumpet the causes of child development and education, early intervention, parent education and family support, and public-private partnerships.

Private philanthropic foundations, both national and community-based, have also focused considerable attention on children and families during this period.[43] Several major initiatives aimed at overhauling public child-serving institutions, such as local schools, child care systems, and state child welfare agencies, are in place.[44] Foundations have assumed the support, either wholly or through public-private partnerships, of numerous research, demonstration, service, and dissemination projects previously considered the job of the government.[45] These private forays into the public domain, while necessary and appealing in the present political climate, represent, at the same time, a loss of democratically elected public supervision of these efforts.

The National Commission on Children's 1991 report, *Beyond Rhetoric: A New American Agenda for Children and Families*, brought together and reinforced many of the themes of the decade.[46] Composed of people from across the political spectrum, the commission counted as one of its major accomplishments its ability to gain consensus on a broad set of recommendations. Among the central recommendations were the following: Proposals *ensuring income security* include a new $1,000 annual refundable tax credit for all children through age eighteen, and the expansion of existing policies such as the Earned Income Tax Credit, child support enforcement, and job training. *Increasing educational achievement* features the expansion of Head Start and a series of educational system reforms including school choice. *Preparing adolescents for adulthood* includes a range of supports and services from tutoring to comprehensive health services to drug and alcohol abuse prevention to opportunities for recreation and cultural enrichment. *Strengthening and supporting families* entails recommendations that both parents share responsibility for planning and supporting their children, that employers establish family-oriented policies and practices, that the availability, affordability, and quality of child care services be improved, and that community-based family support programs be developed. *Protecting vulnerable children and their families* stresses family support and preservation and the coordination of services. The commission also recommended more coordination and collaboration at the federal level to both streamline the family service system and make it more comprehensive. Calling on many sectors of society to *create a moral climate for children*, the commission emphasized parents' responsibility to "be more vigilant and aggressive guardians" of their children's moral development. Significantly, the one major area where the commission failed to reach consensus was in *health care*. While the majority recommended the development of universal health coverage for all pregnant women and children through age eighteen, a substantial minority was unwilling to support this, and other, health policy proposals.

The nascent Clinton administration does appear to have taken the commission's recommendations to heart; the president, after all, was a member. As a result, recommendations virtually ignored by the Bush administration, may well provide the blueprint for child and family policy activity in the 1990s.

A genuine search has been undertaken for common ground on values that both conservatives and liberals consider "profamily." One area of agreement is the recognition of the instrumental value of children to American society[47]—for example, as future workforce participants and contributors to the Social Security system. With declining fertility rates and improved economic conditions for the elderly, children have become more central to our national economy and less central to the economies of their individual families, where they are now increasingly sentimentalized.[48] This formulation of child-as-investment, or "human capital,"[49] argues persuasively for greater public support of, and more active involvement in, children's issues. It also validates other behaviors that mark the private sector, such as the evaluation of these investments in terms of payoffs at a later date, the search for the most cost-effective strategies, and the possible withdrawal of public support should the economic rationale for the investment recede.

An acknowledgment that responsibility for children is to be shared across the established boundaries of public and private domains, of government and family, marks a second area of common ground.[50] Parents and families hold primary responsibility, but community institutions and government are also seen to have legitimate interests in, and responsibility for, child and family well-being. For example, *Beyond Rhetoric* underscored government's role as a support, not a substitute, for families; however, the commission also clearly endorsed having a closely woven, publicly supported safety net for families in crisis.

The White House Conference on Families Redux:
Family Values and the 1992 Presidential Campaign

The Republicans' attempt at reviving the family values debate that had torpedoed the 1980 White House Conference began in the early 1992 primary races. It came to full flower, however, with two later events: Vice President Dan Quayle's condemnation, in May, 1992, of the television character Murphy Brown's decision to bear a child out of wedlock, and the "hard-edged GOP family values blast,"[51] promoting the "cult of the nuclear family"[52] that was delivered by party spokespersons at the Republican National Convention in August of that year. They had calculated, no doubt, that Bill Clinton might be vulnerable to "antifamily" accusations because of the visibility of his nontraditional, working wife, rumors of marital infidelity, and elements of his proposed domestic agenda. Further, they assumed an untapped wellspring of support for a renewed "values war" that pitted the traditional family of bygone days against the more pluralistic image of American families and family roles embraced by the Democratic party. Attacking liberals as major contributors, by their own life-styles and by the policies they promoted, to the disintegration of the American family, had worked successfully in the early 1980s; it seemed worth another go.

It was a mistaken strategy from its inception. To begin, according to Quayle's chief of staff, William Kristol, the voters did not like seeing "a serious issue like family values used cynically," that is, primarily for political purposes.[53] Columnist Meg Greenfield offered that "people resented the intrusion of political figures lecturing them on their moral behavior."[54] And social critic Molly Ivins reported that the great majority of Americans polled after the Republican Convention were offended by the shrillness and vehemence of the attacks; they "didn't care for the gay-bashing, didn't care for the feminist-bashing, didn't care for the Hillary-bashing, and thought the whole exercise was too negative."[55] But the popular backlash ran deeper than annoyance with the messengers and their style of delivery. Demographics played a key role.[56] By identifying a morally superior family type to which only a minority of voters belonged[57]—male breadwinner, female homemaker, and dependent children—the Republicans had alienated many of them. Single-parent families, two-parent working families, extended families of all varieties, struggling in the midst of an economic recession to provide well for their children, deeply resented the implication that they were immoral and dysfunctional.[58] Since both the percentage of single-parent families and the percentage of mothers in the workforce had increased over the decade, there were fewer people to rally around this issue.

Liberals had also worked over the decade to define their own positive, more inclusive and centrist, vision of proper family functioning. Throughout the campaign they refused to cede the "profamily" label to conservatives, as was done in 1980. They argued persuasively that there were more agreements than differences between conservatives and liberals on many fundamental issues: that parents should support their children economically and emotionally; that children should receive love, nurturance, and moral guidance; that families have the responsibility to socialize their children—to teach them good citizenship, the rewards of service, and the value of hard work and discipline; that the family should be a protected, nourishing environment for all family members.[59] Immediately after the Republican Convention, William Bennett, a former Reagan appointee, acknowledged that the difference in values between conservatives and the centrist Democratic Leadership Council, of which Bill Clinton was a member, was "less pronounced" than it had been, and warned his party about attempting to portray the distinctions too starkly. "We shouldn't go at this thing ('values issue') as if it were the forces of light against the forces of darkness; it's a debate, forgive me, within the family."[60]

The "traditional" family of the past, the Republicans' sacred icon, also came under attack in the print media and through increasingly accessible scholarship on the history of the American family.[61] According to social historian Stephanie Coontz, whose provocative book entitled *The Way We Never Were: American Families and the Nostalgia Trap*,[62] was published in the last months of the campaign, the "good old days" in American family life are largely illusory: Many "traditional norms," such as the nuclear family, never actually existed over any sustained period of time. And many worrisome "modern" trends in family behavior, such as premarital sex, are deeply rooted in our past.[63] Throughout the 1980s, the idealization of the nuclear family had almost imperceptibly begun to be replaced by a more realistic, achievable, and sustainable image of a good family. The 1992 family values debate unearthed many families unwilling to embrace a prior image of family life that was, for them, unattainable.

Finally, liberal political pundits simply redefined the term. Assuming diverse family structure, they asked, not what values and composition government should endorse within families, but how government should act to support and value them. "Real family values," according to one columnist, "[are] the kinds of measures that we can take as part of a human community to help each other. . . . [They are] creating a society in which families can flourish."[64] Reframed in this way, President Bush's anemic record in child and family policy, culminating with his second veto of the Family and Medical Leave Act, gave a hollow ring to his espoused commitment to families.[65] As Ivins notes,

> For a political party that has consistently opposed every effort to build a support network for working mothers to then condemn them is despicable. Natal leave, parental leave, day care—the whole complex of programs that exist in other industrialized nations to help working mothers does not exist here, thanks to the Republican party.[66]

A *Boston Globe* editorial on the recent Family and Medical Leave Act's passage is entitled, "Family Values, at Last."[67]

The attack on the family values of the Clintons and the Democratic party was viewed increasingly as a mean-spirited assault on the average, rather than the aberrant, family—on the working mother, hyperfunctional rather than dysfunctional—trying to manage both home and workplace responsibilities.[68] Paradoxically, Bill Clinton's victory helped to demonstrate just how much movement towards the middle had been made since 1980.

IDENTIFYING PROGRESS IN CHILD AND FAMILY POLICY

Social policies are strategies for achieving social purposes or goals. Before proposing or evaluating any specific policy or set of policies, it is critical to establish the current status, and thus the need for the intervention, of the "targets"—in this case, children and families in the United States.[69] As we move into a new millennium, how are families and children faring? How is child and family well-being defined?[70] On which aspects of child and family functioning are data available, and for which should public policies be enacted?[71] How has the condition of children and families changed over time?[72] Answering these questions is well beyond the scope of this chapter. However, a brief note on the social indicators that inform these policy decisions is in order.

Indicators of Child and Family Well-being

Zill, Sigal, and Brim define childhood social indicators as "time series that measure changes (or constancies) in the conditions of children's lives and in the health achievement, behavior, and well-being of children themselves."[73] They identify two related uses of these indicators: The first is descriptive—to identify and understand significant characteristics of children and families, how they change over time, and how broader social change is reflected in them. The composition of families and households; the age, race, and gender of children; the marital status of parents and their ages at marriage; the density of living arrangements, and the like, are often used for this purpose. The second is essentially prescriptive—to identify negative conditions or trends that appear amenable to intervention, and to link a particular phenomenon with a promising, often publicly supported, solution.[74] These negative conditions, such as teen pregnancy or school drop-out rates, are often spoken of as "risk factors."[75]

So, for example, we know that families are becoming smaller, with fewer children in each; since there is no public agreement that this is a problematic situation warranting public intervention, it belongs in the first category. Given our sophisticated medical technology and our espoused commitment to "fair play," the continuing disparity between white and black infant mortality rates, however, clearly belongs in the second.[76] Understandably, policy makers generally use childhood social indicators for the second purpose—to identify problems ripe for public attention.

Social indicators should be able to answer the question of how our children are faring, and they do to a point. Based on available evidence, the National Commission on Children's report states that most children in this country are "healthy, happy and secure."[77] While this is possibly true, it is a difficult statement to make with certainty. One first must ask, "Compared to whom, and with reference to which standards?" Let's look at child health status. Our children are, no doubt, healthier on average than children in Third World countries, or than American children were a hundred years— or even thirty years—ago. But are they healthy enough, given the resources available in this country, or given our values about how healthy we believe children should be?

Two further definitional questions arise: What data are used to determine health status? Who is the typical American child portrayed by them? Our conception of health is necessarily constrained by the available data: For example, because we collect vital statistics as a matter of law, we are able to compute infant mortality rates from birth and death certificates. We maintain records of immunization rates, so we know the number of children both protected and unprotected from certain diseases. And so forth. But the data we have hardly circumscribe the domain of "health" as public health personnel would draw it, or as we each would for ourselves or our own children. Finally, reporting the health profile of the *average* American child obscures the real differences among subgroups of children. Take violent death rates among teenagers: Between 1985 and 1990, the overall rate rose from 62.8 deaths per 100,000 youths (ages fifteen-to-nineteen) to 70.9, representing an average change for the worse of 13%.[78] The rate for white children increased 10%, for African-American children 78%.[79] Thus while the health of all youths declined somewhat on this index, it did so dramatically for African-American youths.

If one is concerned about evidence, then the assertion that American children are "happy and secure" rests on even shakier ground, since there are fewer child status data in these areas.[80] The available information generally describes the most unhappy and insecure members of this group: children who have been abused and neglected, those with severe emotional disturbances, those who have been incarcerated in juvenile facilities, and the like. What characterizes happy and secure children is rarely discussed or reported. Similar limitations pertain in describing family status. Available data are generally confined to those regarding family composition and family economic well-being. Rarely do reports of family health include discussion of internal family functioning—that is, the emotional and interpersonal dimensions of family life. There are at least two obvious reasons for this paucity of data: there are only a limited number of measures with sound psychometric properties in the area, and without broad consensus on what constitutes healthy functioning, there is a reluctance to judge families as either competent or not.[81] And perhaps because our family policies in these domains are generally reserved for those families exhibiting serious dysfunction, policy makers have not demanded more normative descriptions of family life.[82]

These limitations notwithstanding, sound policy decisions should be based on the best data available, and there are sufficient child and family status and trend data to offer some direction.[83] Recent analyses[84] highlight the following:

- Children comprise a smaller percentage of the population (25.6%) than they did in 1980 (28.1%); families with children under age eighteen are a smaller percentage of all households (34.4%) than they were in 1980 (38.4%).

- Married couples with children are no longer the most common household arrangement, as they were in 1980. They now represent 26% of all American households. And fewer children live in two-parent households— 71% compared with 75% in 1980. The percentage of children living in mother-only households grew over the decade.

- Families with children are more common among minorities. While they represent 32% of all white households, they comprise 40% of African-American, 45% of Native American, 47% of Asian-American, and 53% of Hispanic households.

- Today's children are more racially and ethnically diverse, and are more likely to speak a language other than English. Children under age six are more likely to be from minority families than are older children. Almost

14% of school-age children do not speak English at home.

- Eighteen percent of poor families with children are headed by an adult who works full time throughout the year, and 54% are headed by an adult who works part time for a portion of the year.

- The poverty rate for all children is 21.8%; for children under age six it is 24%.[85] The poverty rate for African-American children, however, is roughly double the national average (44.1%), and it is 30.2% for Hispanic children.[86]

- Approximately 11% of all children born in 1990 started out with a combination of three environmental risk factors—a mother who had less than a high school education, was not married to the baby's father, and was younger than twenty when her first baby was born. These children are roughly ten times more likely to be poor, and twice as likely to be ranked in the lower half of their elementary school classes, than children born with none of these risks.[87]

- Of eight indicators used by the Center for the Study of Social Policy to determine national and state trends in child well-being,[88] two have changed for the better since the 1980s: infant mortality and child death rates. The others—the percent of low birth-weight babies, of all births that are to single teens, of youths graduating high school, of children living in poverty, of children living in single-parent households, and teen violent death rate—have changed for the worse.

What lessons should we take from these data? To begin, families are more diverse—racially, ethnically, in family composition, and regarding family roles. Policy should reflect and respect this diversity. Second, the economy has not supported families. Even many working families are falling below the poverty line. As economist David Ellwood states in the National Commission on Children report, "If you work you shouldn't be poor. There are people out there who are playing by the rules and losing the game. Now, who is going to play by the rules if you can't win?"[89] Third, poor children are especially vulnerable to "rotten outcomes,"[90] living as they do in a state of "double jeopardy": They are "more frequently exposed to risks for achieving optimal development such as medical illnesses, family stress, inadequate social support, and parent depression . . . [and] they experience more serious consequences from these risks than do children from higher socioeconomic status."[91] Finally, the dramatic increase in youth violence over the decade, particularly among minority youths, demands public attention.[92]

The present situation is not good. But have we sketched here a portrait of American children and families so devastating that it is unique in our history? Probably not. On a few indices we probably have taken better care of children and had more respect for families in the past, and on others we are inarguably far better off now. On still others, for example, the sexual abuse of children and wife battering, we have no historical basis for comparison. Jeremiads strikingly similar to today's have been expressed by contemporary observers since colonial times.[93] Thus the data need to be considered comparatively and absolutely, within a framework for policy decisions that weighs both utilitarian and ethical concerns.[94]

Policy Dimensions

The data above argue for a more comprehensive and progressive set of child and family policies than we now have. How do we know if we are building toward this end? We propose to view the policy activity of the 1980s along five dimensions:

1. Are these policies child-centered or family-centered?
2. Do they provide families economic support or support for caretaking and nurturance?
3. Are they targeted or universal?
4. Do they promote treatment strategies or preventive strategies?
5. Do they view children as a private or public responsibility?

Progress does not entail solely linear movement along these dimensions—that is, leaving one end and moving toward the other. An enlightened set of policies would not, for example, forsake all targeted policies in favor of universal ones. It is more a matter of balance and inclusion—the extent to which the policies of the last decade reflect the entire range of options, a range which is necessary for a comprehensive approach.

Child-centered or family-centered? Ecological theories of human development are now broadly accepted in developmental psychology. Child development was once viewed as the inevitable unfolding of innate temperament and inherited capacity. It is now increasingly understood as a complex interaction between a child's natural endowments and constitution, and multiple forces in the environment.[95] The most intimate and powerful context affecting children is the family; others include neighbors and community members, formal and informal community organizations and institutions (what Berger and Neuhaus call "mediating structures")[96] and ultimately, governmental policies. Bronfenbrenner describes the child's place in her world as the core piece in a set of nested Russian dolls.[97]

Family systems theory, which informs the clinical field of family therapy, also views much of child development as contextually determined. An outgrowth of general systems theory in the physical and biological sciences,[98] family systems theory sees the family as a unit—an organized whole[99] within which all individuals are interdependent. Individual development and behavior, patterns of interactions between family members, and overall family functioning influence, and in turn are influenced by, one another.[100] Problematic individual behaviors, then—such as teenage drinking—are generally understood as symptomatic of systemic dysfunction, and interventions are focused on the broader system.[101] Systemic attempts to promote the healthy development of individual family members, or to improve family functioning and increase family well-being, rely on the resources of the family.

These two popular disciplines argue for understanding the family and using it to achieve both child-oriented (for example, improved school achievement) and family-focused goals (for example, reduction of intrafamily violence). With some notable exceptions such as Head Start, however, child policies and child-serving institutions do neither.[102] Consider public schools, the medical care system, or the child welfare system. Child protective workers, for example, are essentially disinterested in the domestic violence directed at mothers, though it is likely that witnessing such battery has serious negative consequences for the children,[103] quite apart from the fact that the mothers, themselves, have a right to protection. Shelters for homeless families often do not accept spouses or boyfriends, and a recent national survey found that 40% operated with eligibility policies that excluded adolescent sons.[104]

Families are neglected for many reasons: among the more benign are ignorance of, or disagreement with, systemic theory; resistance to institutional change; nervousness about working with families; and genuine confusion about what constitutes a "proper" family and proper family functioning, and how involved government should become in achieving these ends.[105] However, a portion of this neglect is intentional and punitive. In fact, our commitment to help children has often been compromised by our determination not to help their parents, who, by virtue of their need for assistance, are viewed as shirking their family responsibilities.[106] AFDC grants are so meager in some states that one might question whether we see mothers as legitimate beneficiaries at all, or whether the original title of the legislation—Aid for Dependent Children—is not the more accurate.

Economic functions or caretaking functions? Kamerman and Kahn offer a useful distinction between family policies that help parents in their "breadwinning" roles and those that speak to parents in their nurturing and caretaking roles.[107] The former is most concerned with supporting the family as a viable economic unit, either by maintaining a certain minimal family income or by providing for the care of children while parents work. The latter focuses on the internal life of the family by promoting positive family functioning and individual family member development and well-being. Policies in the United States greatly favor the first.

The basis of our nation's approach is both cultural and developmental. Because we tend to view families as private and to frame issues in economic terms, income security policies appear the least intrusive, most expedient way to offer assistance to families. A developmental theory, informed by Maslow's "hierarchy of need,"[108] would explain that child and family policy is in its early stages, and that policies must focus first on the most basic, immediate needs of families: adequate shelter, food, clothing, health care, child care, and job training and placement. As these material needs are met routinely, the more interpersonal, psychological, or developmental aspects of family life would be addressed. Thus, satisfying the first goal is prerequisite for undertaking the second.

The debate over policies for homeless families is illustrative. Some maintain that homeless families only need housing. Others argue that they often need a broader "economic package," that is, affordable housing, decent jobs, child care, and health care. But still others hold that homeless families often need more than economic assistance, that the factors precipitating their plight and the harmful effects of being homeless call for additional support—a "caregiving package" that includes home management training, mothers support groups, and parent education.[109] This view argues for addressing problems in both the caregiving and economic realms, an approach that is found in the more progressive family policies of some other countries.

Targeted or universal? In general, child and family policy in the United States is targeted rather than universal: in order to receive the benefits of most programs, one must be considered "needy" or unlucky,[110] usually in the extreme. And this is true for both economic and noneconomic types of policy. With regard to economic supports, the United States relies to a far greater extent than other Western industrialized nations on income- and means-tested family programs.[111] AFDC, for example, is provided to the most impoverished families, and assistance is generally withdrawn after a family's economic situations improve somewhat. Support services—health care, child care, dental care—are often unavailable for economically marginal working families. And while former participants in welfare-to-work programs are generally provided these services during a transitional period, they must then absorb the full cost themselves. This extreme targeting of services creates a perverse incentive for many parents either to remain on AFDC or to elect it. Further, since eligibility for these programs varies by program (differing, for instance, for Medicaid, child care, AFDC, WIC) and by state, "families seeking assistance thus encounter a service delivery system that is often confusing, difficult to navigate and indifferent to their concerns."[112] The process of ensuring that no family receives services to which it is not entitled consumes abundant personnel time and public dollars.

Except for public elementary and secondary education, few benefits accrue to children by virtue of their universal status as minors; families also are not eligible for benefits as members of a universal class of child nurturers. For most children and families, early childhood education, post-secondary education, parental leave, and other developmental, educational, and recreational opportunities, are purchased in the marketplace by families able to afford them; children in less advantaged families are effectively denied these opportunities. Services that would be considered beneficial for all children—for example, the individualized educational plan required by P.L. 94–142 (The Education for All Handicapped Children Act)—are available only to "special needs" children.

Universal policies, such as our Social Security insurance or public education, are *immediately* more expensive than those that are targeted to specific, needy subgroups, so that cost containment is often the cornerstone of arguments against the adoption of additional, universal social policies. Yet such policies are attractive for many reasons: they foster a sense of collective identity and civic responsibility; they are politically more stable and dependable; services are often of higher overall quality since they benefit persons of all incomes; and citizens, particularly those who need the help most, are not stigmatized by their use.[113] These virtues are well accepted in other countries, and are held to have a positive impact on national economic growth and security. International comparisons of parental leave and child care legislation, noncustodial child support provisions, and access to health care suggest that the United States is a "family policy laggard"[114] in not providing universal social policies to benefit children and families.[115]

Treatment or prevention? United States child and family policies are overwhelmingly treatment oriented, with only those individuals already in difficulty being eligible; few preventive programs are broadly available. For example, families on the verge of having their children placed in alternative care arrangements are eligible, in fact, are often required, to receive counseling; families in which problems are brewing but not extant often cannot qualify for public services. Furthermore, the preference for treatment means that a more intensive (and more expensive) intervention often is used when a less intensive one would do. For example, many youths incarcerated in detention centers and training schools are "nonserious and nonchronic" offenders; they would be served more appropriately in community-based programs.[116]

This emphasis on treatment over prevention suggests what Grubb and Lazerson call a "negative conception of 'parens patriae'" ("the state as parent").[117] The reliance on treatment precludes helping families negotiate the normal stresses inherent in raising children, for example by offering parent education, or by supporting reduced-hour work policies or parental leave for new parents. The latter type of assistance exemplifies the positive view of the role of the "state's role as parent" embraced by most industrial nations. But it is the negative conception of 'parens patriae' that holds sway here: the state waits until parents fail and families become dysfunctional before assuming the obligation to protect children. 'Parens patriae' applied in this fashion does, no doubt, protect some children from real and imminent danger; it also sacrifices the present and future integrity of many families in crisis.

Our long history of providing public education and public health services (such as immunizations) offers a countervailing, though less popular, model of serving children and families: promoting well-being and preventing problems before they arise. Intervening early is far more effective, and, in the long run, often less expensive, than treating "failures." There is also a more recent, but growing, body of research and practice literature on the benefits of family support and parent education programs.[118]

Implicit in a focus on treatment is the expectation that most "normal" families can get along without any outside help. Substantial social support literature challenges this position. Middle- and upper-class families can either purchase the supportive services they need (babysitting as respite from child caring, marital or family counseling) or in other ways reduce the stresses on their families (for example, by working part time or hiring a house cleaner). Poorer families do not have these options. The need for social supports, however, is normative, not pathological.

Public or private responsibilities? The distinction between "public" and "private" is not as simple as it appears. The terms are often used loosely, and the boundary between public and private rights and responsibilities has shifted over time and continues to shift. The words "private" and "public" and their dichotomy are used in varying ways. Sometimes "private" means the individual and the family, while "public" means the social world outside the family. Advocates of abortion rights, for example, maintain that decisions about abortions are private, that is, they are up to an individual, and are not to be made by the public world or its agents, such as governments. At other times, "private" refers to the private sector, meaning business, while "public" refers to the public sector, meaning local, state, and national government. A still further distinction is sometimes drawn between "private," meaning private social agencies and foundations, and "public," meaning government bodies and agencies at any level.

These multiple definitions can be confusing, and it is not uncommon to find arguments derived from one distinction used to make a case in another. For example, those wanting to avoid any further regulation of business may defend their position against governmental imposition of parental leave by invoking the privacy of individual decisions. By cloaking private corporations in the mantle of the rights enjoyed by private individuals, they argue that government has little right to mandate benefits to those corporations. Decisions about benefits must therefore remain a private matter between employer and employee.

Identifying the family as private, and distinguishing between its concerns and those of the public world outside, reflects our national political culture. Political culture has been defined as the collection of beliefs, attitudes, and values "that people hold toward government and toward each other,"[119] and that "animate the principal institutions of a society."[120] In this country they include, among others, individual freedom, self-sufficiency, democracy, capitalism, autonomy, equality, personal achievement and advancement, and the redemptive virtues of hard work. Indeed, many of these qualities were identified by de Tocqueville in his examination of American democracy in the 1830s.[121]

Some would argue that these values have held the United States in good stead, particularly in the modern era. We have competed well in the global economy, being able to harness, harvest, and use its abundant natural resources. We have produced a well-educated elite, including many a Nobelist. And since the recent fall of Communism in Eastern Europe and the former Soviet Union, the United States is arguably the only remaining superpower—proof, it is said, of the virtues of American capitalist democracy.

Our political culture also has yielded a limited sense of public responsibility. Individual rights are jealously guarded, but few speak of the responsibilities of citizenship, short of paying taxes and voting.[122] Civic behavior is determinedly idiosyncratic, reflecting one's temperament and interests, rather than established norms of participation. Commentators have noted that, in generations past, when the

United States appeared more homogeneous, there appeared to be a more generous civic impulse.[123] Social helping behaviors, they argue, have constricted as the country has become more obviously diverse.

Families generally have been accorded the privacy rights of individuals, with concomitant private responsibilities for raising children. While children's status as independent beings has improved since the time they were considered their fathers' chattel, the sense of children as private possessions lingers.[124] As the argument goes, in an era of birth control, they are, after all, the result of affirmative, personal, adult choices; therefore, both the pleasures and difficulties of raising them should be experienced privately, within the family. In essence, the sum of what each family can provide its own children represents our vision of collective responsibility for children. We then define ourselves as a "child-centered" society.[125]

Mainstream cultural values, including those of independence, self-sufficiency, and privacy, are partly responsible for our national devotion to the private family. The separation of the public world or work from the private world of the family, which has its roots in industrialization, has only strengthened the notion that families should stand or fall on their own.[126] In turn, a rather impoverished set of child and family policies has emerged.

NOTES

1. Children get a good start in budget process (June, 1993). *CDF Reports*, (June, 1993), *14*(7), 1–3; P. Steinfels (December 27, 1992). Seen, heard, even worried about. *New York Times*, 4–1, 12.

2. Attorney General Janet Reno also ranks attending to children and families near the top of her agenda at the Justice Department. See, for example, Justice Dept. choice says violent crime to be a priority (February 13, 1993). *Boston Globe*, 8; L. Rohter (February 16, 1993). Strong hand, sharp eye in Justice Department nominee. *New York Times*, A15.

3. There are 124 new members in Congress; 28 of them are women, and 23 are persons of color. The new face of Congress, (January/February, 1993). *CDF Reports, 14*(3), 1, 4; C. Krauss (November 8, 1992). The old order changes in Congress—a little, *New York Times*, E3.

4. The new face of Congress (January/February, 1993). *CDF Reports, 14*, 4.

5. William Harris, founder and treasurer of KIDSPAC, Cambridge, MA—a political action committee (PAC) that supports candidates who embrace children's issues—found child and family programs and policies increasingly prominent in the 1988 presidential campaign. As he said at the time, "This is not a bumper sticker issue. . . . This is no more kissing babies. This is the real thing." E. J. Dionne, Jr. (September 27, 1987). Children emerge as issue for Democrats. *New York Times*, 36.

6. R. Beck (1973). The White House Conferences on Children: An historical perspective. *Harvard Educational Review, 43*, 653–668; W. N. Grubb & M. Lazerson (1982). *Broken promises: How Americans fail their children*. New York: Basic Books.

7. See, for example, S. Coontz (1992). *The way we never were: American families and the nostalgia trap*. New York: Basic Books; S. Coontz (1988). *The social origins of private life: A history of American families, 1600–1900*. London: Verso; M. Davies (this volume). Who's minding the baby? Reproductive work, productive work, and family policy in the

United States; Grubb & Lazerson (1982), *Broken promises.*

8. These criteria were first proposed and discussed by us (F. Jacobs and M. Davies) in 1991, in: Rhetoric or reality? Child and family policy in the United States. *Social Policy Report, V*(4), 1–25.

9. Beck (1973), The White House Conferences on Children.

10. White House Conference on Families (1980). *Listening to America's families: Action for the 80's.* Washington, D.C.: U.S. Government Printing Office.

11. G. Steiner (1981). *The futility of family policy.* Washington, D.C.: The Brookings Institution.

12. J. Aldous and W. Dumon (1990). Family policy in the 1980s: Controversy and consensus. *Journal of Marriage and the Family, 52*, 1136–1151.

13. J. L. Palmer & I. V. Sawhill (1982). *The Reagan experiment: An examination of the economic and social policies under the Reagan administration.* Washington, D.C.: Urban Institute Press.

14. S. G. Garwood, D. Phillips, A. Hartman, & E. Zigler (1989). As the pendulum swings: Federal agency programs for children. *American Psychologist, 44*, 434–440.

15. J. C. Weicher (1984). The safety net after three years. In J. Weicher (Ed.), *Maintaining the safety net*, 1–19. Washington, D.C.: American Enterprise Institute for Public Policy Research.

16. I. Garfinkel & S. McLanahan (1986). *Single mothers and their children: A new American dilemma.* Washington, D.C.: Urban Institute Press.

17. J. K. Galbraith (1992). *The culture of contentment.* Boston: Houghton Mifflin; L. Mishel & D. M. Frankel (1991). *The state of working America, 1990-1991.* Armonk, NY: M. E. Sharpe.

18. Mishel & Frankel (1991), *The state of working America, 1990–1991*, 13.

19. Mishel & Frankel (1991), *The state of working America, 1990–1991*; K. Phillips (1990). *The politics of rich and poor: Wealth and the American electorate in the Reagan aftermath.* New York: Random House.

20. Center for the Study of Social Policy (1992). *Kids Count data book: State profiles of child well-being.* Greenwich, CT: The Annie E. Casey Foundation.

21. Children's Defense Fund (1992). *The state of America's children 1992.* Washington, D.C.: Author.

22. Children's Defense Fund (1992), *The state of America's children 1992.*

23. S. Danziger & S. Danziger (Winter, 1993). Child poverty and public policy: Toward a comprehensive antipoverty agenda. *Daedalus, 122*(1), 57–84.

24. J. Strawn (1992). The states and the poor: Child poverty rises as the safety net shrinks. *Social Policy Report, VI*(3), 1–19.

25. U.S. Department of Commerce: Bureau of the Census (February, 1992). *Household and family characteristics: March 1991* (Series P–20, No. 458). Washington, D.C.: U.S. Government Printing Office.

26. Strawn (1992), The states and the poor; D. T. Ellwood (1988). *Poor support: Poverty in the American family.* New York: Basic Books.

27. Danziger & Danziger (Winter, 1993), Child poverty and public policy, 69–70.

28. See, for example, M. Finn-Stevenson & E. Trzcinski (1991). Mandated leave: An analysis of federal and state legislation. *American Journal of Orthopsychiatry, 61*, 567–575; Harvard Family Research Project (1990). *Innovative models to guide family support and education policy in the 90s: An analysis of four pioneering state programs.* Cambridge, MA: Author; Center for the Study of Social Policy (1988). *State family preservation programs: A*

description of six states' programs in developing services to keep families together. Washington, D.C.: Author.

29. See, for example, B. Hausman (this volume). Policy entrepreneurship and the emergence of family support programs; L. Hudson & S. Vlodaver (this volume). A season in the sun: The Massachusetts Day Care Partnership Project; Friends of the Family, Inc. (1990). *Maryland's family support centers: Partnerships to strengthen young families.* Baltimore: Author; Commonwealth of Massachusetts, Governor's Day Care Partnership Project (1985). *Final report of the Governor's Day Care Partnership Project.* Boston: Author.

30. See, for example, U.S. House of Representatives Select Committee on Children, Youth, and Families (1987). *The crisis in homelessness: Effects on children and families.* Washington, D.C.: U.S. Government Printing Office; U.S. House of Representatives Select Committee on Children, Youth, and Families (1987). *AIDS and young children: Emerging issues.* Washington, D.C.: U.S. Government Printing Office; U.S. House of Representatives Select Committee on Children, Youth, and Families (1986). *Children in state care: Ensuring their protection and support.* Washington, D.C.: U.S. Government Printing Office.

31. White House Working Group on the Family (1986). The family: Preserving America's future. Unpublished manuscript. Washington, D.C.: U.S. Department of Education.

32. M. W. Edelman (1987). *Families in peril: An agenda for social change.* Cambridge, MA: Harvard University Press.

33. D. P. Moynihan (1987). *Family and Nation.* San Diego: Harcourt Brace Jovanovich.

34. S. Kamerman & A. Kahn (1989). The possibilities for child and family policy: A cross-national perspective. In F. Machiarola & A. Gartner (Eds.), *Caring for America's children,* 84-98. New York: Academy of Political Science.

35. Cited in P. Roby (1973). Young children: Priorities or problems? Issues and goals for the next decade. In P. Roby (Ed.), *Child care—Who cares? Foreign and domestic infant and early childhood development policies,* 123–153. New York: Basic Books.

36. C. Murray (1984). *Losing ground: American social policy (1950–1980).* New York: Basic Books.

37. Working Seminar on Family and American Welfare Policy (1987). *A community of self-reliance: The new consensus on family and welfare.* Washington, D.C.: American Institute for Public Policy Research.

38. R. A. Cloward & F. F. Piven (May 24, 1993). Punishing the poor, again: The fraud of workfare. *The Nation, 256*(20), 693–696; T. Funiciello & S. F. Schram (1991). Postmortem on the deterioration of the welfare grant. In E. A. Anderson & R. C. Hula (Eds.), *The reconstruction of family policy,* 149–163; T.L. Amott (1990). Black women and AFDC: Making entitlement out of necessity. In L. Gordon (Ed.), *Women, the state, and welfare,* 280–298. Madison, WI: University of Wisconsin Press; Kamerman & Kahn (1989), The possibilities for child and family policy; A. Goldman (1988). The politics of welfare reform. Unpublished Masters thesis, Tufts University, Medford, MA.

39. E. C. Kamarck & W. A. Galston (1990). *Putting children first: A progressive family policy for the 1990s.* Washington, D.C.: Progressive Policy Institute.

40. Family Research Council (1992). *Free to be family.* Washington, D.C.: Author, 9.

41. Population Reference Bureau (September, 1992). *The challenges of change: What the 1990 census tells us about children.* Washington, D.C.: Center for the Study of Social Policy.

42. See Committee for Economic Development (1991). *The unfinished agenda: A new vision for child development and education.* New York: Author; Committee for Economic

Development (1987). *Children in need: Investment strategies for the educationally disadvantaged*. New York: Author; Committee for Economic Development (1985). *Investing in our children: Business and the public schools*. New York: Author.

43. A. L. Bailey (1990). Philanthropy and politics: New coalitions. *The Chronicle of Philanthropy, 3*(2), 1, 10–11.

44. For example, the Annie E. Casey Foundation's New Futures Initiative began in 1988 as an effort to address the needs of at-risk youth in five cities; its Child Welfare Reform Initiative aims to improve service systems at both the state and local levels. The Pew Charitable Trusts' Comprehensive Children's Initiative seeks broad impacts for children, families, and the systems that serve them. The Boston Foundation Carol R. Goldberg Seminar has supported community planning efforts for Boston in the areas of health care, parks and open spaces, and child care. The report of its most recent efforts is *Embracing our future: A child care action agenda*, published in 1992.

45. R. Magat (Ed.) (1989). *An agile servant: Community leadership by community foundations*. New York: The Foundation Center.

46. National Commission on Children (1991). *Beyond rhetoric: A new American agenda for children and families*. Washington, D.C.: U.S. Government Printing Office.

47. Grubb & Lazerson (1982), *Broken promises*.

48. V. Zelizer (1985). *Pricing the priceless child: The changing social value of children*. New York: Basic Books.

49. J. S. Coleman (1991). *Policy perspectives: Parental involvement in education*. Washington, D.C.: U.S. Government Printing Office.

50. W. J. Bennett (October, 1990). Children and culture in modern America. Speech delivered at the University of Notre Dame, South Bend, IN.

51. M. Greenfield (September 8, 1992). Enough cant on 'family values.' *Washington Post*, A. 21.

52. K. Pollitt (July 20-27, 1992). Why I hate 'family values' (Let me count the ways). *The Nation, 225*(3), 88–94. 94.

53. E. J. Dionne, Jr. (August 27, 1992). GOP reassesses values war: Collateral damage seen in moral attacks. *Washington Post*, A1, A11.

54. Greenfield (September 8, 1992), Enough cant on 'family values.'

55. M. Ivins (September 14, 1992). Notes from another country. *The Nation, 255*(7), 229, 248–249, 249.

56. See, for example, R. Albelda (December, 1992). Whose values, which families? *Dollars & Sense, 182*, 6–9; A realistic family portrait. (September 21, 1992) *Boston Globe*, 14; T. B. Edsall (July 31, 1992). The 'values' debate: Us vs. Them? At issue is which party best represents heavily white middle class. *Washington Post*, A8; S. Evans & B. Vobejda (August 30, 1992). The 'family values' debate: Emotional issue viewed here as gimmick. *Washington Post*, A1, A8; J. Mann (June 12, 1992). Values: Yours, mine and ours. *Washington Post*, E3.

57. It is estimated that roughly one-quarter of families in the United States are comprised of one working parent and one full time homemaker. U.S. Department of Commerce, Bureau of the Census (1992). *Household and family characteristics: March 1991*, (Series P–20, No. 458). Washington, D.C.: U.S. Government Printing Office.

58. Pollitt (July 20-27, 1992), Why I hate 'family values'; W. Raspberry (August 12, 1992), Chronicles of the 'Nameless Grandmother', *Washington Post*, A21; Evans & Vobejda (August 30, 1992), The 'family values' debate; Greenfield (September 8, 1992), Enough cant on 'family values'; Ivins (September 14, 1992), Notes from another country.

59. D. C. Denison (June 12, 1992). Interview with Marian Wright Edelman. *Boston Globe*, 8. Edelman stated in a later interview that focused primarily on her own family: "The family values talk is just talk. People understand what is real and what is hypocritical. Family and moral values are so central to everything that I am." (Cherishing a sense of place called family: At home with Marian Wright Edelman [October 8, 1992.] *New York Times*, C.1, C.6.)

60. Dionne, Jr. (August 27, 1992), GOP reassesses values war, A8.

61. See, for example, T. Hareven (1992). Continuity and change in American family life, 308–326. In L. Luedtke (Ed.), *Making America: The society & culture of the United States*, Chapel Hill, NC: The University of North Carolina Press. S. Coontz (1988). *The social origins of private life: A history of American families, 1600–1900.* London: Verso; L. Gordon (1988). *Heroes of their own lives: The politics and history of family violence.* New York: Penguin.

62. S. Coontz (1992). *The way we never were: American families and the nostalgia trap.* New York: Basic Books. This volume was widely reviewed in the weeks before the 1992 election. See, for example, D. Katz (November 8, 1992). Ozzie and Harriet lied. *New York Times Book Review, 97,* 21; E. Willis (October 25, 1992). In memory of family, *Boston Sunday Globe*, B. 13–14.

63. Coontz (1992), *The way we never were.*

64. J. Mann (September 25, 1992). A costly veto on values, *Washington Post*, E3.

65. Mann (September 25, 1992), A costly veto on values; A. Rosenthal (July 26, 1992). What's meant and what's mean in the 'family values' battle, *New York Times*, 4–1, 6; E. Robbins (June 7, 1992). Let's disperse the family values smokescreen. *New York Times*, 18; Lip service on family services (January 13, 1992). *Boston Globe*, 10.

66. Ivins (September 14, 1992), Notes from another country, 249.

67. Family values: At last (February 7, 1993). *Boston Globe*, 72.

68. There remains some, probably legitimate, concern about the effects on children of living in single-parent families. For a discussion of some of the issues, see, for example, B. D. Whitehead (April, 1993). Dan Quayle was right. *Atlantic Monthly*, 47–84; C. Teegartin (March 28, 1993). Fragmenting families. *The Atlanta Journal/The Atlanta Constitution*, G1, G3.

69. An excellent recent synthesis of the conceptual challenges to measuring child and family well-being is found in J. Garbarino (June, 1991). *Conceptual issues in the search for social indicators of well-being.* Washington, D.C.: Center for the Study of Social Policy.

70. For a more complete discussion of these issues, and for presentations of these data, see, for example N. Zill (Winter, 1993). The changing realities of family life. *The Aspen Institute Quarterly, 5*(1), 27–51; S. Coontz (1992), *The way we never were*; S. Zimmerman (1992). *Family policies and family well-being: The role of political culture.* Newbury Park, CA: Sage Publications; National Commission on Children (1991), *Beyond rhetoric*; N. Zill II, H. Sigal, & O. Brim, Jr. (1983). Development of childhood social indicators. In E. Zigler, S.L. Kagan, & E. Klugman (Eds.), *Children, families and government*, 188–222. Cambridge: Cambridge University Press; Population Reference Bureau (1992), *The challenge of change: What the 1990 Census tells us about children*, Washington, D.C.: Center for the Study of Social Policy. The U.S. Bureau of the Census conducts annual demographic surveys focused on households and families; see, for example, U.S. Department of Commerce: Bureau of the Census (February, 1992). *Household and family characteristics: March 1991.* Washington, D.C.: Author.

71. See S. Zimmerman (October, 1992). Family trends: What implications for family policy? *Family Relations, 41,* 423–429; M. Campbell (July, 1992). Family policy outcomes: Deciding what to measure. Unpublished manuscript. Washington, D.C.: Council of Gover-

nors' Policy Advisors; A. Cherlin (Ed.) (1988). *The changing American family and public policy*. Washington, D.C.: The Urban Institute Press.

72. Several organizations analyze and report national data on children and families annually; see, for example, Center for the Study of Social Policy (1993). *Kids Count data book: State profiles of child well-being*. Washington, D.C.: Author; Children's Defense Fund (1992). *The state of America's children 1992*. See also N. Zill & C. Rogers (1988). Recent trends in the well-being of children in the United States and their implications for public policy. In A. Cherlin (Ed.), *The changing American family and public policy*, 31–115.

73. Zill et al. (1983), Development of childhood social indicators, 188.

74. There is an extensive literature on how social problems are defined, and why some are successful at achieving a prominent place on the public agenda while others, also worthy, do not. See, for example, J. W. Kingdon (1984). *Agendas, alternative, and public policies*. Boston: Little, Brown; B. J. Nelson (1984). *Making an issue of child abuse*. Chicago: University of Chicago Press; J. B. Williamson, L. Evans, & A. Munley (Eds.) (1981). *Social problems: The contemporary debate*. Boston: Little, Brown.

75. The term "at-risk" holds widely varying meanings according to one's discipline and/ or ideology. For example, for an interesting discussion of 'at-riskness' within an educational context, see J. Frymier & N. Robertson (January, 1991). On being at risk. In W. Schwarz & C. Howley (Eds.), *Overcoming risk: An annotated bibliography of publications developed by ERIC Clearinghouses*, 26–44. Charleston, WV: ERIC/CRESS.

76. These distinctions are not always made so neatly. As with cost-benefit analyses, where one must clearly identify both the party sustaining the costs and the party deriving the benefits (the clients? the government? society at large?), in these cases one must establish whether or not any party is "at-risk," and if so, which one. So while in the first instance above children are not at obvious risk living in smaller families, our society's well-being might be at risk because decreasing birth rates likely result in a shrinking labor pool, fewer working contributors to the Social Security system, and the like.

77. National Commission on Children (1991), *Beyond rhetoric*, xvii.

78. Center for the Study of Social Policy (1993), *Kids Count data book*.

79. Center for the Study of Social Policy (1993), *Kids Count data book*.

80. In an instructive analysis of the Center for the Study of Social Policy's annual Kids Count reports to that date, Zill notes that none of the eight child well-being indicators chosen for the reports pertains to the domain of "emotional well-being," and only one is located within the domain of "moral and social behavior." Four of the indicators relate to "physical health and safety," three to "economic well-being," and one to "academic achievement." See N. Zill (July, 1991). *Improving Kids Count: Review of an annual data book on the condition of children in the 50 states of the U.S.*. Washington, D.C.: Child Trends, Inc.

81. Several chapters in the H. Weiss & F. Jacobs (Eds.) 1988. *Evaluating family programs*. Hawthorne, NY: Aldine de Gruyter, volume address this issue. See, for example, A. Ellwood, Prove to me that MELD makes a difference, 303–313, for a program's perspective on this dilemma, and D. K. Walker & R. W. Crocker, Measuring family systems outcomes, 153–176, for a review of available instruments. There is increasing recent interest, however, in identifying a set of constructs that circumscribe family life (including these affective dimensions). Furthermore, some researchers suggest that "successful" families share a common posture in each. For a review, see M. Krysan, K. Moore, & N. Zill (1990). *Identifying successful families: An overview of constructs and selected measures*. Washington, D.C.: Child Trends, Inc. See D. Olson (July, 1992). *Successful families: Commonalities across theorists, ethnic groups and family structure*. Paper presented at "Successful American

Families: Challenges and Opportunities," sponsored by the National Forum on the Future of Children, and the Johnson Foundation, Racine, WI, for a useful conceptual framework.

82. As a notable exception, the Council of Governors' Policy Advisors has issued a useful guide for state policy makers to help them plan and implement statewide family-centered programming. See J. K. Chynoweth & B. R. Dyer (1991). *Strengthening families*. Washington, D.C.: Council of Governors' Policy Advisors.

83. In an important essay on the development of social policy, Carol Weiss suggests that research ("information") is not neutral—nor is it used by policy makers in a neutral way. It is first filtered through lenses of political ideology and self-interest. See C. Weiss (1983). Ideology, interests, and information: The basis of policy positions. In D. Callahan & B. Jennings (Eds.), *Ethics, the social sciences, and policy analysis*, 213–245. New York: Plenum Press. For a politically conservative presentation of some of these same data, and of others that are considered central to a conservative platform on family policy, see Family Research Council (1992), *Free to be family*.

84. The index year for these data is either 1990 or 1991. Sources include Center for the Study of Social Policy (1993), *Kids Count data book*; Center for the Study of Social Policy (1992), *Kids Count data book*; Population Reference Bureau (1992), *The challenge of change*; Children's Defense Fund (1992), *The state of America's children 1992*; National Commission on Children (1991), *Beyond rhetoric*; U.S. Department of Commerce, Bureau of the Census (1992), *Household and family characteristics: March 1991*.

85. These are 1991 figures. The 1990 figures are 20.6% and 23% respectively. See Children's Defense Fund (1992), *The state of America's children 1992*.

86. Center for the Study of Social Policy (1993), *Kids Count data book*.

87. Center for the Study of Social Policy (1993), *Kids Count data book*. The children ranked in elementary school are aged 7–12.

88. The most recent Kids Count data book presents ten indicators and compares them to figures from 1985. For these current purposes, however, only the eight indicators that were used in earlier data books, and that, therefore, had 1980 comparison figures, are included.

89. National Commission on Children (1991), *Beyond rhetoric*, 78.

90. L. Schorr (1988). *Within our reach: Breaking the cycle of disadvantage*. New York: Doubleday.

91. M. Kaplan-Sanoff, S. Parker, & B. Zuckerman (1991). Poverty and early childhood development: What do we know, and what should we do? *Young Children, 4*(1), 68–76, 68; S. Parker, S. Greer, & B. Zuckerman (1988). Double jeopardy: The impact of poverty on early childhood development. *Pediatric Clinics of North America, 35*, 1–10.

92. See Children's Defense Fund (May, 1993). Stopping the violence. *CDF Reports, 14*(6), 6–7; C. Ronald Huff (1992). The new youth gangs: Social policy and malignant neglect. In I. M. Schwartz (Ed.), *Juvenile justice and public policy*, 20–44. New York: Lexington Books; A. Kotlowitz (1991). *There are no children here: The story of two boys growing up in the other America*. New York: Anchor Books; D. Prothrow-Stith & M. Weissman (1991). *Deadly consequences*. New York: HarperCollins; H. Spivak, D. Prothrow-Stith, & A. J. Hausman (December, 1988). Dying is no accident. *Pediatric Clinics of North America, 35*(6), 1339–1347.

93. Grubb & Lazerson (1982), *Broken promises*.

94. R. M. Moroney (1981). Policy analysis within a value theoretical framework. In R. Haskins & J. J. Gallagher (Eds.), *Models for analysis of social policy: An introduction*, 78–102. Norwood, NJ: Ablex.

95. See, for example, R. A. Hinde (1992). Developmental psychology in the context of

other behavioral sciences. *Developmental Psychology, 28*(6), 1018–1029; J. P. Shonkoff, P. Hauser-Cram, M. W. Krauss, & C. C. Upshur (1992). Development of infants with disabilities. *SRCD Monograph* (Society for Research in Child Development), *57*(6), 1–163; M. Konner (1991). *Childhood.* Boston: Little, Brown; J. Garbarino (1990). The human ecology of early risk. In. S. J. Meisels & J. P. Shonkoff (Eds.). *Handbook of early childhood intervention,* 78–116. Cambridge: Cambridge University Press; A. O. Harrison, M. N. Wilson, C. J. Pine, S. Q. Chan, & R. Buriel (1990). Family ecologies of ethnic minority children. *Child Development, 61,* 347–362; E. E. Werner (1990). Protective factors and individual resilience. In Meisels & Shonkoff (Eds.), *Handbook of early intervention,* 97–116; K. A. Crnic, M. T. Greenberg, N. M. Ragozin, N. M. Robinson, & R. B. Basham (1983). Effects of stress and social support on mothers of premature and full-term infants. *Child Development, 54,* 209–217; J. Garbarino (1982). *Children and families in the social environment.* Hawthorne, NY: Aldine de Gruyter; E. E. Werner & R. S. Smith (1982). *Vulnerable but invincible: A study of resilient children.* New York: McGraw-Hill; M. E. Lamb & M. A. Easterbrooks (1981). Individual differences in parental sensitivity: Origins, components, and consequences. In M. Lamb & L. Sherrod (Eds.), *Infant social cognition: Empirical and theoretical considerations,* 127–153. Hillsdale, NJ: Lawrence Erlbaum; U. Bronfenbrenner (1979). *The ecology of human development: Experiments by nature and design.* Cambridge, MA: Harvard University Press; A. J. Sameroff & M. Chandler (1975). Reproductive risk and the continuum of caretaking causality. In F. Horowitz (Ed.), *Review of child development research, 4,* 187–244. Chicago: University of Chicago Press.

96. P. L. Berger & R. J. Neuhaus (1977). *To empower people: The role of mediating structures in public policy.* Washington, D.C.: American Enterprise Institute for Public Policy Research.

97. Bronfenbrenner (1979), *The ecology of human development.*

98. G. Bateson (1972). *Steps to an ecology of mind.* New York: Ballantine Books; L. von Bertalanffy (1968). *General systems theory.* New York: Braziller.

99. P. Minuchin (1985). Families and individual development: Provocations from the field of family therapy. *Child Development, 56,* 289–302.

100. F. Walsh (Ed.) (1993). *Normal family processes* (2nd Ed.). New York: Guilford Press; N. W. Ackerman (1958). *The psychodynamics of family life.* New York: Basic Books; D. D. Jackson (1965). The study of the family. *Family Process, 4,* 1–20.

101. B. Dym (1988). Ecological perspectives on change in families. In Weiss & Jacobs (Eds.), *Evaluating family programs,* 477–495; S. Minuchin (1974). *Families and family therapy.* Cambridge, MA: Harvard University Press; C. Umbarger (1983). *Structural family therapy.* New York: Grune & Stratton.

102. See, for example, C. J. Dunst, C. Johanson, C. M. Trivette, & D. Hamby (1991). Family-oriented early intervention policies and practices: Family-centered or not? *Exceptional Children, 58,* 115–126; D. K. Walker & R. W. Crocker (1988), Measuring family systems outcomes. In Weiss & Jacobs (Eds.), *Evaluating family programs,* 153–176.

103. L. Davis & B. Carlson (1987). Observation of spouse abuse: What happens to the children? *Journal of Interpersonal Violence. 2,* 278–291; P. Jaffe, D. J. Hurley, & D. Wolfe (1990). Children's observations of violence: Critical issues in child development and intervention planning. *Canadian Journal of Psychiatry, 35,* 466–470; S. Wildin, W. Williamson, W. Daniel, & G. S. Wilson (1990). Children of battered women: Developmental and learning profiles. *Clinical Pediatrics, 30,* 299–304.

104. F. Jacobs, P. Little, & C. Almeida (1993). Supporting family life: A survey of homeless shelters. *Journal of Social Distress and the Homeless, 2*(4), 269–288.

105. See Campbell (July, 1992), Family policy outcomes, for a fuller discussion of appropriate desired effects of family policies.

106. Grubb & Lazerson (1982), *Broken promises*; H. B. Weiss (1989). State family support and education programs: Lessons from the pioneers. *American Journal of Orthopsychiatry, 59*, 32–48.

107. S. Kamerman & A. Kahn (Eds.) (1978). *Family policy: Government and families in fourteen countries*. New York: Columbia University Press.

108. A. Maslow (1954). *Motivation and personality*. New York: Harper & Row.

109. For a fuller discussion, see P. Little (this volume), Municipal policies for homeless families; Jacobs, et al. (1993), Supporting family life; P. Rossi (April, 1993). Adrift in America: Origins and analysis of contemporary family homelessness. Unpublished manuscript, Amherst, MA: Social and Demographic Research Institute; E. Bassuk (December, 1991). Homeless families. *Scientific American, 265*(6), 66–76; E. Bassuk, R. W. Carman, & L. F. Weinreb (Eds.) (1990). *Community care for homeless families: A program design manual*. Washington, D.C.: The Better Homes Foundation, Interagency Council on the Homeless.

110. G. Steiner (1976). *The children's cause*. Washington, D.C.: Brookings Institution.

111. S.B. Kamerman & A. J. Kahn (1989). The possibilities for child and family policy.

112. National Commission on Children (1991), *Beyond rhetoric*, 317.

113. Kamerman & Kahn (1989), The possibilities for child and family policy; R. S. Magill (1984). *Social policy in American society*. New York: Human Sciences Press; R. M. Moroney (1981), Policy analysis within a value theoretical framework.

114. D. Popenoe (1988). *Disturbing the nest: Family change and decline in modern societies*. Hawthorne, NY: Aldine de Gruyter.

115. A. J. Kahn & S. B. Kamerman (1988). Child support in the United States: The problem. In A. J. Kahn & S. B. Kamerman (Eds.), *Child support: From debt collection to social policy*, 10–19. Newbury Park, CA: Sage Publications; S. B. Kamerman (1988). Maternity and parenting benefits: An international overview. In E. F. Zigler & M. Frank (Eds.), *The parental leave crisis: Toward a national policy*, 235–244. New Haven, CT: Yale University Press; C. A. Miller (1987). *Maternal health and infant survival*. Washington, D.C.: National Center for Clinical Infant Programs.

116. I. M. Schwartz & R. Van Vleet (1992). Public policy and the incarceration of juveniles. In I. M. Schwartz (Ed.). *Juvenile justice and public policy*. New York: Lexington Books.

117. Grubb & Lazerson (1982), *Broken promises*.

118. S. Kagan, D. R. Powell, B. Weissbourd, & E. F. Zigler (Eds.) (1987). *America's family support programs*. New Haven, CT: Yale University Press; H. B. Weiss & F. H. Jacobs (1988). Family support and education programs: Challenges and opportunities. In Weiss & Jacobs (Eds.), *Evaluating family programs*, xix–xxix; E. F. Zigler & K. B. Black (1989). America's family support movement: Strengths and limitations. *American Journal of Orthopsychiatry, 59*, 6–19.

119. Zimmerman (1992), *Family policies and family well-being*, 36.

120. S. Feldman & J. Zaller (February, 1992). The political culture of ambivalence: Ideological responses to the welfare state. *American Journal of Political Science, 36*(1), 268–307, 271.

121. See R. N. Bellah, R. Madsen, W. M. Sullivan, A. Swidler, & S. M. Tipton (1986). *Habits of the heart: Individualism and commitment in American Life*, New York: Harper & Row; A. de Toqueville (1969). *Democracy in America*, New York: Knopf.

122. J. Berry, K. Portney, & K. Thomson (1993). *The rebirth of urban democracy,* Washington, D.C.: The Brookings Institution; Who owes what to whom? (February, 1991). *Harper's,* 43–54. United States' voting rates are quite low, in recent years hovering around 50% for presidential elections, and lower for others. Voter turnout for the 1992 presidential election was 55.23%, up from the 1988 figure of 50.11%. (A. Clymer [December 17, 1992]. Election turnout highest since '68. *New York Times,* 16.)

123. N. Glazer (1988). *The limits of social policy,* Cambridge, MA: Harvard University Press; Grubb & Lazerson (1982), *Broken promises.*

124. S. Mintz (1989). Regulating the American family. *Journal of Family History, 14,* 387–408; S. Coontz (1992), *The way we never were.*

125. Grubb & Lazerson (1982), *Broken promises,* challenge this contention. They observe that while Americans often devote themselves wholeheartedly and irrationally to their own children, they harbor little "public love" of "other people's children."

126. See M. Davies (this volume), Who's minding the baby? Reproductive work, productive work, and family policy in the United States, for a fuller treatment of this topic.

2

Who's Minding the Baby?
Reproductive Work, Productive Work,
and Family Policy in the United States

Margery W. Davies

In hopes of providing a framework for understanding contemporary family policy in the United States, in this chapter I explore the political economic history of the work of caring for children and the implications that history has had for family policy. Although family policy includes a wide range of issues from divorce laws to Social Security to provisions for the chronically ill, the central focus of much policy is children: how they are cared for, who is going to do the work, and who is ultimately responsible for them. A historical perspective helps us to understand not only the roots of contemporary family policies, but also their future trajectories, since future policy is generally constrained by what has happened in the past. And unless we look at the political economic context within which policies are made, our grasp of those policies will be shallow.

To name one example, during the past twenty years maternal labor force participation rates in the United States have increased very rapidly.[1] This political economic change forms a central piece of the current political economy of the work of caring for children, which is the backdrop against which the struggle over child and family policy is being played out.

One useful framework to use is the simultaneous analysis of both "productive" and "reproductive" work. "Productive" work is the making of things and other activities ancillary to that production; "reproductive" work is the making of people.[2] Reproductive work includes the care and nurturance of people of all ages. It involves a range of activities from taking care of the daily needs of infants and small children, to the maintenance of a home and the provision of meals for all household members, to the care of the sick and the dependent elderly.

In many cases the distinction between productive and reproductive work is fuzzy. Teaching people to read, for instance, can be seen as part of the work of "making people," since it enables people to have a potentially greater understanding of their world and to communicate with each other in a complex way. But teaching people to read can also be seen as an activity ancillary to, and necessary for, productive work: many of the tasks involved in "making things" these days involve reading. Despite the somewhat fluid boundary between productive and reproductive work, it is still analytically useful to distinguish between them. And in fact, in analyzing women and work it is essential to look at both productive and reproductive labor and to give the latter as much weight as the former. For if we fail to do so, much reproductive work as precisely that—work—slides away from our view and becomes engulfed in notions of family life, interpersonal relations, and emotions.

Using this lens of productive/reproductive work to examine the political economic history of the work of caring for children, it is possible to identify three overlapping historical periods in the post-Columbian United States. The first, from the early seventeenth century until well into the nineteenth, was a time when both productive and reproductive labor took place primarily in the home and on the farm. The second period, which began at the end of the eighteenth century and lasted into the twentieth, developed as productive labor left the home, leaving reproductive labor behind and still outside the market economy. The third period, which began in the nineteenth century but developed much more fully in the twentieth, is when reproductive labor joins productive labor outside the home.[3]

PRODUCTION AND REPRODUCTION IN THE HOME

In primarily agrarian economies, the household is the focus of both production and reproduction. Broadly speaking, this was the dominant political economic organization in the seventeenth and eighteenth centuries. At the first federal census in 1790, 95% of the U.S. population was rural, defined as places with fewer than 2,500 residents.[4] During the nineteenth century, and in some places well into the twentieth, this organization of productive and reproductive labor persisted, although it was being supplanted by other ways of organizing the work.[5]

Much of the production that took place in the home (understood, of course, to mean both home and farm) was production "for use"—people made the things that they needed. People made their own buildings, sometimes with the help of neighbors; grew their own crops, raised their own livestock, and prepared their own food; spun thread, wove fabric, and made clothing; and made a wide variety of household goods from rugs to candles to fuel. Not to overstate the case, there was a certain amount of production "for exchange." Farmers who were able to produce an excess could sell their crops in exchange for goods and services or even cash. Some people who had developed particular skills—blacksmiths, for example— could augment their household production by selling to people from the surrounding community or outlying farms. This "production for exchange" would enable people in turn to purchase items that were hard for them to produce themselves—cooking pots, the service of grinding their grain into flour, the luxuries of glass windows or tea. But even when people were primarily craftsmen or women and no longer farmed, that craft production took place in or next to the household, and giving up farming did not necessarily mean giving up the kitchen garden or a yardful of chickens. By and large the household was the center of production.

The household was also the center of reproduction. Babies were born, the seriously ill were nursed, and people died at home. Although in larger towns and trading centers there were some inns or taverns, people prepared food and ate at home. Despite the organization of grammar and "petty" schools in some communities, children were generally taught at home their sums and reading skills, particularly in the seventeenth century; in the eighteenth century, many different types of schools proliferated, where students learned everything from Latin and Greek to fencing and embroidery.[6]

Not only did reproductive and productive work take place in the same location, but also the distinction between the two was not always very clear. Food is a good example. Growing crops and vegetables and raising livestock should probably be categorized as "productive" work, for they involve the making of things. Likewise, food preparation such as pickling vegetables or curing meat still seems to fall clearly on the side of production. But the preparation of a particular meal, which entails cooking for immediate consumption, not to mention the work of cleaning up afterwards, is a reproductive task, part of the care and nurturance of people. The goal of this work is feeding people, after all, rather than the "production" of a meal, since there is little point in preparing a meal if people are not going to eat it. But without the production of food at the earlier stages, the reproduction of a meal would not be possible. The two kinds of work are interdependent and interwoven. And, interwoven as they are, reproduction emerges as just as important work as production.

In similar fashion, the reproductive work of caring for children was embedded in the productive work of the household.[7] The work all went on at the same time— small children picked up wood chips for kindling while their older brothers and fathers (and probably more often than one might think, their sisters and mothers) chopped wood; babies were rocked in cradles while their mothers or older sisters spun wool; mothers supervised their children's lessons and knitted socks at the same time. Children helped with the productive *and* reproductive work of the household from a young age that might surprise our twentieth-century eyes. Even four- or five-year-olds could feed the chickens, eight-year-olds could carry the noontime dinner pail to people working in the fields, and by the time children were twelve they could put in close to as much work as an adult. The fact that children were working members of the household underscores the interdependence of productive and reproductive work.

This does not mean that there was no gendered division of labor. There were many tasks that were by and large defined as either men's or women's work.[8] To pick out a few examples: Men did the heavy work of plowing fields and, at least in colonial New England, were ultimately responsible for the religious training of their children. Women tended kitchen gardens and were in charge of the care and feeding of infants. But there were also many jobs where everyone turned to, regardless of sex and despite whatever "official" gender definition a job might carry. At harvest, when time was often of the essence, all household members worked in the fields getting in the crops.

Fathers as well as mothers kept vigil at the bedside of a seriously ill child. There are many colonial accounts of widows who became blacksmiths or innkeepers after their husbands' deaths, crossing the gender lines out of socially accepted necessity.[9]

Women primarily undertook reproductive tasks, at least those within the confines of the home itself. Women were mainly responsible for the daily care and supervision of at least small children, cooked meals, did the laundry, and cleaned. But the fact that reproduction was so closely interwoven with production meant that reproductive labor was seen as work. Women were not, however, necessarily deemed as socially important as men. Despite women's central place in not only reproduction but also production, agrarian societies in the United States were generally patriarchal.[10] Men were the ultimate authorities in their households, as well as in the larger social units of community and town. Nonetheless, the interdependence and common location of reproductive and productive work meant that reproductive tasks were seen clearly as necessary, important work.

Within these broad outlines of agrarian economies, there were many variations of the ways in which reproductive and productive work were organized. A few specific historical examples can offer a sense of the complexity of these variations.

In nonfarm households where the primary productive work was a craft or trade, the spheres of production and reproduction were potentially more distinct.[11] First of all, a craftsman was in most cases producing things primarily for their "exchange value"—that is, to be sold or traded to people outside the family unit—rather than for his own family's use. Second, the skills and tasks involved in craft production could be relatively specialized, so that while a craftsman might know all there was to know about his craft, such as cabinet making, he would not have the opportunity to become skilled in other kinds of productive labor such as animal husbandry or shoe making. This specialization would then be self-reinforcing: the more products someone could not produce himself, the more necessary it would be for him to produce his own specialized products so that he could earn enough exchange value to get the things he needed.

Nonetheless, in many craft households productive labor still took place in the same general physical location as reproductive labor. This might be a section of the main living area in a house where shoes were made; or a separate room which served as the workroom for a silversmith; or an outbuilding where a miller ground grain, a blacksmith shod horses, or a glazier made windows and glasses. Even though the specialized work of a craft meant that that labor was only indirectly contributing to the welfare of the household (through the generation of exchange value that could be used to purchase or trade for needed things), as opposed to *directly* contributing through the production of the actual things that would be used in a household, productive and reproductive labor were still closely interwoven through their physical proximity. This made it still possible for reproduction and production to be interwoven. Children from relatively young ages could help with simple tasks in craft production, so that they were engaged in productive labor while their fathers (or, at times, mothers) could be simultaneously engaged in the productive labor of the craft and the reproductive labor of supervising and teaching children.[12] As children grew older they often began to work as full-fledged apprentices to a craft, whether for their parents or for a relative or neighbor.[13]

Even in the agrarian economies of seventeenth- and eighteenth-century North America, there were some people whose productive work took them away from the household entirely. Fishermen and sailors are obvious examples, and even some craftspeople or merchants had a "place of work" that was separate from the home.[14] This separation meant that at least some productive labor left the home, although so-called "domestic production" such as spinning, knitting and weaving, and maintaining a kitchen garden and perhaps some livestock, remained behind. Here, of course, the gender division of labor was highlighted.

For the most part the productive workers who left the home were men, while domestic production was left to the women.[15] While women may have taken a more exclusive role than previously in reproductive labor—being the only ones physically available to keep the toddler from stumbling into the fire or to nurse the seriously ill— it was still possible for some reproductive labor to follow productive labor out of the house. In general this involved older children who helped their fishermen fathers on the boat or apprenticed to their merchant fathers in the storefronts down by the docks. The fact that these children were productive workers themselves does not erase the fact that their elders were doing the reproductive work of teaching them.

The peculiar institutions of slavery and the plantation economy in the South present yet another organization of production and reproduction in an agrarian economy.[16] Both reproduction and production took place on plantations. But the lion's share of production was production for the market rather than for the use of the people who lived on the plantations. Tobacco and cotton, and to a lesser extent such crops as peanuts or rice, were cash crops produced for interregional and international export. In addition, some plantations were so large and home to so many people that even production for use took place on a grand scale. An individual's role in this productive process depended on who you were. White plantation owners and their hired foremen—generally men—supervised the productive labor; the African-American field slaves—male and female—actually did it. The same was true for reproductive labor, although it was generally white women who supervised the African-American house slaves. Preparing food, cleaning, doing laundry, supervising young children, and even nursing infants was all reproductive labor that African-American women and men did under the direction of their mistresses. Certain select tasks, however, were still performed by white minds and hands: the formal education of white children, music and art lessons, and religious instruction were all reproductive work that, in general, white women or hired white teachers did.[17]

Plantations were large enough so that even though both production and reproduction could be said to happen at the same general place, they were physically distinct. The gender division of labor for whites was also quite distinct, with men supervising the productive labor in the fields and plantation workshops, and women in charge of the reproductive work in the house. For the African-American slaves it was a different story. Whether slaves did productive or reproductive work depended not so much on their sex, but on whether they were a field or house slave.

Although slaves could do productive work for their own use—building or repairing their houses, making clothing or furniture—for the most part their productive labor was for the benefit of and controlled by their owners, as was their reproductive labor. The reproductive labor that African-American slaves did for themselves was constrained and molded by the slavery system. Since female slaves, except for the time right around the birth of a child, were working away from their own homes in the service of their owners, they were often not available for reproductive work for their own families.[18] Instead, work such as the care and supervision of very young children or the tending of the sick fell to people who were too old and worn out to spend much time working for their owners, or to somewhat older children. Slave narratives tell often of the mother who worked from dawn to dusk taking care of her owners' house and children and was therefore not able to care for her own as she longed to do. Furthermore, slave families were often broken apart by the market in human flesh—children sold away from their parents and parents from children. Even though these dispersed families often made heroic efforts to keep in touch with one another and even to reunite, the care and nurturance of family members was often perforce a community responsibility.

Finally, there were some reproductive tasks that sometimes simply did not happen for some slaves. Education is a prime example. There were no schools for slave children: in the nineteenth century, southern states made educating slaves a crime. Although some whites did educate some slaves, this was rare; African-American slaves also taught each other.[19]

Implications for Family Policy

The fact that households and families were so central to productive, as well as reproductive, work meant that they were central social and economic institutions of agrarian society. As such, it was clearly in the overall community's interest to keep them in good functional order. Many of the family policies of the time reflected the primacy of maintaining families.

In colonial New England, the mid-Atlantic, and the South a system of "outdoor relief" provided poor families who were not making ends meet with financial and in-kind support.[20] Families who did not measure up to community norms in raising their children were sanctioned.[21] If parents were not providing the proper religious training, for instance, they were ordered to do so. While this oversight of family life by the community was particularly marked and has been much written about in Massachusetts, it was also present further south, at least for white families.[22] For African-American families, slavery brought with it policies that actively broke apart families, rather than supported them and helped them to function.

One notable feature of the combination of production and reproduction in the home is the absence of the notion of a distinction between the *private* life of the family and the *public* life of the community. Rather, family life was in some sense public or at least community life, for families were the essential cells of communities. It is not surprising, then, that community family policies were designed to regulate what went on inside families and to maintain them, not out of some notion of protecting the rights of individuals within families, but instead out of the necessity of keeping a society's primary economic units in good working order. Families were "a little commonwealth,"[23] the smallest unit of social or public life, rather than the private enclave of a "haven in a heartless world."[24] It is with the advent of industrialization in the United States in the nineteenth century that this precise notion of two distinct spheres, private family life and public community (read "government" or "business" or even "work") life began to develop.

PRODUCTION LEAVES THE HOME

The onset of industrialization in the United States is often dated to the 1790s, when Samuel Slater's carding and spinning machines were placed in small textile mills throughout New England.[25] Landmark moments in the history of industrialization in the nineteenth-century United States are legion, and it will suffice to mention only a few to remind us of the scope of political economic change. In 1793, in the context of strong demand for American cotton created by the mechanization of spinning in England, the cotton gin was invented to separate the seeds from the cotton fibers. Ramifications of this invention included establishing cotton as the southern plantation economy's main crop, and helping to create the impetus for a North American textile industry.[26] Among the first and most famous of this textile industry's mills were the ones in Lowell, Massachusetts.[27] Here the "noble experiment" of a largely female workforce, drawn from New England farms and employed and housed in what the mill owners touted as the ideal modern conditions, was quickly eclipsed by the militant "turn-outs" of the "Lowell girls" themselves in the 1830s, and their replacement, beginning in the 1840s, by thousands of immigrants from Europe.

Systems of communication and transportation, essential parts and products of industrialization, were also expanding during the nineteenth century.[28] Samuel Morse developed both the electric telegraph and the Morse Code in the 1830s. The Western Union Telegraph Company completed a transcontinental line in 1861. Steam engines, a novelty in the 1820s, were by 1860 chugging along rail lines throughout the country. The Golden Spike, which connected lines from the east and west coasts in 1869, marked not only the interconnection of the entire country by rail, but also the fact that the economy had changed to the point where people could well see the usefulness and profitability of such a far-flung transportation network.

In 1886 the Haymarket "riots" crystallized several developments that were part and parcel of industrialization: the growth of an urban working class that, at times, organized and protested over working conditions such as pay and hours; the development of political groups whose generally left-wing politics were forged in the class relations engendered by capitalist industrialization; and the vehemence of class conflict where (to oversimplify) workers and owners fought over hours, pay, and the organization of work itself.[29]

Industrialization in the nineteenth-century United States was a ragged process over both time and place—most advanced in urban areas (virtually by definition, since it was the process of industrialization itself that gave rise to rapid urban growth), and quite distant, apparently, from the agrarian life of both the older East and the westward-moving "frontier." But even that agrarian life was influenced by industrialization: the textile mills of Britain and New England drove up demand for southern cotton, thereby maintaining, at least for a time, a plantation system based on slave labor. The migration of European-Americans to farms on the western plains was hastened and cemented by the railroads. Tools and household goods that farm families purchased rather than made for themselves began to come from factories instead of local craftsmen. Varied and complicated as it was, industrialization nonetheless entailed several general characteristics that had crucial bearing on the organization of productive and reproductive work.

In the first place, industrialization by and large meant that production, which in an agrarian economy had been centered in the household, left the home. Textile production is a classic example. Housing looms and spinning jennies that were manyfold more powerful than the looms and spinning wheels of the preindustrial household, textile mills removed an arena of production from the home. People working in factories, on machines driven initially by waterpower, could produce far more cloth than they could working individually in their homes on machines powered by humans. A particular feature of capitalist industrialization is that only a few people had access to enough money to purchase the land, buildings, and industrial machinery necessary to establish a factory; the remainder of the people involved in this industrial enterprise were brought in as workers who were hiring out their labor.

There are several ramifications of the removal of production from the household. First of all, the departure of production from the home was equated with the departure of "work" from the home.[30] The "making of things," involving as it does the creation of physically tangible objects, often appears more like "real work" than does reproductive labor, the "making of people," which often involves the creation of less tangible products such as a well-behaved child or a good meal. In addition, the more that the growth of industrialization moved people's lives into a money economy, the more important seemed those activities which could procure money. As money became more important, "work" became defined, bit by bit, as that activity for which one is paid money. Since it was by and large productive work that earned money, at least in the first stages of industrialization, then it was production and production alone that merited being called work.

Second, the manufacture of products outside the home made their manufacture within the home less necessary.[31] Textiles woven in factories were soon inexpensive enough, and often considered of superior quality to home-produced goods, so that people on farms as well as in cities preferred "store-bought" to "homespun." It is of course important to remember that one of the reasons that factory-made textiles were cheap enough for the mass market was that they were made by cheap labor—from the slaves of southern plantations who picked the cotton to the Yankee farmgirls, and then, very quickly, the impoverished immigrants who ran the looms in New England mills. Furthermore, each particular product has its own particular story and timing— women in their homes were still knitting wool into sweaters and socks long after they no longer wove cloth, just as many families kept up a kitchen garden, and perhaps a cow and some chickens, long after they started to rely on stores for flour and sugar. The process of the replacement of production within the household by production outside of it is complex and varied. Nonetheless, the basic point is that this process was self-reinforcing: when family members left the household to work for wages, by and large in the performance of production, their labor was no longer available for production within the household, while their wages *were* available to purchase the products that they and other wage workers like them were making. The more that family members worked outside the home, the more necessary did their wages become to buy the things they were no longer making for themselves.

For the most part, the family members who left the household for jobs related to production outside the home were men.[32] This stems in part from the gendered division of labor within an agrarian economy. Although there is debate over how that division was defined—some argue that men were primarily responsible for work outside the house and women for work within it,[33] while others draw the line between production for exchange (male) and production for use (female)[34]—there is agreement that "men's work" and "women's work" were distinguished from each other. A man who was no longer needed to work the farm—a second or third son who did not stand to inherit the family farm; or all the men from a family farm that was failing—had expendable labor that could be put to work in the factories and cities of the industrializing United States.[35] Certainly in the earlier decades of industrialization, there was enough work in the home so that women, whose primary responsibility it had been even in preindustrial times, remained there if the family could afford for them to do so.

The corollary of defining only production as work is the redefinition of reproduction as something that is not work. When production and reproduction both took place in the household, and when they were woven together in a relatively seamless way, reproduction was as much a part of work as production was. But when production left the home, particularly when this meant that male labor left the home in societies where men were thought to be more important, it came to seem that work left the home.

This is not of course to say that all work actually did leave the home.[36] Reproductive work, in general, still took place there. Children continued to be born at home, the sick of all ages were nursed there, and it was at home that people died. It is true that during the course of the nineteenth century, and particularly in towns and cities, more and more of some reproductive tasks were performed for wages by non-family members. Over time male doctors and female nurses replaced the "nurses and midwives" of the agrarian era, for instance, but for many years they still rendered their services in families' homes. Institutions such as hospitals only began in the latter half of the nineteenth century, and nursing homes to care for the dependent elderly or chronically ill were a twentieth-century innovation.[37] Meals continued to be prepared at home, although nonfarm families relied more and more on peddlers, markets, and stores to purchase their food, even if they still kept a kitchen garden. Until processes of food preservation and storage were industrialized (milk pasteurization and reliably safe canning procedures did not really get established until the beginning of the twentieth century; freezing foods to preserve them was a process developed in the 1930s), individual families did the work of preserving fruits and vegetables, often by drying them or storing them in root cellars. Children were cared for at home, although with the advent of public education in the midnineteenth century, their formal education in academic subjects left the home.[38] But for all this reproductive work that remained in the home, its characterization changed bit by bit from a part of all the varied work that took place in the household, to "women's work"—somehow not as real or as worthwhile as the work that men did outside the home, work which never really received the gendered qualifier of "men's work" and therefore came to be considered generic work. Reproductive labor had now become "family life."

This redefinition of reproductive labor as an activity that is not work was a gradual process and affected different women in different ways.[39] One of the paramount measures of success for the men who worked in production outside the home was the ability to earn money. The more money earned, the more successful one was. To demonstrate this success, men could purchase bigger and better land, houses, and other forms of property, and could also purchase labor to help with the reproductive work that remained in their homes. Their wives and daughters thereby could be relieved of many reproductive tasks, and devote themselves to what were considered more refined pastimes, such as decorative needlework, art and music, a cultivated social life replete with calling cards, teas, and formal visits, and even charity and volunteer work conducted through churches and other social organizations. The reproductive labor of cleaning, buying and preparing food, doing laundry and ironing, and work-a-day sewing could be carried out by hired labor—servants. The "lady of the house" supervised this reproductive labor, and there was of course wide variation in how much reproductive labor she and her family were able to hire. Some families could only afford to hire extra help at spring-cleaning time, others were able to have a "girl" in to help every day, while the richest could hire several servants, from cook to chambermaid to gardener.

The women who were hired as servants to do reproductive labor in other people's homes no doubt saw themselves and were seen by others as working, and were in fact paid wages for their work. But the standards of what was desirable were being set by the more affluent families. In the first place, the long-term impact of hiring servants at relatively low wages to perform a host of reproductive tasks was to define those very tasks as being menial (worthy of being done by servants rather than employers) and not of great value (worthy only of the relatively low wages paid to servants). To the extent that affluent middle-class families set the ideological norms, the role of women vis-à-vis what was considered work changed markedly from what it had been in the preindustrial household. The "lady," while being ultimately responsible for the smooth operation of the household, and still expected to be knowledgeable about the tasks involved, did not roughen her own hands with this menial work. Instead, her responsibility was to maintain and cultivate the arts, to orchestrate a family's social life among others of its class, and to maintain and promote high moral standards. All these activities were valued by nineteenth-century norms, but none were defined as work.

Middle-class ladies therefore did not "work." And since they still retained central responsibility for raising and caring for children,[40] over time that aspect in particular of reproductive labor was no longer seen as work. Instead, middle-class women presided over "the family," "the home," and "domestic life," while their husbands operated in the world of work. The departure of production from the household, accompanied by the redefinition of reproduction, has given rise to some very powerful conceptual dichotomies that have had and continue to have profound influence: the private world of the family versus the public world of work; women's work, centered on reproduction versus men's work, centered on production; family versus work; private versus public.[41]

Families were no longer the "little commonwealths" of preindustrial times, the essential cells of society where both production and reproduction took place. Instead, they were diametrically opposed to the world of work as it was developing in the industrializing United States. Work was dominated by money and all the venal interests that went with it, by rough behavior that included everything from swearing to the necessity of making harsh decisions such as firing employees, and by affairs of the world from politics to war. Families were supposedly havens from this world of work. Families were places where feelings and sentiment were more important than money, where gentle behavior and social graces were cultivated and preserved, and where spiritual and moral values were passed on, rather than the more worldly and even amoral behavior and values that were tolerated in the work world. Families were private and the domain of women; work was public and the domain of men. No longer working together, as they had in preindustrial households, women and men reigned over separate spheres as industrialization changed the organization of all work.[42]

Middle-class families promoted and aspired to this ideal. And in fact many of them were able to attain it, although the ideology of a perfect and complementary division between two separate spheres masked the unhappy lives of many middle-class men who could not quite meet the demands of the work world and many middle-class women who chafed at the restrictiveness of their exclusively domestic roles. Furthermore, for many families in the United States, this ideal was not only unattainable, but established an invidious standard which they failed to reach. As immigrants from Europe and Asia, African-Americans moving off southern share-cropping farms, and poorer native-born Americans from throughout the country moved into the cities of the industrializing United States, they were hard put to emulate middle-class life.[43]

In the first place, the men in these working-class families often had to take the least desirable jobs that industrialization had to offer—"nonskilled" factory work where the hours were long, the wages low, and job security nonexistent; the lower rungs of commercial life from carters to longshoremen to peddlers; the hod-carriers of the building trades. They were often not able to earn enough money so that other family members could stay out of the labor force. And enter it those family members did—wives and children old enough worked as servants, took in laundry, took in boarders, made jewelry at their kitchen tables on a piecework basis, worked in small sweatshops sewing clothing and putting feathers on hats, and worked the line in factories.[44] One common pattern of maternal employment among working-class women, for instance, was to stay in the labor force while their children were very young, the children being cared for by a grandmother, aunt, neighbor, or even by each other. When the children were old enough to enter the labor force themselves and contribute to the family income, the mothers would leave it, to return to their homes full time and perhaps to even realize the dream of a stay-at-home mother.

The concept of the "family wage" illustrates this belief in the separate spheres of work and family. This wage, ideally paid to the male breadwinner, was supposed to be enough to support the needs of the entire family. Interestingly enough, the very notion of a family wage points up the fact that family and work were not really all that separate, for it defines the very existence of a family as being dependent on a wage, and the existence of the wage earner as dependent on a family. In poor and working-class families, it was frequently impossible for a sole male breadwinner to earn an entire family wage, in which case other family members perforce contributed to it.

No matter how separate "family" and "work" actually were as industrialization proceeded, the fact that they were defined as different was crucial. The development of a belief in the private family, where women were responsible for reproduction, set apart from the public work world, where men were responsible for production, had many ramifications, not the least of which was for the development of child and family policy.

Implications for Family Policy

The essential impact of the privatization of families and the development of a family/work duality was that families were expected to manage on their own with neither direct support nor direct interference from the surrounding community.[45] Over time, this stance often was portrayed as one where the sanctity of the private family was being protected from unwarranted intrusions by the public world and its agent, the government. When communities did explicitly concern themselves with families, it was frequently in a punitive way, rather than the basically supportive spirit of the outdoor relief policies of the seventeenth and eighteenth centuries. While towns in colonial New England sometimes refused aid to certain "strangers" for whom the community deemed it was not responsible, poverty was generally viewed as one understandable piece of the social hierarchy.

But by the beginning of the nineteenth century, distinctions were being drawn between the deserving and the undeserving poor. Their budgets strained by the increasing numbers of the poor, municipalities began establishing almshouses and workhouses, which were seen as less expensive and more efficient ways of providing for the poor. Although some of these institutions were initially designed to teach "able-bodied paupers" the proper attitudes and habits of industry whereby they could overcome their individual moral failing of poverty, by the latter half of the nineteenth century many had become houses of filth and pestilence where the insane, the diseased, and the merely poor were kept together.[46]

One way in which people pushed for policies that would support families and prevent poverty rather than punish it was the struggle over wages, hours, and working conditions, which was a product of capitalist industrialization and which was solidly underway by the midnineteenth century.[47] At first glance these fights between workers and owners appear to have been exclusively about the world of "work" and wages, but they were closely connected to the world of "family" and reproductive work as well. People who were selling their productive labor in factories for wages were keenly aware that the welfare of their families and their ability to continue doing unwaged reproductive labor depended upon the deal they could strike with their employers. Far from being divorced from the world of work, the world of families was inextricably bound up with it. This connection emerged explicitly when workers called and organized for being paid a "family wage," named as such at the time.[48] The connection was also there when some male workers and unions tried to push women out of their particular type of employment, arguing that the lower wages women would accept would rob male workers of the "family wage" that was their due.[49]

Although campaigns for higher wages, shorter and less tiring hours, and safer working conditions were important to the welfare of families, they were nonetheless part of a structural organization of society and whole way of thinking which perpetuated the notion of a private family and a public world of work. Rather than granting support outright to families for the reproductive work they were doing, the society at large channeled that support through wages. Since for the most part these wages were earned by men, this left women and children in families in a vulnerable position, dependent as they essentially were on the good will of husbands and fathers.

Connected to families and family policy as they may have been, struggles over the "family wage" were nonetheless still indirect family policy. Direct involvement in family policy was not a top priority of governments in the nineteenth century at any level—municipal, state, or federal. The ideology of separate spheres, of the private world of the family and the public world of "work" and of political activity, grew in strength as the nineteenth century wore on. In fact, many of the child and family policies, as well as other social welfare policies, that were constructed in the nineteenth century were initiated and carried out by private agencies and groups. These agencies and groups, in turn, were often started by women who saw themselves engaged in "social housekeeping" rather than public life outright.[50]

There were many middle-class women in the nineteenth century who embraced the notion of separate spheres for men and women and the attendant ideology of one of women's domestic roles being the upholding and promotion of higher moral values. These values included everything from personal rectitude and the avoidance of such transgressions as swearing, drinking, and sexual licentiousness, to Christian religious principles and teachings, to compassion and charity towards the less fortunate. Thus many women saw it as their duty to "do good works" and to concern themselves with these issues outside as well as inside the home. Far from intruding in the male public world, these women construed their involvement in social welfare as "social housekeeping," whereby they attempted to keep the house in order for as many people as possible.[51] Growing as it did out of a middle-class and primarily white base, this conglomeration of social welfare efforts also worked, sometimes very explicitly, to impose the values and norms of the white middle class on the people who were being "helped," who were for the most part poor and frequently newly arrived immigrants from "other" cultures. The "social housekeeping" often initiated by women in the second half of the nineteenth century ranged from visiting nursing and hospitals for the poor; to the establishment of orphanages and a foster care system for children who were sometimes true "orphans," but just as often from families who were having a hard time providing for them; to the temperance movement. By the turn of the century, these efforts included "social work" centers such as Hull House in Chicago and public health initiatives such as safe milk stations, where women could procure nonspoiled milk for their children and sometimes other medical care.

These late nineteenth-century social welfare movements remained in the private sector. Often begun by women as an extension of their reproductive work within the private family, the institutions that got established often kept going on a combination of "private" volunteer efforts by women seeking to do charitable good works and of "private" donations from individuals, churches, and sometimes even businesses seeking to do the same with money instead of labor. Social welfare was still a matter of private and individual good will rather than a public or social, that is, governmental, responsibility. The one primary exception to this general nineteenth-century rule was the advent of universal public education.[52]

Some historians of education have pointed out that the establishment of public education met a political-economic need—employers in the industrializing United States needed a labor force that was punctual, knew how to follow rules and cooperate with extrafamilial authorities, and at least for some jobs, how to read and compute. Public schools could train such a labor force, as well as attempt to inculcate

"American" mores and values into an immigrant population. There were many factors that gave rise to "universal" public education (unequal as it may have been and become across class and race lines), including a push from working-class groups for access to education. But it can also be seen as an instance where the community takes responsibility for and is the location of reproductive work—the formal education of children—that had heretofore been found primarily in the home. Public education was one of the first places where reproductive work followed productive work out of the home. This is a process that has been proceeding—with fits and starts—throughout the twentieth century.

REPRODUCTION LEAVES THE HOME

During the course of the twentieth century, the process of industrialization that began in the nineteenth century has expanded and deepened. The agrarian economy which had predominated in the seventeenth and eighteenth centuries and had survived in many places, notably the West and the South, in the nineteenth century, has been supplanted. Even within the agricultural sector, industrylike practices and work relations have accompanied the rise of large farms and ranches; the "family farm" is dying out. This continuing development of industrialization has engendered some profound demographic shifts, including the concentration of more and more people in cities and the increasing participation of women in the labor force. (See Table 1.)

The expansion of industrialization has affected reproductive work in a number of ways. In the first place, more and more aspects of reproduction that had taken place in the home, even during the first decades of industrialization, began to move out. All sorts of housework, which up until the twentieth century had been very labor intensive (whether that labor came from family members or from servants), began to change with the advent of "labor-saving" devices.[53] Perhaps most significant among these was the introduction of running water and plumbing systems, which saved many back-breaking trips to the local pump or backyard well. Electrification also had a big impact, since electricity both provided lights that did not need repeated cleaning and filling as kerosene lamps had done, and made possible a legion of housework tools from vacuum cleaners to clothes washing machines to refrigerators. The industrialization of food processing meant that preserving and canning fresh produce was no longer work that individual families needed to do (granted that food processing is in that gray area where production—the making of things—and reproduction—the making of people, in this case feeding them—meet).

There has been considerable debate over whether these labor-saving devices have actually lessened the load of reproductive work within the home. Some argue that along with the new machinery came new, more ambitious, standards of housewifery and cleanliness—kitchen floors must now be spotless; underwear changed daily; meals must be fancier; a fresh dress every day for the modern

Table 1:

Women's Labor Force Participation Rates by Marital Status and by Racial Ethnic Group, 1920 and 1980

	1920		1980	
	Married	Other	Married	Other
Native American	8.9	19.8	47.9	47.6
Chicana	n.a.	n.a.	46.1	52.6
European American	6.5	45.0	48.1	51.1
African-American	32.5	58.8	60.5	49.4
Chinese-American	18.5	38.7	60.8	55.0
Japanese-American	18.5	38.7	56.1	62.3
Filipina-American	18.5	38.7	70.6	64.5
U.S. Puerto Rican	n.a.	n.a.	44.8	36.6
Island Puerto Rican	13.1	32.2	29.2	28.9

Source: Adapted from Amott & Matthaei (1991), *Race, Gender, and Work* (Boston: South End Press, 1991), Table 9–3.

schoolgirl replaced the pinafore worn by her nineteenth-century predecessor.[54] Furthermore, the panoply of products, once produced in the home, that were now sold in the market meant that people responsible for the smooth operation of a home had a big new job: shopping.[55]   Many writers have emphasized the roles that the twentieth-century culture of consumption has played: as a force driving demand in an expanding capitalist economy so that new industries would have a market for their products; as a fundamental measuring stick of class status that encourages people to consume more and more "things" in order to raise their position within the finely grained class hierarchies in the United States; and as a mechanism for keeping women identified with their homes and the consumption attached to them.[56] But it is also true that the labor-saving devices do in fact save labor: a refrigerator can save on daily trips to the store; an electric washing machine involves much less physical labor than a tub and a scrubboard; and many women know full well that it is not necessary to spend hours shopping for "bargains" that save only a dollar or so.

Other aspects of reproductive work have also left the home. Over the past 100 years large portions of the work of caring for the dependent elderly, the sick, and even of providing emotional support and nurturance have been transferred to the cash nexus and the "public" world of work. Even considering the lower life expectancy of people in the United States prior to the twentieth century, there were still many elderly people who lived to become infirm in a variety of ways—unable to walk very well, incontinent, senile, for example—and who needed help caring for themselves.

This had been work for which family members had been responsible.[57] Wives cared for husbands (and, to a lesser extent, husbands for wives); daughters took care of parents, sometimes by having them move in with them and sometimes through frequent daily visits; and it was certainly not unheard of for sisters to care for their aging siblings. While it is true that much of this work, shouldered primarily by women, goes on to this day within the home, it is also true that nursing homes, which are a twentieth-century development, have taken over part of it.

Although people who are mildly ill are still nursed at home, the organization of U.S. health care in the twentieth century has meant that the acutely ill are generally nursed in hospitals. Prior to 1900, most ill people, no matter how desperately sick, were nursed at home. Although doctors and nurses were hired to provide medical advice and nursing care, much of the reproductive labor required to care for the sick came from family members. By the middle of the twentieth century, the acutely ill were routinely hospitalized; those who could afford it took themselves and especially their children to the doctor for sore throats, earaches, and annual check-ups; and babies were born almost exclusively in hospitals and then remained there with their mothers for as long as two weeks of rest and recuperation.[58] A considerable amount of the reproductive work involved in caring for the sick had left the home.[59]

Another aspect of reproductive work that has been taken over in part by the public world of the market is the provision of emotional support and nurturance.[60] People now pay for everything from dating services, to psychotherapy, to educational week-end workshops on topics such as "enhancing your self-esteem," to body massage. This is not to say that previously, individual families had been the only locations and sources of emotional sustenance. Certainly churches and other religious and community organizations played a significant role in providing people with a sense of belonging and advice about personal problems. And it is also not to imply that families in the past were necessarily happy places where everyone's needs for emotional support were fulfilled.[61] In fact, we know that *not* to be the case. It is simply to point out that significant portions of some of the reproductive labor of making people feel cared for have moved outside the home—there is now a market in sympathetic understanding and guidance in personal problems.

One part of reproductive labor which, until the past twenty years, has remained primarily in the home is the care of pre-school-age children, generally speaking, children from birth to five years. The middle-class norm was that mothers should care for young children at home.[62] The middle-class mothers who hired child care help so that they could "continue their careers" were very much the exception until the 1970s. And mothers from poorer families, whose earnings could be crucial to maintaining the necessary family wage, often traded babysitting with a neighbor or even had a family member who could do the work without being paid. These mothers also often stayed at home and did piecework, took in boarders, or did laundry for wages; children were sometimes left home alone. There were also some day nurseries.[63] In recent years, however, the care of young children has begun to move out of the home.[64] This is because during the twentieth century, the labor force participation rates of women, particularly married women and the mothers of younger and younger children, have steadily increased.[65]

These women have been drawn into the labor force partly because of the expansion of production and all of the ancillary activities associated with that expansion.[66] As firms have grown in both size and complexity, not only has the number of people directly involved in production increased, but also the number of people in support activities for that production. Large industrial companies with many factories require large office staffs to coordinate production and sales. Advertising firms that promote the sale of products; insurance firms that sell protection for corporate as well as individual property; legal firms that sell the services of protecting individual interests as well as those of particular corporations within the complex world of both national and international competition and government regulations; governmental bureaucracies that have kept pace with the increasingly complex societies that industrialization and urbanization have wrought— all of this work is connected to the industrialization of production. And much of this work has been done by women.[67]

As reproduction has begun to leave the home as well during the twentieth century, women have also been employed to do reproductive work in the labor market. Many of the jobs that are part of reproductive labor—work in education, health care, and social services—are often referred to as the "service sector." Primary and secondary education has expanded along with the population, while post-secondary education has grown from serving a very thin slice of the rich and middle class in the nineteenth century to enrolling a larger and larger percentage of the populace during the twentieth, particularly after World War II. The health care system, including doctors and nurses, all sorts of other hospital personnel, and the employees of the health insurance industry, has mushroomed and is still growing. Social services, employing everyone from social workers to psychologists, have increased. This service sector has grown by leaps and bounds over the past century, and many of the women who have entered the labor force have gotten jobs there.

By and large, women entered the labor force out of need, and not unconstrained choice. Many of these were single women or widows, but a sizeable percentage of married women were also in the labor force. A watershed was reached in 1987, when the U.S. Census Bureau announced that more than half of mothers of children under the age of one were in the labor force.[68] More and more mothers from all families, including middle-income and affluent ones, are staying in the labor force, precisely as a means of maintaining their families' economic position. The stagnation of real wages has meant that family members have to work harder just to stay in the same place. In part because of the feelings of economic insecurity that this situation has engendered, many mothers stay in the labor force at the time of the birth of a child. This is not necessarily because they need their earnings at that particular moment, but rather because they know that their family cannot long go without their earnings and they are afraid to give up the job that they have for fear of not being able to get another one as good.[69]

This long-range trend of increasing female, and particularly maternal, labor force participation shows no signs of being reversed. Mothers in large numbers are going to be working outside the home, at least for the foreseeable future.[70] But women have been and still are second-class citizens in the labor force. Why? The answer is bound up with notions of the private family and women's primary identification as mothers within it.

As discussed above, the departure of production from the home that took place in the nineteenth century brought with it the advent of a cultural norm that the family was a private place, the sphere of women, in which something other than work took place. Work was what men did in the public world to earn wages; what women were doing within private families may have been valuable, but it was not work. It was running a house, raising a family, being a mother or housewife—but not named as work. This distinction between the private world of the family and the public world of work had several ramifications for the women who did enter that public world of "work."

In the first place, it was assumed that they were only temporary members of the labor force, and that they would be leaving before long to take up their primary calling as wives and mothers.[71] Many of the single women who were in the labor force in the nineteenth century and the first half of the twentieth did in fact follow this pattern after they married, assuming that their families could manage without their individual contribution to the family wage. Furthermore, the operation of a "marriage bar" in some occupations meant that women were actively pushed out of the labor force when they married.[72] Many states in the nineteenth century (and even into the twentieth) had laws which prohibited schoolteachers from being married and required them to resign when they did so.[73] Since women were therefore only "temporary workers," they were not considered to merit some of the advantages that came with the better jobs that the labor market had to offer—training, promotions, higher wages, and job security. And since they were only temporary members of the labor force, and not primarily responsible for the family wage, it did not really matter if they were in general paid lower wages than men for their work.[74] The widespread notion that women were only working for pin money only justified the situation.

These stereotypes about women in the labor force and the lower wages and status which they justified were particularly harmful to women whose need to be in the labor force was indeed great. Single women who were supporting themselves and often other family members, widows who were their children's sole source of support, and married women whose earnings were absolutely crucial were often in the labor force permanently. But they were paid the same lower wages as the women whose labor force tenure was relatively short.

Second, as industrialization progressed, money became an increasingly important measure of the worth of both things and labor. Work outside the home that earned money became more valuable than the work inside the home that did not. This devaluation of reproductive labor tended to color the status of *all* labor performed by those people—women—who were primarily responsible for reproductive labor.

Women's work was, first and foremost, reproductive labor. Reproductive labor, no longer worth as much as productive labor, was devalued. Therefore, all women's labor was devalued: women's work by definition was not worth as much as men's work. So even if the work that women were doing took place outside the home for wages, it was worth less simply because it was women's work.

Third, the stricter gender division of labor that accompanied the development of the separate spheres of women's work in the private family and men's work in public outside the home legitimized the very concept of "women's work" and "men's work."[75] Employers could refuse to hire women, and male employees could both oppose the employment of women in their occupations and keep women out of their unions, supporting their positions by maintaining that the job in question was not properly women's work. It is important to stress that arguments about what did and did not constitute women's work were often opportunistic. People could make the argument that women's "greater dexterity" made them ideal typists at the same time that they neglected to mention that that very dexterity might also make them ideal surgeons. The notion of an appropriate "women's work" made discrimination against women in various occupations relatively easy. Women who entered this sex-segregated labor force were thereby crowded into a limited number of occupations, and the resultant competition for employment tended to keep wages low.

Many of the jobs in the labor market defined as women's work were in fact reproductive work. It is not that women always followed their work out of the home: Women have in general been the primary cooks within the home but their numbers are few among the ranks of the great chefs or the food servers (waiters) in expensive restaurants; women were the primary healers of the sick in the home, but in the labor force they tend to be the lower-paid nurses rather than the higher-paid doctors. But it is true that when reproductive tasks left the home, women tended to take jobs in which they did not have to contend with the argument that they were trying to do men's work.

In part because much of this reproductive work has been defined as women's work, it too has been devalued. Female nurses, who do much more of the routine caregiving work of tending to the sick, are valued less than male doctors.[76] Elementary school teachers, who are mainly women and who teach children, have less status and less pay than college professors, who are still primarily men and who teach adults.[77] And child care workers, who do the quintessential reproductive work of taking care of children, earn very low wages.[78] Anyone who has tried to run a preschool classroom of ten three- and four-year-olds for an entire morning knows how much work and skill is involved in doing a good job. And yet, as a recent study of child care in Boston found:

> The disgracefully low salaries of child care workers are at the heart of a critical issue in the child care industry. Although Boston is privileged to have one of the best trained pools of child care providers in the country, these professionals are earning roughly half the salaries of comparably educated workers in other professions, and often less than they could earn working at McDonald's. In addition to low salaries,

they typically receive few, if any, job benefits, and function under highly stressful working conditions. At these salaries, they cannot afford to pay back the loans they took out to get their bachelor's and master's degrees.

As a result, there is a high rate of turnover among child care providers, although study after study shows that the quality of care is inextricably linked to hiring and keeping good teachers with whom the children can develop lasting, positive attachments.[79]

The devaluation of the work of caring for children has become quite entrenched by this latter half of the twentieth century. When the work is done by unpaid labor in the home, many people do not even recognize it as work. The idea that mothers caring for children in the home are "just housewives" has widespread currency, from the women themselves who often feel that they are not doing anything important to popular jokes. The cruelly small allotments of Aid to Families with Dependent Children, one of the few places where governmental policy pays for that labor directly, only serve to emphasize that devaluation. When the work is done by paid labor outside the home, the compensation is generally miserly. Extremely low wages for day care workers, coupled with the stress of working in an occupation that demands a high level of skill to be done well, have resulted in very high turn-over rates among those workers. The low status of the work of caring for children seems to have infected the general attitude towards children in the United States. When over 21% of all children are living in poverty, and only 10-42% of children starting school in nine major cities in 1991 had received their preschool vaccinations at the appropriate time, the welfare, health, and education of all children could not be said to have been top national priorities.[80] Despite the efforts of a wide range of child advocates and professionals, in fields ranging from public education to social work to health care to academia, to counter this trend, the devaluation of the work of caring for children has not yet been turned around. The story of child and family policy in the United States in the twentieth century is a good case in point.

Implications for Family Policy

As both reproductive work and reproductive workers have left the home during the course of the twentieth century, there have been some public policies that have been developed to take the place, at least partially, of both the work and the workers. These policies have been implemented by a variety of agents: the federal government, state governments, local and municipal governments, nonprofit or voluntary agencies and organizations, and even some for-profit enterprises.[81] Nonetheless, many maintain that the aggregate of policies from all levels of government and private agencies still adds up to only a threadbare patchwork.[82]

Now that so many mothers are in the labor force on a more or less permanent basis, and even many middle-class families find it difficult to manage on a single contribution to the family wage, there may be an emerging recognition that the work of caring for children is work for which *all* families in the United States should receive social support. As reproduction and reproductive workers have joined production outside the home, the political economic basis for community responsibility for reproduction is at hand. Structural shifts in the economy have made the old arrangement of the productive worker earning a family wage in the public labor market in order to support unpaid reproductive workers caring for people in the home no longer viable. If political will can match economic reality, the work of caring for children will begin to receive the value and support that it so richly deserves.

NOTES

1.   U.S. Department of Commerce: Bureau of the Census (1992). *Statistical abstract of the United States: 1992* (112th ed.). Washington, D.C.: Government Printing Office. Series No. 621: Labor force participation rates for wives, husbands present, by age of own youngest child: 1975 to 1991.

2.   Many people have drawn this distinction. Particularly good discussions can be found in E. Zaretsky (1986). *Capitalism, the family, and personal life* (Rev. ed.). New York: Harper & Row; J. A. Matthaei (1982). *An economic history of women in America: Women's work, the sexual division of labor, and the development of capitalism.* New York: Schocken Books; L. A. Tilly & J. W. Scott (1978). *Women, work, and family.* New York: Holt, Rinehart & Winston; and C. Lasch (1977). *Haven in a heartless world: The family besieged.* New York: Basic Books.

3.   This schema should not obscure the fact that historical change is a ragged process in which the complexity of any given place and moment is far more complicated than any analytic framework can hope to credit. Despite dividing U.S. history into three periods where the political economy of productive and reproductive labor is organized differently, it is certainly possible to see all three organizations existing at the same time. In the United States today, for example, there are still rural pockets where families engage in a great deal of production for use in their own homes; families where most reproductive labor takes place in the home while some members earn money by engaging in production in the labor force; and families where the "making of people" takes place at least as much outside the home and in the market economy as it does within the home.

4.   U.S. Department of Commerce, Bureau of the Census (1975). *Historical statistics of the United States: Colonial times to 1970.* Part 1. Series A57–72: Population in urban and rural territory, by size of place: 1790 to 1970. Washington, D.C.: Government Printing Office.

5.   D. C. North (1961). *The economic growth of the United States, 1790–1860.* Englewood Cliffs, NJ: Prentice-Hall.

6.   J. Spring (1986). *The American school, 1642–1985: Varieties of historical interpretation of the foundations and development of American education.* New York: Longman; L. A. Cremin (1970). *American education: The colonial experience, 1607–1783.* New York: Harper & Row.

7.   J. Boydston (1990). *Home and work: Housework, wages, and the ideology of labor in the early republic.* New York: Oxford University Press; S. Coontz (1988). *The social origins of private life: A history of American families, 1600–1900.* London: Verso; J. Demos (1970). *A little commonwealth: Family life in Plymouth Colony.* New York: Oxford University Press.

8. Boydston (1990), *Home and work*; R. S. Cowan (1983). *More work for mother: The ironies of household technology from the open hearth to the microwave.* New York: Basic Books; M. P. Ryan (1983). *Womanhood in America: From colonial times to the present* (3rd ed.). New York: Franklin Watts; Matthaei (1982), *An economic history of women in America*; A. Clark (1919). *Working life of women in the 17th century.* London: G. Routledge & Sons.

9. M. B. Norton (1980). *Liberty's daughters: The revolutionary experience of American women, 1750–1800.* Boston: Little, Brown; E. Dexter (1924). *Colonial women of affairs: A study of women in business and the professions in America before 1776.* New York: Houghton Mifflin; Clark (1919), *Working life of women in the 17th century.*

10. Boydston (1990), *Home and work*; Matthaei (1982), *An economic history of women in America*; H. Hartmann (1979). Capitalism, patriarchy, and job segregation by sex. In Z. R. Eisenstein (Ed.), *Capitalist patriarchy and the case for socialist feminism*, 206–247. New York: Monthly Review Press.

11. C. Bridenbaugh (1950). *The colonial craftsman.* New York: New York University Press.

12. Boydston (1990), *Home and work*, 42–43.

13. W. J. Rorabaugh (1986). *The craft apprentice: From Franklin to the machine age in America.* New York: Oxford University Press; Bridenbaugh (1950), *The colonial craftsman.*

14. M. Rediker (1987). *Between the devil and the deep blue sea: Merchant seamen, pirates, and the Anglo-American maritime world, 1700–1750.* New York: Cambridge University Press.

15. Boydston (1990), *Home and work*; Matthaei (1982), *An economic history of women in America.*

16. T. L. Amott & J. A. Matthaei (1991). *Race, gender, and work: A multicultural economic history of women in the United States.* Boston: South End Press; J. Jones (1985). *Labor of love, labor of sorrow: Black women, work and the family, from slavery to the present.* New York: Basic Books; D. G. White (1985). *Ar'n't I a woman? Female slaves in the plantation South.* New York: Norton; P. Giddings (1984). *When and where I enter: The impact of black women on race and sex in America.* New York: William Morrow; Matthaei (1982), Chapter 4: Women's work and the sexual division of labor under slavery, *An economic history of women in America*, 74–97; H. G. Gutman (1976). *The black family in slavery and freedom, 1750–1925.* New York: Pantheon; E. D. Genovese (1974). *Roll, Jordan, roll: The world the slaves made.* New York: Random House; J. C. Spruill (1972). *Women's life and work in the Southern colonies.* New York: W.W. Norton. (Original work published 1938.); E. D. Genovese (1969). *The world the slaveholders made: Two essays in interpretation.* New York: Pantheon.

17. W. J. Fraser, Jr., R. F. Saunders, Jr., & J. L. Wakelyn (Eds.) (1985). *The web of southern social relations: Women, family, and education.* Atlanta, GA: University of Georgia Press; Spruill (1972), *Women's life and work in the southern colonies.*

18. Jones (1985), *Labor of love, labor of sorrow*; White (1985), *Ar'n't I a woman?*; Gutman (1976), *The black family in slavery and freedom.*

19. P. S. Foner & J. F. Pacheco (1984). *Three who dared: Prudence Crandall, Margaret Douglass, Myrtilla Miner—Champions of antebellum black education.* Westport, CT: Greenwood Press; Genovese (1974), *Roll, Jordan, roll*, 561–566.

20. M. B. Katz (1986). *In the shadow of the poorhouse: A social history of welfare in America.* New York: Basic Books; W. I. Trattner (1984). *From poor law to welfare state: A history of social welfare in America* (3rd ed.). New York: Free Press.

21.   Demos (1970), *A little commonwealth*.

22.   B. L. Bellows (1985). "My children, gentlemen, are my own": Poor women, the urban elite, and the bonds of obligation in antebellum Charlestown. In Fraser et al., *The web of southern social relations*, 52–71.

23.   Demos (1970), *A little commonwealth*.

24.   Lasch (1977), *Haven in a heartless world*.

25.   North (1961), *The economic growth of the United States*.

26.   R. Fogel & S. Engerman (1974). *Time on the cross: The economics of American Negro slavery*. Boston: Little, Brown.

27.   A. Kessler-Harris (1982). *Out to work: A history of wage-earning women in the United States*. New York: Oxford University Press; T. Dublin (1979). *Women at work: The transformation of work and community in Lowell, Massachusetts, 1826–1860*. New York: Columbia University Press; H. Josephson (1949). *The golden threads: New England's mill girls and magnates*. New York: Duell, Sloan, & Pearce; C. Ware (1931). *The early New England cotton manufacture*. Boston: Houghton Mifflin.

28.   A. D. Chandler, Jr. (1977). *The visible hand: The managerial revolution in American business*. Cambridge, MA: Harvard University Press; North (1961), *The economic growth of the United States*.

29.   H. Zinn (1980). Chapter 10: The other Civil War. *A people's history of the United States*, 206–246. New York: Harper Collins; N. Ware (1964). *The industrial worker, 1840–1860*. Chicago: Quadrangle Books. (Original work published 1924.); P. Foner (1947–1964). *A history of the labor movement in the United States*. 4 volumes. New York: International Publishers.

30.   N. Folbre (Spring, 1991). The unproductive housewife: Her evolution in 19th-century economic thought. *Signs: Journal of Women in Culture and Society, 16*(3), 463–484.

31.   Kessler-Harris (1982), Chapter 2: From household manufactures to wage work, *Out to work*, 20–44; Matthaei (1982), *An economic history of women in America*; R. M. Tryon (1917). *Household manufactures in the United States, 1640-1860: A study in industrial history*. Chicago: University of Chicago Press.

32.   F. D. Blau & M. A. Ferber (1992). *The economics of women, men, and work* (2nd ed.), 22–24. Englewood Cliffs, NJ: Prentice-Hall; U.S. Department of Commerce: Bureau of the Census (1975). *Historical statistics of the United States, Colonial times to 1970*, Part 2. Series D75–84: Gainful workers, by age, sex, and farm-nonfarm occupations: 1820 to 1930. Washington, D.C.: Government Printing Office.

33.   R. W. Smuts (1971). *Women and work in America*. New York: Schocken Books; E. Abbott (1910). *Women in industry, a study in American economic history*. New York: D. Appleton.

34.   Matthaei (1982), *An economic history of women in America*.

35.   In fact, one of the most famous instances of women being employed in productive work in the early days of U.S. industrialization illustrates this point of a family's expendable labor being drawn into production outside the home. The "Lowell girls" were young women from the farms and small towns of New England who composed, for a few years during the 1830s and 1840s, the majority of the factory workforce in the new textile mills in Lowell, Massachusetts. They were able to take these jobs precisely because their labor was no longer absolutely essential to their families' household economies, and could be more useful earning wages in the factories. They were soon supplanted by the cheaper labor of Irish immigrants, both male and female, who fled for their lives to the United States from the potato famine of the 1840s.

36. Cowan (1983), *More work for mother*; S. Strasser (1982), *Never done: A history of American housework*. New York: Pantheon.

37. S. M. Reverby (1987). *Ordered to care: The dilemma of American nursing, 1850–1945*. New York: Cambridge University Press; P. A. Kalisch & B. J. Kalisch (1986). *The advance of American nursing* (2nd ed.). Boston: Little, Brown; B. Melosh (1982). *"The physician's hand": Work culture and conflict in American nursing*. Philadelphia: Temple University Press; P. Starr (1982). *The social transformation of American medicine*. New York: Basic Books; G. B. Risse, R. L. Numbers, & J. W. Leavitt (Eds.) (1977). *Medicine without doctors: Home health care in American history*. New York: Science History Publications/ USA; B. Ehrenreich & D. English (1973). *Witches, midwives, and nurses: A history of women healers*. Old Westbury, NY: The Feminist Press.

38. Spring (1986), *The American school, 1642–1985*; C. Kaestle (1983). *Pillars of the republic: Common schools and American society, 1780–1860*. New York: Hill & Wang; M. B. Katz (Ed.) (1973). *Education in American history: Readings on the social issues*. New York: Praeger; M. B. Katz (1968). *The irony of early school reform: Educational innovation in mid-19th century Massachusetts*. Boston: Beacon Press.

39. Amott & Matthaei (1991), *Race, gender, and work*; E. C. DuBois & V. L. Ruiz (Eds.) (1990). *Unequal sisters: A multicultural reader in U.S. women's history*. New York & London: Routledge.

40. In the United States, at least, it was only the wealthiest of families who employed nursemaids or governesses.

41. Coontz (1988), *The social origins of private life*; Zaretsky (1986), *Capitalism, the family, and personal life*.

42. G. Matthews (1987). *"Just a housewife": The rise and fall of domesticity in America*. New York: Oxford University Press; Matthaei (1982), Chapter 5: The development of separate sexual spheres of activity and of masculine and feminine self-seeking, *An economic history of women in America*, 101-119; D. S. Smith (Winter-Spring, 1973). Family limitation, sexual control, and domestic feminism in Victorian America. *Feminist Studies, 1*, 40–57. Reprinted in N. F. Cott & E. H. Pleck (1979), *A heritage of her own: Toward a new social history of American women*. New York: Simon & Schuster; N. F. Cott (1972). *The bonds of womanhood: Woman's sphere in New England, 1780–1835*. New Haven, CT: Yale University Press; B. Welter (Summer, 1966). The cult of true womanhood: 1820–1860. *American Quarterly, 18*(2), 151–174.

43. Amott & Matthaei (1991), *Race, gender, and work*; DuBois & Ruiz (Eds.) (1990), *Unequal sisters*; E. Ewen (1985). *Immigrant women in the land of dollars: Life and culture on the Lower East Side, 1890–1925*. New York: Monthly Review Press; Jones (1985), *Labor of love, labor of sorrow*.

44. S. P. Benson (1986). *Counter cultures: Saleswomen, managers, and customers in American department stores, 1890–1940*. Urbana, IL: University of Illinois Press; C. Stansell (1986). *City of women: Sex and class in New York, 1789-1860*. New York: Knopf; J. M. Jensen & S. Davidson (Eds.) (1984). *A needle, a bobbin, a strike: Women needleworkers in America*. Philadelphia: Temple University Press; F. E. Dudden (1983). *Serving women: Household service in 19th-century America*. Middletown, CT: Wesleyan University Press; Kessler-Harris (1982), *Out to work*; E. H. Pleck (1979). A mother's wages: Income earning among married Italian and black women, 1896–1911. In Cott & Pleck, *A heritage of her own*, 367–392; D. Katzman (1978). *Seven days a week: Domestic service in industrializing America*. New York: Oxford University Press; M. Cantor & B. Laurie (Eds.) (1977). *Class, sex, and the woman worker*. Westport, CT: Greenwood Press.

45.   F. Jacobs (this volume). Child and family policy: Framing the issues; F. Jacobs & M. Davies (this volume). On the eve of a new millennium.

46.   M. Abramovitz (1988). *Regulating the lives of women: Social welfare policy from colonial times to the present*. Boston: South End Press; Katz (1986), *In the shadow of the poorhouse*; Trattner (1984), *From poor law to welfare state*.

47.   Stansell (1986), *City of women*; S. Wilentz (1984). *Chants democratic: New York City and the rise of the American working class*. New York: Oxford University Press; Dublin (1979), *Women at work*; D. Montgomery (1979). *Workers' control in America: Studies in the history of work, technology, and labor struggles*. Cambridge: Cambridge University Press.

48.   R. Rothbart (Winter, 1989). "Homes are what any strike is about": Immigrant labor and the family wage. *Journal of Social History, 23*(2), 267–284; M. May (1987). The historical problem of the family wage: The Ford Motor Company and the five dollar day. In N. Gerstel & H. Engel Gross (Eds.), *Families and work*, 111–131. Philadelphia: Temple University Press; Matthaei (1982), *An economic history of women in America*, 121.

49.   J. Andrews & W. D. P. Bliss (1974). *A history of women in trade unions*, Vol. 10 of *Report on condition of women and child wage-earners in the United States*, Senate Doc. 645, 61st Congress, 2nd Session. New York: Arno Press. (Original work published 1910, Washington, D.C.: Government Printing Office.); H. Sumner (1974). *A history of women in industry in the United States*, Vol. 9 of *Report on condition of women and child wage-earners in the United States*, Senate Doc. 645, 61st Congress, 2nd Session. New York: Arno Press. (Original work published 1910, Washington, D.C.: Government Printing Office.)

50.   Abramovitz (1988), *Regulating the lives of women*.

51.   Ryan (1983), *Womanhood in America*, 198–210; B. L. Epstein (1981). *The politics of domesticity: Women, evangelism, and temperance in 19th-century America*. Middletown, CT: Wesleyan University Press.

52.   Spring (1986), *The American school, 1642–1985*; Kaestle (1983), *Pillars of the republic*; Katz (1968), *The irony of early school reform*.

53.   Cowan (1983), *More work for mother*; Strasser (1982), *Never done*.

54.   Cowan (1983), *More work for mother*.

55.   N. Y. Glazer (1993). *Women's paid and unpaid labor: The work transfer in health care and retailing*. Philadelphia: Temple University Press.

56.   S. Strasser (1989). *Satisfaction guaranteed: The making of the American mass market*. New York: Pantheon; Matthaei (1982), *An economic history of women in America*, 235–245; W. D. Wandersee (1981). *Women's work and family values, 1920–1940*, 7–26. Cambridge, MA: Harvard University Press; S. Ewen (1976). *Captains of consciousness: Advertising and the social roots of the consumer culture*. New York: McGraw-Hill.

57.   J. Demos (1979). Old age in early New England. In D. D. Van Tassel (Ed.), *Aging, death, and the completion of being*. Philadelphia: University of Pennsylvania Press. Also in M. Gordon (Ed.) (1983), *The American family in social-historical perspective* (3rd ed.). New York: St. Martin's Press; H. Chudacoff & T. Hareven (1978). Family transitions into old age. In T. Hareven (Ed.), *Transitions, the family and the life course in historical perspective*, 217–243. New York: Academic Press; D. H. Fischer (1978). *Growing old in America*. New York: Oxford University Press.

58.   Starr (1982), *The social transformation of American medicine*; M. J. Vogel (1979). The transformation of the American hospital, 1850–1920. In S. Reverby & D. Rosner (Eds.). *Health care in America: Essays in social history*, 105–116. Philadelphia: Temple University Press.

59.   Interestingly enough, the contemporary "crisis" in health care has brought with it

a rapid increase in the use of outpatient services and radical decreases in the average length of hospital stays, such that many patients now recuperate primarily at home, cared for by the unpaid labor of family members and the cheaper-than-hospital-costs paid labor of home health care aides and visiting nurses. One of the criticisms of this trend has been that the changes are being made at the expense of women, who are being expected to take up once again the unpaid reproductive work of nursing the sick, even at a time when many of them have jobs outside the home in the labor force as well.

60. W. Kaminer (1992). *I'm dysfunctional, you're dysfunctional: The recovery movement and other self-help fashions.* Reading, MA: Addison-Wesley; Lasch (1977), Chapter 1: Social pathologists and the socialization of reproduction, Chapter 5: Doctors to a sick society, *Haven in a heartless world,* 3–21, 97–110; D. B. Meyer (1965). *The positive thinkers: A study of the American quest for health, wealth, and personal power from Mary Baker Eddy to Norman Vincent Peale.* Garden City, NY: Doubleday.

61. S. Coontz (1992). *The way we never were: American families and the nostalgia trap.* New York: Basic Books.

62. Ryan (1983), *Womanhood in America,* 259–278; S. Fraiberg (1977). *Every child's birthright: In defense of mothering.* New York: Basic Books; J. Bernard (1974). *The future of motherhood.* New York: Penguin Books.

63. E. Boris & C. R. Daniels (Eds.) (1989). *Homework: Historical and contemporary perspectives on paid labor in the home.* Urbana, IL: University of Illinois Press; L. Gordon (1988). Chapter 5: "So much for the children now, so little before": Child neglect and parental responsibility. *Heroes of their own lives: The politics and history of family violence, 1880–1960,* 116–167. New York: Viking Penguin; M. O. Steinfels (1973). *Who's minding the children? The history and politics of day care in America.* New York: Simon & Schuster.

64. C. D. Hayes, J. L. Palmer, & M. J. Zaslow (Eds.) (1990). Chapter 2: Trends in work, family, and child care. *Who cares for America's children? Child care policy for the 1990s,* 16–42. Washington, D.C.: National Academy Press.

65. Between 1975 and 1991, for instance, the labor force participation rate for wives with husbands present increased from 37% to 60% for women with children under six, from 33% to 57% for women with children under three, and from 31% to 56% for women with children one year old or younger. U.S. Department of Commerce: Bureau of the Census (1992). *Statistical abstract of the United States: 1992,* Series No. 621: Labor force participation rates for wives, husbands present, by age of youngest child: 1975 to 1991.

66. L. Y. Weiner (1985). *From working girl to working mother: The female labor force in the United States, 1820–1980.* Chapel Hill, NC: University of North Carolina Press; Chandler (1977), *The visible hand.*

67. S. H. Strom (1992). *Beyond the typewriter: Gender, class, and the origins of modern American office work, 1900–1930.* Urbana, IL: University of Illinois Press; C. S. Aron (1987). *Ladies and gentlemen of the civil service: Middle-class workers in Victorian America.* New York: Oxford University Press; G. S. Lowe (1987). *Women in the administrative revolution: The feminization of clerical work.* Toronto: University of Toronto Press; Benson (1986), *Counter cultures;* M. W. Davies (1982). *Woman's place is at the typewriter: Office work and office workers, 1870–1930.* Philadelphia: Temple University Press.

68. U.S. Bureau of Labor Statistics (August 12, 1987). Over half of mothers with children one year old or under in labor force in March 1987. Press release. USDL 87–345. 769–P. Washington, D.C.: Government Printing Office.

69. F. D. Blau & M. A. Ferber (1992). Chapter 4: The allocation of time between the household and the labor market. *The economics of women, men, and work,* 72–118.

70.   Hayes et al. (1990), *Who cares for America's children?.*

71.   Weiner (1985), Chapter 2: The discovery of "future motherhood," *From working girl to working mother*, 31–46.

72.   Strom (1992), *Beyond the typewriter*.

73.   C. Goldin (1990). *Understanding the gender gap: An economic history of American women*, 160-179. New York: Oxford University Press; Spring (1986), Chapter 5: Organizing the American school: The 19th-century school-marm, *The American school, 1642–1985*, 112–148; Kessler-Harris (1982), *Out to work*, 235.

74.   Goldin (1990), *Understanding the gender gap*; A. Kessler-Harris (1990). *A woman's wage: Historical meanings and social consequences*. Lexington, KY: University of Kentucky Press.

75.   Goldin (1990), *Understanding the gender gap*; Matthaei (1982), Chapter 9: The development of sex-typed jobs, *An economic history of women in America*, 187–232; R. C. Edwards, M. Reich, & D. M. Gordon (Eds.) (1975). *Labor market segmentation*. Lexington, MA: D. C. Heath.

76.   Reverby (1987), *Ordered to care*; Melosh (1982), *"The physician's hand."*

77.   Spring (1986), *The American school*.

78.   M. Whitebook, C. Howes, & D. Phillips (1989). *Who cares? Child care teachers and the quality of care in America*. Executive summary, National Child Care Staffing Study. Oakland, CA: Child Care Employee Project; K. Modigliani (1986). But who will take care of the children? Childcare, women and devalued labor. *Journal of Education, 168*, 46–69.

79.   The Boston Foundation Carol R. Goldberg Seminar on Child Care (1992). *Embracing our future: A child care action agenda*. Boston: The Boston Foundation.

80.   Children's Defense Fund (1992). *The state of America's children 1992*. Washington, D.C.: Children's Defense Fund.

81.   Jacobs (this volume), Child and family policy.

82.   F. H. Jacobs & M. W. Davies (Winter, 1991). Rhetoric or reality? Child and family policy in the United States. *Social Policy Report, 5*(4). Society for Research in Child Development, 1–25; Hayes, et al. (1990), *Who cares for America's children?*; J. S. Lande, S. Scarr, & N. Grunzenhauser (Eds.) (1989). *Caring for children: Challenge to America*. Hillsdale, NJ: Lawrence Erlbaum Associates; S. B. Kamerman & A. J. Kahn (Eds.) (1978). *Family policy: Government and families in fourteen countries*. New York: Columbia University Press.

3

Dependent Children and Their Families: A Historical Survey of United States Policies

Cherilyn E. Davidson

Since the seventeenth century, community responses to high-risk families have ranged from support enabling them to continue to care for their children, to policies and practices that have removed children to be cared for elsewhere. When analyzed historically, these policies can be seen in terms of a dynamic tension between those that preserve families and those that, in essence, dissolve them. An understanding of historical patterns of the types of care, the groups who had the authority to design and implement the care, and the families affected by these decisions, enables us to analyze present practices on behalf of children and families and to contemplate future ones.

Dependent children are those who have been cared for by their communities because of their parents' inability to care for them in ways that met community standards. Historically, dependent children in the United States have been cared for through five primary programs: outdoor relief, almshouses, orphanages, foster care, and public welfare. The categories of families eligible for community care and sustenance have developed and changed over time. Analysis of the types of dependent care and the changing definitions of dependency reflects an overall pattern that can be discerned beneath the complexity of child welfare policy. These historical trends illuminate the current status of dependent children and the policies used to serve them.

OUTDOOR RELIEF

During the colonial period, the primary goal was community survival, which depended on every individual's labor within the confines of a family's farm or shop. The poor and indigent were expected to work, and having a trade was considered necessary for full participation in the community. Until roughly fifty years after the American Revolution, this country remained a collection of preindustrial, semiautonomous states. Every hand was needed and the institutional care of dependent families, such as almshouses in England, did not meet the needs of the new republic.[1] Instead, the primary response to destitute families unable to sufficiently provide for themselves was outdoor relief.

Outdoor relief was the provision of goods—usually in the form of coal, food, and other household supplies—and the abatement of taxes.[2] "Outdoor" relief was given to a family that lived outside, as compared to inside, a debtor's prison or workhouse such as those in England.[3] But the colonists did not leave all English practices behind. They brought with them the tradition of the 1601 Elizabethan Poor Laws which, in addition to providing some outdoor relief, also dealt with destitute families by removing children and placing them with other families in the community.[4]

In colonial communities, out-of-home placement, although not as commonly used for dependent children as outdoor relief, was implemented in two ways. The first consisted of placing children under the age of five or six in the homes of other families. This "boarding out" placement was paid for by the natural family or by the community with small, regular sums of money or goods.[5] The second, less frequently used method, was indenture or apprenticeship, which provided for children, usually over seven years of age, who were considered old enough to work.[6] This contractual agreement commonly provided the child with room, board, clothing, and training in exchange for the child's labor.[7]

Those responsible for making decisions about dependent families and their children were community-appointed Overseers of the Poor, also patterned after the English system.[8] Most communities appointed their own overseers, some by municipal decision and some under colonial law. For example, a Virginia statute of 1646 codified the community's right to remove children and place them in situations of apprenticeship if their parents had failed to instruct them satisfactorily in catechism, reading, and writing.[9] In 1735, Boston legislated responsibility for neglected children to Overseers of the Poor.[10] Between 1790 and 1825, numerous states passed legislation authorizing overseers to bind out or commit to almshouses dependent, illegitimate, poor, delinquent, neglected, orphaned, or fatherless children. Included were children found begging on the streets and those whose parents were beggars.[11] Despite instances of child removal, public welfare officials more routinely assisted indigent children with family aid. Infants, in particular, were provided for by community payments to their mothers or wet nurses.[12]

During the colonial and post-Revolutionary eras, dependent children under the jurisdiction of the overseers came from three groups: the fatherless or those whose fathers were absent, destitute families, and those whose families failed adequately to educate them. Townspeople commonly viewed female-headed families as unable to prepare children for independent living. In response, towns authorized overseers to remove children from such "neglectful" mothers and to board them out to father-headed working families. Thus, under colonial Poor Laws, single mothers did not have the right to care for their own children.[13] For those children who were not fatherless, but who were otherwise dependent upon the community, outdoor relief was the norm. When outdoor relief was insufficient to stabilize a family, boarding out and indenture were usually within the same community, so that familial relationships were not completely severed.[14]

The provision of supplies to needy families in their homes first peaked between 1650 and 1825, an apogee which was unparalleled until the twentieth century when Aid to Dependent Children (ADC) and Aid to Families with Dependent Children (AFDC), or public welfare, were implemented. Outdoor relief, although continued on a much reduced scale between 1825 and 1935, did not remain the primary response to dependent families. Many towns grew after the Revolution and outdoor relief came to be seen as an inadequate means to care for the needy. In response to the expense and a growing intolerance for the poor, communities established congregate living arrangements for families, modeled after those legislated by England's Elizabethan poor laws.[15]

ALMSHOUSES

By the second quarter of the nineteenth century, industrialization and mechanization reduced the demand for unskilled child labor. Vast numbers of youths, both with and without their families, emigrated to the United States. The net effect of these trends was an oversupply of child labor and a vastly increased number of poor families.[16] The primary response to these families was placement in almshouses, buildings maintained at public expense for the internment of paupers, the infirm, and the mentally ill, as well as law-breakers and alcoholics.[17] Although some children were committed to almshouses without their families, it appears that the majority were there with one if not both parents.[18] In many almshouses, the majority of inmates were women. Many entered with their children; others were unmarried and pregnant.[19] A secondary response was the early development of institutions for children called orphanages or children's asylums, although these did not become a major response to dependent children until the latter half of the nineteenth century.[20]

Almshouse care of dependent children and their families lasted from the 1790s to the early 1920s. Almshouse populations of children were: 1,000 in 1790, when the primary response was outdoor relief; 17,000 in the 1850s, at the height of almshouse use;[21] 9,000 in the 1880s;[22] and less than 3,700 by 1910,[23] when orphanage and foster care were primary. During the 1850s, over 25% of the population in New York City's almshouses,[24] and over 50% in Boston,[25] were children. Between 1880 and 1920, over 75,000 children resided in almshouses nationwide.[26]

The provision of outdoor relief diminished as punitive attitudes towards the poor grew, and it came to be seen as an ineffective use of a community's limited financial resources. The poor were no longer one's relatives or neighbors, no longer belonged to one's church, and no longer came from one's country of origin. Commerce developed and altered the social structures of many towns and small cities. The agrarian village economy was shifting to small town commercialism, with wider gaps between the "haves" and the "have-nots." The poor became a class distinct from the middle class, and as a result, class differences began to have a greater influence upon decisions of how to care for indigent families. The poor were no longer seen as blessed, meek, unfortunate individuals, but as people who had brought their misfortune upon themselves and were deserving of punitive scorn. Poverty was redefined as a moral condition and the indigent became the undeserving poor.[27]

In the 1820s, both the Poor Law Commission and the secretary of state in New York reported that outdoor relief to families was the most wasteful aid, with almshouses the most economical alternative. It was recommended that every county maintain its own poorhouse.[28] Because the majority of children in almshouses were there with at least one parent, almshouses can be viewed as another form of family preservation.[29] Indenture was utilized for many able-bodied older children, but younger children commonly stayed with their families. Within the almshouses' crowded and unsanitary confines, child mortality rates were alarmingly high, as a result of poor nutrition and the rapid spread of communicable diseases.[30]

Children who were likely to be considered dependent came from families like those of the colonial and post-Revolutionary period: white, destitute, and fatherless. However, during this period a new concern developed—child maltreatment. By 1825, it became public duty in a number of states to intervene in cases of cruelty or neglect of children.[31] In 1833, New York City established municipal power to remove maltreated children from their families.[32] The distinction was also made between delinquent and dependent children. Delinquent children, primarily older boys, were often removed from almshouses and adult prisons and placed in specialized reformatories or penal institutions for children.[33] New York City and other municipalities continued placing most dependent children in almshouses, but were substantially increasing the number of orphanages.

By the 1850s, "scientifically" administered orphanages were hailed as better for children than the squalid life in almshouses. Advocates for orphanage care proposed that children could be trained to be functional, productive members of the community if removed from their destitute parents and reared in what was considered to be a more morally instructive environment.[34] These philosophical arguments were instrumental in out-of-home care becoming the primary response to dependent children and remaining so for the next eighty years.

ORPHANAGES

In the late 1840s and 1850s, a massive influx of European immigrants led to an unprecedented number of poorly supervised, indigent children in Eastern seaboard cities.[35] By the end of the Civil War, resources to care for poor children and the children of deceased soldiers were seriously depleted. The philosophical shift to family dissolution as the means to deal effectively with dependent children resulted in more children being placed in large, congregate care orphanages than were maintained in almshouses or in their own homes through outdoor relief.

The growing unpopularity of almshouses also contributed to the proliferation and increased use of orphanages. After the Civil War, children of deceased soldiers often were treated as paupers and confined to almshouses, a practice many thought appallingly disrespectful. Private investigations of almshouses uncovered disturbing conditions. In 1867, one found that children were kept in locked cells and cared for by inmates, many of whom were insane or feeble-minded. In 1872, another found children who were abused, sick, ill-fed, and poorly clothed.[36] A number of state governments and private associations responded by establishing special institutions for the care and education of war orphans.[37]

During the last quarter of the nineteenth century, efforts were begun to remove children from almshouses. New York was the first to take action, and in 1874 passed the Children's Act, which ordered the removal of children between the ages of two and sixteen from almshouses.[38] Other states followed suit, many making it illegal to place a child in a poorhouse or almshouse unless mentally ill or retarded, physically handicapped, or so diseased that the child was considered unfit for family foster care. Children who were deaf or blind were also removed and placed in specialized institutions.[39] Life in the poorhouse, it was argued, was demoralizing, dangerous, and apt to foster dependency in children.[40]

Many state Boards of Charities were established between 1865 and 1890 to investigate and supervise the system of charitable and correctional institutions.[41] Frequently, one of their first official acts was to remove children from the state's almshouses and place them either in institutions or in fosterlike homes. Some of these foster families were paid small sums by community or private funding sources; others were uncompensated.[42] By 1910, only thirteen of the forty-eight states did not have state boards to supervise the organizations that cared for dependent children.[43]

Policies for dependent children and their families shifted to favor orphanages gradually rather than radically. The first private orphanage was established by the Ursuline Convent in New Orleans in 1727; the first public orphanage was established in Charleston, South Carolina, in 1790.[44] In 1790, when outdoor relief was still the primary means of caring for dependent children, there were approximately 200 children in orphanages. By 1800, eight private institutions for children had been founded,[45] and by 1824, the number climbed to twenty-six. By 1850, private charitable groups had established 56 of the 116 children's institutions in the United States;[46] and even though this was the height of almshouse care, there were 7,700 children in orphanages.[47] By the turn of the century, there were 93,000 children in orphanages.[48] Orphanage use predominated from the 1860s through the 1930s, when 1600 existed nationwide. The apex of orphanage care was reached in the mid-1930s, when it was estimated that there were over 144,000 children in this type of institutional care, representing 58% of the dependent children in out-of-home care.[49] Despite this, by the end of the 1930s, the number of dependent children maintained in their own homes surpassed the number of those in out-of-home care.[50] Nevertheless, as late as 1970, there were still over 55,000 children in institutions for neglected and dependent children.[51]

One nineteenth-century justification for removing children as young as toddlers from their parents was that society's respectable classes could best be protected from a militant working class by breaking up poor families, destroying the trade unions, and weakening the working-class urban political base.[52]   Whether the families affected were in almshouses or in urban slums, a primary aim was to stabilize society by removing children from the dangerous influence of their poor families and the environments in which they lived.[53] Philanthropic reformers, as well as officials and legislators, advocated removing poor children from their families to prevent the transmission of dependence from one generation to another. Despite the fact that removal of children from their parents who remained in the almshouse was a painful process to witness, it was "evident that the only hope of rescuing the child from a life of pauperism was to separate it from its parent or parents."[54]

Public responsibility in general for children was expanding, with orphanages and nurseries for children of "bad" parents, and education and health services for children of "good" parents.[55] The punitive attitude towards the poor had been tempered; it was reserved for the indigent adult who had failed to make something of himself or herself with the opportunities available. The poor child, however, came to be viewed as an individual who was malleable, trainable, and ultimately salvageable if removed from the pauperizing influence of his or her indigent parents.[56]

During the mid-1800s, the private sector, consisting of religious organizations, philanthropic groups, and middle-class helping societies, rose in dominance in the care of dependent children. The increased reliance on charitable work empowered these organizations to intervene in families as extensively as any branch of government.[57] The middle class had the resources, the time, and the motivation to respond to the "dangerous classes." The Child Saving Movement, which defined the destitute parent as the primary negative influence upon a child, "rescued" children from almshouses and placed them in institutions.[58]   Later, the Movement played a substantial role in moving over 100,000 children from the East Coast to families in the Midwest.[59]

Empowered by the states, private organizations fueled the Child Saving Movement by publicizing the conditions in the almshouses and advocating for state laws that removed children from them.[60] Private organizations also established the majority of orphanages, although they were publicly subsidized and often provided with land grants. These orphanages commonly demanded parental relinquishment so that their governing boards had complete power over the children "in loco parentis," or in place of the parent. Finally, private agencies, as well as their supporters in state government, espoused the ideology that they were saving "good" children from "bad" parents.[61] Criteria for "bad" parenting included poverty, being husbandless, or being a newly arrived non-Protestant immigrant.[62] Whether by means of orphanages or fosterlike homes, the goals of the Movement were to save children from the gross poverty and "moral depravity" of their parents.[63] The antialmshouse legislation of the 1870s, and the child abuse and neglect legislation of the 1890s, gave both public and private officials the power to remove poor children from their families.[64]

Orphanages commonly maintained flexible admissions policies, accepting children from the courts, from Overseers of the Poor, and from heads of households. The institutions often modeled their regimented functioning on an ideal of the well-ordered family, but familial intimacy was not a priority. Known as the Jacksonian model of institutionalization, it was common practice for children to march in lines to most activities that were begun at the same time every day. Eating and sleeping were undertaken in large halls that often accommodated over a hundred children at a time, in institutions that housed many hundreds.[65]

Because many orphanages only accepted children for placement on the condition that their families relinquish all rights to them, children often were prevented from maintaining familial contact.[66] The orphanages were free to enforce discipline and "rehabilitation."[67] Children were not typically returned to their families, because destitute families were considered "unworthy," and unlikely to change. Children would benefit most if reared in an atmosphere that was conducive to learning good work habits, which destitute families were thought unable to provide.[68] Except for some private charity to families, this was a period in which the removal of children from troubled or destitute homes was the norm. This approach left parents to their own devices for survival, allowing many to work, free from child care responsibilities. Interestingly, some orphanages allowed parents to visit if they paid for part of their children's care.[69] For children whose parents had been forced to surrender them to the custody of institutions, indenture was their means of returning to the community.[70]

The children who were most often considered for orphanage care were similar to their counterparts of earlier periods: white, poor, and fatherless. The majority were not true orphans; an estimated 90% had one or both parents living.[71] The majority of institutions did not serve children of color, and only a few orphanages were built to care specifically for African-American children.[72]

By the end of the nineteenth century, many orphanages began to resemble the almshouses they were designed to replace. Overcrowding was widespread, care inadequate, and disease rampant; children released from them were often unprepared to function autonomously.[73] In 1897, the New York State Board of Charities closed a nursery institution that housed over 400 children under the age of six on the grounds that it provided poor care, had irregularities in the use of its monies, spent very little on its wards, had unchecked contagion of disease, had no system of placing out or returning the children to the community, and acted to keep children within the institution for funding purposes.[74]

Foster homes became the alternative for children for whom homes could be found; for them, the orphanage became a short-term receiving school.[75] But institutional care was not over; it continued to grow well into the twentieth century. The institutions were "down-sized" and many implemented the "cottage" system: small groups of children who lived together in familylike settings with one or two houseparents or child care workers. In the mid-1930s, when the greatest number of children were in orphanages, it was estimated that 1,200 orphanages housed less than 100 children, 400 housed less than 500 children, 22 orphanages had populations between 500 and 1,000 children, and only 3 had child populations of more than 1,000.[76]

The orphanage care that began in the mideighteenth century continues in a limited fashion today. Institutional care is now recommended only for a small percentage of children who, because of special needs, require an environment "more restrictive" than a family foster home.[77] These include group homes, which are therapeutically oriented foster homes; residential treatment centers, which are small therapeutic institutions; and locked or secured psychiatric facilities or hospitals.

EARLY FOSTER CARE

Foster care, the out-of-home placement of children in family homes, became a widespread practice in the twentieth century. This challenge to orphanage care began in the midnineteenth century, and was implemented in one of three ways: indenture, in which the child worked for his or her keep; boarding-out, which was a paid placement; or placement in a "free" or unpaid home.[78] The number of children in foster care, however, did not surpass the number in orphanages until the 1940s. By then, the number of children maintained in their own homes through public aid or "welfare" had surpassed the number of children in out-of-home care.[79] Before this shift to the family preservation policy of welfare, foster care was a reality in the lives of many.

The midnineteenth century found many communities sapped of financial resources by the Civil War and, particularly in the East, cities were filled with vagrants, many of whom were children.[80] In response to the overwhelming prospect of supporting tens of thousands of destitute children, the Children's Westward Migration began. Members of the Child Saving Movement advocated, lobbied, and policed poor neighborhoods and children's institutions, separating many immigrant, poor, and working-class children from their parents. Sent west by train, the children were chosen at auctionlike meetings by rural families from throughout the East and Midwest.[81] The children were primarily Catholic immigrants; the majority of homes into which they were placed were Protestant.[82] Proponents of westward migration argued that institutional life produced young adults who lacked drive and motivation, and were prone to remain burdens to the community. Their philosophy of child development was that the then-idealized rural family life was the best way to rear healthy, well-adjusted children who valued work and community moral standards.[83] By the early part of the twentieth century, over 100,000 such children had been placed.[84] The most active of these child-saving agencies was the New York Children's Aid Society, which by the mid 1890s had placed over 90,000 in rural homes.[85]

This large-scale westward migration of young, healthy, dependent children had its roots in colonial indenture and boarding-out, and ultimately evolved into the current practice of foster placement. However, unlike current practice, in which foster care is considered temporary, care in the nineteenth and early twentieth centuries was most commonly a final measure. Many children were removed from their families without the full legal consent or understanding of their parents,[86] and were often placed miles, if not states, away.[87] Parents frequently were not given any information of their children's whereabouts, effectively severing parental custody rights.[88]

By the end of the 1800s, states began to regulate the private sector's care of dependent children in response to two issues: pressure from non-Protestant religious groups that objected to the forced conversion of their children placed in Protestant homes, and the high costs associated with orphanage care—costs often subsidized by public dollars. State Boards of Charity began not only to regulate the care of children in the orphanages, but to demand that homes used for foster placement be screened and licensed. Children placed in these homes had to be regularly supervised, and not simply placed and abandoned. These efforts were pioneered by the first board, formed in Massachusetts in 1863, which advocated against the development of large, congregate care institutions for the "dependent classes," and championed the placement of children in family foster homes that had been chosen to meet their individual needs.[89]

The children placed in early foster homes were similar to those of previous periods: white and poor. By 1899 most states had enacted laws that authorized the removal of victims of child abuse and neglect from their homes, and as a result, some children were in out-of-home placement for reasons of maltreatment.[90] However, poverty, the primary reason for placement during the previous two centuries, remained the main rationale for taking children from their families.

PUBLIC WELFARE

The midtwentieth century witnessed a dramatic return to the support of dependent children within their families. As in previous shifts in policy, economic, philosophical, and moral arguments were brought to bear. Proponents argued that it was more economical to pay a single mother to care for all of her children than to pay different boarding homes to care for each. They maintained that "mother love" was needed by all children, as evidenced by the fact that most institutionalized infants during this period did not survive, and children reared in orphanages did not thrive.[91] Punitive attitudes towards the poor were now tempered by the realization that industrial capitalism had increased the divisions between classes, and that for some, existence in the lower classes was a chronic, if not inevitable, condition. Progressive movement ideology reflected attempts to temper the effects of industrialization on the poor.

This position was best articulated by President Theodore Roosevelt in his opening remarks for the first White House Conference on the Care of Dependent Children in 1909. "Home life is the highest and finest product of civilization. Children should not be deprived of it except for urgent and compelling reasons."[92] The conference concluded with goals that have yet to be met more than eighty years later: poverty alone should not disrupt the home; children of worthy parents or deserving mothers should be kept with their parents at home; and efforts should be made to eradicate the causes of dependency with such aid as may be necessary.[93]

Historical change is seldom a well-delineated affair, and the shift to policies preserving the family, likewise, came gradually. Roosevelt's conference confronted the fact that thousands of dependent children were still in almshouses, many more were in foster homes, and an estimated two-thirds of the children in out-of-home placements remained in orphanages.[94] By the mid-1920s there were 139,000 dependent children in orphanages, with 73,000 in foster care, and another 121,000 maintained in their homes under state-funded mothers' aid programs.[95] In 1933, there were 144,000 children in orphanages and 105,000 in foster homes; by 1951, 86,000 children were in orphanages and 128,000 in foster homes.[96]

Six major initiatives testify to the dramatic shift in twentieth-century policy from family dissolution to family preservation. On the state level, these were maternal custody rights, enforced maternal care of infants, and Mothers' Pension Laws. On the federal level, they were the Social Security Act of 1935 (Public Law [P.L.] 74-271), the Child Abuse Prevention and Treatment Act of 1974 (P.L. 93-247), and the Adoption Assistance and Child Welfare Act of 1980 (P.L. 96-272).

State Legislation

Many states began to award custody of children to their mothers, preventing the automatic out-of-home placement of children due to a father's absence. Previously, mothers were not eligible for custody if their children's fathers died or abandoned their families, and frequently the state would take custody. In 1858, Kansas was the first state to enact maternal custody legislation, giving women the power to be made guardians of their children; in 1880, Oregon gave mothers equal statutory rights to the custody of their children. Other states soon followed suit.[97]

Many states also implemented statutes that actually *required* mothers to care for their infants under six months of age. In response to the 80-100% mortality rates common in foundling homes or baby asylums,[98] it became illegal to relinquish infants. Advocates argued that every child needed and deserved the love that only a mother could bestow. In 1915, Maryland became the first state to prohibit the separation of children under the age of six months from their mothers, except for reasons of the mother's or child's ill health. Other states followed, and by the 1920s the prevailing philosophy was that unwed mothers should keep and rear their children. By the 1930s, mothers were again given the right to decide whether or not to keep their infants, and social agencies were forced to develop alternatives for unwanted babies.[99] Adoption became an increasingly popular alternative due to a trend of decreasing birthrates, and the weakening of suspicions that children born out-of-wedlock were genetically inferior.[100] Psychodynamic theory influenced this trend by positing that motherhood was more than simply a biological relationship, and that the emotional aspects of the relationship were primary.[101] By the 1940s, all states had revoked the legislation or regulations which had enforced the care of infants by their mothers[102]—a complete reversal of philosophy in less than forty years.

The third instrumental category of state legislation was Mothers' Pension Laws. Between 1911 and 1937, states enacted legislation to fund new heads of households empowered by the maternal custody statutes. These pension laws had their historical roots in colonial outdoor relief; their contemporary version is Aid to Families with Dependent Children (AFDC). They began the practice of states' support of needy children in their own homes, for which widowed mothers and, in some locales, destitute families with fathers in residence, were eligible.[103] The philosophy behind this movement was that a "worthy, morally fit" mother was the best guardian of her children.[104] It was also argued that poverty was too pervasive a problem to be dealt with by private philanthropy alone, and that paying mothers was more economical than either maintaining families in almshouses or maintaining children in paid foster homes.[105] The result was that indigent, widowed, white women were no longer automatically dispatched to almshouses, and their dependents to orphan asylums.[106]

Federal Legislation

The Great Depression strained the public welfare capacities of the states to their breaking points. By 1935, every state but Georgia and South Carolina, the two states with the greatest percentage of African-American citizens, had Mothers' Pension Laws, but the demand for support for destitute families was too great.[107] The federal government responded by taking primary fiscal responsibility for dependent children and their families through enactment of the Social Security Act of 1935 and its Aid to Dependent Children (ADC), or public welfare.[108] Because of the depth of the Depression, the number of dependent children publicly maintained in their homes did not surpass the number in out-of-home care until the 1940s.[109]

The Social Security Act had an enormous impact on this dependent population. Title IV of the Act, *Grants to States for Aid to Dependent Children*, provided federal matching funds for mothers' pensions, and sharply reduced the rate of children entering out-of-home care. Title V of the Act, later known as Title IV-B, provided federal assistance in the provision of child welfare services—services that were later expanded in federal legislation: P.L. 93-247 in 1974 and P.L. 96-272 in 1980.[110] Aid to Dependent Children, later amended and titled Aid to Families with Dependent Children (AFDC), became the most successful measure to prevent children's out-of-home placement.[111]

The Social Security Act was a major point of transition. It gave the federal government responsibility for dependent children and their families, and altered the definition of children considered dependent and at risk of out-of-home placement. The Act removed fatherless children as a group likely to be placed outside the home, and by doing so encouraged a focus on children who were at higher risk, such as maltreated children. The states still had primary child welfare responsibility, although minimum standards were set by the federal government through the allocation of federal monies.[112]

Later in the twentieth century, additional in-kind, or noncash, benefits were added by the federal government to the cash benefits for dependent families and their children. In the 1950s, the School Lunch Program was enacted. During the War on Poverty in the 1960s, the Food Stamp Program, and the WIC nutrition program (Women, Infants, and Children Supplemental Nutrition Program) were implemented. Medical care through Medicaid and EPSDT (Early Preventive Screening, Detection, and Treatment), and housing subsidies, including those available through Section 8 of P.L. 93–383, and public housing, became part of the public welfare benefit package.[113] The family preservation policies of the twentieth century, like those between 1650 and 1850, enabled many poor families to care for dependent children within their households. From 1932 to the present, more dependent children have been cared for at home than in all out-of-home facilities combined.[114]

Although most dependent children were with their families by midcentury, advocates for children were touched by the plights of those who remained in out-of-home care. Spurred by the Civil Rights Movement and the subsequent deinstitutionalization movement of the 1950s and 1960s, the many problems of the foster care system once again gained notoriety. These challenges were fueled by service monitoring and developmental psychological research. Maas and Engler described "foster care drift": the movement of foster children from placement to placement, seemingly without plans for stability. Their study revealed few attempts to rehabilitate families or to encourage visitation; most cases had no plans to either return children or to find them permanent homes. Thus, despite the fact that the majority of children had come into state custody for temporary placement, most remained for years.[115] Fanshel and Shinn found unnecessary use of foster care; inappropriate, unstable, and unnecessarily restrictive placements; and inadequate monitoring of the quality of care and appropriateness of placement. They also found that children of color had a higher incidence of out-of-home placement, not necessarily related to need.[116]

The negative psychological sequelae of foster care for children were publicized. Bowlby analyzed the negative effects of maternal deprivation and foster care on children, and advocated prevention through family support measures.[117] Long-term damage to self-esteem, identity, sense of belonging, and ability to establish meaningful relationships was associated with removal from the home and placement in foster care.[118] By the late 1970s, Goldstein, Freud, and Solnit argued that the "best interests of the child" standard for removing children from their homes was too imprecise and should be limited, considering the fact that foster care represented a known risk to children's mental health.[119] They stated that removal of a child from his or her home should only be practiced when a child is in such danger that "intrusion will be more beneficial than injurious to the child."[120]

The second instrumental piece of federal legislation was the Child Abuse Prevention and Treatment Act of 1974 (P.L. 93–247), which provided states funds to identify, prevent, and ameliorate the effects of abuse and neglect. Heightened public awareness of child maltreatment, garnered through publication of research such as the "Battered-Child Syndrome,"[121] fueled passage of the legislation. The Act established a National Center on Child Abuse and proposed the mandated reporting of child maltreatment. This Act, together with federal legislation that funded foster care to a much greater extent than prevention of maltreatment, resulted in a rapid increase in foster care placement.[122]

The tension between keeping children in, and removing them from, their families continued through the 1960s and 1970s. The number of children in foster care by the end of the 1970s was estimated to be between 500,000 and 1.5 million, while 8 million dependent children were receiving care in their own homes. Although foster care was less utilized than AFDC, its costs made it a major child welfare expenditure.[123] A powerful new coalition across political ideologies began forming to promote family preservation policies in child welfare.[124]

The Adoption Assistance and Child Welfare Act of 1980 (P.L. 96–272) is, to date, the federal legislation most supportive of the implementation of family preservation policies. The Act provides federal payments to states for child welfare and family support services, and attempts to change the federal incentive structure to favor prevention of out-of-home placement over the use of foster care. P.L. 96–272 reflects the major themes of ten years of reform activities: prevention of out-of-home placement; reunification of children with their natural families; and permanent placement of those who cannot be reunified. The Act also mandates a number of family preservation actions, the most important of which are reasonable efforts by child welfare agencies to prevent the removal of children and to make possible their return home; services to improve home conditions; and families' notification of and inclusion in the periodic review hearings on behalf of their children.[125]

By 1984, the number of dependent children maintained through AFDC in their own homes was close to 7.5 million, while the number of children in foster care nationally had been reduced to less than 250,000. The average length of placement had been reduced as well. As late as 1960, less than 25% of children in foster care were returned to their natural families. Recently, because of the implementation of the P.L. 96–272, the rate of reunification approached 95%.[126] The reduction in placements did not mean that families were necessarily being provided supportive services. In many states, the courts, acting in accordance with the regulations of P.L. 96–272, simply made it more difficult for social service agencies to remove children from their families.[127] Although by 1993, twenty-three states had legislated family preservation programs,[128] other states are still in the process of legislating family preservation, and a sound definition of reasonable efforts to prevent the unnecessary placement of children. These services in other states are not necessarily absent, but are being provided on a restricted scale.[129] Since the recent federal Omnibus Budget Reconciliation Act of 1993 (P.L. 103–66) includes almost one billion dollars for states to spend on family preservation and family support services, more states are likely to follow suit.[130]

DEFINING DEPENDENT CHILDREN

Dependent children are those who have become the public's responsibility. The characteristics of this group and their families have changed over time, not only because of sociodemographic shifts, but also because of changing community standards of what distinguishes a "good" family from a family at "high risk." In the seventeenth century, dependent children and their families were primarily white and poor. They were not orphans, and although considered neglected by colonial Poor Law standards because of their poverty or the absence of a male to head the household, the majority of these children would not be defined today as abused.[131] Children of color were not labeled and cared for as dependents by white communities. Most African-American families were composed of slaves who readily adopted African-American orphans and cared for those who were less fortunate among themselves.[132]

The pattern of defining poor, white, fatherless children as dependent continued throughout the 1700s. During the 1800s, however, an additional characteristic emerged. Not only were the majority of dependent children white, poor, and fatherless, but they also were recent immigrants, as compared to the "mainstream" families that had been in this country for more than a generation.[133] Families of color continued to be denied the benefits of public social welfare programs.[134] Few orphanages accepted African-American or Native American children, although several were built specifically for African-Americans during this period. Their existence is noted at least in part because two were burned down by whites during the draft riots of the Civil War.[135] After Emancipation, African-American freedwomen continued to care not only for their own families, but also for the dependents in their local communities. By 1880, African-Americans supported numerous societies dedicated to charitable and social services in their communities.[136] The group dependent upon mainstream child welfare services and aid remained white, poor, and fatherless.

The group's composition changed a number of times during the 1900s. Early in the century, the fatherless or "half orphans" left the ranks of dependent children, as a result of the states' legislation of mothers' guardianship, Mothers' Pensions Laws, and the federal Social Security Act of 1935. Although unclear whether by statute or merely by practice, the recipients of Mothers' Pensions had to be physically, mentally, and morally fit to rear their children. Divorced, abandoned, nonmarried, and minority mothers were often not deemed worthy, which effectively limited aid to white widows.[137] Despite the fact that 10% of the U.S. population was African-American during the first decades of the twentieth century, and a disproportionate percentage of the poor, it is reported that 96% of the families receiving benefits from Mothers' Pensions were white, 3% were African-American, and less than 1% were other races.[138] These figures highlight the racial discrimination in care that had existed for centuries.

African-Americans, restricted from mainstream aid, continued to care for their own dependents. Throughout this century, African-American female volunteer beneficial societies continued to meet vital social welfare needs within their communities, both rural and urban.[139] Although most New Deal welfare programs, including Aid to Dependent Children, officially tried to prohibit discrimination, African-American civil rights were not protected because implementation of the programs relied on state and local administration.[140] Nonetheless, ADC opened the way for states' Mothers' Pensions to be given to African-American families, and by midcentury, children of color began to appear in the group of dependent children cared for publicly. Because of the linkage of Aid to Families with Dependent Children (AFDC) funds to foster care placements, African-American, Hispanic, and Native American children soon began to appear in ever-increasing numbers in publicly financed foster care.[141] More recently, in response to the high placement rate of Native American children, which was over 50% of some tribes' children, the U.S. Congress enacted the Indian Child Welfare Act.[142] This Act increased tribal control over the foster placement and adoption of Native American children through the funding of Native placements.[143]

Now no longer segregated from public services, children of color are over represented in the ranks of dependent children. This trend reflects multiple factors, the most salient of which is poverty. Other factors include unequal access to resources, adolescent motherhood, the recent proliferation of substance abuse, and racially prejudicial attitudes towards approaches to parenting among cultural minorities.[144] Over 50% of the foster children in this country today are children of color, and it has been estimated that African-American children today are three times more likely to be placed in foster care than are white children. Since the 1980 passage of P.L. 96-272, the number of white children in foster care has declined, while the number of low-income minority children has risen.[145] The increased popularity of adoption of white infants since the 1940s, and the opposition to transracial adoption since the 1970s, has left many older minority children in foster care.[146]

The group of children now considered dependent continues to be children of primarily poor families, but the group is now multiracial and multiethnic. The passage of the Child Abuse Prevention and Treatment Act[147] in 1974 highlighted the plight of maltreated children, while the Adoption Assistance and Child Welfare Act[148] decreased the out-of-home placement of children by mandating that reasonable efforts be made to prevent placement and to secure reunification. Therefore, those currently at high risk of placement form a group much more saturated with children who have been victims of serious physical or sexual abuse, or neglect. Child maltreatment, drug abuse, family violence, homelessness, and poverty, often in combination, now constitute the risk factors that are likely to lead to a young child's removal from his family.[149]

In addition to these children, new categories of children requiring community support and care have emerged. These include children who are dependent on advanced medical technology, such as respirators for infants born so prematurely that their lungs fail to function adequately; those who have AIDS or are HIV-positive and are often left as "boarder babies" in hospitals or are orphaned by the AIDS epidemic; and those who have been born chemically affected because of *in utero* exposure to drugs such as alcohol or cocaine. While family preservation has been the predominant policy of the last sixty years, the community and other family support services available to these children and their families no longer appear adequate to the task of caring for them. In the absence of funding for strong community-based services, home for greater numbers of these children may be in the institutional care of residential treatment centers and chronic-care hospitals.[150]

POLICIES FOR DEPENDENT CHILDREN TODAY

Taking the broadest view, we see in the seventeenth and eighteenth centuries an extended period of family preservation policy where outdoor relief was the main support. The nineteenth-century almshouses continued to preserve family units, but by midcentury, family dissolution policy was in the ascendant; children were routinely placed in orphanages or foster homes. By the 1940s the introduction of public welfare policies at both the state and federal level ushered in a second era of family preservation policy, which continues to this day. Despite the current dominance of family preservation policy, there is reason to believe that family dissolution responses are becoming more prevalent.

The economic position of families is shifting and creating a different context for policy formation. Poor and homeless families are on the increase. There are almost thirty-two million poor Americans today, an increase of over six million since the 1970s.[151] Unfortunately, half of this increase is children, and nearly two million of the new poor are under six.[152] Children under the age of six are especially vulnerable: one in four is now poor.[153] Each year in this country, 10,000 children die from the effects of poverty.[154] Poverty among children has grown 33% since 1970, and in 1990, 12.6 million U.S. children, 18% of those under eighteen years of age, lived in poverty. These families are considerably poorer than those of the 1970s; approximately 40% of poor children live in families with incomes less than one half of the federal poverty level of $12,675 for a family of four.[155] A substantial percentage of these families are marginally housed or homeless; an estimated 100,000 children and their parents are homeless each day.[156] Families with children are the most rapidly growing group in the homeless population, particularly in urban areas, and many shelters for the homeless report that over half of those seeking shelter are families with children.[157]

Within this context, the recent increase in the number of child maltreatment reports plays a particular role. The number of reports of maltreatment has risen dramatically. In 1991, it reached 2.7 million, up from only 150,000 in 1960.[158] Formulation of the battered-child syndrome and the mandating of reporters of child abuse and neglect[159] have helped propel this widespread problem into national prominence. Attention has been directed to maltreatment as an individual, as opposed to a systemic, problem. The media's presentation of individual cases of child maltreatment often helps people focus their concern on individual children, but it remains more difficult to mobilize and maintain concern for the overwhelming problems of "state sanctioned" maltreatment: children's poverty, homelessness, inadequate access to resources, and lack of civil rights.[160]

"Other people's children," especially the poor and children of color, are still not a priority in this country.[161] Despite the fact that the number of poor children has increased since the 1970s, the number of dependent children on AFDC has steadily decreased during this same period, from 7.9 million children in 1972 to less than 7.4 million in 1987.[162] In 1973, AFDC benefits were provided to 83.6% of poor children; by 1987 AFDC benefits reached only 59.8%.[163] This decrease in public expenditures, as in earlier periods, may support the expediency of out-of-home care over the investment of time and resources necessary to implement a comprehensive family preservation policy, and may herald a shift in the dominant policy.

Today, children's out-of-home placements are increasing rapidly, especially in states where there are large populations of poor, drug-addicted women bearing infants.[164] Some placements are in family foster homes; others are in institutions. In 1990, there were over 360,000 children in foster care nationwide, up from 276,000 in 1987.[165] Not surprisingly, a disproportionate number are children of color.

In addition to the increased use of foster care, another indication of a shift in thought is that the spread of civil rights has not reached foster children. The primary goal of out-of-home placement is to protect children, and yet children in foster care are at higher risk of maltreatment than those in their own homes.[166] Despite this, the U.S. Supreme Court has yet to grant foster children the rights of adults. Children removed from their families under the guise of protection *do not* have a clearly established constitutional right to be free from harm while in the custody of the state, as guaranteed by the due process clause of the Fourteenth Amendment.[167]

Another indication of a shift in policy is that more than half a million juveniles are currently incarcerated in detention facilities. Another 400,000 are reportedly held, against federal regulation, in adult jails.[168] While most of these children are charged with delinquency, only a small percentage of these charges are for serious or violent acts. Many children are incarcerated for statutory offenses such as running away, and others are maltreated children for whom there is no other place.[169]

In addition to the children in jails and foster homes, there is a rapidly increasing number of children whose parents have AIDS. At least 30,000 children in the United States have lost one or both parents to AIDS, and over the next seven years that number is expected to triple. Orphanages are promoted as an alternative by those who fear that there are few options for these children other than the streets.[170] Then there is the group of "boarder babies," infants who are HIV-positive and who are medically able to go home, but remain hospitalized because there is no home or functioning parent to whom to return. A U.S. Department of Health and Human Services survey of 851 hospitals in 1991 found 22,000 such infants.[171] AIDS has created the new orphans of the twenty-first century. The Centers for Disease Control estimated for the year 1991 that 10,000-20,000 children were infected with HIV, almost 80% of whom share the disease with their mothers.[172] Whether in foster homes, institutions, or hospitals, these placements, like those of the early nineteenth century, may indicate a change of practice. Considering that this is happening in the face of federal family preservation legislation (P.L. 96-272, 1980), it is particularly indicative of a shift to family dissolution policy.

Even opposition to institutionalization, which has held sway for most of the twentieth century, is eroding. According to psychologist Sally Provence, a long-time advocate of deinstitutionalization: "Residential care may be a placement of choice for infants in some circumstances: some fragile infants who no longer need hospital care; infants of dysfunctional parents; and healthy infants without families."[173] Some policymakers also support the return to institutionalization for maltreated infants and toddlers,[174] while others see out-of-home placement for the 375,000 infants born drug-exposed each year becoming more likely.[175] Former "drug czar" William J. Bennett stated that orphanages and institutions could be used as nurturing environments for the children of drug addicts.[176] Political scientist Charles Murray was lauded by prestigious news commentators on national television when he advocated removing children from poor, unwed teen mothers on welfare and placing them in "nurturing orphanages" as a way to combat the decay of our society.[177] These pronouncements suggest a return to the institutionalization of a now newly defined group of dependent children, reminiscent of arguments made a century ago.

The dynamic tension between family dissolution and family preservation policies continues. Currently, the trend appears to be that of family preservation. We are now witness to the effects of the prevailing social and economic trends and policies of the past decade: the upsurge in the survival of extremely low birth weight infants; infants exposed prenatally to drugs; AIDS orphans; and children living in chronic poverty. Should these problems go unchecked, the new millennium may bring a shift from family preservation policy to that of family dissolution for these new high-risk populations and others dependent on our care.

NOTES

1. M. D. Speizman (1981). Child care: A mirror of human history. *Children and Youth Services Review, 3*, 213–232; D. J. Rothman (1972). Of prisons, asylums, and other decaying institutions. *The Public Interest*, (26), 3–17.

2. G. Guest (1989). The boarding of the dependent poor in colonial America. *Social

Service Review, 63(1), 92–112; Rothman (1972), Of prisons, asylums, and other decaying institutions.

3. R. H. Bremner (Ed.) (1970, 1971, 1974). *Children and youth in America: A documentary history* (Vol. 1: 1600–1865, Vol. 2: 1866–1932, Vol. 3: 1933–1973). Cambridge, MA: Harvard University Press.

4. J. Giovannoni & R. Becerra (1979). *Defining child abuse.* New York: Free Press.

5. Rothman (1972), Of prisons, asylums, and other decaying institutions.

6. Giovannoni & Becerra (1979), *Defining child abuse.*

7. L. Costin & C. A. Rapp (1984). *Child welfare policies and practice.* New York: McGraw-Hill; G. Abbott (1938). *The child and the state* (Vol. 2). Chicago: The University of Chicago Press.

8. M. Abramovitz (1985). The family ethic: The female pauper and public aid, pre–1900. *Social Service Review, 59*(1), 121–135.

9. Giovannoni & Becerra (1979), *Defining child abuse.*

10. H. Folks (1902). *The care of destitute, neglected and delinquent children.* New York: The Macmillan Company.

11. Costin & Rapp (1984), *Child welfare policies and practice.*

12. P. F. Clement (1979). Families and foster care: Philadelphia in the late nineteenth century. *Social Service Review, 53,* 407–420.

13. Abramovitz (1985), The family ethic.

14. Guest (1989), The boarding of the dependent poor; J. Demos (1986). *Past, present, and personal: The family and the life course in American history.* New York: Oxford University Press; Giovannoni & Becerra (1979), *Defining child abuse.*

15. Speizman (1981), Child care; Bremner (1970), *Children and youth in America* (Vol. 1).

16. S. W. Downs & M. W. Sherraden (1983). The orphan asylum in the nineteenth century. *Social Service Review, 57,* 272–290.

17. Speizman (1981), Child care; Rothman (1972), Of prisons, asylums, and other decaying institutions.

18. M. B. Katz (1986). *In the shadow of the poorhouse: A social history of welfare in America.* New York: Basic Books.

19. Abramovitz (1985), The family ethic; D. J. Rothman (1971). *The discovery of the asylum: Social order and disorder in the new republic.* Boston: Little, Brown; Folks (1902), *The care of destitute, neglected and delinquent children.*

20. Speizman (1981), Child care.

21. Downs & Sherraden (1983), The orphan asylum in the nineteenth century.

22. Bremner (1971), *Children and youth in America* (Vol. 2).

23. Downs & Sherraden (1983), The orphan asylum in the nineteenth century.

24. H. W. Thurston (1930). *The dependent child.* New York: Columbia University Press.

25. Folks (1902), *The care of destitute, neglected and delinquent children.*

26. Thurston (1930), *The dependent child.*

27. M. B. Katz (1989). *The undeserving poor: From the war on poverty to the war on welfare.* New York: Pantheon.

28. Guest (1989), The boarding of the dependent poor; Abramovitz (1985), The family ethic; R. A. Meckel (1985). Protecting the innocents: Age segregation and the early child welfare movement. *Social Service Review, 59*(3), 455–475; Costin & Rapp (1984), *Child welfare policies and practice*; Abbott (1938), *The child and the state.*

29. Abramovitz (1985), The family ethic; Folks (1902), *The care of destitute, neglected and delinquent children.*

30. Katz (1986), *In the shadow of the poorhouse*; Costin & Rapp (1984), *Child welfare policies and practice*; Bremner (1970), *Children and youth in America* (Vol. 1); Thurston (1930), *The dependent child.*

31. Costin & Rapp (1984), *Child welfare policies and practice*; Folks (1902), *The care of destitute, neglected and delinquent children.*

32. Giovannoni & Becerra (1979), *Defining child abuse.*

33. Bremner (1970), *Children and youth in America* (Vol. 1).

34. Katz (1986), *In the shadow of the poorhouse*; Speizman (1981), Child care; Rothman (1972), Of prisons, asylums, and other decaying institutions; Bremner (1970), *Children and youth in America* (Vol. 1).

35. Speizman (1981), Child care.

36. Bremner (1971), *Children and youth in America* (Vol. 2); Folks (1902), *The care of destitute, neglected and delinquent children.*

37. E. O. Lundberg (1947). *Unto the least of these.* New York: Appleton-Century-Crofts.

38. Katz (1986), *In the shadow of the poorhouse*; Bremner (1971), *Children and youth in America* (Vol. 2); Thurston (1930), *The dependent child*; Folks (1902), *The care of destitute, neglected and delinquent children.*

39. Bremner (1971), *Children and youth in America* (Vol. 2); Folks (1902), *The care of destitute, neglected and delinquent children.*

40. Katz (1986), *In the shadow of the poorhouse.*

41. Costin & Rapp (1984), *Child welfare policies and practices.*

42. Lundberg (1947), *Unto the least of these.*

43. Bremner (1971), *Children and youth in America* (Vol. 2).

44. Speizman (1981), Child care.

45. Costin & Rapp (1984), *Child welfare policies and practice.*

46. Downs & Sherraden (1983), The orphan asylum in the nineteenth century.

47. Downs & Sherraden (1983), The orphan asylum in the nineteenth century.

48. U.S. Congress (1909). *Proceedings of the conference on the care of dependent children*, Document No. 721. Washington, D.C.: Government Printing Office.

49. M. Wolins & I. Piliavin (1964). *Institution or foster family: A century of debate.* New York: Child Welfare League of America; H. W. Hopkirk (1944). *Institutions serving children.* New York: Russell Sage Foundation.

50. Bremner (1970), *Children and youth in America* (Vol. 1); Hopkirk (1944), *Institutions serving children.*

51. S. B. Kamerman & A. J. Kahn (1976). *Social services in the U.S.: Policies and programs.* Philadelphia: Temple University Press.

52. Katz (1986), *In the shadow of the poorhouse.*

53. Rothman (1971), *The discovery of the asylum.*

54. W. P. Letchworth (1874), cited in Katz (1986), *In the shadow of the poorhouse*, 107.

55. P. Robertson (1974). Home as a nest: Middle class childhood in nineteenth-century Europe. In L. deMause (Ed.). *The history of childhood: The untold story of child abuse*, 397–431. New York: Peter Bedrick.

56. Speizman (1981), Child care.

57. Giovannoni & Becerra (1979), *Defining child abuse.*

58. Folks (1902), *The care of destitute, neglected and delinquent children*; C. L. Brace

(1880). *The dangerous classes of New York and 20 years work among them.* New York: Wynkiip and Hallenbeck.

59. Katz (1986), *In the shadow of the poorhouse*; Costin & Rapp (1984), *Child welfare policies and practice*; Brace (1880), *The dangerous classes of New York.*

60. Costin & Rapp (1984), *Child welfare policies and practices.*

61. Katz (1989), *The undeserving poor.*

62. Giovannoni & Becerra (1979), *Defining child abuse.*

63. Brace (1880), *The dangerous classes of New York.*

64. Lundberg (1947), *Unto the least of these*; Brace (1880), *The dangerous classes of New York.*

65. Speizman (1981), Child care; Rothman (1972), Of prisons, asylums, and other decaying institutions; D. Gilbert (1944). A community changes its children's institutions. *Child Welfare League of America Bulletin, 24*(9), 5–9; Hopkirk (1944), *Institutions serving children*; Folks (1902), *The care of destitute, neglected and delinquent children.*

66. Giovannoni & Becerra (1979), *Defining child abuse.*

67. Speizman (1981), Child care.

68. Katz (1986), *In the shadow of the poorhouse*; Costin & Rapp (1984), *Child welfare policies and practice*; Speizman (1981), Child care.

69. Katz (1986), *In the shadow of the poorhouse*; Clement (1979), Families and foster care; Hopkirk (1944), *Institutions serving children.*

70. Abramovitz (1985), The family ethic.

71. Thurston (1930), *The dependent child.*

72. S. M. Stehno (1988). Public responsibility for dependent black children: The advocacy of Edith Abbott and Sophonisba Breckinridge. *Social Service Review, 62*(3), 485–503; A. H. Taylor (1976). *Travail and triumph: Black life and culture in the South since the Civil War.* Westport, CT: Greenwood Press; Bremner (1970), *Children and youth in America* (Vol. 1); Hopkirk (1944), *Institutions serving children.*

73. Folks (1902), *The care of destitute, neglected and delinquent children.*

74. Bremner (1971), *Children and youth in America* (Vol. 2).

75. Gilbert (1944), A community changes its children's institutions; Brace (1880), *The dangerous classes of New York.*

76. Hopkirk (1944), *Institutions serving children.*

77. U.S. Congress (1980). *Public Law 96–272: Adoption Assistance and Child Welfare Act of 1980.* Washington, D.C.: Government Printing Office.

78. U.S. Children's Bureau (1936). *The abc of foster-family care for children* (Bureau Publication No. 216). Washington, D.C.: U.S. Government Printing Office.

79. Bremner (1970), *Children and youth in America* (Vol. 1).

80. Speizman (1981), Child care.

81. Katz (1986), *In the shadow of the poorhouse*; Abramovitz (1985), The family ethic; Meckel (1985), Protecting the innocents; Bremner (1971), *Children and youth in America* (Vol. 2); Hopkirk (1944), *Institutions serving children.*

82. Speizman (1981), Child care.

83. Bremner (1971), *Children and youth in America* (Vol. 2); U.S. Congress (1909), *Proceedings of the conference on the care of dependent children*; Folks (1902), *The care of destitute, neglected and delinquent children*; Brace (1880), *The dangerous classes of New York.*

84. Katz (1986), *In the shadow of the poorhouse*; Meckel (1985), Protecting the innocents; Bremner (1971), *Children and youth in America* (Vol. 2); Brace (1880), *The*

dangerous classes of New York.

85. Katz (1986), *In the shadow of the poorhouse.*

86. Giovannoni & Becerra (1979), *Defining child abuse.*

87. Costin & Rapp (1984), *Child welfare policies and practice*; Brace (1880), *The dangerous classes of New York.*

88. Katz (1986), *In the shadow of the poorhouse.*

89. Costin & Rapp (1984), *Child welfare policies and practice*; Wolins & Piliavin (1964), *Institution or foster family*; Lundberg (1947), *Unto the least of these*; K. H. Welch (1940). *The meaning of state supervision in the social protection of children* (Bureau Publication No. 252). Washington, D.C.: U.S. Government Printing Office; U.S. Congress (1909), *Proceedings of the conference on the care of dependent children*; Folks (1902), *The care of destitute, neglected and delinquent children.*

90. Costin & Rapp (1984), *Child welfare policies and practice.*

91. U.S. Congress (1909), *Proceedings of the conference on the care of dependent children.*

92. U.S. Congress (1909), *Proceedings of the conference on the care of dependent children.*

93. U.S. Congress (1909), *Proceedings of the conference on the care of dependent children.*

94. Wolins & Piliavin (1964), *Institution or foster family.*

95. Bremner (1971), *Children and youth in America* (Vol. 2).

96. Wolins & Piliavin (1964), *Institution or foster family.*

97. Bremner (1971), *Children and youth in America* (Vol. 2).

98. U.S. Congress (1909), *Proceedings of the conference on the care of dependent children.*

99. Costin & Rapp (1984), *Child welfare policies and practice*; U.S. Children's Bureau (1936), *The abc of foster-family care for children.*

100. V. A. Zelizer (1985). *Pricing the priceless child: The changing social value of children.* New York: Basic Books.

101. L. J. Yarrow (1979). Historical perspectives and future directions in infant development. In J. D. Osofsky (Ed.), *Handbook of infant development.* New York: John Wiley; S. I. Harrison & J. F. McDermott (1972). *Childhood psychopathology.* New York: International Universities Press.

102. Costin & Rapp (1984), *Child welfare policies and practice.*

103. Lundberg (1947), *Unto the least of these.*

104. U.S. Congress (1909), *Proceedings of the conference on the care of dependent children.*

105. M. H. Leff (1973). Consensus for reform: The mothers'-pension movement in the Progressive era. *Social Service Review, 47*(3), 397–417; Lundberg (1947), *Unto the least of these*; Abbott (1938), *The child and the state*; U.S. Congress (1909), *Proceedings of the conference on the care of dependent children.*

106. Rothman (1972), Of prisons, asylums, and other decaying institutions.

107. Bremner (1971), *Children and youth in America* (Vol. 2); Lundberg (1947), *Unto the least of these.*

108. U.S. Congress (1935). The Social Security Act. P. L. 74–271, 49 Stat. 620.

109. Bremner (1971), *Children and youth in America* (Vol. 2); Wolins & Piliavin (1964), *Institution or foster family.*

110. M. A. Jones (1985). *A second chance for families: Five years later.* New York: Child

Welfare League of America; Costin & Rapp (1984), *Child welfare policies and practice*.

111. Jones (1985), *A second chance for families*; M. J. Cox & R. D. Cox (1984). Foster care and public policy. *Journal of Family Issues, 5*(2), 182–199.

112. Costin & Rapp (1984), *Child welfare policies and practice*.

113. Children's Defense Fund (1988). *A call for action to make our nation safe for children: A briefing book on the status of American children in 1988*. Washington, D.C.: Author.

114. Jones (1985), *A second chance for families*; Bremner (1971), *Children and youth in America* (Vol. 2).

115. A. R. Gruber (1978). *Children in foster care*. New York: Human Services Press; H. S. Maas & R. E. Engler (1959). *Children in need of parents*. New York: Columbia University Press.

116. D. Fanshel & E. Shinn (1978). *Children in foster care*. New York: Columbia University Press.

117. J. Bowlby (1962). *Separation anxiety: A critical review of the literature*. New York: Child Welfare League of America.

118. A. N. Maluccio, E. Fein, J. Hamilton, J. L. Klier, & D. Ward (1980). Beyond permanency planning. *Child Welfare, 59*(9), 515–530; Fanshell & Shinn (1978), *Children in foster care*; Gruber (1978), *Children in foster care*; Maas and Engler (1959), *Children in need of parents*.

119. J. Goldstein, A. Freud, & A. J. Solnit (1979). *Before the best interests of the child*. New York: Free Press.

120. Goldstein et al. (1979), *Before the best interests of the child*, 137.

121. C. H. Kempe, F. N. Silverman, B. F. Steele, W. Droegemueller, & H. K. Silver (1962). The battered-child syndrome. *Journal of the American Medical Association, 181*, 17–24.

122. Jones (1985), *A second chance for families*.

123. National Black Child Development Institute (1989). The status of black children. *Black Child Advocate*. Washington, D.C.: Author; Children's Defense Fund (1988b). *A children's defense budget: An analysis of the FY 1989 federal budget and children*. Washington, D.C.: Author; J. Jones (1985). *Labor of love, labor of sorrow: Black women, work, and the family from slavery to the present*. New York: Vintage Books.

124. M. Novak (1987). *The new consensus on family and welfare*. Washington, D.C.: American Enterprise Institute for Public Policy Research.

125. U.S. Congress (1980), *Public Law 96–272*.

126. Children's Defense Fund (1988b), *A children's defense budget*; B. A. Pine (1986). Child welfare reform and the political process. *Social Service Review, 60*(4), 339–359; C. Sudia (1986). Preventing out of home placement of children. *Children Today, 6*, 4–6, Washington, D.C.: U.S. Department of Health and Human Services.

127. U.S. Congress (1980), *Public Law 96–272*.

128. J. Zalenski (January, 1993), Information specialist at the National Resource Center on Family-Based Services. Personal communication.

129. M. P. Bribitzer & M. J. Verdieck (1988). Home-based family-centered intervention: Evaluation of a foster care prevention program. *Child Welfare, 67*(3), 255–266.

130. U.S. House of Representatives (August 4, 1993). *Omnibus Budget Reconciliation Act of 1993*. Conference Report of the Committee on the Budget, House of Representatives (Report 103–213). Washington, D.C.: U.S. Government Printing Office.

131. Katz (1986), *In the shadow of the poorhouse*; T. J. Stein (1984). The Child Abuse

Prevention and Treatment Act. *Social Service Review, 58*(3), 302–314.

132. Jones (1985), *Labor of love, labor of sorrow.*
133. Abramovitz (1985), The family ethic; Lundberg (1947), *Unto the least of these.*
134. Jones (1985), *Labor of love, labor of sorrow.*
135. Bremner (1971), *Children and youth in America* (Vol. 2).
136. Jones (1985), *Labor of love, labor of sorrow.*
137. Lundberg (1947), *Unto the least of these.*
138. Bremner (1971), *Children and youth in America* (Vol. 2).
139. Jones (1985), *Labor of love, labor of sorrow.*
140. Katz (1986), *In the shadow of the poorhouse.*
141. Stehno (1988), Public responsibility for dependent black children; Bremner (1971), *Children and youth in America* (Vol. 2); Hopkirk (1944), *Institutions serving children.*
142. M. Henry (Ed.) (1990). Eskimos and Indians say recent rulings undermine tribal rights in adoption. *Youth Law News, 11*(4), 23; U.S. Congress (1978). *Public Law 95–608: Indian Child Welfare Act of 1978.* Washington, D.C.: Government Printing Office.
143. Costin & Rapp (1984), *Child welfare policies and practice.*
144. P. L. Hogan & S. F. Siu (1988). Minority children and their child welfare system: An historical perspective. *Social Work, 33*(6), 493–498; Abramovitz (1985), The family ethic; Kamerman and Kahn (1976), *Social services in the U.S.*; A. Billingsley & J. M. Giovannoni (1972). *Children of the storm: Black children and American child welfare.* New York: Harcourt Brace Jovanovich.
145. National Black Child Development Institute (1989), The status of black children; Stehno (1988), Public responsibility for dependent black children.
146. Costin & Rapp (1984), *Child welfare policies and practice.*
147. U.S. Congress (1974), *Public Law 93–247.*
148. U.S. Congress (1980), *Public Law 96–272.*
149. U.S. Congress: Select Committee on Children, Youth, and Families (1989). *Born hooked: Confronting the impact of perinatal substance abuse.* Washington, D.C.: U.S. Government Printing Office.
150. P. G. Anderson (1989). The origin, emergence, and professional recognition of child protection. *Social Service Review, 63*(2), 222–243; M. F. Granger, S. Rosen, J. Yokoyama, & M. Tasker (1989). Transitional group homes for children with HIV: Support for children, families, and foster parents. *Zero to Three, 9*(3), 14–18; S. Provence (1989). Infants in institutions revisited. *Zero to Three, 9*(3), 1–4.
151. U.S. Department of Commerce: Bureau of the Census (1990). *1990 Census of population and housing: Summary of social, economic, and housing characteristics.* Washington, D.C.: Government Printing Office.
152. J. D. Weill (1990). Child poverty in America. *Youth Law News, 11*(6), 1921.
153. Children's Defense Fund (1992). *The state of America's children 1992.* Washington, D.C.: Author.
154. Children's Defense Fund (July, 1991). Child welfare reform. *CDF Reports*, 1.
155. Children's Defense Fund (July, 1991). Cuts in aid push more children into poverty. *CDF Reports*, 6; Weill (1990), Child poverty in America.
156. Children's Defense Fund (July, 1991), Child welfare reform.
157. Little (this volume). Municipal policies for homeless families.
158. Children's Defense Fund (1992), *The state of America's children 1992*; T. Demchak (1988). Abused and neglected children. *Youth Law News, 9*(1), 23–28.
159. U.S. Congress (1974), *Public Law 93–247.*

160. B. J. Nelson (1984). *Making an issue of child abuse: Political agenda setting for social problems.* Chicago: University of Chicago Press.

161. W. N. Grubb & M. Lazerson (1982). *Broken promises: How Americans fail their children.* Chicago: University of Chicago Press.

162. Children's Defense Fund (1988), *A children's defense budget.*

163. Weill (1990), Child poverty in America.

164. U.S. Congress: Select Committee on Children, Youth, and Families (1988). *Continuing crisis in foster care: Issues and problems.* Washington, D.C.: U.S. Government Printing Office.

165. National Commission on Child Welfare and Family Preservation (1990). *A commitment to change: Interim report from the American Public Welfare Association.* Washington, D.C.: Author; U.S. Congress: Select Committee on Children, Youth, and Families (1988), *Continuing crisis in foster care.*

166. National Center on Child Abuse Prevention (1986). *Deaths due to maltreatment soar: The results of the 89th Annual 50 State Survey.* Chicago: National Committee for the Prevention of Child Abuse.

167. B. Grimm (1989). Courts agree: Foster children have fewer rights than prisoners. *Youth Law News, 10*(6), 1–7.

168. Children's Defense Fund (1988), *A children's defense budget.*

169. D. Lambert (1988). Children in institutions. *Youth Law News, 9*(1), 10–15. For an interesting differentiation of the treatment of white males, girls, and children of color, see K. H. Federle & M. Chesney-Lind (1992). Special issues in juvenile justice: Gender, race, and ethnicity. In I. M. Schwartz (Ed.), *Juvenile justice and public policy*, 165–195. New York: Lexington Books.

170. *Time* (November 1, 1993), 76–80.

171. *U.S.A. Today* (December 2, 1993), 1.

172. Granger et al. (1989), Transitional group homes for children with HIV.

173. Provence (1989), Infants in institutions revisited, 4.

174. Anderson (1989), The origin, emergence, and professional recognition of child protection; C. G. Sankey, E. Elmer, A. D. Halechko, & P. Schulberg (1985). The development of abused and high-risk infants in different treatment modalities: Residential versus in-home care. *Child Abuse and Neglect, 9*, 1–10.

175. Children's Defense Fund (1991), Child welfare reform; Granger et al. (1989), Transitional group homes for children with HIV; D. R. Weston, B. Ivins, B. Zuckerman, C. Jones, & R. Lopez (1989). Drug exposed babies: Research and clinical issues. *Zero to Three, 9*(5), 1–7.

176. Sanctuaries suggested for addicts' children (April 29, 1990). *New York Times*, section I, 15; Not exactly the way to attack drugs (April 30, 1990). *Los Angeles Times*, B6.

177. This week with David Brinkley (November 28, 1993). ABC News.

The author acknowledges the generous support and inspiration provided by Dean Paula Meares of the School of Social Work, University of Michigan, and Professor Nora Gustavsson of the School of Social Work, University of Illinois.

4

Congressional Responses to Families in the Workplace: The Family and Medical Leave Act of 1987–1988

Katharine Karr Kaitin

Women of child-bearing age are the fastest growing segment of the workforce. The increasing number of women entering the workforce has changed both the private life of the family and the public world of the workplace. Whereas in 1950, 65% of married mothers stayed at home, by 1989, 58% of married mothers were in the labor force.[1] According to Census data, mothers of children under one are remaining in the job market at ever-increasing rates, rising from 31% in 1976 to 53% in 1990.[2] Yet in this country, less than 40% of women with newborn infants are entitled to job-protected leave with partial wage replacement to care for a newborn child.[3] Although job-protected leave is offered by 51% of small companies and 80% of firms with more than 100 employees,[4] prior to 1993, there was no national, standardized policy of job protection for parents who took time off from work for the birth, adoption, or serious illness of a child.

While the child development research community does not recommend one genre of early care over another, many believe it is in the best interests of families to have parents care for their newborns.[5] Indeed, there is a consensus in the academic community that a federal parental leave policy should grant parents at least four to six months of leave to provide security for new families, and to allow them time to find the best child care options available for their infants.[6]

In 1985, Representative Patricia Schroeder (D-CO) introduced the Parental and Disability Leave Act. The initial draft intended to provide eighteen weeks of job-protected leave for workers to care for newborn, newly adopted, or seriously ill children, and twenty-six weeks in the case of their own prolonged medical illness.[7] Furthermore, the legislation offered universal employer coverage before a preliminary compromise raised the employee exemption to five.[8]

In 1987, the bill, retitled the Family and Medical Leave Act (FMLA), gained popular support, greater visibility in the media, and momentum with each congressional term. Due to the willingness of advocates to compromise on several key issues, the bill attracted enough support to be passed by both the House and Senate, but was vetoed in 1990 and 1992 by then-President Bush. The legislation received considerable attention during the 1992 presidential campaign. In February, 1993, President Clinton signed the Family and Medical Leave Act, making it the corner-stone of his administration's family policies.[9] This chapter recounts an earlier piece of the FMLA's history—one critical to its eventual passage.

FAMILY LEAVE POLICIES PRIOR TO 1993

Prior to 1993 in the United States, the average maternity leave was six to eight weeks, frequently administered in a haphazard and arbitrary fashion.[10] Often defined as a disability or sick leave, and only covering the time of physical disability around the birth of a child, it was rarely extended to fathers or adoptive mothers.[11] Although certain states enacted parental-leave legislation, there were few guidelines for private employers regarding models of leave. Even today, when a company establishes a clear policy, management can convey subtle contradictory messages,[12] or make it impractical for a worker to use a family-work program.[13] New parents may be led to believe that it is not in their best interests to utilize the entire leave period,[14] and that workers ought to be able to manage their private lives without the company's "help."[15] While advocates for family leave define it as a labor standard that should be available to all qualified employees, the business community generally considers it to be one of many possible fringe benefits offered by employers to attract new workers and maintain a workforce; benefits typically cover vacation time, health-care benefits, and the provision of partial wage replacement to employees when they are unable to work.[16]

When the Family and Medical Leave Act of 1987 was introduced, four states had enacted parental-leave legislation, and twenty-seven other states had considered maternity or parental leave bills.[17] Five states (California, Rhode Island, New York, New Jersey, Hawaii), and Puerto Rico now offer qualified workers temporary disability insurance, which offers partial wage replacement to workers unable to work due to non-job-related injuries or illnesses.[18] In the absence of a state-mandated leave policy, employers determine the specifics of any policy or fringe benefits they may offer. Furthermore, workers must meet certain employer-mandated requirements to take advantage of leave policies, such as working a forty-hour week or being employed by the company for over one year.

Some members of the child development community have expressed concern regarding early nonparental infant care. Specifically, Belsky asserted that early full-time infant care may interfere with the attachment process between parent and child, and cause the infant to exhibit increasing avoidant behavior of his or her mother,[19] which may be associated with increased aggressiveness and diminished compliance with adults in later years.

On the other hand, Gamble and Zigler,[20] in a review of the research on the effects of infant day care, conclude that there are "no strikingly negative psychological consequences accruing to infants who experience regular nonparental care." Other experts contend that infants will do well in quality child care settings, and that outcomes like diminished compliance may merely reflect greater independence. A study conducted by Howes and Olenick[21] showed that children in high-quality day care settings demonstrated high degrees of self-regulation, while those in low-quality settings lagged behind both the children in the high-quality settings and those cared for by their mothers. Notwithstanding these debates among child development researchers, more and more parents are returning to work soon after the birth of a child, due, in part, to the constraints of workplace policies.

International Perspective on Parental Leave

By 1988, the fact that the United States was the only developed nation in the world besides South Africa without a family leave policy had become part of the litany for reform among advocates for the Family and Medical Leave Act. Supporters often pointed to exemplary European leave policies; Sweden's parental-leave policy, which is the oldest and most extensive, was the most frequently cited model because, among other aspects, it is gender-neutral.[22] However, even some poorer countries (e.g., Cuba, Ghana, Brazil) have some kind of national policy that provides for a parenting leave, usually offered in a protectionist model aimed at new mothers and infants.[23] Eighty-five countries provide workers with income protection and health care during pregnancy and maternity leave, as well as coverage for other illness.[24] Advocates for the U.S. legislation asserted that parental- rather than maternal-leave policy would protect women from gender bias in the workplace.

Proposed Study

The Family and Medical Leave Act is a particularly interesting piece of legislation in light of the apparent conflict between "business" and "family" interests. This case study examines the evolution and promotion of the legislation through the end of the 100th Congress in the fall of 1988.

It has three major objectives:

1. To describe the sociopolitical context in which the Family and Medical Leave Act developed.
2. To identify the key actors, institutions, and constituency groups that played a forceful role in the evolution of the legislation.
3. To identify factors accounting for the FMLA "stalling" in the legislative process.

Data have been collected from primary and secondary sources. The author conducted key informant interviews with thirty-one individuals who have special knowledge and/or involvement in this issue (see appendix), using a semistructured interview schedule which was constructed and administered for this purpose. Secondary sources included legislative documents, congressional hearings, and relevant sociological and child development research.

HISTORICAL BACKGROUND

The debate over the Family and Medical Leave Act emerged from a long history of government intervention in women's labor force participation. Both advocates and opponents could link their positions to those taken by like-minded activists over the last 100 years. Proponents found support for the principles behind the FMLA in the long tradition of women's rights laws, beginning in the nineteenth century with early attempts to improve the quality of women workers' lives.[25] These efforts culminated in the now-famous Brandeis brief in the case of *Muller v. Oregon*.

Louis Brandeis,[26] then an attorney for the National Consumers' League, argued that women's physical weakness, dependency on men, and likelihood of becoming mothers entitled them to special working conditions; in *Muller v. Oregon*, the Court upheld this protective legislation for women.[27] Some feminists objected to this protection, believing that the principle of equality was more important than that of protection, and that the fight should be for better conditions for all workers.[28] Yet the courts consistently overruled universal protection for workers, because men had a "Constitutional God-protected" right to work and to freedom of contract,[29] i.e., to work for as many hours a day as they chose. Labor leaders used the principles established in *Muller v. Oregon* to fight for legislation granting maximum hours and minimum wages for women workers. As the legislation was enacted and the concept gained a measure of social credibility, advocates went back to the courts to expand these protective measures to cover all workers.

Ultimately, in a series of decisions in the 1920s and 1930s, the Supreme Court of the United States found that the freedom to contract was not so overarching that maximum hours and minimum-wage legislation were an unconstitutional burden on that freedom.[30] With the "rebirth" of the women's movement in the 1960s and 1970s, a number of new organizations again took up the struggle to gain equality for women, both in the workplace and in society at large. The courts and women's groups revisited the notion of special protection versus equal rights. Many labor organizations and women's groups took the fight to "bring women into full participation in the mainstream of American society"[31] to the federal government, seeking legislative support for their goals. Some inroads were made as the government was goaded into ending certain discriminatory practices, such as routinely firing women once they became visibly pregnant or had given birth. Among the landmark pieces of legislation resulting from this movement was the Pregnancy Discrimination Act, passed by the U.S. Congress in 1978.

The Pregnancy Discrimination Act

In 1978, Congress took steps to end discrimination against women workers in situations where any disability benefits were offered to qualified workers. The Pregnancy Discrimination Act of 1978 (Public Law [P.L.] 95–555) was an amendment to Title VII of the Civil Rights Act of 1964, which outlawed discrimination on the basis of race, color, religion, national origin, or sex in employment practices.[32] The Pregnancy Discrimination Act amendment to Title VII mandates that "women affected by pregnancy, childbirth, or related medical conditions shall be treated the same for all employment-related purposes . . . as other persons not so affected but similar in their ability to work."[33] Any employer who offered disability benefits to qualified employees would have to extend those benefits to mothers taking maternity leave.

Most importantly, the Pregnancy Discrimination Act established the principle that there had to be equal treatment for men and women when they were unable to work because of medical conditions. However, this provided limited protection as employers who provided no disability benefits were not obliged to offer any benefits to pregnant women. Further, the Pregnancy Discrimination Act did not force employers to recognize workers' needs and responsibilities outside the workplace that might have an impact on their labor force participation.[34]

While these issues were not being forcefully addressed in any federal policy arena, activity on the issue of job-protected maternity leave was occurring on the state level. Legislation was passed in nine states mandating benefits for workers taking maternity leave. Some state laws (e.g., those in California) offered up to four months of job-protected unpaid leave.[35] However, some of these laws were soon challenged as being discriminatory, in that they offered women a benefit that was not available to men. The case that attracted the most attention was *California Federal Savings and Loan (CalFed) v. Guerra*, commonly called the Garland case.

The Garland Decision

In 1982, Lillian Garland, a receptionist at the CalFed bank in West Los Angeles, gave birth to a baby girl. Due to complications during delivery, her physician prescribed three months of leave to recuperate. When she returned to the bank, her position had been filled. Because she could not pay her monthly rent, she moved in with a friend and let the estranged father of her child care for the baby until she could find a job; by early 1983 he had sued for, and won, custody.

Garland filed suit against CalFed, citing a 1978 California state law, an amendment to the state's Fair Employment and Housing Act, which holds that any company with fifteen or more workers must offer up to four months of unpaid leave for pregnant women. Workers are promised either the same jobs or jobs of comparable worth upon returning to the workplace, and leave is available to pregnant women whether or not their employer offers a disability leave. The State of California censured the bank for not reinstating Garland upon her return to the workplace, and CalFed challenged the California law in federal court.

The bank argued that the California maternity leave statute was in direct conflict with the Pregnancy Discrimination Act of 1978 because it could only apply to, and benefit, women. In 1984, the U.S. District Court for the Central District of California ruled in favor of the bank in *California Federal Savings and Loan v. Guerra*, stating: "California employers who comply with state law are subject to reverse discrimination suits under Title VII [of the Civil Rights Act], by temporarily disabled males who do not receive the same treatment as female employees disabled by pregnancy."[36] The case was appealed to the U.S. Court of Appeals.

A few local feminist and labor groups, including 9 to 5 and the Coalition for Reproductive Equality in the Workplace, were outraged by the Court's decision and immediately launched an appeal to the Appellate Court.[37] Prominent feminists derided the notion that this law discriminated against men, maintaining that it instead equalized the status of men and women in the workforce; the extended leave would allow women and men to have children without risking their jobs. However, the entire women's movement did not rally around this position because groups such as the National Organization for Women (NOW) and the Women's Legal Defense Fund (WLDF) were adamantly committed to equal rights treatment for women, and disagreed that new mothers should constitute a protected class.[38] They maintained that historically these kinds of protective measures had resulted in discrimination against female workers.[39] Furthermore, extended-leave policies should not just be maternal but be available to all workers.

After the District Court handed down its decision, U.S. Representative Howard Berman (D-CA), who as a state legislator had sponsored the California maternity leave statute, was urged by some feminist constituents to act on the federal level to protect women workers. Although he was committed to legislating maternity leave,[40] Berman was confronted by Washington-based feminist lobbyists, like the WLDF, who ardently opposed legislation that would offer special protection to female employees. Washington-based groups interested in these issues continued to meet on their own, and became the core of the coalition advocating the FMLA.[41]

Meanwhile, the U.S. Court of Appeals reversed the decision of the District Court in the Garland case, holding that the Pregnancy Discrimination Act "does not demand that state law be blind to pregnancy's existence," and further, that the intention of Congress was "to construct a floor beneath which pregnancy disability benefits may not drop—not a ceiling above which they may not rise."[42] Again the case was appealed, this time by the bank, and finally in January, 1987, the U.S. Supreme Court upheld the California state law by a six-to-three vote. The Court ruled that a state may legally require an employer to provide special job protection for workers temporarily disabled by pregnancy. Justice Thurgood Marshall stated that whereas the California statute does not violate federal law nor discriminate against men, it does promote equal employment opportunity; by "taking pregnancy into account, California's pregnancy disability leave statute allows women as well as men to have families without losing their jobs." Further, the Supreme Court determined that the California statute does not compel employers to treat pregnant workers better than other disabled employees, but merely establishes the benefits that employers must, at a minimum, provide to pregnant workers. Indeed, California employers were free, if not urged, to give comparable benefits to other disabled workers.

The question of "special protection" vs. "equal rights" was taken up on the federal level, where various women's and labor groups had been meeting with Representative Berman and other members of Congress and their staffs. They were trying to craft a federal policy that would permit parents to take leave in the event of the birth or illness of a child.[43] Key groups at that point included WLDF, NOW, the Junior League, NOW-Legal Defense and Education Fund, the National Council of Jewish Women (NCJW), and the Women's Equity Action League (WEAL). This coalition drafted its own version of the legislation, which provided for universal, non-gender-based parenting leave based on the principles of equal rights.

This version of the bill was significantly broader than the maternity leave bill that Representative Berman had originally intended to introduce. Representative Berman felt certain that his legislation had a greater chance of being acted upon by Congress than the more comprehensive version,[44] and was unwilling to act as its chief sponsor. The coalition found a new sponsor in Representative Patricia Schroeder, in what was considered by many to be a perfect fit. H.R. 2020, "The Parental and Disability Act," was introduced in the 99th Congress in April, 1985. Receiving some attention from policy makers and the media, the bill moved successfully through several committee hearings. It was reintroduced in the 100th Congress as The Family and Medical Leave Act, reflecting in its title the lobbying efforts of two movements.[45] The change from "parental" to "family" came from the provision to include leave to care for family members other than children. "Disability" was changed to "medical" when "differently abled" groups contacted sponsors, raising objections to the term "disability." In their own quest for equal treatment by employers, they did not want the term "disability" to be associated with being unable to work.[46]

THE FAMILY AND MEDICAL LEAVE ACT OF 1987

The Family and Medical Leave Act of 1987 (House of Representatives [H.R.] 925 and Senate [S.] 249) would have required businesses to provide job security for certain workers who took leave to care for a newborn, newly adopted, or seriously ill child, and for those who took leave due to their own prolonged medical illness or to care for a sick parent. Workers would have been entitled to unpaid leave with continued health benefits paid for by employers, but perhaps most importantly, workers would have been guaranteed either their old job back, or one of similar status, upon returning to the workplace. While some workers might have taken advantage of the entire leave period, the loss of income would have greatly reduced the period of leave for many.

As the FMLA made headway through the legislative process, lobbyists on both sides of the issue remained intensely involved in negotiations. The FMLA coalition attracted many groups to actively advocate passage of the bill, as well as support from numerous and diverse organizations. The U.S. Chamber of Commerce mounted a strong opposition to the bill, and from the beginning attached the term "mandated benefit" to the legislation, deeming it an unprecedented intrusion into the workplace by government.[47]

The most serious challenge to the FMLA was a competing parental-leave bill that had been introduced by Representative Marge Roukema (R-NJ), ranking minority member of the Subcommittee on Labor Management Relations of the House Education and Labor Committee. Unlike the FMLA, this bill exempted companies that employed 100 or fewer employees, offered fewer weeks of leave, and was generally more restrictive. Policy makers and advocates sat down with Roukema's legislative staff "and came up with a compromise that was very hard fought," said Sammie Moshenberg, legislative director for the National Council for Jewish Women (NCJW), a prominent member of the FMLA coalition.[48] Coalition members and staffers alike claimed a substantial victory with Roukema's support.[49] Several other Republicans were also willing to sign on and work on the legislation, including Representatives Olympia Snowe (R-ME), Nancy Johnson (R-CT), and James Jeffords (R-VT).[50]

This changed a number of aspects of the bill. The Parental and Medical Leave Act of 1986 (the family leave bill that had been introduced in the 99th Congress) had had an employee exemption number of fifteen, which was raised in the 100th Congress to fifty in the first three years, then thirty-five thereafter. Family leave was reduced from eighteen to ten weeks, which could be taken every two years, and medical leave was reduced from twenty-six weeks to fifteen weeks over a one-year period. A key employee provision was also added, allowing employers to exempt an employee in the top 10% salary range if the employer could show substantial economic necessity.[51] Despite these compromises, certain coalition members still hoped to pass a less compromised bill on the Senate side.

However, according to Sammie Moshenberg, this new alliance still did not "turn [around] the Chamber and the National Association of Manufacturers, who would have been opposed to it if one person got one day of leave, because of philosophical opposition to government mandated benefits."[52] The business community remained adamant in its opposition to the House legislation. Virginia Thomas, policy director of the U.S. Chamber of Commerce, noted that "the changes we have seen are quite modest . . . we haven't seen any significant ones."[53] Even some organizations within the coalition were unhappy with the compromises, believing that they had gone too far, and turned their attention to the Senate version, where they hoped fewer concessions would be necessary. "It is almost a basic civil rights issue. We are not interested in discriminating against anyone in this legislation," said one advocate.[54]

As the 100th congressional session drew to a close, the Senate sponsor, Christopher Dodd (D-CT), put together a new draft of the FMLA, S. 2488, which went to markup quickly, and soon thereafter to the full Senate Education and Labor Committee. In the fall of 1988, S. 2488 was brought to the floor of the Senate. Through a procedural maneuver, an antichild pornography bill, sponsored by outgoing Senator Strom Thurmond (R-SC), was attached to the FMLA. Coalition leaders were unhappy with the addition, not only because the Thurmond amendment was controversial, but because they believed that the FMLA should stand on its own merits.

In an effort to delay voting on the bill, Senate Republicans started a filibuster, leading the Democratic leadership to attach yet another bill, the Act for Better Child Care (ABC), which would have provided $2.5 billion annually for child care and related services to low-income families.[55] While ABC had already failed to move through Congress, it had attained greater visibility in the media and policy arena. In fact, some proponents of the FMLA believed that attachment of ABC should have made an irresistible package, winning support for the legislation as a whole.[56]

Yet advocates such as Pat Reuss, the legislative director of the Women's Equity Action League, felt that legislators had lost sight of the significance of the FMLA. "I am convinced that [Senate Majority Leader Robert Byrd (D-WV)] wouldn't care if there was a small employee exemption of 300. I think that is dangerous because it sets a dangerous precedent."[57] Furthermore, as it was an election year, legislators' motives seemed politically rather then ideologically driven. However, Republicans were not swayed by the attachment of either amendment.[58] On the floor of the Senate, they successfully blocked a vote on the bill with a procedural filibuster. Senator Byrd pulled the FMLA from the floor on October 7, 1988, accusing the Republicans of obstructionism and an unwillingness to support profamily legislation.[59]

INFLUENCES ON THE FMLA

In its important work in child and family policy development, the National Academy of Sciences identifies the following six influences in the policy formation process:[60] (1) contextual factors such as political, demographic, or economic conditions, which provide the background for the policy process; (2) principles or ideas that influence or guide the decisions of policy makers; (3) activities of constituents (e.g., lobbyists); (4) key actors and institutions, or principal government participants; (5) the media's presentation of the social problem and the policy process; and (6) research, which is introduced to explore problems, build general knowledge, or support the positions of participants. The four salient forces in the formation of the Family and Medical Leave Act were contextual factors; principles or ideas that influence policy makers; constituent activities; and key actors and institutions. The remaining two influences, research and the media, were less significant.[61]

Contextual Factors

The most frequently cited influence on every stage of this bill's progress was the growing recognition of changing demographics of the workplace. Due to the economic climate, women were entering the workforce in ever-increasing numbers, and a dire need had arisen for social policies that were cognizant of the new roles of working mothers. Workers and policy makers alike were growing more concerned about companies that offered fringe benefits in uneven and arbitrary ways. For example, workers testified at both the Senate and House hearings about new mothers getting only two weeks of maternity leave, or employees getting shabby treatment by managers when family emergencies arose.[62] This testimony was thought to have had a powerful impact on actors in the policy process.[63]

According to Donna Lenhoff, policy director for the Women's Legal Defense Fund (WLDF), "you get social change by a million people knocking on a million doors real, real hard and then when one of the doors opens everybody rushes in that door and knocks at the next door."[64] For public interest groups and child welfare activists, this was a time of many groups beating on many doors. While the FMLA was not ideologically competitive with other legislation such as the Act for Better Child Care (ABC), certain child care advocates chose to focus their energy on ABC, believing it to be more important, even if that meant the exclusion of the FMLA.[65] A member of the FMLA coalition noted that while everyone working on the parental-leave bill was also working on ABC, "there were those in the ABC Coalition who felt it had to be an either/or situation, and wanted it to be their bill."[66]

In the 1988 presidential campaign, the Democratic nominee, Governor Michael Dukakis of Massachusetts, was running against Vice President George Bush. Parental leave, like child care, had been raised as a presidential campaign issue, thus giving these issues more visibility than they had received for a decade.[67] In fact, despite his strong opposition to the FMLA and "mandated benefits," Bush announced to a group of women supporters that no woman should lose her job because she had had a child.[68] In spite of his intentions, his speech was credited with being the strongest influence in getting the FMLA considered during the 100th congressional session.[69] By merely mentioning family-leave policy, Bush was credited with forcing the Democratic, congressional leadership to move on the FMLA, and thereby thwart a Republican effort to gain control of family policy issues. This was especially true when candidate Dukakis did not lend express support to the bill. "There ha[d] been a gradual move forward, steady, but if not for Bush, it would not [have] come up for a vote."[70]

Principles and Ideas

The theoretical underpinnings of the debate between advocates and opponents of the Family and Medical Leave Act centered on the role of the federal government in the private sector. The Chamber of Commerce supported the concept of free enterprise, which it interpreted as allowing the marketplace to determine what kind of fringe benefits employers extend to their employees, and when.[71] Advocates for the FMLA believed that taking responsibility for the welfare of families is an appropriate role for the federal government. "The government is supposed to facilitate a decent quality of life for Americans, which includes economic situations, not just a climate where businesses can thrive, but where people can afford to live and work."[72]

In fact, FMLA advocates argued that family leave does not define a new relationship between government and the private sector, but instead falls under the rubric of minimum labor standards. They maintained that it is a basic protection for workers, which has historical precedent in such legislation as the Occupational Safety and Health Act and child labor laws. These standards arose in response to specific problems, where the voluntary actions of employers were inadequate.[73] In fact, "all major labor legislation came at a time when the country was demographically going through a real change . . . and the business community was just not responding . . . the government stepped in and set these minimum standards."[74]

While the FMLA gained attention because the presence of women in the workforce had a tremendous impact on the kind of care they gave their families, concern for children and infants was not a driving force. Even FMLA advocates acknowledged that support came from workers, acting on their own behalf, not from parents concerned about their children's welfare, per se.[75] This may be due, in part, to the legislation being labeled a labor bill rather than a profamily bill. "Families have not seemed to be able to mobilize around issues that are central to families. Families are made up of children and parents taking care of children, or their parents. It is not a voting block," said Laura Loeb, director of public policy for the Older Women's League. Employers have not evidenced a tremendous amount of concern for employees, let alone for employees' infants and children.[76] In fact, it seemed to be a basic premise that women who choose to have children should consequently deal with the resulting work and family stress on their own.[77]

Further, the issue of child care and its relation to parental leave did not enter this discussion in a central way. Infant care or the needs of families were surmounted by policy makers' concerns about employers coping with these kinds of leave policies.[78] This focus was evident in the compromise legislation on the House side, as policy makers attempted to appease small business concerns regarding the implementation of these policies.[79]

Constituent Pressure

The Family and Medical Leave Act was notable for attracting a broad range of supporters, and over 100 diverse lobbying groups endorsed the legislation. Approximately thirty groups came together to actively promote the bill, and these core groups became known as the FMLA coalition. While sharing no common bottom line, they worked by consensus: every time a decision had to be reached, a representative from each organization had to be present for the discussion.[80] While this made for a slow and unwieldy process, it was still surprisingly effective in getting members to work together as a fairly cohesive group, despite dissimilar political philosophies.[81]

The coalition was managed by Donna Lenhoff, director for Legal Policy and Programs for the Women's Legal Defense Fund and author of the original Family and Medical Disability Act.[82] She, and other feminist activists, were credited for the invention and promotion of the FMLA and its attendant gender-neutral leave policies. In actively advocating the FMLA, they raised the concept of "parental leave" on the national agenda, believing that taking responsibility for the welfare of families was an appropriate role for the federal government.[83] Robin Lipner, legislative assistant to Representative Schroeder, characterized the role of the women's community as "significant—critical in developing, moving, lobbying for the FMLA."[84] Once the bill was introduced, labor groups signed on and played a key role in the promotion of the legislation, and indeed the bill was recast as a piece of labor legislation by policy makers and the U.S. Chamber of Commerce. Yet its roots are firmly in the feminist community and ideology as articulated by Lenhoff: "in the long run, women's interests are best served by insuring that they have equal opportunity to participate both in the nurturing sphere and in the employment sphere."[85]

Like its advocates, the opponents of the Family and Medical Leave Act also came from a variety of backgrounds, and did not necessarily share a common bottom line. Economic conservatives, who were against mandated benefits, joined forces with social conservatives, who were against anything that would "seduce" young mothers into the workforce.[86] Some members of the conservative New Right believed that the FMLA was a "yuppie" ("Young Urban Professional") bill which only wealthier families could afford due to the unpaid leave component.[87] Other conservatives believed that the legislation was an effort to extend the welfare state to working-class people, with the benefits of the welfare state to be provided by employers rather than by the government.[88]

Opponents maintained that these issues should be worked out in labor contracts in the private sector, because job-protected leave is one of any number of benefits which might be attractive to employees.[89] If business is forced to offer this benefit, employers might be forced to drop other potentially more valuable benefits.[90] While certain factions opposing the Family and Medical Leave Act took dissimilar positions on the legislation, they all tended to align themselves with the Chamber of Commerce, which fought the bill due to a belief that it was a federal attempt to mandate benefits rather than to enact minimum labor standards. Further, the Chamber contended that workers could have abused or taken advantage of the leave policies as the bill read in 1987. The legislation was considered not only too lenient but lacking in structure, especially regarding parental leave. As its spokesperson and policy director, Virginia Thomas, noted

> You can give men and women fifteen weeks off for bonding with a child, but how do we know they are actually doing that, as opposed to getting a baby sitter and going on vacation? That is said flippantly, and I hope would be the exception rather than the rule, but the abuse potential with a lot of leave—we can't be policing that.[91]

Actors and Institutions in the Policy Process

House sponsors of the FMLA were able to reach a compromise with several key actors, but were ultimately unable to bring the bill up for a vote. The Senate leadership scheduled their vote on the legislative calendar right after acting on two labor bills, minimum wage and the sixty-day plant-closing notification. The Family and Medical Leave Act was perceived by many policy makers as a labor bill too, and members were once again confronted with highly divisive lobbying by business and labor groups. Members were not about to commit themselves unless they had to vote on the bill.[92] "They were under such pressure from the business community and the coalition that their attitude was 'It is a lose-lose situation. Why get myself in trouble if I am never going to have to vote? Don't send me into an election year alienating either women or the business community.'"[93]

Media Presentation

Advocates gave credit to the newsmakers for covering the FMLA from its inception.[94] When the bill was first introduced in the 99th Congress, proponents held a series of hearings to make the case for the legislation, and the former director of the Congressional Caucus for Women, Michele Lord, remembers that the media took up the issue of parental leave with enthusiasm. Yet by 1988, the Family and Medical Leave Act had not received tremendous media attention, and the media did not play a particularly forceful role in shaping the legislation.

Research: A Knowledge-building Force

Diverse fields of research played prominent roles in the initial promotion of the parental-leave legislation. Large-scale studies of implementation costs were undertaken by both sides of the parental-leave controversy, and cost estimates were hotly debated through much of the policy process. Proponents of the FMLA turned to child and family development research to define and rationalize their policy proposal.

The target constituency for the FMLA is families, and the bill was promoted and lobbied by representatives of the child development research community. Experts such as pediatrician T. Berry Brazelton of Harvard University and psychologist Edward Zigler of Yale University were very active in their support, linking research and public policy. Not only did their voices lend authority to the issues raised by advocates, but their testimony was considered immensely helpful in putting a human face on the demographic figures behind the Family and Medical Leave Act.[95] Indeed, research on the needs of children, infants, and families was considered critical in raising the issues of work and family conflict.[96]

Yet while these scholarly figures were frequently cited as having had an impact on members of Congress, "bonding," or more accurately "attachment," dropped out of the parental-leave discussion. Members of Congress were uncomfortable with the idea. "They didn't understand what [attachment] was or what it meant. In fact, the child development part of the overall debate has been dropped. Initially, Brazelton and other researchers were very prominent in the debate, but members of Congress couldn't relate to their testimony," said Michele Lord.[97]

Policy makers were more interested in the controversial debate around the cost to employers of implementing family leave policies. In 1987, the Chamber of Commerce estimated that enactment of the legislation would cost businesses approximately $2.6 billion per year. Faced with this seemingly inflated figure, both House and Senate sponsors requested that the General Accounting Office (GAO) conduct a cost estimate of implementing the FMLA. The GAO report estimated that, at an employee exemption level of fifty or fewer, the cost would be $188 million per year, and at thirty-five approximately $212 million per year. These lower figures likely were due to a different methodology for estimating the cost of training temporary workers, determining how many workers would take the full leave and how many would actually be replaced by temporary workers. The GAO reports indicated that workers' absences are typically handled by reallocating their work among other employees, and therefore cause no additional cost to employers.[98]

Nonetheless, the data the Chamber was advancing gained both publicity and support, swaying votes in its favor. Donna Lenhoff, of the WLDF, and leader of the FMLA coalition, decided that the coalition needed quantitative data of its own regarding the cost of *not* having a federal family leave policy;[99] a volume entitled *Unnecessary Losses*[100] was a response to this need. The authors' research indicated that, while there may be minor costs to businesses to implement parental-leave policies, the lack of these policies has costs for taxpayers, workers, and society by increasing unemployment and transfer payments for these workers. "It costs society in general because of lost productivity costs, when skilled workers lose jobs."[101]

THE RESULTING LEGISLATION

As with most legislation, the Family and Medical Leave Act was a compromise bill with no single author and little of the original intent. Responsibility for many of the concessions, as well as the defeat of the legislation, was laid at the feet of the business community, even though the coalition leaders knew that compromises would have had to be made during the policy process.[102] The Chamber of Commerce maintained, however, that "it may have looked like they were accommodating business, but they weren't. They were very unwilling to compromise on things we brought up."[103]

The Unpaid Leave Component

The issue of paid leave was first raised when the legislation was originally brought to the attention of members of Congress and their staffs. Many would-be supporters and several proponents questioned the value of the legislation without wage replacement.[104] However, advocates were quite sure that they would not be able to find a sponsor in Congress for any kind of paid-leave legislation. Neither Representatives Schroeder nor Berman would introduce it, "because they thought they would be laughed right out of their Congressional seat. That is a political reality so—should we have done nothing or should we have gone with unpaid leave?"[105]

The coalition members did choose to do something, believing that any leave was better than none at all. Still, there are those who pointed to the unpaid component and called this a yuppie bill targeted at the middle class.[106] Advocates denied this, offering Lillian Garland, the receptionist whose firing led to the CalFed case, as an example of someone who would have benefited from the FMLA, and was clearly not a yuppie.[107]

In fact, despite this compromise, the coalition believed their bill would be valuable and effective, for it is lower- and middle-income people who can least afford to lose their jobs. Furthermore, they would retain their health benefits while on leave, and if unable to afford to take the full amount of leave, could at least target the leave they did use for family emergencies.[108] Furthermore, women in higher-paying positions do not necessarily have more disposable income than those in the middle or lower socioeconomic status groups, for their income may primarily or wholly support their households.[109]

Having compromised on the issue of paid leave, advocates went on to negotiate labor standards and related points. Supporters considered the FMLA a minimum labor standard, and placed it squarely in the tradition of federal government labor legislation that dates back 50 to 100 years. They reasoned that just as it was appropriate for the federal government to establish the forty-hour work week, minimum wage, safety, and health requirements, and child labor standards, so was it appropriate for the federal government to address the needs of the current workforce. Business, on the other hand, called it a benefit, like vacation and pension plans, which have always been the right of employers to determine, based on their own calculations of workers' needs and their bottom-line desire to attract a stable workforce.

In the process of negotiation, the Family and Medical Leave Act of 1987 ended up with one of the highest employee exemption figures of any piece of labor legislation.[110] Moreover, the legislation's intent, which was to provide workers with a reasonable period of job-protected leave, was considerably compromised, raising concerns that, if enacted, the FMLA could have promoted a rather low ceiling for benefits, instead of inspiring business to do more.[111] However, proponents familiar with labor legislation were not convinced that this was a real risk. "Minimum wage, OSHA set a floor, and most employers go well above that and we certainly hope that will be the case for this bill as well.[112] Furthermore, the bill incorporated remedies that would enable qualified workers whose employers were not complying with the intent of the laws to avail themselves of an appeals process.

Early versions of the Family and Medical Leave Act provided leave specifically to biological parents, raising concerns that it could be regarded as discriminating against nonbiological parents, and nonparents in general.[113] Advocates interpreted the FMLA as emerging from the same set of legal guidelines that informed the Pregnancy Discrimination Act of 1978; namely, that it was constitutionally correct to make leave policies available to all employees, regardless of gender. When the bill was introduced in 1985, advocates had fought long and hard to include parental, rather than just maternal, leave in the legislation.

Furthermore, it was considered essential for families to decide on an individual basis what sort of leave-taking would work best for them.[114] The family leave provision, which permitted workers job-protected leave to care for family members, addressed many of these concerns. The provision for elder care, a stipulation in the Roukema compromise on the House side, gave relief to advocates uncomfortable with the previous draft of the legislation, which only extended the leave to parents.[115]

Some advocates of the FMLA were disturbed by the legislation defining or equating maternity leave with disability leave, preferring that public policy take the unique characteristics of childbirth into account.[116]

> It is like a woman is cured of having a child, and when she comes back to work she is supposed to function as if everything is just fine and there has been no change in her life. That has made it possible for companies to ignore the child care needs of employees.[117]

Opponents of the Family and Medical Leave Act claimed that, although the legislation is gender-neutral, employers will still discriminate against women of child-bearing age. As one informant noted, it is easy for an employer to determine which candidate for a job is of child-bearing age merely by looking at her.[118] Advocates believed this was a specious argument, since medical leave is just as likely to be taken by a middle-aged man who suddenly has a heart attack. Further, women are the fastest growing segment of the labor force, so right behind that woman there is likely to be another woman waiting to be hired.[119]

The FMLA also held significant implications for older and retired workers. While the elder care provision might provide comfort to certain workers whose parents needed their direct attention, medical leave was construed as a provision that would most likely benefit older workers, because they tend to be more prone to illness and chronic diseases. Furthermore, job-protected leave makes it more likely that workers would be able to stay with a single job and a single employer, which would have positive implications for pension security and thus be a significant asset at the time of retirement.[120]

THE FMLA: "STALLED" IN THE POLICY PROCESS?

The Family and Medical Leave Act, perhaps because it was sometimes referred to as the parental-leave bill, was popularly perceived as giving a new mother job-protected leave to spend a few weeks at home with her new baby. However, the legislation could effect large-scale social change in the American workplace. Its intention was to make the workplace more friendly and accommodating to the needs of workers, "more understanding of the fact that people have other needs in their lives that need not interfere with their being good workers, but on the other hand require certain accommodations so that both can be done," according to Jackie Ruff, of Senator Dodd's office. In trying to achieve this goal, some very basic social principles were tested, and the legislation "stalled" in the political process.

Carol Weiss's analysis of the policy formation process can shed some light on this "stalling."[121] Her thesis is that every policy results from a complex interaction of three forces: ideology, interests, and information. Ideology refers to the philosophical, moral, and political values that are at the core of the position taken by an actor. Interests are primarily defined as self-interests, including the pursuit of power, reputation, or rewards. Information includes the social science research to which policy makers have been exposed, including biased or invalid understandings of those data. When these forces are in alignment or harmony, both within categories and across them, policy proposals are most likely to succeed.

Ideology played a powerful role in the promotion, evolution, and "stalling" of the Family and Medical Leave Act. Both sides of the debate were driven by principles and values they held close to their hearts. Ideologically, business has been uncomfortable with taking responsibility for the families of workers, and has generally opposed the concept, if not always the fact, of government intervention. Yet the growing change in family structure as mothers enter the labor force, which led to the conceptualization of federal family leave policy, has lent demographic urgency to the advocates' belief that family and work life are mutually interdependent and that government intervention is sometimes appropriate.

Moreover, other policy analysts, such as Hyde and Essex, Strober and Dornbusch, and Zigler and Frank, have called for public policy that assists all citizens in meeting their private needs, and that enables adults to reconcile home and work responsibilities.[122] The women's community has been aware of these gender issues from the inception of the women's movement, and the drive to make the leave for new parents a "parenting" rather than a "maternal" leave stems from that background.[123] "It was their feeling that special treatment legislation, going back 100 years, usually backfired in the faces of those they were trying to protect in terms of discrimination," said Michele Lord, former director of the Congressional Caucus for Women.

To advocates, much of the significance of the FMLA, at least symbolically, was in society's growing recognition that, after an infant is born or a worker has a heart attack, there are long-lasting repercussions both for the individual and the family. The majority of families now face the task of combining work and family life, with women making sacrifices to take advantage of the equal opportunity they should have in the workplace. Psychologist Edward Zigler points out that there used to be a definite, impermeable boundary between the workplace and home.[124] He refers to the long tradition in America that families are a kind of encapsulated, sacrosanct, isolated entity. "I take care of my family. You take care of your family. Your kids are not a responsibility of mine—my kids are not a responsibility of yours. That is a uniquely American view."[125]

This notion was challenged here by legislation that could have been construed as crossing the barrier between public and private domains. Advocates were asking the federal government to give families protection in the marketplace, due to the reluctance of the business community to meet the changing needs of the American worker. Congress and the business community, however, seemed to share a common ideology about workers, which resulted in their failure to act on the bill. Indeed, supporters noted that because members of Congress tended to be older and had traditional family lives in which they did not often participate actively,[126] their lack of personal exposure to any of the work and family issues that the FMLA targets may have made their ideology incompatible with that of the proponents of the bill.[127] Even the most conservative members of Congress supported a straight disability leave for women bearing children;[128] that position, however, was ideologically irreconcilable with the equal rights stance of the FMLA coalition.[129]

For policy to proceed, it is necessary for interest groups to convince policy makers that it is in their—the policy makers'—best interests to promote a particular policy initiative. In the 100th Congress, both parties were perceived as being somewhat aware of family issues, and for the most part, advocates and lobbyists no longer felt that members of Congress needed to be educated about the fact that women are in the workforce.[130] Yet it was very difficult to get the House and Senate leadership to be actively interested in this issue. The dearth of female policy makers in leadership positions, who may have been more empathic to the issues, may have hindered the bill.[131] The FMLA further suffered because it was perceived as a piece of labor legislation. While this was logical due to its impact on workplace policies, labor bills historically have been difficult for Congress to pass. Further, the FMLA was characterized as a hybrid issue, both a labor and a women's bill, and neither constituency had a particularly strong voice representing them in the Congress.[132] The business community, on the other hand, had the powerful U.S. Chamber of Commerce representing them in their lobbying effort.

Furthermore, FMLA coalition leaders maintained that business interests not only had significantly more personal access to members of Congress, but combined it with the possibility of large financial contributions. Indeed, congresspersons were perceived as caring more about one "small businessman than the sixty people who work for [him], because he is the one they see at Rotary—at the country club on Saturday."[133]

At the time the Family and Medical Leave Act was being prepared to go to the floor of the Senate, the Children's Defense Fund and other child advocacy groups were lobbying very heavily for the Act for Better Child Care (ABC), despite the bill having been tabled for the legislative year. While the link between the parental-leave bill and the child care bill was evident to some advocates, they believed that there was an explicit decision made by the architects of the ABC bill to distance themselves, and not to lobby one single parental-leave and child care bill.[134] The mandated benefits concept would have brought on a whole different debate which they did not want applied to the child care bill.[135]

Interestingly enough, most groups in the FMLA coalition were very supportive of ABC, and many were working on that legislation. "Almost everyone in the parental leave coalition was also working on the child care bill. In my own organization, I could not tell you which was a greater priority."[136] Clearly, some of the resources of the FMLA coalition were drained by being involved with more than one "hot" piece of legislation, while the U.S. Chamber of Commerce and National Association of Manufacturers were able to devote seemingly endless resources to the defeat of the Family and Medical Leave Act.[137]

In the end, it seemed obvious to many in the FMLA coalition that the Chamber of Commerce was largely responsible for the defeat of the legislation in 1988.[138] The Chamber was unlikely to change its position on the FMLA or on any other bill that it believed intruded in the workplace. While recognizing the value of these family-oriented policies, it encouraged its constituency to implement them on a nonmandated basis. Beyond the strength of the opposition, the bill may have also been defeated due to coalition members having insufficient evidence of strong backing from voters back home. They never had the financial resources that the Chamber had to crank out letters to members and gain active support on the grassroots level.[139] As one member stated, "We haven't been able to translate [our support] into letters coming into the offices, and politicians haven't perceived these as issues that are going to move them out of office."[140]

After the defeat of the FMLA at the end of the 100th Congress, advocates planned to organize a grassroots campaign to gain support from working families when they reintroduced the legislation. Despite the fact that polls indicated popular support for the FMLA, it seems unlikely that there would be a massive grassroots movement without a tremendous amount of organization, because the primary constituency constantly fluctuates.[141] The FMLA was unusual in the canons of U.S. social policy in that it targets average families going through usual, stressful, and relatively short-term transitions. Constituents tended to be unaware that there were no laws requiring job-protected leave until they were in the midst of a family crisis or transition, and then realized there was no appropriate leave-taking policy at their place of employment. In the case of parental leave, their need tended to be short-term, and for most working parents, attention rapidly turned to child care issues soon after the arrival of their child.

In the event that a worker needed to take leave to attend to a sick child, a sick parent, or the adoption of a child, it was highly unlikely that the worker would be able to take any time to advocate the FMLA. The motivation behind the legislation was to help workers confronted with the stress of work while needing to attend to family matters. This may be the most transient and least politically active constituency any legislation could target.

On the other hand, the business community was very resourceful in making its position known to members of Congress through mailings and other grassroots activities. "When we go into Congressional offices, we hear that the mail coming in was sometimes 90–10 or 95–5 against the legislation," said Virginia Thomas, policy director of the U.S. Chamber of Commerce. This was a clear measure of the strength of the anti-FMLA groups, and especially of the influence and power of the small-business community. If indeed letterwriting and grassroots activity are such powerful influences in the policy process, constituent activities can be seen as elemental in the outcome of legislation. Advocates could not prove that it would have been in the best interests of members of Congress to vote for the Family and Medical Leave Act when it appeared to be against the stated point of view of their constituents.

Information was the third contested element in the progress of the FMLA, and both sides of the debate had research supporting their positions. Advocates presented objective, demographic data and explicit case studies of individuals affected by the lack of leave policies, and appealed to the personal knowledge of members of Congress. They also presented strong academic support for the concept of helping families through stressful times. The business community countered with data indicating that the cost of implementing the FMLA would break the backs of small businesses. Although the data of the Chamber of Commerce were successfully challenged by research conducted by the General Accounting Office, they left their mark.[142]

The attempt to embody the ideas of the child development research community in the promotion of the FMLA could not overcome the substantive interests of the business community. Expert data and testimony from the field of child development were instrumental in the initial promotion of the Family and Medical Leave Act. Indeed, research on the needs of infants played a significant role in the formation of the parental leave component of the legislation. Furthermore, the concept of mothers taking leave to care for newborns gave proponents a strong ideological vision for reference in their promotion of the bill. However, vision must be supported by interests,[143] and families' interests appeared notably weaker than those of the business community.

THE FMLA: PUBLIC POLICY SYMBOL?

Discussion about the Family and Medical Leave Act changed over the years, as did its focus. When it was first introduced, compelling arguments were made about supporting average families going through expected but stressful transitions. Policy makers stated that a primary reason for passing the bill would be "to give parents time to bond with their infants," or to protect the jobs of parents who took leave to care for seriously ill children.

However, the Chamber of Commerce, representing business interests, stepped into the debate, and the thrust of its objection was economic. This changed the focus of the debate to the workplace, and the data that were raised reflected the fear of business owners that these policies would be too expensive. They also worried that these labor standards or "benefits" would eventually be expanded to include paid leave. The issue of mandating benefits became explosive, as the business community rallied its forces to keep the federal government out of the workplace.

While the FMLA coalition was unable to gather the kind of support that opponents directed against the legislation, "success" has many definitions within the legislative process. It takes time to enact policy, and although the legislation did not pass, the FMLA was moved forward in the policy process. "In terms of advancing the issue and improving the prospects, [we feel] we did very well in the last Congress. To get all the attention, and move it as far along . . . we [will be] starting from a point that is further advanced."[144]

While the FMLA was hampered by a number of forces, such as its representation as a labor bill, the lack of visible grassroots support, and the reluctance of members to vote for these bills, perhaps most significant was the lack of deep commitment on the part of Congress and the White House to these kinds of reforms. Theodora Ooms, of the Family Impact Seminar, asks:

> Who within the [Reagan or Bush] administrations [wa]s working on issues of good child care policy and good parental leave policy? People are reacting, but there is no responsibility within government, saying, 'These are important issues.' [It is] important not to pass legislation, without acknowledging that it has largely symbolic value, and more needs to be done.[145]

Resistance to social legislation that appears to muddy the boundary between public and private responsibility for the welfare of families may well account for the failure of Congress to pass what many considered a tiny piece of profamily legislation at that time. For the federal government it would have been essentially revenue neutral, and it would have affected only 42–50% of the workforce. The fact that the leave would have been unpaid probably would have shortened the period of leave for most workers. But for many, just having paid medical insurance available, and a job to go back to, would have greatly eased an already stressful event.

Now that the FMLA has been enacted, there is some consensus that it will have a relatively minimal effect on the workplace as a whole. In fact, although President Clinton signed the Family and Medical Leave Act early in the 103rd Congress, many supporters felt that with the president's support, a stronger bill could have been drafted.[146] However, as both sides have indicated, perhaps the single most important point about the Family and Medical Leave Act is its symbolic value, and the fact that not only has it elevated the debate on these issues, but also it has shifted it to the center of public attention.

APPENDIX: LIST OF INTERVIEWS

J. Terry Bond: Director of the Center for the Study of the Child, National Council of Jewish Women, New York City, December, 1988.

Steven Crowne: Attorney, Former President, Lexington Chamber of Commerce, Lexington, Massachusetts, May, 1988.

Ann Dalton: Director of Public Policy, Association of Junior Leagues, New York City, December, 1988.

Fred Feinstein: Counsel and Staff Director, Subcommittee on Labor Management Relations of the House Education and Labor Committee, Washington, D.C., September, 1988.

Dana Friedman: Senior Research Associate, Work and Family Information Center, The Conference Board, New York City, December, 1988.

Mary Jane Gibson: Representative, Massachusetts House of Representatives, Boston, Massachusetts, November, 1988.

Maureen Goggin: Executive Director, Congressional Caucus for Women, Washington, D.C., September, 1988.

Jill Kagan: Professional Staff, House Select Committee on Children, Youth and Families, Washington, D.C., September, 1988.

Azar Kattan: Deputy Director, Congressional Caucus for Women, Washington, D.C., September, 1988.

Ann Kurkjian: NOW Legal Defense and Education Fund, Washington, D.C., September, 1988.

Donna Lenhoff: Director for Legal Policy and Programs, Women's Legal Defense Fund, Washington, D.C., November, 1988.

Robin Lipner: Legislative Assistant, Office of Representative Pat Schroeder, Washington, D.C., September, 1988.

Laura Loeb: Director of Public Policy, Older Women's League (formerly at Congressional Caucus for Women), Washington, D.C., November, 1988.

Michele Lord: Research Associate, Bank Street College of Education (Former

Director of Congressional Caucus for Women), New York City, December, 1988.

Susanne Martinez: Legislative Counsel, Office of Senator Alan Cranston, Washington, D.C., September, 1988.

Monica McFadden: Director of Public Policy, Business and Professional Women's Organization (BPW), Washington, D.C., November, 1988.

Margaret Meiers: Senior Associate in Programs, Catalyst, New York City, December, 1988.

Carol Miller: Legislative Associate, Business and Professional Women's Organization (BPW), Washington, D.C., November, 1988.

Sammie Moshenberg: Director of Washington Legislative Office, National Council for Jewish Women, Washington, D.C., November, 1988.

Theodora Ooms: Director, Family Impact Seminar, Washington, D.C., September, 1988.

Joseph Piccione: Policy Analyst, National Forum Foundation, Washington, D.C., September, 1988.

Joseph Pleck: Henry R. Luce Professor of Families, Change, and Society, Wheaton College, Norton, Massachusetts, December, 1988.

Edward Remsburg: Corporate Benefits, Digital Equipment Corporation, Massachusetts, January, 1990.

Patricia Reuss: Legislative Director, Women's Equity Action League, Washington, D.C., November, 1988.

Jackie Ruff: Senate Committee on Children, Drugs, Youth and Alcoholism (Office of Senator Christopher Dodd), Washington, D.C., November, 1988.

Helen Sayles: Assistant Vice President, Manager of Human Resources Department, Liberty Mutual, Boston, Massachusetts, January, 1990.

Mike Schwartz: Resident Fellow in Social Policy, Free Congress Foundation, Washington, D.C., September, 1988.

Roberta Spalter-Roth: Director of Research, Institute for Women's Policy Research, Washington, D.C., September, 1988.

Virginia Thomas: Policy Director, U.S. Chamber of Commerce, Washington, D.C., November, 1988.

Rebecca Tillet: Legislative Director, National Women's Political Caucus, Washington, D.C., September, 1988.

Edward Zigler: Sterling Professor of Psychology and Director of the Bush Center in Child Development and Social Policy, Yale University, New Haven, Connecticut, October, 1988.

NOTES

1. Department of Labor Report (February, 1990). *Congressional Digest, 69* (2), 34.

2. E. Eckholm (October 6, 1992). Finding out what happens when mothers go to work. *New York Times*, A1, A21.

3. S. B. Kamerman (1991). Parental leave and infant care: U.S. and international trends

and issues, 1978–1988. In J. S. Hyde & M. J. Essex (Eds.), *Parental leave and child care: Setting a research and policy agenda*, 11–23. Philadelphia: Temple University Press; S. B. Kamerman & A. J. Kahn (1987). *The responsive workplace: Employers and a changing labor force.* New York: Columbia University Press; S. B. Kamerman (1983). Fatherhood and social policy: Some insights from a comparative perspective. In M. Lamb & A. Sage (Eds.). *Fatherhood and family policy*, 23–37. Hillsdale, NJ: LEA Associates.

4.   E. Trzcinski (1991). Employers' parental leave policies: Does the labor market provide parental leave? In Hyde & Essex (Eds.), *Parental leave and child care*, 209–228.

5.   D. Phillips, K. McCartney, & S. Scarr (1987). Child-care quality and children's social development. *Developmental Psychology, 23*(4), 537–543; T. Gamble & E. Zigler (1986). Effects of infant day care: Another look at the evidence. *American Journal of Orthopsychiatry, 56*(1), 26–42.

6.   T. B. Brazelton (1988). Issues for working parents. In E. F. Zigler & M. Frank (Eds.), *The parental leave crisis: Toward a national policy*, 36–54. New Haven: Yale University Press.

7.   Interview with Michele Lord, Research Associate, Bank Street, (Former Director of the Congressional Caucus for Women), New York, December, 1988.

8.   A. Radigan (1988). *Concept and compromise: The evolution of family leave legislation in the U.S. Congress.* Washington, D.C.: Women's Research and Educational Institute.

9.   Family values, at last (February 7, 1993). *Boston Globe*, 72; R. W. Apple (February 6, 1993). A case of double jeopardy over attorney general. *New York Times*, A1, A8; A. Clymer (February 5, 1993). Congress passes measure providing emergency leaves. *New York Times*, A1, A14. While Congress received some attention for passing the FMLA, the media coverage of the signing of the bill was limited due to the president being challenged by Republicans both for his desire to lift the ban on homosexuals in the military and his inability to appoint a suitable attorney general. (This is reflected in the *New York Times*, which covered the signing of the FMLA in an article describing the "flap" over the attorney general.)

10.   S. B. Kamerman (1983). Child-care services: A national picture. *Monthly Labor Review, 106*(12), 35–39.

11.   Hyde & Essex (1991), *Parental leave and child care.*

12.   Kamerman (1991), Parental leave and infant care; S. B. Kamerman, A. J. Kahn, & P. Kingston (1983). *Maternity policies and working women.* New York: Columbia University Press.

13.   M. E. Starrels (September, 1992). The evolution of workplace family policy research. *Journal of Family Issues, 13*(3), 259–278.

14.   Catalyst (1986). *Report on a national study of parental leaves.* New York: Catalyst.

15.   Starrels (September, 1992), The evolution of workplace family policy research.

16.   Kamerman & Kahn (1987), *The responsive workplace.*

17.   C. Harrison (1988). A richer life: A reflection on the women's movement. In S. E. Rix (Ed.), *The American woman 1988–89: A status report*, 53–77. New York: W.W. Norton.

18.   M. Piccarillo (1988). The legal background of a parental leave policy and its implications. In Zigler & Frank (Eds.). *The parental leave crisis*, 293–314; L. W. Gladstone, J. D. Williams, & R. S. Belous (1985). *Maternity and parental leave policies: A comparative analysis* (Report No. 85–148 GOV). Washington, D.C.: Congressional Research Service.

19.   J. Belsky (1988). A reassessment of infant day care. In Zigler & Frank (Eds.), *The parental leave crisis*, 100–119; J. Belsky (1986). Infant day care: A cause for concern? *Zero to Three, 6*(5), 1–7.

20. Gamble & Zigler (1986), Effects of infant day care.

21. C. Howes & M. Olenick (1986). Family and child care influences on toddler compliance. *Child Development, 57*, 206–216.

22. J. P. Allen (1988). European infant care leaves: Foreign perspectives on the integration of work and family roles. In Zigler & Frank (Eds.), *The parental leave crisis*, 245–275.

23. P. Pizzo (1988). Uncertain harvest: Maternity leave policies in developing nations. In Zigler & Frank (Eds.), *The parental leave crisis*, 276–292.

24. Kamerman (1988), Maternity and parenting benefits: An international overview. In Zigler & Frank (Eds.), *The parental leave crisis*, 235–244.

25. Interview with Donna Lenhoff, Director for Legal Policy and Programs, Women's Legal Defense Fund, Washington, D.C., November, 1988.

26. Muller v. Oregon was decided by the U.S. Supreme Court in 1908. Louis Brandeis served as an associate justice of the Supreme Court from 1916 to 1939.

27. Kamerman et al. (1983), *Maternity policies and working women*.

28. Interview with Lenhoff, November, 1988.

29. A. Kessler-Harris (1982). *Out to work: A history of wage-earning women in the United States*. New York: Oxford University Press; Interview with Lenhoff, November, 1988.

30. J. A. Baer (1978). *The chains of protection: The judicial response to women's labor legislation*. Westport, CT: Greenwood Press.

31. Interview with Lenhoff, November, 1988.

32. Gladstone et al. (1985), *Maternity and parental leave policies*.

33. Radigan (1988), *Concept and compromise*.

34. W. Williams & S. Marshall (1985). Legal issues. In S. Orr & G. Haskett (Eds.), *Parental leave: Options for working parents*, 13–14. Association of Junior Leagues.

35. M. H. Strober & S. M. Dornbusch (1988). Public policy alternatives. In M. Strober & S. Dornbusch (Eds.), *Feminism, children, and the new families*. New York: Guilford Press.

36. Radigan (1988), *Concept and compromise*; California Federal Savings & Loan, Assoc., et al., Petitioners, v. Mark Guerra, Director, Department of Fair Employment and Housing, et al. *United States Supreme Court Reports*, October Term, Volume 479 U.S., Lawyers' Edition, Volume 93: Edd 2d (1986). Rochester, NY: The Lawyers Co-operative Publishing Co; Editorial Staff, United States Supreme Court Reports. California Federal Savings & Loan, Assoc., et al., Petitioners, v. Mark Guerra, Director, Department of Fair Employment and Housing, et al. *Decisions of the United States Supreme Court: 1986–87 Term*. Lawyers Edition. Rochester, NY: The Lawyers Co-operative Publishing Co.; California Federal Savings & Loan Association v. Guerra, 758 F.2d 390 (9th Cir. 1984).

37. J. Leo (August 18, 1986). Are women "male clones"? *Time*, 63–64.

38. B. Kantrowitz (February 17, 1986). The parental leave debate: How much is enough? *Newsweek, 107*, 64.

39. Piccarillo (1988), The legal background of a parental leave policy; Kamerman, Kahn, & Kingston (1983), *Maternity policies and working women*.

40. Radigan (1988), *Concept and compromise*.

41. W. L. Clay & F. L. Feinstein (Fall, 1987). The family and medical leave act: A new federal labor standard. *ILR Report, 25*(1), 28–33.

42. California Federal Savings & Loan Association v. Guerra, 758 F.2d 390 (9th Cir. 1985).

43. Clay & Feinstein (1987), The family and medical leave act.

44. Radigan (1988), *Concept and compromise*.

45. Interview with Lord, December, 1988.

46. Interview with Lord, December, 1988.

47. J. Rovner (November 21, 1987). Revised family-leave measure ok'd by divided house panel. *Congressional Quarterly*, 2884.

48. Interview with Sammie Moshenberg, Director of Washington Legislative Office, National Council for Jewish Women, Washington, D.C., November, 1988.

49. While not joyous over the terms of the compromise, coalition members knew they had no choice but to make concessions if they wanted to move the FMLA through the policy process. Interviews #2, #3. Key informants were offered anonymity. A link-file system, which assigned numbers to each interview, was developed for that purpose.

50. Interview #2; Radigan (1988), *Concept and compromise.*

51. Family & medical leave compromise stirs controversy among supporters (September/October/November, 1987). *National NOW Times*, 8; Rovner (November 21, 1987), Revised family-leave measure ok'd by divided house panel.

52. Interview with Moshenberg, November, 1988.

53. Interview with Virginia Thomas, Policy Director, U.S. Chamber of Commerce, Washington, D.C., November, 1988.

54. Interview with Ann Dalton, Director of Public Policy, Association of Junior Leagues, New York, December, 1988.

55. D. Stipek & J. McCroskey (February, 1989). Investing in children: Government and workplace policies for parents. *American Psychologist, 44*(2), 416–423.

56. Interview with Jackie Ruff, Senate Committee on Children, Drugs, Youth and Alcoholism (office of Senator Christopher Dodd), Washington, D.C., November, 1988.

57. Interview with Patricia Reuss, Legislative Director, Women's Equity Action League, Washington, D.C., November, 1988.

58. "The people who are opposed to this bill don't want a compromise and have said that even if all their amendments are adopted, they still wouldn't vote for it on final passage," said Representative Clay. Rovner (November 21, 1987), Revised family-leave measure ok'd by divided house panel.

59. M. Morehouse (October 8, 1988). *Senate Democrats are stymied on so-called 'Family Issues.'* Washington, D.C.: Congressional Quarterly, Inc.

60. C. D. Hayes (Ed.) (1982). *Making policies for children: A study of the federal process.* Washington, D.C.: National Academy Press.

61. Interview with Dana Friedman, Senior Research Associate, Work and Family Information Center, The Conference Board, New York, December, 1988; Interview with Lenhoff, November, 1988; Interview with Monica McFadden, Director of Public Policy, Business and Professional Women's Organization, Washington, D.C., November, 1988.

62. For example, see Committee on Labor and Human Resources (1988). *Hearings before the Subcommittee on Children, Family, Drugs and Alcoholism of the Committee on Labor and Human Resources, United States Senate, One hundredth Congress, first session, on S.249, to grant employees parental and temporary medical leave under certain circumstances, and for other purposes, Part 1 and 2.* Washington, D.C.: U.S. Government Printing Office.

63. Interview with Lord, December, 1988; Interview with Susanne Martinez, Legislative Council, office of Senator Alan Cranston, Washington, D.C., September, 1988; Interviews #2 and #4.

64. Interview with Lenhoff, November, 1988.

65. Interviews #2; #16; #33.

66. Interview #21, a core member of the FMLA coalition.

67. D. Harbrecht & S. B. Garland (September 26, 1988). A Bush flip-flop gives new life to the parental leave bill. *Business Week*, (3071), 61.

68. Supporters were hopeful that the Democratic candidate, Governor Michael Dukakis, would back the Senate version. However, advocates like Reuss believe that "we weren't successful with Mike Dukakis but in a funny way we were with Bush," in that Bush addressed the topic of a working woman's right to stay home with her newborn child. Governor Dukakis never forcefully challenged the Republicans on the family leave issue.

69. Harbrecht & Garland, A Bush flip-flop, 61.

70. Interview with Ann Kurkjian, NOW Legal Defense and Education Fund, Washington, D.C., September, 1988. Many other interviewees agreed that this was true, including Laura Loeb, director of Public Policy, Older Women's League, Washington, D.C., November, 1988; Carol Miller, Legislative Associate, Business and Professional Women's Organization, Washington, D.C., November, 1988; Reuss, November, 1988.

71. Interview with Thomas, November, 1988.

72. Interview with Moshenberg, November, 1988.

73. Clay & Feinstein (1987), The family and medical leave act.

74. Interview with Lord, December, 1988.

75. Interview with Moshenberg, November, 1988.

76. Interview with McFadden, November, 1988; Interview with Margaret Meiers, Senior Associate in Programs, Catalyst, New York, December, 1988.

77. E. Galinsky (1986). *Investing in quality child care: A report for AT&T*. New York: Bank Street College; Interview with Meiers, December, 1988.

78. Interview with Lenhoff, November, 1988; Interview with Loeb, November, 1988; Interview with Reuss, November, 1988.

79. Interview with McFadden, November, 1988; Interview with Kurkjian, September, 1988; Interview with Robin Lipner, Legislative Assistant, Representative Pat Schroeder, Washington, D.C., September, 1988.

80. Interview with Reuss, November, 1988.

81. Interview with Lord, December, 1988; Interview with Reuss, November, 1988.

82. "If there is any leader, Donna would be it . . . the WLDF is not a grassroots organization . . . had never been as actively involved in the advocacy element of moving legislation as it has been now," said Loeb, November, 1988. In her November, 1988 interview, Lenhoff credited Representative Howard Berman for the original concept of a national leave bill, stating that "it would be a natural extension of the theory of the Pregnancy Discrimination Act." She also praised the training she received from Judy Lichtman, president of the Women's Legal Defense Fund, and Wendy Williams and Susan Ross, law professors at Georgetown University.

83. Interview with McFadden, November, 1988; Interview with Moshenberg, November, 1988. Even the leader of the opposition to the FMLA, Virginia Thomas of the U.S. Chamber of Commerce, acknowledged, "I will give the other side of that battle credit . . . they really have raised the issue to a better level of debate . . . . The debate has raised the consciousness of employers."

84. Interview with Lipner, September, 1988.

85. Interview with Lenhoff, November, 1988.

86. Interview with Joseph Piccione, Policy Analyst, National Forum Foundation, Washington, D.C., September, 1988.

87. Interview with Piccione, September, 1988; Interview with Mike Schwartz, Resident

Fellow in Social Policy, Free Congress Foundation, Washington, D.C., September, 1988.

88.   Interview with Thomas, November, 1988; Interview with Piccione, September, 1988; Interview with Schwartz, September, 1988.

89.   Interview with Thomas, November, 1988; Interview with Schwartz, September, 1988; J. E. Ellis (August 31, 1987). Parental leave is snowballing. *Business Week*, 32–33.

90.   Interview with Thomas, November, 1988.

91.   Interview with Thomas, November, 1988.

92.   Interview with Lord, December, 1988; Interview with Miller, November, 1988; Interview with Moshenberg, November, 1988.

93.   Interview with Miller, November, 1988.

94.   Interview with Meiers, December, 1988; Interview with Moshenberg, November, 1988; Interview with Martinez, September, 1988. While not an advocate, she did give credit to newspaper articles for bringing the need for the FMLA to her attention.

95.   Interview with Edward Zigler, Sterling Professor of Psychology and Director of the Bush Center in Child Development and Social Policy, Yale University, October, 1988. Most of the members of the FMLA Coalition and the policy makers agreed that "they had been very useful." (Lenhoff, November, 1988).

96.   Interview with Dalton, December, 1988; Interview with Fred Feinstein, Counsel and Staff Director, Subcommittee on Labor Management Relations of the House Education and Labor Committee, Washington, D.C., September, 1988; Interviews #2, and #3.

97.   Interview with Lord, December, 1988.

98.   U.S. General Accounting Office (1988). *Parental leave: Estimated cost of revised parental and medical leave act proposal* (/HRD–88–132). Washington, D.C.: U.S. Government Printing Office; U.S. General Accounting Office (1988). *Parental leave: Estimated cost of revised parental and medical leave act* (/HRD–88–103). Washington, D.C.: U.S. Government Printing Office; U.S. General Accounting Office (1987). *Parental leave: Estimated costs of H.R. 925, the family and medical leave act of 1987* (/HRD–88–34). Washington, D.C.: U.S. Government Printing Office.

99.   Interview with Roberta Spalter-Roth, Director of Research, Institute for Women's Policy Research, Washington, D.C., September, 1988.

100.   R. M. Spalter-Roth & H. I. Hartmann (1990). *Unnecessary losses: Costs to Americans of the lack of family and medical leave*. Washington, D.C.: Institute for Women's Policy Research; R. M. Spalter-Roth & H. I. Hartmann (1988). *Unnecessary losses: Costs to Americans of the lack of family and medical leave: Executive summary*. Washington, D.C.: Institute for Women's Policy Research.

101.   Interview with Spalter-Roth, September, 1988.

102.   Radigan (1988), *Concept and compromise*.

103.   Interview with Thomas, November, 1988.

104.   "Because of the political climate, the legislation does not include the partial wage replacement that experts consider to be a key component of a national leave policy mode. The bill does, however, propose a commission to study existing and proposed family or medical leave policies that provide for wage replacement." P. Schroeder (1988). Parental leave: The need for a federal policy. In Zigler & Frank (Eds.), *The parental leave crisis*, 326–332.

105.   Interview with Lenhoff, November, 1988; Schroeder (1988), Parental leave.

106.   Interviews #28 and #29.

107.   Interview with Zigler, October, 1988; Interview with Feinstein, September, 1988.

108.   Interview with Dalton, December, 1988; Interview with Moshenberg, November, 1988; Interview with Reuss, November, 1988.

109. Interview with J. Terry Bond, Director of the Center for the Study of the Child, National Council of Jewish Women, New York, December, 1988.

110. In the interview with Lord, she stated, "what they don't understand is that there are serious consequences to raising the small employer exemption.... You are setting a precedent for a minimum labor standard, so that instead of the 15 number that you are more likely to find, people will start thinking of 50 or 100."

111. Interview with Lord, December, 1988.

112. Interview with Feinstein, September, 1988.

113. Interview with Dalton, December, 1988; Interview with Reuss, November, 1988; Interview with Lipner, September, 1988.

114. Interview with McFadden, November, 1988; Interview with Lipner, September, 1988; Interview #4.

115. Interview with Joseph Pleck, Henry R. Luce Professor of Families, Change, and Society, Wheaton College, Norton, MA, December, 1988; Interview with Lenhoff, November, 1988; Interview with Reuss, November, 1988.

116. Interview with Friedman, December, 1988; Interview with Meiers, December, 1988; Interview with Loeb, November, 1988.

117. Interview with Friedman, December, 1988.

118. Interview with McFadden, November, 1988.

119. Interview with Kurkjian, September, 1988; Kamerman & Kahn (1987), *The responsive workplace.*

120. Interview with Feinstein, September, 1988.

121. C. Weiss (1983). Ideology, interests, and information. In D. Callahan & B. Jennings (Eds.), *Ethics, the social sciences, and policy analysis*, 213–245. New York: Plenum Press.

122. Hyde & Essex (1991), *Parental leave and child care*; Strober & Dornbusch (1988), Public policy alternatives; Zigler & Frank (Eds.) (1988), *The parental leave crisis*, xv-xxv.

123. Interview with Lenhoff, November, 1988; Interview with Reuss, November, 1988.

124. Interview with Zigler, October, 1988.

125. Interview with Zigler, October, 1988.

126. Interviews #6; #25; #34.

127. Interview with Pleck, December, 1988.

128. Interview with Bond, December, 1988.

129. Interview with Lenhoff, November, 1988; Interview with Reuss, November, 1988; Interview with Ruff, November, 1988.

130. Interview with Loeb, November, 1988.

131. Interview with Loeb, November, 1988.

132. Interview with Loeb, November, 1988; Interview with Reuss, November, 1988.

133. Interview with Reuss, November, 1988.

134. In fact, in a telephone interview, a highly placed staffer at the Children's Defense Fund (CDF) stated that, although CDF supported the FMLA, they had nothing to do with it, as they were too busy with ABC.

135. One policy analyst noted that there were "problems with the way CDF handled ABC, one of them is that they have not always moved towards family leave at all .... ABC was always totally consuming to CDF."

136. Interview with Moshenberg, November, 1988.

137. Interview with Lenhoff, November, 1988; Interview with Moshenberg, November, 1988; Interview with Ruff, November, 1988; Interview with Zigler, October, 1988.

138. Interview with Moshenberg, November, 1988; Interview with Ruff, November,

1988. "I see the Chamber of Commerce as the straw that broke this camel's back . . . . That is who the opposition was, that is what the problem was," said Donna Lenhoff, of the WLDF (November, 1988).

139. Interview with Lenhoff, November, 1988.

140. Interview with Loeb, November, 1988.

141. Interview with Reuss, November, 1988.

142. U.S. General Accounting Office (1988), *Parental leave* (/HRD–88–132); U.S. General Accounting Office (1988), *Parental leave* (/HRD–88–103); U.S. General Accounting Office (1987), *Parental leave* (/HRD-88-34).

143. Hayes (Ed.) (1982), *Making policies for children.*

144. Interview with Ruff, November, 1988.

145. Interview with Theodora Ooms, Director, Family Impact Seminar, Washington, D.C., September, 1988.

146. "The bill is a real disappointment . . . . More than half the workers in the country aren't covered," said Jill Ireland, President of NOW [as cited in E. Neuffer (January 31, 1993). Prospects for family leave bill darken. *Boston Globe*, 15.] However, the congressional sponsors of the bill, Representative Schroeder and Senator Dodd, both felt it was important to have something on the books, and that they would "revisit the legislation down the road."

5

Policy Entrepreneurship and the Emergence of Family Support Programs

Bonnie Hausman

Scholars, practitioners, and advocates may have despaired of achieving a national-level policy for children and families since the ideologically polarized White House Conference on Families in 1980.[1] Nevertheless, teams of individuals in several states: government officials, service providers, community activists and philanthropists—policy entrepreneurs—have dramatically altered the policy landscape on behalf of families and children. By launching programs to improve child development outcomes that emphasize parent education and support services, these policy entrepreneurs have invigorated the policy environment of contemporary social welfare and education administration.

During the 1980s, many state agency executives were alarmed by social indicators that suggested increasing family dysfunction and unfavorable child outcomes. Although much of the concern focused on the problems of "underclass" families, evidence of declining family well-being extended across race and class lines.[2] For example, data revealed the extent to which suburban families were increasingly affected by demographic, labor force, and family structure changes during the last twenty years.[3] Whether inadequately funded, wrongly conceived, or poorly implemented, it appeared that existing income support strategies and social welfare services were failing to achieve remediative objectives. Agencies were simply overrun with families and children needing intensive services. In the absence of federal guidance, state policy leaders searched for innovative preventive approaches.

Within this context, the family support and education model emerged as a logical policy response. By contrast with traditional strategies, it aims to improve child outcomes by changing parental behaviors and family functioning.[4] These programs share a set of common principles: supporting family strengths over remediating weaknesses, fostering self-sufficiency through nonhierarchical peer supports, strengthening family and community support networks and respecting cultural differences.[5] Through home visits or within community-based settings, family support and education programs provide a wide range of instrumental, social, educational, and emotional support to parents—mostly mothers, but fathers are included—throughout the childrearing years. Services frequently offered include peer support groups that permit exchange of experiences; home visitations; sessions to transmit information about effective parenting strategies; family recreational activities; diagnostic developmental evaluations; individual counseling and referrals for medical, job training, or social services; and other opportunities to create social support networks and improve self-esteem.[6]

Although the family support model has been cited as an "innovative" approach, in fact it has a venerable history in this country, dating back to the informal family support networks established in colonial America. The most direct antecedents, however, are "the community action programs of the 1960s, the child advocacy programs of the 1970s, and the long and diverse history of family service agencies."[7] In the 1980s, promotion of family support and parent education programs became an ideological movement among believers as much as an approach to comprehensive social service delivery among practitioners. Heather Weiss, director of the Harvard Family Research Project, has aptly characterized the family support model as "old wine in new bottles."[8] Advocacy of family support is, then, an exercise in putting old wine into new bottles . . . and attempting to sell it. Observation of the process by which these programs have been put to market in new bottles by teams of entrepreneurs in state government is the central focus of this chapter.

POLICY ENTREPRENEURSHIP

Scholars of the policy-making process have applied a model of private-sector entrepreneurial leadership to the public sector: "advocates who are willing to invest their resources—time, energy, reputation, money—to promote a position in return for anticipated future gain in the form of material, purposive, or solidary benefits."[9] King and Roberts have also borrowed the public-private analogy: "As business entrepreneurs assume financial risks to create products and open new markets, so do policy entrepreneurs risk their political capital by espousing innovative and controversial policy ideas."[10] Others have described activities of key actors in administrative agencies who influence the "issue-attention cycle."[11] A profile of policy entrepreneurs reveals that they are found as often inside as outside of government— as agency civil servants, legislators, and elected executives. Their functions (intellectual, strategic, and activist) and ingredients (ideology, information, and interests) have also been identified.[12] The literature on private-sector entrepreneurship distinguishes managers from leaders.[13] Whereas managers focus primarily on coping with organizational complexity, leaders engage in changing processes: *setting* a new vision and direction, *aligning* people toward the new direction, and *inspiring* people to forge ahead despite numerous obstacles. Applied to the public sector, this means that managers focus on providing more efficient services, while leaders focus on transforming the mission or direction of the agency.

Although analysts of corporate innovation have noted the important role of team work in successful innovation, observers of public-sector management, with few exceptions, have not described collaborative teams.[14] Instead, the public-sector management literature has canonized the individual charismatic policy leader, largely ignoring the elaborated, highly differentiated groups that launched important innovations.

A more elaborated model of public-sector innovation is presented in this cross-state analysis of family support program development and implementation. The three state programs examined in this case study—Kentucky's Parent and Child Education (PACE), Missouri's Parents as Teachers (PAT), and Maryland's Family Support Centers (FSC)—vary by auspices (education or social welfare); funding authority (budgetary or statutory); scale (pilot or statewide); eligibility (targeted or universal); model of service delivery (voluntary or mandatory, centralized or decentralized); and staffing (professional or volunteer). Data from each state also suggest variations in culture and tradition, yielding somewhat unique program provisions. Nonetheless, cross-site comparisons reveal an instructive set of similarities in the activities of the programs' proponents.

Semistructured field and telephone interviews with legislators, committee chairs, agency managers, program directors, child advocates, and key foundation and community leaders provide the primary data source for this multisite case study. Approximately fifty interviews were conducted from states reported here during the two-and-a-half-year course of the project (see the Appendix); programs were observed during site visits in the states between January, 1987, and January, 1989. Information was obtained from archival records: agency memoranda, letters, and both formal and informal meeting agendas. Updated information was obtained by the author through personal and telephone interviews through December, 1993. Most data were collected as part of a study of state-sponsored family support and education programs reported previously.[15]

The following section describes programs and details the most salient features of formulation and implementation in each site. Cross-site findings are then summarized. The final section offers practical and theoretical conclusions, with special emphasis on factors that affect national family policy development.

THE STATE PROGRAMS

Kentucky: Parent and Child Education

Kentucky's Parent and Child Education (PACE) began as a $1.2 million pilot program administered by the Kentucky Department of Education (KDE). Initiated in 1986 to combat illiteracy, PACE provides education and support services to parents who have not completed high school and to their preschool children.[16] While the children attend preschool, parents participate in literacy, parent education, and support sessions. Because PACE's goal is to reverse Kentucky's pattern of undereducation and negative attitudes toward schooling, all centers are located within public schools.

PACE evolved as a result of collaboration between two colleagues at the KDE: Sharon Darling, then director of the Division of Adult and Community Education, and Jeanne Heberle, then Kindergarten Program Consultant, Division of Program Development.[17] During their daily 120-mile commute to work, Darling and Heberle routinely argued the merits of adult remediation versus preschool preparation. This ongoing dialogue strengthened their conviction that working with the two generations together was the most effective means of breaking the cycle of intergenerational illiteracy. Their own program experiences were validated by data showing Kentucky's poor performance on school outcomes. Sixty percent of the adults in fifty-one of Kentucky's school districts had not graduated from high school, placing Kentucky first among states in the number of adults over twenty-five without high-school diplomas.[18] More important, in Darling's own adult literacy classes less than 10% of the parents of her adult students had completed high school. Darling had heard about the developing Even Start program in Washington, D.C., and knew that a similar approach was needed in Kentucky. By 1985, Kentucky's leaders had also become keenly aware of the strong link between the state's poor standing educationally and its slow economic development. General Motors' choice of Tennessee over Kentucky as a site for its Saturn plant was believed to have resulted from an examination of these data.

During the summer of 1985, Darling and Heberle approached Representative Roger Noe, chairman of the House Education Committee, to explore their idea of beginning a statewide intergenerational literacy program. Noe was receptive, and together they developed a plan of action. First, Noe approached the superintendent of public instruction with a request that the Kentucky Department of Education develop a model for intergenerational literacy programs. In response to Noe's request, the superintendent then asked Darling to submit a proposal for intergenerational literacy services. Darling later reflected on the irony of being asked to develop a proposal that was originally her concept (with Heberle): "Something happens when one or two people who have worked together over the years really push for a new policy—it looks as if it is initiated from above when it really comes from below."[19]

Within twenty-four hours, Darling and Heberle assembled the PACE model, combining what was known about effective adult, parent, and early childhood education programs. Darling explained:

> Although there were many alternative configurations that could be just as effective, we selected only those models with a good research base, confining ourselves to those tested and reported in the National Diffusion Network. We knew we had to

select models with a good research base or we could easily be blown out of the water.[20]

In the spring of 1986, when the General Assembly was in special session to consider education reform bills, the PACE bill—House Bill (H.B.) 662—ranked only twenty-second on a list of twenty-three legislative priorities. Nevertheless, it was submitted and, to the proponents' surprise, passed easily. More surprising yet was the successful outcome of the appropriations process: PACE was given a fiscal note of $1.2 million for a two-year pilot program in twelve school districts.

This success rested on several well-considered strategic decisions. Noe and his colleague in the Senate, Paris Hopkins, linked H.B. 662 to the welfare-reform movement, using language about self-sufficiency that would later prove so effective during promotion of the federal Family Support Act of 1988. They distinguished this preventive initiative from the spate of remediation proposals generally endorsed by their liberal colleagues in the Kentucky State House, repeatedly prefacing their appeals with: "This was not another one of Roger Noe's programs of services targeted to welfare recipients." Further, the PACE team apparently correctly interpreted Kentucky's strong profamily sentiment to mean that any program taking mothers away from their children would fail. Instead, they emphasized PACE's intent to provide services to mothers and children in close physical proximity. "PACE flew because it did not separate children from families. Despite Kentucky's heavily Democratic party leanings, it is a conservative and profamily state."[21]

No one expected revenue for PACE in a year when the K-12 education budget was being cut. But when a vocational bill was defeated on an unforeseen technicality and funds became available, Darling, who was observing floor debate at the statehouse, "grabbed them for literacy (PACE)!"

Darling and Heberle's first administrative objective was to create a coherent management entity to ensure a quality PACE program from the Adult Basic Education Division. Subsequently, other objectives developed: Darling left the Department of Education and began to focus on replicating PACE beyond Kentucky, whereas Heberle channeled her energy to program implementation within Kentucky. Heberle established a competitive grants-selection process and chose school districts as pilot sites that would serve as effective bases of political support. The law restricted participation to those school districts with high concentrations of adults without high-school diplomas. In the first year Heberle's division staff selected six sites and opened eight new centers with additional funding. The "social pork barrel" worked to their advantage: legislators from nonqualifying districts quickly recognized the tangible economic benefits—an extra $50,000—accruing from PACE and agreed to reduce the eligibility standard from 60% of resident adults without high-school diplomas to 40%!

The toughest problem during the first year was managing the recruitment and retention of program participants. The literacy program was first advertised in local newspapers—a classic implementation error. When many fewer registered than expected, program administrators initiated a massive recruitment effort—"pavement pounding"—throughout the participating school districts. When a few districts failed to recruit enough parents, an "appetizer" program, HomeBased Instruction, was developed to familiarize parents with the program in their own homes before introducing them to school-based classes.

PACE's recruitment was more successful in the second year because "the word spread" that PACE was helpful. However, *retaining* enrolled students continued to be difficult. Heberle closed two sites in conformity with guidelines requiring that centers maintain a minimum enrollment of ten parents. To explain why they had dropped out, several participants described the verbal and physical threats they received from family members after they had enrolled in the PACE program. When they showed signs of becoming literate, and perhaps more independent, family members grew resentful. One grandmother told her daughter, "If you go to PACE, don't come home!"[22]

Early assessments also showed that attrition was associated with a lack of support at home for literacy. In most cases, program dropouts either had husbands or mothers who were unsupportive of their ambitions. A phrase heard repeatedly by the women enrolled in PACE from their mothers, grandmothers, aunts, and sisters was, "You're just tryin' to get past your raisin'!" In fact, a range of early program experiences revealed the tightly woven family system that nurtures and sustains illiteracy. Throughout the first two years, Heberle and her center directors modified the PACE model, refining the afternoon sessions to incorporate research knowledge about family support and to help women address the more subtle issues of family illiteracy: self-esteem and family dynamics.

> We started teaching the concept of self-image to women who hadn't even heard the word before. These were women who had never thought about how they perceived themselves or how these feelings were transmitted to their children. Many came to understand how they (and their children) have been held back by negative self-images. There have been a lot of eye-opening discussions, and the women feel they have brought their learning into their homes.[23]

These discussions became the cornerstone of PACE's family support component. Experiences in the field highlighted the importance of addressing family tensions that develop when one member becomes, in essence, upwardly mobile.[24] Other components of the PACE model—definitions of eligibility and professional requirements for the providers—were added later. Evaluation findings attest to PACE's success. According to Heberle, since PACE started "70% percent or more of the adult participants have either received a GED or raised their level by two grades."[25]

During PACE's early administrative phase, Heberle looked to increase its visibility. Representative Noe persuaded Heberle to apply for the Ford Foundation-Harvard University Innovations in State and Local Government Award, not only for the financial support ($100,000), but also for the publicity with which to protect PACE within the Kentucky General Assembly. However, when Noe lost his election bid for superintendent of public instruction in 1988, his priority shifted to more global agency budget issues and PACE's funding was compromised. However, after persistent lobbying by Heberle in 1990, the General Assembly increased PACE's budget to $3.2 million, and the program was expanded to thirty-three classrooms in thirty counties and school districts.[26] Afterwards, however, the General Assembly moved PACE and the new Office of Adult Education from the Kentucky Department of Education to a new administrative entity, the Workforce Development Cabinet.

PACE won the Innovations Award in 1988, as well as a Council of State Governments Innovations Award in 1990. This success generated substantial positive publicity, but also created a dilemma. Waves of requests from policy makers outside Kentucky flooded in as officials in those states learned about PACE and hoped to replicate it in their own states. Although Darling was eager to replicate PACE with foundation sponsorship beyond Kentucky, she was especially concerned about the "policy grabbing": "It is so important for each state to consider its own constellation of resources. There are many ways to be successful—many configurations that could be just as effective. Some states just want to pick off the pieces, take PACE, and run—even if it is not really appropriate."[27]

Experience implementing PACE taught Darling and Heberle that program models cannot be "bought," but must be adapted to fit the circumstances—the problems, resources, and administrative structures—in each state's environment. Darling was the first to acknowledge that PACE was only a starting point, and that the program model would, over time, be refined and reformulated to meet the unique and changing needs of families in Kentucky and beyond.

Maryland: Family Support Centers

Maryland's family support centers (FSCs) are community-based centers administered by an independent nonprofit organization, Friends of the Family, in partnership with the Maryland Department of Human Resources (DHR) and several local and national private foundations.[28] By providing a supportive familylike environment and a range of services, the centers aim to help adolescents postpone childbearing or second pregnancies. In addition, they encourage employment, self-sufficiency, and sound parenting skills among Maryland's youngest families. Friends of the Family started in fiscal-year (FY) 1986 with four centers and a budget of $400,000; by FY 1991 there were thirteen centers with a budget of over $4 million.

The genesis of Maryland's family support centers was marked by the arrival of Frank Farrow, a "think-tanker and a networker," who became director of the Social Services Administration (SSA) within Maryland's Department of Human Resources. Farrow connected with a small group of social welfare professionals, foundation executives, and child advocates to discuss the rising incidence of child abuse and neglect. Among this group was Jan Rivitz, executive director of the Aaron and Lillie Straus Foundation; Sandra Skolnik, executive director of the Maryland

Committee for Children; Rosalie Streett, then director of the Community Adolescent Health Centers, Johns Hopkins University; and Frank Sullivan, director of Day Care and Special Programs within SSA. As Streett recalled:

> We met to brainstorm what needed to be done on behalf of children. We were looking for a way to take advantage of a new climate of innovation in the agency, and we were committed to prevention. But [we] had much to sort out philosophically: We addressed such questions as, "What is a family?"; "What do families need?"; and "How does one achieve healthy development in children?" These issues seem so simple, but they needed to be hammered out.[29]

In attempting to develop an effective intervention, Farrow shared his vision of a comprehensive community-based service model gained from his observation of the Family Focus program in Chicago.[30] Farrow, Skolnik, Streett, and Sullivan debated the merits of "empowerment" over deficit models and affirmed traditional principles of child development: love, attention, and extended family supports. After several weeks of informal meetings, they articulated a philosophy of prevention and a commitment to comprehensive, community-based services. As Rosalie Streett summarized it, "All centers should have a pregnancy prevention component because it is not good for adolescents to be parents, and it is not good for babies to have adolescent parents."[31]

Although they preferred a universal, nontargeted approach, and believed that they could have "sold" family support as a solution to a broad range of social problems, those involved in the early discussions with Farrow agreed that a focus on adolescent pregnancy prevention was the most politically practical. Farrow believed that DHR's secretary, Ruth Massinga, would be more receptive to a program that addressed the adolescent pregnancy problem directly, and that targeting services to a high-risk population would make it easier to generate support within DHR and their other audiences—the Office of Management and Budget (OMB), the governor, and the legislature:

> In retrospect, perhaps we should have insisted from the beginning on a universal access program. The jury is still out on that.... We took advantage of an opportunity and we couldn't have done it differently, but once you get into targeted programs for at-risk families, can you get out of it?[32]

Massinga and Sullivan, meanwhile, expressed reservations about lodging preventive family support centers within DHR. Massinga was not enthusiastic about a universal, nontargeted approach and was reluctant to sponsor the proposal in her annual budget request to the governor. Sullivan's skepticism was based on his assessment of the proposal's political feasibility. He had visited Chicago to observe the Family Focus model and to assess its potential for replication in Maryland. He returned even more skeptical about grafting an Illinois program onto the Maryland context. Sullivan's view was that Family Focus, a product of private philanthropy, never had to justify its approach to a broader political audience. He had learned about Family Focus's struggle with the conservative right-to-life opposition in southern Illinois and warned about similar opposition from well-organized groups in Maryland. Also, Sullivan was pessimistic about the likelihood that nontargeted prevention programs could be incorporated successfully into an agency with a deeply entrenched treatment philosophy and strong political connections to the social work profession.

These warnings helped to forge a political strategy consisting of several simultaneous streams of action: participating in several legislative commissions; recruiting key supporters from the private sector; securing Governor Hughes's approval; and finally, involving key moderate right-to-life lobbyists and legislators. As a first step, Farrow orchestrated his own appointment to several key legislative commissions. Operating on the premise that commission recommendations would influence OMB decisions, he promoted the family support concept so consistently that during 1985 several reports cited family support and teen pregnancy as high priority issues for the coming legislative session.

The second stream of action consisted of strengthening DHR's budget request to the governor and the General Assembly. Farrow aggressively sought a partnership with two Baltimore philanthropic foundations: the Aaron and Lillie Straus and the Morris Goldseker Foundations. Although Rivitz had been involved from the outset in planning discussions, she and other foundation executives were reluctant to fund any programs without prior assurances that the public sector would ultimately underwrite them. "It is better strategy to grab the state from the beginning and hook it then," said Rivitz.[33] When Farrow secured Massinga's commitment of $50,000, he succeeded in leveraging $75,000 from both the Straus and Goldseker Foundations.

Farrow and his colleagues then turned to the third stream of action: winning gubernatorial support. Farrow, Streett, and Skolnik recruited to the cause everyone important in the private and public worlds of Maryland politics; they all visited the governor during the winter of 1985 to talk about family support. Using their social and professional networks, Skolnik and Streett organized a series of social "parlor meetings" where they engaged Governor Hughes in policy discussions with child development experts, social welfare professionals, and key supporters in the philanthropic community. These social gatherings broadened the base of constituent support among influential persons who were eventually recruited to persuade Governor Hughes to include a line item for the proposal in his annual budget. When the governor finally endorsed the proposal, Farrow and the others developed a successful strategy to shepherd the Governor's Allowance through the General Assembly. "The key," said Streett, "is knowing how the system works and mobilizing advocates who already work well together."[34]

Once initial funding was confirmed, the team decided to create a separate administrative entity, Friends of the Family, with Streett as executive director. Friends of the Family's independence would protect DHR from any negative publicity that might result from the program experiment and would ensure a level of flexibility that a bureaucratic agency could not provide. They established a grants selection process, distributed requests for proposals (RFPs), received thirty applications, and selected four sites.

Even before the centers opened, however, Farrow, Skolnik, and Streett suspected that the original funding would be insufficient. Although they acquired a discretionary grant from the U.S. Department of Health and Human Services (HHS) to fund one demonstration center, they knew they needed additional funds from the state. Thinking that their task would be easier the second time around, they approached legislators for a modest increase. This time, however, consistent with Sullivan's warnings, right-to-life activists mounted opposition to the family-planning component of the proposal. In response, the team enlisted the support of the executive director of the Maryland Catholic Conference, Richard Dowling, who represented the moderate Catholic right-to-life groups. Dowling's support effectively divided the right-to-life coalition in the Maryland General Assembly; his active partnership in the coalition was pivotal.

The team further divided the right-to-life block in the General Assembly by recruiting four additional legislators generally allied with right-to-life groups. These four legislators collaborated on a letter to the governor and their colleagues urging increased funding for family support centers (including the family-planning component). "Prevention programming is an area where we can and should work together."[35] The appeal drew 135 signatures from the General Assembly's 185 members, representing a rare cross-section of legislators. Suddenly the family support centers became "a program of the 'middle ground,' one everyone could rally around—a 'neat compromise.'"[36] Temporarily, at least, the proposal united both prochoice and right-to-life groups, easing a longstanding polarization in the General Assembly. Said Streett, "We were successful because we talked to the moderate right-to-lifers—those the liberals always ignore. We told them, 'We have the program you have always wanted: a program to strengthen the family.'"[37]

Only the Family Protection Lobby, the most conservative of the right-to-life groups, remained opposed. Responding to the letter from the moderates, the Lobby distributed a formal response to all their colleagues in the General Assembly denouncing the proposal and accusing the moderates of promoting the belief that "the best way to stop teen pregnancy is to teach kids how to have sex without becoming pregnant."[38] This exaggerated, if not false, claim backfired, unifying support for the proposal.[39]

With the coalition of the prochoice and moderate right-to-life legislators established, Farrow, Skolnik, Streett, and Sullivan thought they would easily shepherd the family support line item through the budget subcommittees. However, a near-fatal error at the eleventh hour nearly killed the proposal. During one of Skolnik's midnight watches over budget proceedings, she discovered that several supporters had inadvertently voted against the Omnibus budget where the family support center proposal was embedded. Skolnik mobilized Streett, and together they requested a special Saturday subcommittee session (a rare event) to reverse the error and approve the Omnibus budget.

As the program entered its sixth year in 1991, Friends of the Family had expanded to thirteen sites with multiple foundation sponsors. Like Missouri's PAT and Kentucky's PACE, Friends of the Family has been awarded the Ford Foundation-sponsored Innovations in State and Local Government Award at Harvard University's Kennedy School of Government. Meanwhile, Streett has reflected on the challenges of managing an array of providers: "If there is one key lesson, it is the value of maintaining the principles of family support—partnership in decision-making and flexibility—throughout the process. These principles were played out in the development of the program and are still operating at all levels."[40]

Missouri: Parents as Teachers[41]

Parents as Teachers (PAT) began in 1981 as a pilot program, New Parents as Teachers (NPAT), in four school districts. Its purpose is to promote healthy child development by assisting parents in their roles as their children's first teachers. In 1984, PAT was extended by the Missouri General Assembly to each of its 543 school districts. As of early 1993, Missouri was the only state requiring school districts to provide parent education services (home visits, developmental screenings, and group meetings) to parents with children birth through age four. By 1991, with a budget of over $3 million, PAT had served more than 60,000 families.

PAT was initiated by public-spirited educators who had formally discussed early childhood education reforms since the 1950s. Jane Paine of the Danforth Foundation spearheaded the reform notion, persuading the then commissioner of education, Arthur Mallory, to hire Mildred Winter to head the Early Childhood Division at the Missouri State Department of Elementary and Secondary Education (MSDESE). Paine, Commissioner Mallory, and Winter adopted a position statement affirming the mission of the agency to assist parents during the preschool years and enlisted the support of former Governor Christopher (Kit) Bond.[42] They organized a series of conferences to learn about various models of intervention with families, and brought Burton White, then director of the Brookline Early Education Project (BEEP), and David Weikart of the High/Scope Educational Research Foundation, to present data about the effectiveness of their approaches.

Winter recalls having made two discrete decisions at the conferences: the first, to embrace prevention over remediation; and the second, to submit an early childhood bill with a parent education component in the next legislative session. The team concurred that a prevention model with parent education services was superior to, and more cost-effective than, a model like High/Scope that directed services to preschoolers. "I appreciated the High/Scope model of buying early-childhood education for three-to five-year-olds, but I was concerned that the child still returns to families who are out there possibly doing damage down the road."[43]

Sponsorship of parent education bills ultimately spanned three gubernatorial administrations. Despite the defeat of Bond in the 1976 gubernatorial election, early childhood bills were submitted in every legislative session during the Teasdale administration (1976–1980). Although the bills passed consistently in the House, they lost in the more fiscally conservative Senate, where they were always attacked as a "communistically inspired scheme."[44] Nevertheless, sponsors "hung in there year after year," educating their colleagues about prevention.

When Bond was reelected in 1980, Paine, Mallory, Winter, White, and Bond decided to launch a pilot program—New Parents as Teachers (NPAT)—for 300 first-time parents in four school districts. Winter and White developed a parent education curriculum that emphasized the phases of child development and began a pilot experiment. With no direct state funding, they assembled a combination of Danforth Foundation grants, federal block grant funds, and contributions from the participating school districts. They selected four districts willing to comply with the demands and constraints of a research demonstration project, and collected data on parent and child outcomes. This research paved the way for an independent outcome evaluation, central to the larger political strategy promoting statewide expansion.[45]

Governor Bond decided to take advantage of the 1984 election year and launch the campaign for statewide expansion even before the pilot programs were evaluated. With a state constitutional limitation of two terms in office, Bond had decided to run for the U.S. Senate; he wanted to leave a parent education program as a legacy to the state. During his campaign, he and Burton White traveled together throughout the state to enlist public and private support for PAT. Bond's "new father" status heightened his personal commitment and lent credibility to his sponsorship. His popularity advanced PAT demonstrably during the 1984 session; his vigorous promotion gave the issue prominence and symbolic significance.

Promoting a statewide parent education program required more than speaking engagements throughout Missouri; it required a specific strategy to mobilize a broad-based coalition. Toward this end, Paine and Winter added a new partner, Carolyn Losos, who agreed to chair the supervisory committee consisting of key MSDESE officials, as well as an advisory committee, Committee on Parents and Teachers (CPAT), comprised of supporters from both the private and public sectors. CPAT, under the leadership of Losos ("Mildred's right arm"), was effective both as a political vehicle to mobilize community support and as a fundraising body. Meanwhile, Paine, Winter, Mallory, Bond, and White further broadened their political base of support by talking with state commissioners about the virtues of early childhood prevention programs such as PAT. They presented evaluation data from Head Start, High/Scope, and BEEP that demonstrated the long-term positive effects of preschool and family-oriented interventions, and cited data on rising costs of addressing juvenile delinquency, incarceration, and special needs remediation.

Efforts to expand the scope of support throughout the Missouri state government also provided the PAT team with important data on how to craft the bill. In drafting the specific elements of a new PAT bill (Senate Bill [S.B.] 658), Bond, Winter, and

Paine also benefited from the pilot experience. They knew which elements of the program must be preserved and which must be adapted. According to Duncan Kincheloe, Governor Ashcroft's assistant, the bill was drafted so that all its components were aligned with known political preferences. For example, sponsors knew that the child-focused models such as High/Scope were unacceptable both for substantive and political reasons: "There is *no way* PAT would be acceptable to the legislature if services were directed to children and not parents. This is only acceptable . . . because services are being offered to *parents*."[46]

The decision to make the program universal rather than targeted, voluntary (for parents) rather than mandatory, and to limit its scope (no district obligation beyond the level of state reimbursement), were all *justified* on substantive grounds, but *imperative* on political grounds. "To be politically acceptable in this state, the program needs to be a universal one so that all families benefit; once a decision is made in Missouri that services are important, you can't tell a substantial sector that these services will be unavailable to them."[47]

Commissioner Mallory, Kincheloe, and others believed that the program must be voluntary; Mallory did not want the perception to develop that Missouri requires "at-risk" families to participate. "It would be bad for welfare departments or courts to sentence people to PAT."[48] In short, the sponsors believed that to be acceptable in Missouri, a program must be provided to *families*; it must be *universal*; and it must be *voluntary*. Even the system of reimbursement to districts based on participation rather than eligibility was a decision to avoid unpopular entitlements. Therefore, the language and provisions of S.B. 658 were based on an assessment of Missouri's political climate, not only a hard-nosed evaluation of empirical data. One state representative described the bill's responsiveness to Missouri's political culture in this way: "This program embodies everything essential for political appeal in Missouri."[49] In the commissioner's words: "Parents as Teachers is just the right fit for Missouri."[50]

Once the specific components of S.B. 658 were prepared, Governor Bond and his assistant, Jane Nelson, crafted a new, three-part legislative strategy that involved forming a bipartisan alliance in the legislature, introducing the bill first in the Senate to create ownership there, and exploiting gubernatorial leverage over legislative pay increases. Bond succeeded in recruiting the support of Harry Wiggins, Senate Majority Floor Leader, so that PAT sponsorship became a bipartisan effort. In addition to arranging a friendly committee assignment for the bill, Wiggins agreed to support Bond's threat to veto legislative pay increases until PAT had passed both houses. One observer commented that "the Governor laid it on the line that he wanted this bill passed in order to sign their pay increase."[51] Another close observer reflected, "By 1984, it was unwise to be a legislator and not support this program."[52]

After S.B. 658 passed in the Senate, it had to overcome subcommittee scrutiny based on a misconception about the bill's providing public funds to parochial schools. According to Representative Annette Morgan, "Once people in the legislature were satisfied that S.B. 658 did not give aid to private schools, all opposition withered."[53] Sponsors then expected the bill to sail unopposed through the House, where similar bills had passed before. They were surprised when, during the final hours of legislative debate, a rural legislator, concerned that the bill would favor urban over rural districts, attempted to defeat it by attaching a provision that made PAT mandatory for school districts. The legislator's strategy backfired when the amended bill passed easily in both houses and radically transformed PAT from a voluntary to a mandatory (for districts, not parents) statewide program.

When PAT moved from a four-site pilot to a statewide program, allocations per site were reduced. Concerned that reducing funding from a well-endowed pilot experiment to a modest statewide effort would compromise the model, White withdrew his support. In the subsequent eight years, PAT's program directors have modified and elaborated the program model in response to parent requests and the needs of distinct populations. PAT has added a range of components, including literacy programs, in-service professional training, programs for teenage mothers, and services for families with special-needs children. The enormous popularity of Parents as Teachers has prompted many school districts to provide additional subsidies to local programs. Meanwhile, the level of state reimbursement aid has expanded gradually from 20% to 35% of total costs.

When Parents as Teachers received the Ford Foundation's Innovations in State and Local Government Award in 1987, school districts in several states approached MSDESE for information about the program. Winter and Paine established the PAT National Center to respond to numerous requests for technical assistance and training. In 1992, the PAT National Center, under the leadership of Winter, supervised 207 programs in thirty-six other states, a total of 750 PAT programs. To oversee the model's dissemination, Winter appointed to the board of the National Center key leaders from Missouri's public and private sectors, as well as respected academic researchers and foundation executives.

THE COMPONENTS OF POLICY DEVELOPMENT

The cross-state data presented in this chapter provide evidence that successful innovation on behalf of children and families has been a function of effective policy entrepreneurship. At first glance, one individual in each site stands out, but closer scrutiny reveals coordinated action by entrepreneurial teams. This looks less like a "leader with helpers," and more like a teamwork approach to problem solving. Each team began in a "brainstorming" mode, airing philosophy and goals, articulating preferences and beliefs, and outlining objectives. Team members searched for funding support, built supportive alliances, and assembled necessary resources. They also timed the presentation of their initiatives to coincide with sudden opportunities, exploiting the weaknesses and excesses of their opponents. Entrepreneurs persisted over many years, maintaining their particular policy goal as their first priority.

Once programs were in the field, the teams adopted a flexible, responsive management style within the framework of independent administrative entities. During the early implementation phase, program directors in all sites modified the original model to fit community preferences. This profile of operations resembles what Elazar has described as the major transformation in state government during the 1980s—away from managing federal entitlements, towards designing new approaches to governance.[54]

These themes, drawn from the three cases, are elaborated in the following pages.

Entrepreneurial Teams

Entrepreneurs in the three sites did not work alone, but in tandem with like-minded colleagues, operating with a common objective and a well-defined division of labor. Peter Drucker has described private-sector project groups where each team member contributes unique skills to the overall effort. Likewise, policy entrepreneurs assumed responsibility for tasks consistent with their distinctive competencies.[55] Although they frequently performed several tasks during one or more phases of the policy-initiation process, the individuals differentiated themselves as visionaries, communicators, internal systems technicians, and alliance builders. These tasks correspond to the three functions of policy entrepreneurship—the intellectual, strategic, and activist—described by King and Roberts.[56]

Observation of entrepreneurial teams suggests that these functions rise to prominence at different stages of policy development and implementation. In the initial phases of formulation when the program is freshly conceived, the visionary predominates. The visionaries in Kentucky (Darling and Heberle), Maryland (Farrow), and Missouri (White and Winter) were more active in this early stage. Later, as the innovation evolved from pilot to institutionalized status, team members whose expertise was highly specific and technical were increasingly valued to guide the program's implementation. Thus, Heberle, Sullivan, and Nelson offered strategic and technical advice. As alliance builders, Noe, Skolnik, Losos, and Paine were crucial, whereas individuals with special communication skills—Heberle, Streett, and Winter—were especially central to program operations. Although these individuals were active during the initial formulation stages, they assumed greater responsibility once the programs were in the field and managing program personnel effectively was essential.

The shifts in each team's leadership reflected their focus on entrepreneurial management. At critical junctures the teams transferred leadership (and visibility) to a different member to promote a larger objective. Peter Drucker's private-sector case description of Henry Ford's team applies here. Drucker shows how successful entrepreneurs adopted low profiles during a critical phase of product development in order to maximize the expertise of other team members. The policy entrepreneurs observed here also retreated at critical points in order to exploit the talents of team members toward common objectives. For example, Paine and Winter had Bond and White assume most of the public persuasion tasks, while Darling and Heberle gave public credit to Roger Noe. Farrow encouraged Massinga's growing "ownership" of the family support experiment (despite her initial skepticism) while he carried the mission to social welfare and public policy circles beyond Maryland. If a team's common objectives are splintered by the emergence of team members' divergent agendas, public support for the project is compromised and program growth stalled, as in the case of Kentucky's PACE.

Brainstorming

The brainstorming, or initial phase of policy development, conforms most closely to the "garbage can model of organizational choice," a time when, according to Cohen, March, and Olsen, "a collection of choices [go] looking for problems . . . [and] solutions [go] looking for issues to which they might be the answer."[57] Like their private-sector counterparts awash in problems to which they might attach themselves, our public managers required an initial brainstorming stage during which they could articulate a vision, assemble a team, and outline strategies for grafting an idea onto the local policy scene. In all cases, a small group of colleagues coalesced around a charismatic individual with confirmed beliefs about the virtue of family-oriented programs. This individual orchestrated discussion and facilitated the group's articulation of what should be done for children and families.

This was not rational policy analysis, where experts evenhandedly evaluated a broad range of policy alternatives. Rather, it was an informal, sometimes messy, process.[58] In Kentucky, the initial idea and planning occurred during a daily commute to work, and in Maryland, discussions occurred in small pubs after work hours. Although in Missouri policy development appeared more formal, brainstorming actually occurred over several years and focused on finding the correct problem to link with a favorite belief or treasured policy choice.

Once a vision was articulated, lengthy discussions ensued about how to market the solution. Would family support be sold as an answer to the high costs of remediation (Missouri), as education reform (Kentucky), or as a solution to teen pregnancy (Maryland)? Uncertain about how best to sell their vision, they delayed the definition of their core problem.

During the brainstorming phase, entrepreneurs exhibited a "bias toward action."[59] They were eager to launch new programs, on a pilot basis if necessary, without pausing to resolve design issues or create the perfect program. During the early brainstorming phase, the entrepreneurs made several key decisions:
- to begin prevention-oriented programs for families
- to seek funding either from line-item budgetary additions or through statutory changes
- to begin quickly with modest pilot centers and build a political constitu-

ency favoring prevention
- to market their proposal as a solution to a still undefined problem
- to build alliances sufficient for agency, legislative, or gubernatorial approvals

The Imaginative Search for Dollars

Policy entrepreneurs engaged in imaginative searches for private and public funding, even during an era of state budget surpluses! They successfully sought funding from several public sources: state, federal, and local, either through budgetary or statutory changes.[60] Kentucky's entrepreneurs claimed "found" money—sources earmarked for another program that suddenly became available. The Maryland team solicited grants from private foundations before going to either the DHR, the legislature, or the governor for public funds. Putting together the financial package required a capacity to network both privately and publicly. Missouri was the only state to begin *without* any state funding, yet the Missouri team assembled an amalgam of federal block grant funds and combined them with local school district and private foundation funding.

Observation of fundraising strategies across sites teaches that although the initial formulation phase is simplified by relying on a single funding source, long-term success depends on assembling a combination of private and public sources. Diversifying financial support requires building alliances, an activity that some groups prefer to accomplish at the outset, while others defer.

Building Alliances

In his classic, *The Semi-Sovereign People*, Schattschneider described the process of "broadening the scope of the conflict" by which policy leaders gradually expand the ever-widening circle of support by defining a problem consistent with the objectives of a broad range of interests.[61] Levin and Ferman demonstrated that policy leaders (in their case, in youth-employment programs) wield a "political hand" to make partners of potential opponents.[62] In the sites observed here, wielding a political hand involved artful "packaging" for broad appeal, holding opposition at bay, agreeing to compromise, and recruiting adversaries to the partnership.

Artful packaging required developing rationales to defend the proposal as the best solution to the state's foremost problem. The Missouri team presented their proposal as the solution to the high costs of educational remediation, the Maryland team presented the FSCs as a solution to adolescent pregnancy, and the Kentucky team packaged PACE as the first piece of comprehensive education reform. Whether the label was education reform and self-sufficiency in Kentucky, comprehensive family services in Maryland, or early intervention in Missouri, entrepreneurs carefully packaged proposals to sell their products to an ever-widening circle of state officials, legislators and, in two of the three cases, governors as well.

"Wielding a political hand" also involved framing issues to avoid the points of greatest resistance: the specter of government bureaucrats dictating child-rearing or family-planning practices, creating another welfare-reform program for poor people, or siphoning off public funds for parochial schools. Entrepreneurs in Kentucky and Missouri knew that "separating" mothers and children must be avoided. PACE advocates also skirted opposition by promoting PACE as the first piece of a larger education-reform package, rather than as another of Noe's "liberal welfare programs for poor people." In Missouri, they directed PAT's services to parents rather than to children and side-stepped another potential land mine: the church-state issue. Loose language in the original bill nearly ignited the controversy over state support for private schools. Until intent was clarified and language altered so that it was clear PAT would not subsidize private religious instruction, the bill was in jeopardy.

The third—and classic—political hand strategy was compromise. Entrepreneurial teams in all sites sacrificed favorite provisions and modified proposals to bring them into alignment with local attitudes and practices. In the beginning, proposals were only vaguely defined visions. Over time they were crafted, provision by provision, to fit the particular concerns of local constituencies. For example, entrepreneurs in Maryland preferred a universal delivery approach, but to appeal to social services personnel, they proposed a model that would target services.

Finally, entrepreneurs built coalitions by "co-opting" the potential opponents, incorporating the more moderate groups into policy making sessions to isolate the most vociferous opponents. In Maryland, Streett and Skolnik did not avoid abortion-funding controversy, but rather addressed it head on. They convinced legislators that they could avoid the costly and damaging divisions that had resulted during annual Medicaid-funding debates if they supported this prevention proposal. Also, they isolated and discredited the ultraconservative right-to-life groups by talking to moderate conservatives. PAT's sponsors asked key Senate leaders to sponsor the bill. By drawing Senator Wiggins into the inner circle, Missouri's sponsors transformed a historically oppositional Senate into a powerful ally. And Missouri entrepreneurs also neutralized potential critics by recruiting them for supervisory and advisory committees.

Creative Timing

John Kingdon describes the importance of timing in successful policy entrepreneurship by citing a political appointee: "You keep your gun loaded and you look for opportunities to come along . . . . Have idea, will shoot."[63] Behn, as well as Sanger and Levin, also use the weaponry metaphor as they describe the "ready-fire-aim" approach, the desire to get programs in the field while the opportunity exists and fine-tune or "target" later.[64] In these cases, program sponsors were eager to get pilot programs operating, knowing that they could perfect a program or develop a constituency for expanded services later. They understood from experience that once programs provided needed services in communities, they would assume a life of their own.

On the other hand, Kingdon warns:

> We should not paint these entrepreneurs as superhumanly clever. It could be that they are—that they have excellent antennae, read the windows [of opportunity] extremely well, and move at the right moments. But it could as easily be they aren't. They push for their proposals all the time; long before a window opens, they try coupling after coupling that fails; and by dumb luck, they happen to come along when a window is open.[65]

Kingdon is not alone in suggesting the power of luck; other serious scholars of the policy process also have made this observation.[66] However, observation of the family support entrepreneurs exposes the uncanny talent for exploiting opportunities in a timely manner. Our entrepreneurs exhibited an exquisite sense of timing, knowing not only *how*, but *when* to maximize opportunities and make optimal use of their own equity and leverage. They presented their proposals to coincide with an election year, exploited the weaknesses or excesses of their opponents, and capitalized on legislative surprises and budgetary windfalls.

Election-year politics played a pivotal role in two sites: Maryland and Missouri. Maryland's entrepreneurs took advantage of the legislators' eagerness to compromise during an election year and their vulnerability on the abortion issue. Bond also used election-year politics to achieve his objective.

Timing also involved maximizing political opportunity by responding quickly to serendipitous events. Not only did entrepreneurs accumulate requisite political capital in terms of credibility, power, or popularity; they knew, simply, when to buy and when to sell. Bond knew when his popularity was at its peak, and threatened to veto a bill that would increase salaries of state legislators. Farrow, too, enhanced his leverage with Secretary Massinga when he successfully shepherded her agency's full budget request through the General Assembly. Kentucky's Darling grabbed unclaimed dollars for literacy the moment they became available, not waiting for a better, perhaps more lucrative offer, later.

Exploiting the excesses of opponents was an especially effective strategy. In Maryland, the right-to-lifers went too far and alienated moderates, allowing entrepreneurs to solidify their coalition. The eleventh-hour attempt by a Missouri legislator to defeat S.B. 658 backfired, and it passed overwhelmingly. Thus, outcomes depended not only on good investments but on an intuitive understanding of when to reap profits. Equally important was the willingness to sacrifice an uncertain higher profit for a certain lower one. Entrepreneurs did not engage in lengthy debates about whether to take advantage of the moment; they acted swiftly and decisively.

Persistent Investment

The significance of persistence cannot be underestimated, and as Kingdon suggests, "in combination with the other qualities, it is disarmingly important. In terms of our concept of entrepreneurship, persistence implies a willingness to invest large and sometimes remarkable quantities of one's resources."[67] Our policy entrepreneurs demonstrated extraordinary persistence, "hanging in there year after year," marketing different versions of the same idea before realizing success, learning through error and adapting to new understandings.

Although Maryland's formulation phase was shorter than in Missouri, the Maryland entrepreneurs demonstrated persistence between 1983 and 1985, participating in numerous legislative commissions, endless organizational meetings, and informal gatherings. Farrow's long hours on various commissions, Skolnik's midnight vigils during budget subcommittee hearings, and Streett's persistent efforts to form alliances with conservatives in the legislature were all pivotal. Missouri's entrepreneurs engaged in repeated efforts through two divided gubernatorial administrations. Despite their failure throughout the 1970s and early 1980s, they started pilot programs and applied understandings gained from the pilots to revise their proposal. (In this regard, Kentucky's experience was unusual because of its rapid formulation.)

All policy entrepreneurs were realistic about the enormous expenditure of capital required in launching a new initiative, and were critically aware of balance sheets. They knew the extent of their power, the limits of their own political capital, the scarce resources of state government, and the limited time for achieving their objectives. Despite their awareness of resource constraints and time limitations, all teams were undaunted by obstacles, vigilant in search of opportunities, and persistent in making their policy solution a first priority, for when a competing priority emerged, the program suffered.

This was especially apparent in Kentucky. When Noe, PACE's foremost advocate in the General Assembly, lost his election for superintendent of public instruction in 1986, he turned his attention to internal issues at KDE. With Noe's priority shifted from PACE to other KDE matters, and Darling's focus on replication beyond Kentucky, PACE's expansion bill failed and its growth in 1988 was compromised. Without the extensive history of coalition building, as in Maryland and Missouri, PACE lacked a reservoir of supportive legislators on which to draw when Noe's priority changed. Moreover, without the political groundwork laid in the General Assembly, PACE's position in the Kentucky statehouse and in the Department of Education was compromised until 1990, when Heberle's persistent lobbying resulted in a budget that was doubled. By contrast, in Maryland and Missouri, Streett and Winter never let up, giving the programs their exclusive attention, and gradually building the alliances that would prove so critical during the program's later management phase.

Creating Independent Administrative Entities

Program expansion was greatest in Maryland and Missouri, where policy teams established independent administrative entities to manage program development. Administrative independence was important everywhere, but especially in social services agencies, where the organization's mission, objectives, and incentive structure contradicted the prevention philosophy of the fledgling family support programs.

Streett cites the creation of Friends of the Family, a private, nonprofit entity, as the most significant decision she remembers making. During the first year of operation, the FSCs' managers knew that organizing pregnancy-prevention services within the context of a government agency would be difficult, if not impossible—hence the establishment of Friends of the Family. As Streett indicated, "If we had chosen to go through the state, it would have been a mistake. Friends of the Family allowed us to be flexible and responsive to the changing needs of our families as well as to nourish the partnership between the public and private sectors."[68]

Missouri's team also established an independent body to administer Parents as Teachers. As a new and highly publicized initiative, PAT received inquiries about the model and requests for assistance from educators outside the state. At the outset, PAT's managers were alert to the tradeoff inherent in administering a new statewide program, and simultaneously disseminating it nationally. Tensions arose at MSDESE about whether PAT would siphon off the state's scarce administrative resources. Creating the National Center became an administrative solution to protect PAT as well as its parent agency during the initial management phase of operations. More importantly, it served as a political vehicle to incorporate nationally respected experts, some of whom were initially critical of the PAT management for attempting to disseminate an "immature" model.

A Flexible, Pragmatic Management Style

Sanger and Levin have profiled the public-sector manager as a "tinkerer."[69] Others have characterized the management style of policy entrepreneurs as "groping along" or "management by wandering."[70] This present investigation has revealed a flexible, pragmatic style of public management consistent with the tinkering, groping, and wandering described elsewhere. Just as formulation was a messy nonrational process, so too was the early phase of implementation. Policy entrepreneurs engaged in an iterative process of learning, molding, adapting, or "fine-tuning" their original program design to fit new understandings gained from practice in the field. By continually surveying the market to understand the consumer, the entrepreneur-managers made midcourse corrections.

During the five years the centers have been operating, FSC program managers added literacy programs, summer camps, and in-home services to the original core model to respond to the needs of Maryland's most troubled families. A literacy program component was also added to the Parents as Teachers program in Missouri centers, and a family support component was added to PACE in response to the adjustment difficulties experienced in families with a newly literate mother. The words of Streett capture the essence of this successful operating style: "We never say we have planned it all, primarily because as our families change, the programs change too. Building in flexibility is what we did right."[71]

CONCLUSIONS

Observation both of the formulation and implementation of state family support policy has led to several unexpected findings. First is the centrality of the highly differentiated team, not the individual policy or "public entrepreneur" that has been canonized in the political science literature.[72] The entrepreneurial teams in this study, including the chief executives who were active in developing the family support programs, repeatedly emphasized their prominence. Within the team framework, members assumed the refined roles of visionary, networker, communicator, and technician.

This investigation of family support and education programs was not constructed in an effort to democratize the theory of policy entrepreneurship. No questions were asked about team work, yet data continually pointed in this direction. A comparison of the literature with the field experience leads to the inevitable question: Why the past absence of discussion about the innards of the entrepreneurial enterprises, so thoroughly dissected in every other way? Perhaps past studies of entrepreneurial leadership were confined to hierarchical bureaucracies, not the "softer" human services agencies where policies and decision-making orientations may be less strictly stratified. Or, perhaps the human services and education agencies foster a uniquely team-oriented, democratic decision-making style that has not been sufficiently identified. Without a more rigorous and systematic comparative analysis, we cannot speculate about whether there is something intrinsic to the human services enterprise that would produce this outcome. I would speculate, to the contrary, that the true nature of team efforts has remained invisible because we have looked for a single entrepreneurial hero.

A second surprising finding is the thorough merging of formulation and implementation. Policy entrepreneurship observed here has blurred what, heretofore, had been thought to be solid distinctions between the formulation and implementation stages of policy development. The litany of program changes and modifications during implementation highlights the dual role of state-level entrepreneurs as formulators and implementers, that is, as program designers and program managers. In short, it is no longer clear where design ends and management begins.

Analysts of the policy-implementation process have often cited "separation of formulators from implementers" as a primary cause of implementation failure.[73]

Without a later-stage "fixer," programs were destined to implementation failure.[74] The advantage of hindsight tells us that our understanding of implementation failures derived from evidence gathered during the post-Great Society era. Therefore, our postulates about implementation are bound in the Great Society time warp, when national policies were invented and enforced in Washington, but administered by distant managers. Experience during that era taught us about the complexity of implementing federally sponsored and designed programs buttressed by a complex system of regulations and enforcement strategies. Local implementers were bound to a vision owned by distant, external officials. The renaissance of entrepreneurial state government, then, has collapsed formulation and implementation into a single science of policy development; our diagram of policy development, once linear, now looks to be a spiral construct, or in the words of Levin and Sanger, "iterative, incremental, and adaptive."[75] Policy entrepreneurship in the states has also altered the lexicon of implementation: regulation writing, compliance, and enforcement have been supplanted with a new vocabulary: technical assistance, facilitation, partnership, and capacity-building.

Finally, this observation of policy development raises a theoretical question about the two, heretofore distinct, models of policy formulation: the rational model and the pragmatic experimenter.[76] Judging from this observation, policy-making behavior is sometimes experimental, sometimes rational. On the one hand, policy entrepreneurs were eager to experiment with a beloved program model in the field. On the other hand, they were also remarkably "rational" in their approach. Although entrepreneurs were not performing mathematical calculations to determine optimal policy choices, they did consciously plan strategies to build alliances and design politically palatable program models. It appears that successful entrepreneurship involves a combination of belief, rationality, and experimentation—a combination that can be construed as "cultural entrepreneurship."

> Cultural entrepreneurship is the art of leading others to alter their core beliefs about social realities and possibilities.... Good ideas percolate to the top, are championed by public entrepreneurs, and are politically accepted only in a culture that values innovation for the good that it accomplishes, not merely the money it saves.[77]

Drucker also has noted that "to build entrepreneurial management into the existing public-service institution may ... be the foremost political task of this generation."[78]

The events described in this chapter demonstrate that entrepreneurial management on behalf of families was well underway during the recent decade. If these observations are to inform the debate over how to structure new government activity to strengthen families, we must first consolidate the lessons from our state entrepreneurial teams about the importance of administrative flexibility and local control. If our recollection of the Great Society disappointments has faded, observation in these three sites serves as a poignant reminder that distant sponsors, designers, monitors, and enforcers do not breed sustained policy innovations. To the contrary, effective policy development happens when flexibility is built in and the fine-tuning is left to the locals. Perhaps the words of a Maryland entrepreneur express it best: "Building in flexibility is what we did right."

APPENDIX: LIST OF INTERVIEWS

Timothy Armbruster: Executive Director, Morris Goldseker Foundation, Maryland, March, 1987.

Donna Bagley: Coordinator, Parents As Teachers (PAT), Missouri, February, 1987.

Sharon Darling: Director, Division of Adult and Community Education, Kentucky Department of Education, Kentucky, October, 1987; April 1988.

Richard Dowling: Executive Director, Maryland Catholic Conference, February, 1987.

Frank Farrow: Director of Children's Services Policy, Center for the Study of Social Policy, Washington, D.C., formerly Director, Social Services Administration, Maryland Department of Human Resources, March, 1987.

Wayne Goode: State Senator, Missouri, December, 1987.

Linda Hamburg: Coordinator, Early Childhood Education, Missouri, November, 1987.

Jeanne Heberle: Director, Parent and Child Education (PACE), Kentucky Department of Education, formerly Coordinator of Program Development, Division of Early Childhood Education, Kentucky Department of Education, October, 1987; March, 1988; April, 1988; May, 1988; October, 1988; December, 1993.

Barbara Hoffman: State Senator, Maryland, March, 1987.

Mary Kasten: State Representative, Missouri, February, 1987.

Duncan Kincheloe: Assistant to Governor Ashcroft, Missouri, February, 1987.

Betsy Krieger: Director, Waverly Family Center, Maryland, March, 1987.

Carolyn Losos: Director, Leadership St. Louis, Missouri, October, 1987.

Arthur Mallory: Commissioner of Education, Missouri, February, 1987.

Ruth Massinga: Secretary, Department of Human Resources, Maryland, March, 1987.

Wanda Moore: Coordinator, Ashland Parents As Teachers Program, Missouri, February, 1987.

Annette Morgan: State Representative, Missouri, February, 1987.

Jane Nelson: Assistant Legal Counsel to Governor Christopher Bond, Missouri, February, 1987.

Roger Noe: State Representative, Kentucky, June, 1988.

Judith Noland: Coordinator, Parents As Teachers, Missouri, October, 1987.

Jane Paine: Program Officer, The Danforth Foundation, Missouri, February, 1987; February, 1988.

Julie Plax: Coordinator, Ladue Early Childhood Center, Missouri, February, 1987.

Jan Rivitz: Executive Director, The Aaron and Lillie Straus Foundation, Maryland,

March, 1987.

Samuel Rosenburg: State Delegate, Maryland, 1987.

Sandra Skolnik: Executive Director, Maryland Committee for Children, March, 1987.

Kay Steinmetz: State Representative, Missouri, December, 1987.

Rosalie Streett: Director, Friends of the Family, formerly Director, Community Adolescent Health Centers, Johns Hopkins University, Maryland, September, 1986; March, 1987; October, 1988; November, 1988.

Frank Sullivan: Director of Human Resources, Rhode Island, formerly Director, Day Care and Special Programs, Social Services Administration, Maryland Department of Human Resources, May, 1987; December, 1987; December, 1988.

Sue Treffeisen: Training Coordinator, Parents As Teachers, Missouri, December, 1987.

Julie Wernick: Program Officer, Morris Goldseker Foundation, Maryland, October, 1988.

Burton White: Director, Center for Parent Education, Newton, Massachusetts, formerly Director, Brookline Early Education Project and Senior Project Consultant to Missouri State Department of Elementary and Secondary Education, August, 1986.

Pam Whitehead: PACE Center Director, formerly a preschool teacher, Bell City School District, Kentucky, February, 1988.

Harry Wiggins: State Senator, Majority Floor Leader, Missouri, February, 1987.

Mildred Winter: Director, Parents As Teachers Network Center, Missouri, November, 1986; February, 1987; September, 1987; October, 1987; February, 1988.

NOTES

1. Family policy is used here as it has been defined by Shirley Zimmerman: "A perspective for understanding and thinking about policy in relation to families . . . and also as a way of conveying the idea of a cluster of policy measures with identifiable family context that then finds expression in family-related program activities." See S. L. Zimmerman (1992). *Family policies and family well-being: The role of political culture.* Newbury Park, CA: Sage Publications, 3; also, G. Y. Steiner (1981). *The futility of family policy.* Washington, D.C.: Brookings Institute. A debate earlier in the century ensued regarding federal and state roles in child and family policy when the issue of a Children's Bureau arose. See J. L. Aber (1983). The role of state government in child and family policy. In E. F. Zigler, S. L. Kagan, & E. Klugman (Eds.) *Children, families and government*, 96–116. Cambridge: Cambridge University Press.

2. P. Uhlenberg & D. Eggebeen (Winter, 1986). The declining well-being of American adolescents. *The Public Interest*, (82), 26–38.

3. D. Blankenhorn, S. Bayme, & J. B. Elstain (Eds.) (1990). *Rebuilding the nest.* Milwaukee: Family Service America; A. Cherlin (Ed.) (1988). *The changing American family and public policy.* Washington, D.C.: The Urban Institute Press; A. Cherlin (1988). The family. In I. V. Sawhill (Ed.), *Challenge to leadership*, 147–171. Washington, D.C.: The

Urban Institute Press.

    4. F. H. Jacobs & M. W. Davies (Winter, 1991). Rhetoric or reality?: Child and family policy in the United States, *Social Policy Report, 5*(4), 1–25.

    5. E. Zigler & K. B. Black (1989). America's family support movement: Strengths and limitations. *American Journal of Orthopsychiatry, 59*(1), 6–19.

    6. For a fuller definition, see B. Weissbourd & S. L. Kagan (1989). Family support programs: Catalysts for change. *American Journal of Orthopsychiatry, 59*(1), 20–31.

    7. S. B. Kamerman (September, 1988). Poverty, politics, and family policy. *Readings: A Journal of Reviews and Commentary in Mental Health*, 4–8.

    8. Heather B. Weiss, personal communication, undated.

    9. J. W. Kingdon (1984). *Agendas, alternatives, and public policies*. Boston: Little, Brown, 188.

    10. P. J. King & N. C. Roberts (1987). Policy entrepreneurs: Catalysts for policy innovation. *Journal of State Government, 60*, 172–178, 173.

    11. A. Downs (Summer, 1972). Up and down with ecology. *The Public Interest, 32*, 38–50; Also see Kingdon (1984), *Agendas, alternatives, and public policies*; B. J. Nelson (1984). *Making an issue of child abuse: Political agenda setting for social problems*. Chicago: University of Chicago Press; R. W. Cobb & C. D. Elder (1972). *Participation in American politics: The dynamics of agenda-building*. Boston: Allyn and Bacon.

    12. King & Roberts (1987), Policy entrepreneurs; C. H. Weiss (1983). Ideology, interests and information. In D. Callahan & B. Jennings (Eds.), *Ethics, the social sciences and policy analysis*, 213–245. New York: Plenum Press.

    13. J. P. Kotter (1990). What leaders really do. *Harvard Business Review, 90*(3), 103-111.

    14. T. J. Peters & R. H. Waterman, Jr. (1982). *In search of excellence: Lessons from America's best-run companies*. New York: Warner Books; see 125–134, on the importance of project teams.

    15. The author wishes to thank Heather Weiss of the Harvard Family Research Project for the opportunity to work on the State Case Studies Project. While the views herein are solely the responsibility of the author, the initial research and analyses for this chapter were conducted under the auspices of the Harvard Family Research Project. See Harvard Family Research Project (1990). *Innovative models to guide family support and education policy in the 1990s: An analysis of four pioneering state programs*. Cambridge, MA: Harvard Graduate School of Education; H. B. Weiss (1989). State family support and education programs: Lessons from the pioneers. *American Journal of Orthopsychiatry, 59*(1), 32–48.

    16. H. 662, 127th Leg., Reg. Sess., 1986 KY Acts 824–25.

    17. B. Hausman & K. Parsons (1989). PACE: Breaking the cycle of intergenerational illiteracy. *Equity and Choice, 5*(3), 54–61.

    18. R. Noe (Spring/Summer, 1989). Accelerating the 'PACE' against illiteracy. *Yale Law and Policy Review, 7*, 442–448.

    19. Interview with Sharon Darling, Director, Division of Adult and Community Education, Kentucky Department of Education, April, 1988.

    20. Interview with Darling, April, 1988.

    21. Interview with Jeanne Heberle, Director of PACE, Kentucky Department of Education, formerly Kindergarten Program Consultant, Division of Program Development, Kentucky Department of Education, May, 1988.

    22. Interview with Heberle, October, 1987.

    23. Interview with Pam Whitehead, PACE Center Director, February, 1988.

24. Hausman & Parsons (1989), PACE, 59.

25. J. Heberle (1990). PACE: Parent and Child Education in Kentucky. *Family Resource Coalition Report, 9*(3), 13.

26. Heberle (1990), PACE.

27. Interview with Darling, April, 1988.

28. B. Hausman (1990). Maryland. In Harvard Family Research Project, *Innovative models to guide family support and education policy in the 1990s*, 69–83.

29. Interview with Rosalie Streett, Executive Director, Friends of the Family, Maryland, September, 1986.

30. Bernice Weissbourd, President of Family Focus, Inc., was one of the founders of the contemporary family support movement.

31. Interview with Streett, March, 1987.

32. Interview with Streett, November, 1988.

33. Interview with Jan Rivitz, Executive Director, The Aaron and Lillie Straus Foundation, Maryland, March, 1987.

34. Interview with Streett, September, 1986.

35. Letter to Governor Harry Hughes, December 17, 1985. Signed by 135 Delegates and Senators of the Maryland General Assembly.

36. Interview with Frank Sullivan, Director, Human Resources, Providence, RI, formerly Director of Day Care and Special Programs, Social Services Administration, Maryland Department of Human Resources, May, 1987.

37. Interview with Streett, September, 1986.

38. Letter from Jim Wright, The Family Protection Lobby, December 30, 1985.

39. Interview with Samuel (Sandy) Rosenberg, Delegate, Maryland General Assembly, Maryland, March, 1987.

40. Interview with Streett, November, 1988.

41. See also B. Hausman (1989). Parents as teachers: The right fit for Missouri. *Educational Horizons, 67*(1 & 2), 35–39; reprinted in *Journal of Educational Public Relations* (1991), *13*(4), 11–16.

42. Senator Bond was elected to the U.S. Senate for a second term in 1992. During his first term he introduced S.551, Parents as Teachers: The Family Involvement in Education Act of 1991.

43. Interview with Mildred Winter, Executive Director, Parents as Teachers Network Center, November, 1986.

44. Interview with Arthur Mallory, Commissioner, Missouri State Department of Elementary and Secondary Education, February, 1987.

45. J. Pfannenstiel & D. A. Seltzer (1985). *Evaluation Report: New Parents as Teachers (Missouri Department of Elementary & Secondary Education)*. Overland Park, KS: Research and Training Associates, Inc.

46. Interview with Duncan Kincheloe, Assistant to Governor Ashcroft of Missouri, February, 1987.

47. Interview with Kincheloe, February, 1987.

48. Interview with Mallory, February, 1987.

49. Interview with Mary Kasten, State Representative, Missouri House of Representatives, February, 1987.

50. Interview with Mallory, February, 1987.

51. Interview with Annette Morgan, State Representative and Chairperson, Missouri General Assembly, February, 1987.

52. Interview with Burton White, Center for Parent Education, Newton, MA, August, 1986.

53. Interview with Morgan, February, 1987.

54. D. J. Elazar (February, 1981). States as polities in the federal system. *National Civic Review, 17*, 77–82.

55. See P. F. Drucker (1985). *Innovation and entrepreneurship: Practice and principles*. New York: Harper & Row, 197–205, on the internal differentiation by ability.

56. King & Roberts (1987), Policy entrepreneurs.

57. M. Cohen, J. March, & J. Olsen (1972). A garbage can model of organizational choice. *Administrative Science Quarterly, 17*, 1–25, cited in Kingdon, 90.

58. "Everything is as sloppy as it sounds!" Interview with Streett, September, 1986.

59. M. B. Sanger & M. Levin (1992). Using old stuff in new ways: Innovation as a case of evolutionary tinkering. *Journal of Policy Analysis and Management, 11*(1), 88–115.

60. A budgetary change, that is, obtaining a line-item addition to their agency's budget, involved an endorsement from the secretary and the governor prior to legislative approval. A statutory change, on the other hand, required legislative authorization and allocation.

61. E. E. Schattschneider (1960). *The semi-sovereign people*. New York: Holt, Rinehart, & Winston.

62. M. Levin & B. Ferman (1985). *The political hand*. New York: Pergamon Press.

63. Kingdon (1984), *Agendas, alternatives, and public policies*, 193.

64. See R. Behn (1991). *Leadership counts*. Cambridge, MA: Harvard University Press, 136; M. Levin & B. Sanger (January, 1990). *The practitioner as tinkerer: Learning from analysis and learning from the field*. Paper presented at the Graduate School of Public Policy workshop on practitioner competency, University of California at Berkeley, for their reference to Peters and Waterman's "Ready, Fire, Aim" description of the public management context.

65. Kingdon (1984), *Agendas, alternatives, and public policies*, 192.

66. Behn (1991), *Leadership counts*.

67. Kingdon (1984), *Agendas, alternatives, and public policies*, 190. The author also wishes to acknowledge the contribution of Drew Altman to this analysis in his Address to the Gordon Public Policy Center, Brandeis University, May 8, 1990.

68. Interview with Streett, November, 1988.

69. Levin & Sanger (1990), *The practitioner as tinkerer*.

70. O. Golden (1990). Public sector human services programs: The implications of innovation by 'groping along.' *Journal of Policy Analysis and Management, 9*(2), 219–248; R. Behn (1988). Management by 'groping along.' *Journal of Policy Analysis and Management, 7*(4), 643–663.

71. Interview with Streett, November, 1988.

72. There is an extensive body of literature on executive and entrepreneurial leadership. See, for example, J. W. Doig & E. C. Hargrove (Eds.) (1987). *Leadership and innovation: A biographical perspective on entrepreneurs in government*. Baltimore: The Johns Hopkins University Press, for a succinct summary of the organizational and entrepreneurial literature. Also, see E. Lewis (1980). *Public entrepreneurship: Toward a theory of bureaucratic political power*. Bloomington, IN: Indiana University Press.

73. J. Pressman & A. Wildavsky (1973). *Implementation*. Berkeley: University of California Press.

74. E. Bardach (1977). *The implementation game*. Cambridge, MA: M.I.T. Press.

75. Sanger & Levin (1992), Using old stuff in new ways, 104.

76. Sanger & Levin (1992), Using old stuff in new ways.

77.   M. Barzelay & R. Leone (1984). Creating an innovative managerial culture: The Minnesota "Step" strategy. *Journal of State Government, 60*(6), 161–171, 170–171.

78.   Drucker (1985), *Innovation and entrepreneurship*, 187.

6

Municipal Policies for Homeless Families

Priscilla M. D. Little

The profile of homelessness in the United States changed dramatically over the 1980s. Throughout the 1970s, unemployed single men with substance abuse problems or mental illness comprised the vast majority of the homeless; since the early 1980s, however, homeless families are increasing—both in absolute numbers and as a proportion of the total homeless population.[1] Recent estimates suggest that between one-quarter and one-third of individuals without residence are members of homeless families.[2] These statistics reflect only the "literal" homeless; in 1989, up to 186,000 children and their parents were described as marginally housed,[3] and "at risk" of becoming homeless, due to a combination of economic and social factors.[4]

The lack of affordable housing appears to be the primary cause of family homelessness; thus, an increase in the affordable housing supply is critical to solving this crisis.[5] However, recent research suggests that interpersonal characteristics of homeless family members, particularly parents, may contribute to their homeless status. For example, homeless families appear to lack the supports (intimate relationships, extended kin networks, local neighborhood support) available to housed families of similar family composition and socioeconomic status (SES).[6] Developmental research also suggests that children in shelters are at high risk for health and educational problems, developmental and emotional delays, and family dissolution.[7] Were policy makers to attend to these provocative findings, policies would be more comprehensive, providing a range of family support services in addition to affordable, safe housing.

Some commentators question the appropriateness of government intervention in family homelessness, given that internal family behavior is not the usual domain of public policy;[8] others grant a public role but argue about which level of government (federal, state, local) should be responsible for assisting homeless families. Although there has been some federal, state, and county policy activity,[9] the immediacy of the problems faced by homeless families has compelled many cities to take primary responsibility for their well-being.

This chapter examines homeless policy formation at the municipal level in three cities—Atlanta, St. Louis, and Seattle—with a particular focus on how each city addresses the *noneconomic* needs of its homeless families.[10] The first section provides a brief overview of the characteristics of homeless families and the putative impact of homelessness on children and families. Next, the three case studies of policy formation are presented. They highlight the events in each city that led to an institutionalized municipal response to homelessness, and detail prevailing attitudes toward homeless families. Cross-case analyses follow, revealing factors that influence these local policies for both the general (individual adult) population and for homeless *families*.

Data for this study were collected from May, 1988, to September, 1988, as part of a larger investigation of municipal responses to homeless families.[11] Data sources included (1) archival materials at the local, state, and federal level (i.e., agency reports, legislative materials, internal memoranda); (2) twenty-three field interviews with researchers, advocates, program directors, and key city employees responsible for designing and implementing homeless services (see appendix A);[12] and, (3) policy and child development journals.

CHARACTERISTICS OF HOMELESS FAMILIES

While there is no "typical" homeless family, studies have repeatedly verified that homeless families tend to share the following set of characteristics: They are living below the poverty line (often on public assistance); they are primarily female-headed, and have one or two children under the age of eighteen. Members of racial minorities are overrepresented in this population. Mothers tend to be in their midtwenties, about half of whom have never been married. Often they are fleeing an abusive domestic situation.[13] From one-third to one-half are reported to have mental disorders ranging from "problems with their nerves," to established clinical diagnoses.[14] Although there is little information on the prevalence of drug and alcohol abuse among adults in homeless families, anecdotal evidence suggests that it is a vastly underreported problem, especially in large urban areas.[15]

Furthermore, it appears that, compared to housed poor families, homeless families may have diminished social supports or have "exhausted" the supports they once had.[16] Bassuk and Rosenberg report that homeless mothers' support networks tend to be fragmented and include more men, while housed mothers tend to have more frequent contact with their own mothers, other female relatives, and extended family members.[17] Bassuk, Rubin, and Lauriat also report that one-fourth of homeless mothers in an earlier study could not name any supports; almost one-quarter of the mothers in that sample viewed their child as their major emotional support.[18] Twenty-five percent of mothers in McChesney's Los Angeles-based study identified relationship (as opposed to economic) events as the precipitating factor for their present episode of homelessness.[19] Maza and Hall conclude that "the role of a family's social support system is critical in determining when the family will seek help from service providers,"[20] suggesting that the lack of social supports among homeless families partially accounts for their present episode of homelessness.

The Impact of Homelessness on Children and Families

Parker, Greer, and Zuckerman suggest that living in poverty places children in "double jeopardy." They are exposed to a greater number of risks (for example, physical illness, family stress, accidents, and parental depression), and the consequences of these risks tend to be more serious for them and their families than for other children.[21] Extending this model, homeless children may be said to live in "triple jeopardy," since prior family vulnerabilities often contribute to their becoming homeless and magnify the impacts of homelessness on child development, health, and family functioning.

Children's health. Recent studies comparing the health status of homeless children and that of poor, housed children have concluded that homeless children are at substantially higher risk of experiencing chronic health problems, immunization delay, and elevated lead blood levels.[22] While studies generally do not differentiate between problems resulting from shelter living in itself, and those related to living in chronic poverty, the hygienic conditions in shelters likely amplify the already poor health of many homeless family members, especially the youngest children.[23]

Education. Homelessness poses two major threats to an educational program. First, homeless children are less likely to attend school on a regular basis than housed children;[24] second, even those children who do attend school often experience learning difficulties that inhibit their academic progress. The National Coalition for the Homeless identifies several barriers to successful schooling: local residency requirements, transportation difficulties, inadequate health and immunization records, and guardianship requirements.[25]

Developmental and emotional problems. Several teams of researchers have found emotional and developmental problems among homeless children, including developmental delay, and sleep, behavior, and psychiatric problems.[26] Although some of the problem behaviors reported in the literature (for example, aggression, shyness, withdrawal) may be viewed as adaptive rather than negative, they represent a deviation from the expected developmental course. Homelessness appears to distort the mother-child relationships in ways detrimental to the child as an individual and the family as a whole.[27] In their observational study of mother-child interaction in a public night shelter in Atlanta, Boxill and Beaty conclude that shelter living lends itself to "public mothering," and the "unravelling of the mother role" (similar to role reversal). Previously private family lives become "public lives with permission."[28]

Like the health risks described above, many of the emotional and developmental problems observed in homeless children may predate their episode of homelessness. However, the sudden disruption of family life, crowded living conditions, lack of privacy, and the acute stress experienced by homeless mothers, likely exacerbate existing problems, and may create new ones.

Family dissolution. Perhaps the most direct consequence of homelessness is the separation of children from their parent(s). Wright suggests that while most homeless families have dependent children, only about half have their children living with them.[29] This is attributed to several factors. Anticipating homelessness, some parents voluntarily place their children in foster care directly prior to their episode of homelessness; other children are removed from families because of abuse and neglect, homelessness often being considered a form of neglect.[30] Homeless facility requirements may also inadvertently contribute to family dissolution. Many family shelters have eligibility requirements; the most frequently cited restriction is the refusal to accept adolescent males, or any males over the age of fourteen, including fathers.[31] One result of these regulations is that many older homeless children leave their families and try to make it on their own.[32]

In summary, research on homeless children and families suggests that they appear particularly vulnerable to psychological, emotional, and developmental risk. Housing assistance alone may not be sufficient to guarantee either long-term, independent living, or the healthy child and family development that likely has been compromised by episodes of homelessness.

THREE CASE STUDIES OF MUNICIPAL POLICY FORMATION

Each of the three cities profiled in this section—Atlanta, St. Louis, and Seattle—achieved national recognition as a "model" city for homeless services. The Atlanta Task Force for the Homeless, an advocacy organization closely aligned with the National Coalition for the Homeless, demonstrated the power of extragovernmental groups in policy and program development. St. Louis's reputation had two bases: first, the St. Louis Salvation Army Emergency Lodge is a well-respected, comprehensive program for homeless families; second, St. Louis's Homeless Services Network Board is considered an exemplary public-private partnership. Seattle's reputation had less to do with a specific organization or program than with the general aura of "goodwill" and sense of active concern prevalent throughout public and private organizations in the city. Yet while each city is a model, the characteristics of their approaches to the issue, homeless family populations, and shelter systems differ substantially from one another (see appendix B).

Atlanta

Atlanta was described as being in a "peculiar" situation vis-à-vis homelessness in the city. The Georgia State Plan of Improvement, passed by the state legislature in 1954, specifically mandated Fulton County (*not* the city) to provide health and human services to all its residents, including the citizens of Atlanta. This, of course, included services to homeless persons. At the time of this study, however, county support for these services was limited. County commissioners had taken some steps to alleviate *general* (individual adult) homelessness in Metropolitan Atlanta, but had done little for homeless families. Since Atlanta comprises only a portion of the county, no doubt commissioners from outlying areas were more interested in other issues—those perceived as directly affecting their own constituents.[33]

The City of Atlanta had no legal obligation to support health and human services, being responsible only for providing police, fire, and sanitation services. Yet it *did* attend to the needs of its homeless citizens, contracting for homeless services (as opposed to providing direct service), and assigning mayoral staff to address the problem. The main coordinating agency for city involvement in homeless services was the Office for Community and Citizen Affairs (OCCA), run by the Office of the Mayor. The director of OCCA, Connie Curry, spent approximately 70% of her time on homeless issues. Atlanta could not look to the state for much support, sitting as it does in what was described as an "unresponsive state full of Reagan Democrats."[34] According to Curry (OCCA), the lack of concern for homelessness at the state level could be attributed to the "urban-rural split" that exists in the state legislature. Thus, Atlanta is an interesting case study of how, despite a lack of legal obligation or support from other levels of government, a city came to respond to a social issue such as homelessness.

In 1974, Mayor Maynard Jackson introduced a revision to the City Charter to create the Bureau of Human Services, through which the City of Atlanta could coordinate resources for social services. Then, when federal Community Development Block Grant (CDBG) funds became available to cities in the mid-1970s, the Bureau of Human Services began contracting with nonprofit agencies to provide necessary services. This was viewed by the city council and others as the city's chance to help develop and support social service programs without directly providing the service itself. At this point, the city was contracting for social services, but none of the services were specifically targeted toward any homeless population.

After becoming mayor in 1981, Andrew Young placed the Bureau of Human Services in the Department of the Mayor, and renamed it the Office for Community and Citizen Affairs (OCCA). It remained the lead agency for distributing social service CDBG funds, and Connie Curry remained its director. Since 1981, OCCA has been actively involved in shaping Atlanta's policy response to its general homeless population. The Office contracted with several organizations to provide emergency (short-term) shelter and supported homeless initiatives to establish transitional (long-term) shelter.

Key informants identified several forces that led to the city's current level of participation. First, the origin of Atlanta's response lay in the spirit of volunteerism in the private sector. "In the absence of strong leadership from the City, the volunteer community came in and picked up the slack. . . . The spirit of volunteerism in Atlanta is high."[35] This spirit was seen as an outgrowth of the "deep emotional commitment to issues" that evolved during the Civil Rights era in the South. In fact, many homeless advocates in Atlanta at the time of this study were actively involved in that 1960s movement.

The fact of homelessness in Atlanta, and individual reactions to it, also was considered to have a moral impact on the community at large. John Abercrombie, Director of Charis Community Housing, felt that because the bulk of the response to homelessness lay in churches and synagogues, the moral impact reached thousands of people through their parishes: "It leads to a tremendous personalizing of the issue."[36] For example, in the five months between November, 1981, and March, 1982, over 900 people volunteered their time to the first "nontraditional" shelter in Atlanta: a large, church-based facility operated by the Central Presbyterian Church. Since the opening of that shelter, fifty-seven other church-based shelters opened in the Metro Atlanta area, reflecting the continued spirit of volunteerism and caring among the private, religious sector.

The Atlanta Task Force for the Homeless (ATFH), a coalition closely aligned with the National Coalition for the Homeless in Washington, D.C. and New York, was a third and powerful influence. The Task Force began in 1981 as a "group of folks" who worked in downtown shelters meeting for breakfast. It formed originally to share information on the homeless services each member provided; however, the group soon realized its potential for political advocacy, and the Atlanta Task Force for the Homeless was born. For the first few years, the Task Force devoted much of its energy to persuading congregations and organizations to open shelters and to add other services gradually. Then, in response to a 1985 report on homelessness in Atlanta and a follow-up report recommending immediate and long-term actions,[37] the Task Force became the coordinating agency for homeless services in Atlanta. Incorporated in 1986, it began to coordinate emergency shelter activity, help develop homelessness prevention and service policy, and disseminate national and Atlanta-based data on homelessness and model services.

The media also played a major role in focusing attention on Atlanta's homeless throughout the 1980s. As a major urban center in the Southeast, Atlanta supports many regional news bureaus, including *Time* and *Newsweek;* it also is home to a major television network (Cable Network News, CNN). The strong presence of national media in Atlanta was thought to contribute to a "nationalizing" of the city's problems, in this case, homelessness. "When news of homelessness hits the papers, the reporters do not report homelessness in Fulton County; they report homelessness in Atlanta."[38] To a city undergoing major economic redevelopment, "bad press" was understandably unwelcome. Thus, business interests were served by paying attention to the homeless problem.

Finally, several informants pointed to the central role of two particular individuals in shaping Atlanta's policy. While opinion regarding the role of the mayor varied, there was general consensus that his understanding of the issue and support for services had increased since the early 1980s, when he first came into office. The city's homeless activities reflected this progression. Connie Curry, a long-time social activist, has been involved with human services in Atlanta since 1974. When the ATFH asked the city for representation in 1982, Curry was one of the first "city" people to serve on the Task Force. Despite occasional tensions between the city and the ATFH, she continued to be an active participant in Task Force activities.

Attitudes towards homeless families. "In summary, we know now that most families live in shelters because they are poor—because they can not find housing that they can afford."[39] This conclusion to the "Homeless Family" section of the ATFH's major document on homelessness accurately reflected the widely shared belief that homeless families in Atlanta primarily need economic, not emotional, support. While the report recognized the "at risk" nature of children and families living in shelters, it implied that homelessness is the cause, not a symptom or a result of, family disruption; thus, the report's long-term prevention strategies centered around income maintenance, job training, and housing.

Despite the emphasis on economic supports, the report *did* recommend that the Task Force work with shelter providers to establish minimum guidelines for the management of all family shelters. This recommendation grew out of a study of the effects of public night shelter in Atlanta on mother-child interactions.[40] Findings suggested that homeless families needed more private space within shelters and greater understanding by shelter staff of the needs of homeless mothers for autonomous parenting. When the study was made public in 1987, an informant described it as "preaching to the choir," in that it only influenced those who were already sensitive to the needs of families living in emergency shelter, and then only slightly.[41] Although the results of the study influenced the Task Force recommendations regarding the *immediate* needs of sheltered homeless families, the emphasis on housing and economic support in the Task Force's influential report[42] overshadowed the importance of noneconomic support services for homeless families.

Echoing the Task Force position, Boxill, also the director of a homeless facility, defined homeless families as those in which something unpredictable had happened, such as an eviction or a domestic dispute, and they had no available resources to cope with the crisis.[43] She believed that families are usually homeless for economic reasons, and that they generally do not have exaggerated problems distinct from those of other families living in poverty. However, once homeless, these families needed a shelter environment that would support and protect their privacy.

The belief that homeless families are not unlike other poor families except in regard to their housing status was generally accepted in Atlanta;[44] given this ideological position, the strong emphasis on affordable housing was understandable. Most providers in Atlanta agreed on two points: services for homeless families (economic and noneconomic alike) should not be segregated from services for the homeless population in general, and services for homeless families should not be segregated from services for other poor families.[45]

Two main rationales for this approach were cited. First, to segregate the homeless population weakens the argument that housing is at the root of their problems. According to Beaty, arguing for the provision of social services to homeless families "gives ammunition to the politicians," who prefer the view that homeless families "need to be fixed."[46] This shift of blame for being homeless removes pressure from the system to provide affordable housing.[47] Secondly, segregated homeless services create another service system, with the risk of service duplication and fragmentation. "Why pour more money, more time, into new services for a population because they have been somehow excluded from existing services?"[48] Using this argument, the ATFH, for example, asserted that existing city and county social service agencies should be held responsible for *all* their clients, including homeless families, and that emergency service providers should continue to provide *emergency services only.*

In Atlanta, broad-based community advocacy strongly influenced the policy process. Religious organizations played an important role in providing emergency shelter, and the OCCA's efforts were commendable. But Atlanta's response to homelessness rested largely in the hands of the ATFH, whose philosophy was that housing is the solution to homelessness. This assumption that homeless families are like other poor families, except that they need housing, was reflected in the service system, which was largely night-only congregate shelter provided by private religious groups.[49] Although the City of Atlanta did support these shelter efforts beyond simply a "fear of bad press," the types of shelter available to homeless families in Atlanta suggested that a commitment to the distinct needs of homeless *families* had not yet been clearly articulated.

St. Louis

St. Louis's homeless problem was small relative to the other cities in this study. Nonetheless, in 1988, there were over 1,000 bedspaces of shelter provided per night to homeless men, women, and children, and the city had committed substantial resources to the problem. St. Louis's approach to homeless services was considered thoughtful and innovative. The city's motivation for becoming involved, however, was seen by some as less than wholly commendable: A class action suit was filed for noncompliance with the Missouri State Charter regarding the provision of support for *all* city residents, including the poor.

According to Judy Weilepp, project director of St. Louis Health Care for the Homeless Coalition, St. Louis's original response to homelessness was "a matter of giving the right person the right job at the right time."[50] In the late 1970s, the Community Development Agency (CDA) of the City of St. Louis was responsible for long-range planning and the awarding of CDBG funds. Its director, Dan Spade, was quite taken with two proposals that came across his desk: the first, from the Salvation Army, to open St. Louis's first family shelter; the second, to establish an agency solely devoted to relocating individuals who were being displaced by downtown renovations.

The Salvation Army had been actively involved in providing "stop-gap" emergency shelter for families since the 1940s, but the establishment of its Salvation Army Emergency Lodge would represent a major shift in the Salvation Army's approach—a shift from crisis intervention and emergency service to crisis prevention and long-term, comprehensive support for families. By granting the funds to operate the lodge, the city would be supporting this shift. Further, the city seemed to feel somehow responsible for the displacement of people in the downtown area; while not exactly a homeless issue per se, people were being forced out, and a "Relocation Clearinghouse" might assist the city in handling its displaced citizens. Thus Spade backed both proposals, and from 1978 to 1981 approximately $1.5 million was allocated for the two projects.

Until the mid-1980s, the CDA's award of CDBG funds for the Salvation Army Emergency Lodge and the Relocation Clearinghouse was the extent of city recognition of the growing homeless problem. Beginning in 1983, however, several events spurred St. Louis on to "institutionalize" its response to homelessness.

First, in the early 1980s, homelessness finally became visible. This, in turn, led to complaints, primarily from local business people, about the effects of this problem on their businesses. In conjunction with this increasing visibility of homeless persons, by 1983, Larry Rice, an outspoken minister, had begun "kicking up sand" on behalf of the homeless.[51] He criticized the city for being unresponsive to the plight of homeless people in St. Louis, staging several "press stunts" that attracted much publicity. While not entirely accurate in his accusations, these press events served to further sensitize the community to the issue. Although Mayor Vincent Schoemehl countered Rice's arguments by citing the Salvation Army Emergency Lodge and the Relocation Clearinghouse as examples of city efforts, Rice kept the pressure on nonetheless.[52]

Research also played a crucial role early in the process. In the initial Emergency Lodge proposal, the Salvation Army hired an independent research team to assess citywide need for homeless services and to document the development of the Salvation Army program. The team began collecting data, including profiles of clients served by the lodge, from June, 1979, to May, 1981. The Relocation Clearinghouse also began to collect data on its clients. In 1983, shortly after Rice began his homeless crusade, these data were released publicly. They suggested that the homeless problem in St. Louis, specifically the homeless *family* problem, was much more severe than the city had admitted previously.[53] The data were used to fuel Rice's and other advocates' allegations of public neglect.[54]

In December, 1984, Mayor Schoemehl received a letter from attorneys acting on the behalf of several homeless individuals asserting that the city had the power and duty to provide shelter and services for all homeless. The following month (January, 1985) representatives from the city met with the attorneys who had drafted the letter. The city did not dispute the nature and scope of the problem, but questioned whether it had a legal obligation to provide homeless services. In response to this hesitation, the plaintiffs' attorneys threatened the city with a class action suit, insisting that it was in violation of Section 205.580 of the Missouri Charter, which states that "Poor persons shall be relieved, maintained, and supported by the county of which they are inhabitants."[55] The term "poor persons" was defined to include all homeless persons residing in St. Louis. Further, although the section referred to county involvement, the counsel argued, nonetheless, that the City of St. Louis, under Section 1.080, was subject to Section 205.580.[56]

In a futile attempt to avoid the suit, the mayor immediately appointed a task force to study the problem; despite this action, the class action suit was filed in February, 1985. For the next ten months, the city and the plaintiffs negotiated, culminating with the signing of a Consent Decree which obligated St. Louis to meet the needs of homeless citizens as described in the 1985 *Mayor's Task Force on the Homeless Report.*[57] Furthermore, in order to monitor its ongoing efforts, the Consent Decree required the city to provide the plaintiffs' counsel with monthly reports from providers of homeless services.

Throughout the negotiation process, the Mayor's Task Force on the Homeless played a crucial role in determining the shape of the final Consent Decree. Chaired by George Eberle, the Task Force had ninety days to examine the needs of the homeless in St. Louis and to develop recommendations of steps to address those needs. The major recommendation was to request a plan from the St. Louis Housing Authority, which would either contract with existing agencies, or establish a Housing Authority Program for the Homeless to rehabilitate 150 units for emergency housing and permanent housing for large families. The second was to establish a central management group to coordinate and integrate existing homeless services in the metropolitan area. Included in this group's responsibilities would be central intake; coordination of available bedspace; collection of accurate data; establishment of minimum shelter standards; provision of transportation; creation of adequate day shelter and support services (transitional housing, job placement, child care); and the development of a legislative program to address these problems.

The Task Force concluded that while the city should not be forced to provide shelter care directly, it should enable private agencies to do so by contributing funds to their operating costs. The mayor immediately endorsed this position. By 1985, the Board of Aldermen had approved $310,000 to establish the "Homeless Services Network" for the purposes of implementing the Task Force recommendations. The city's Department of Human Services (DHS) was designated as the city's lead coordination agency; the Homeless Services Network Board was established as a voluntary coalition of homeless service providers to work with DHS on implementing the recommendations.

When the Consent Decree was signed in November, 1985, several of the Task Force recommendations already had been implemented. Why is it that the city responded so promptly once the class action suit was filed? First, according to Eberle, "we didn't make unreasonable demands."[58] The original funding was generated from existing general revenue sources, thus it did not pose a financial drain on the city budget. Second, Eberle asserted, there was a high level of consensus among Task Force participants concerning the role of the city: "We all wanted to do something, and we all knew that creating more shelter wasn't the answer." Furthermore, using DHS as a vehicle for the creation of the Homeless Services Network Board meant that an existing mechanism was being used instead of creating a new service system. Finally, Rose Terranova, director of DHS, received the "full support of the Mayor."[59]

Attitudes toward homeless families. St. Louis's mixture of both emergency shelter and comprehensive support programs for homeless families reflected two distinct, conflicting attitudes regarding the needs of homeless families. On the one hand, informants argued that homeless families need *housing* first, which should be secured as soon as possible. "The first thing you need to do when a family is homeless is figure out how they can pay rent. . . . We haven't paid enough attention to moving people out of shelters quick enough."[60] Should families really need "life" support services (that is, family support, counseling, or parent education), then the city government should improve its mental health system, not expand its shelter system.

Sue Taylor, the former administrator of the Salvation Army Hospitality House, presented an alternative view: "When I see a homeless family, what I see *first* is a dysfunctional family, not a poor family."[61] Taylor observed that the homeless family population had changed since the early 1980s; in 1980, only 6% to 8% of women with children seeking shelter cited domestic violence as the primary reason for leaving home; by 1988, over half of the women calling the Relocation Clearinghouse cited it as such. Taylor felt that a substantial percentage of the callers were young girls, in conflict with their parents, who no longer wanted to live at home.

Dorothy Dailey, Homeless Services Coordinator for St. Louis, articulated a midground between these two positions. She felt that the city had "played up" the economic aspects of homelessness because "people can relate to no money but how can they relate to something called 'dysfunction'? . . . If we [the city] said that homeless families were dysfunctional, we wouldn't get as much support."[62] Like Eberle, she feared that the shelter system had become so developed that it represented a viable alternative living arrangement for many young mothers. However, she also supported Taylor's position that homeless families need more than permanent housing in order to stabilize their living situations. To that end, the city contracted with a large multiservice center to provide a *mandatory* parent-education and living skills program to homeless mothers prior to their placement in permanent housing. While Dailey recognized that the program would not benefit everyone who participated, the program's director suggested that at the very least, an episode of homelessness gave the program a brief opportunity to work with these high-risk families. "It is a unique opportunity to teach these women something, anything. . . . It gives them a support group, some structure to their day, and it gets them to think about their kids as *kids*. . . . Some will benefit, some will not."[63]

Acknowledging that homeless families often lack social supports or adequate family functioning prior to becoming homeless, DHS had begun to discuss ways to identify currently housed families at risk for homelessness due to these problems. In 1988, however, the city's homeless efforts were based in contractual agreements with private agencies to ensure emergency and longer-term housing, transportation, data collection, and some family support services for families already without homes. St. Louis had "a whole continuum of shelters from mass shelter to smaller shelter; it [the shelter system] covers a broad spectrum for families."[64] This spectrum seemed to reflect the varying perceptions of the service needs of homeless families, and the best ways to fill them.

Seattle

The origin of Seattle's response to homeless families can be traced to the battered women's "safe houses" that appeared in the city in the mid-1970s.[65] Sponsored partially by state funds, these shelters were viewed as forerunners of Seattle's present-day, extensive family shelter network. The 1970s also saw the emergence of several youth hostels in Seattle; while these originated as "flop-houses" for the "down and out," other services soon became attached to them. In 1972 the Seattle Emergency Housing Service (SEHS) was established, and in 1975 it received major funding from the local United Way. Its opening marked the first homeless family shelter in Washington State.[66]

By the early 1980s, nontransient, nonbattered street people needing shelter became visible in sections of the city. Individual, community-based, nonprofit shelters, some religiously affiliated, began responding to this new population. In addition, there was a strong advocacy group, the Seattle Emergency Housing Coalition, (renamed the Seattle/King County Emergency Housing Coalition [S/KCEHC] in 1990) ready to tackle new homeless issues. When homeless *families* began to appear in large numbers by the mid-1980s, the homeless service community was ripe to respond. What had begun as a largely private agency response became a public effort.

Several factors promoted this municipal involvement. As in other cities, increasing visibility of the homeless in the downtown area was an early catalyst. In the 1970s Seattle's public laws for drunken behavior were repealed; this led to an increase in the numbers of homeless persons on the streets. As their numbers increased, the downtown area reportedly became an uncomfortable place for many, and businesspeople in the area began to demand that the city do something to attract shoppers back.[67]

The city articulated, and accepted, its responsibility to house all its citizens. In 1979, before most cities were even considering issues of hunger and homelessness, the Survival Services Unit of the Department of Human Resources was formed with the following mission:

- to disseminate information on hunger and homelessness to the population at large
- to administer all hunger and homelessness programs funded by federal Community Development Block Grants (CDBG) and general revenue

- to coordinate existing programs and systems and initiate new programs and comprehensive solutions
- to participate in community coalitions and provide them limited staffing[68]

Concurrent with the formation of the Survival Services Unit in 1979, Seattle also began to make creative use of federal CDBG funds. The federal government intends the bulk of each city's CDBG money to be used for physical improvements, not human services; since 1979, however, Seattle has obtained a waiver to use a greater percentage of these funds for human services (usually capped at 25%). Karen Dawson, Coordinator of Survival Services for the Department of Human Resources, identified the waiver of the 25% CDBG cap as the primary reason that Seattle was ahead of other cities; it was channeling a substantial portion of its CDBG funds into the Survival Services Unit. By the early 1980s, Seattle had an institutionalized response to adult homelessness—a mechanism that could be reenacted in the service of homeless families.

Seattle has a long-standing reputation as a giving, caring, and collaborative community. "We have a 'we can do it' attitude across the board on all issues; we don't give up."[69] As a result, several informants described Seattle as a "city of coalitions." The first and oldest homeless coalition is the Seattle/King County Emergency Housing Coalition (S/KCEHC). What began as a small advocacy group for "safe, sane, sanitary shelter," grew into a coalition of over sixty organizations. According to its cochair, Ruthann Howell (also director of the Salvation Army Social Services), S/KCEHC was a powerful force in the community, acting as "catalyst" for city, county, and state involvement.[70]

A second coalition was established briefly in 1983, when the S/KCEHC banded together with the Food Bank Coalition and the Community Health Clinic Coalition to form the Survival Services Coalition (SSC). This was the first time that different coalitions had coalesced to lobby for direct city funding (for food, emergency shelter, and health care) as a group, rather than through individual applications for CDBG funds. Once funded, the SSC allocated these monies, removing the city from the awkward political situation of having to award funds for one shelter to the exclusion of another.

In 1984, two significant events occurred: First, a subgroup within the SSC received a substantial grant through the Robert Wood Johnson Health Care for the Homeless Project. The Seattle project ensured improved health care for all homeless persons through coordination of a citywide network of existing health care providers. Second, the Mayor's Task Force on Street People and the Homeless was formed to address issues of homelessness in the downtown area. Under the supervision of mayoral staff, the Task Force included government officials, service providers, business representatives, the Seattle Housing Authority, the United Way, the Private Industry Council, and members of the public-at-large. While not a "coalition" per se, the Task Force also expressed Seattle's spirit of coalition building and cooperation.

In 1986, the Task Force published a comprehensive strategy for the downtown homeless, focusing on adult men and women who, at that time, comprised the majority of Seattle's homeless population. Although the city had been actively involved in promoting homeless services since 1979, the *Strategy for the Downtown Homeless*[71] was the first attempt to directly address the needs of the single-adult homeless population.

The business community exerted its own pressure on Mayor Charles Royer to respond to the homeless problem in downtown Seattle; however, much of Seattle's responsiveness was attributed to Royer himself, a liberal mayor with a long-standing commitment to human services. "If a mayor doesn't assign direct staff on an issue, it is likely the issue will not receive the attention it needs. . . . There has always been mayoral staff assigned to the homeless issue in the Department of Human Resources. . . . The Mayor's office is the key. . . . He (Royer) has always been the leader."[72] When Royer convened the Mayor's Task Force on Street People and the Homeless in 1984, he appeared eager not only to placate irate businessmen, but also to address and solve some of the long-term issues of homelessness.[73]

Finally, individuals with a mission—visionaries—have made a substantial difference. "There are individuals here [in Seattle] who are willing to go the extra mile to get things done."[74] Three such visionaries were identified as being instrumental in shaping Seattle's response to homelessness: Mayor Royer; Martha Dilts, founder of the Seattle Emergency Housing Service; and Karen Dawson, of the Survival Services Unit.[75]

Shortly after the publication of the *Strategy for the Downtown Homeless* in 1986, several members of the Mayor's Task Force (including Karen Dawson and Marty Curry) spent six months researching local and national responses to *family* homelessness. They produced the *Homeless Family Strategy*,[76] one of the nation's first citywide blueprints for addressing the needs of homeless families as distinct from other homeless populations. The *Strategy* outlined policies on housing, support services, employment and income supports, and intergovernmental coordination at each of four phases of family homelessness: prevention, emergency response, transitional services, and housing stabilization. It is this comprehensive strategy specifically for homeless *families* that distinguished Seattle from other cities.

Attitudes towards homeless families. "The focus of the City is definitely on *families.* . . . We are still turning families away and until that stops, that will be our focus."[77] Although Dawson clearly articulated the city's priority, there was dissent among service providers on the best approaches to problems, particularly the wisdom of inequitable services for different homeless populations. Sylvie McGee, director of the Washington State Coalition for the Homeless, agreed that there are clinical issues necessitating the separation of homeless populations, but noted, "We [advocates] can't just focus on the salable, and I think there is a tendency in Seattle city government to capitalize on the tragedy of homeless families to the exclusion of other, equally needy populations."[78]

While there appeared to be considerable concern for, and activity on behalf of, homeless families, opinions varied among service providers regarding the causes of family homelessness. Interviews with program directors revealed the following range of opinion: "Homelessness is an economic issue; housing is the answer;"[79] "Ten years ago families were homeless for economic reasons. Period. Now, they have real screwed up lives and housing won't solve their problems;"[80] "Homeless families are a major symptom of the Reagan administration; there has been a devolution of support for children."[81]

Resulting from the variation in perceived causes of the problem, there was an equally wide range of opinion and practice regarding services for homeless families. Directors expressed the following: "I think family support is a classist notion;"[82] "I think kids lose out when they look at the family as a whole; their needs are so different;"[83] "Shelter is not the solution; support services must be balanced with independence."[84]

According to Marty Curry at the Health and Human Services Strategic Planning Office (HSSPO), "The level of success among service providers is too varied and inconsistent, and they don't do enough follow through to find out how successful they really were."[85] Therefore, HSSPO considered it essential to establish citywide service guidelines, ensuring every homeless family the same opportunity for stabilization regardless of its shelter or transitional experience. However, service providers have met this proposal with opposition, arguing that since homeless families are homeless for a variety of reasons, there is no one "correct" service orientation and that diversity of services is what makes Seattle's policies so unique.[86]

In summary, as Joan Haynes, project director of the Health Care for the Homeless Project, suggested, "There is a program for everyone here . . . but there is no consensus on what services should be provided for each [homeless] group."[87] David Okimoto, director of Human Resources, concluded, "We still don't have a system of care for homeless families. We just have a range of services."[88] While Okimoto's statement captured the city's frustration in trying to develop a unified systemwide approach to family homelessness, the "range of services" available to homeless families in Seattle was impressive. Over half of the family shelters in 1988 served homeless families exclusively. Further, they did so predominantly via year-round, 24-hour facilities, most of which offered family support services including parent education, family and individual therapy, and child care. All residential facilities for homeless families excluded single adult males, reflecting the city's orientation toward homeless families as a distinct subgroup of the general homeless population.

FACTORS ACCOUNTING FOR POLICY FORMATION

General Homeless Policy

Cheryl Hayes[89] proposes six categories of influences on child policy at the federal level: media presentation, constituent activities, actors and institutions, contextual factors, principles and ideas, and research. While the policies under discussion here were all affected, to some degree, by these factors, three appear particularly influential to the development of general homeless policy—that is, policy for homeless adults. They include the visibility of the homeless problem (within the "media" category); the existence and/or character of local and state homeless coalitions (within the "constituent" category); and the existence of visionaries in the community who actively worked to engage local government in the issue (within the "actors and institutions" category).

Visibility. One of the earliest catalysts for city involvement was the growing visibility of the homeless population in downtown areas. As the numbers of single homeless adults increased, local businesses began exerting pressure on city governments to address the problem. For example, the press in St. Louis publicized data revealing a growing homeless problem in that city; this prompted the mayor to begin formulating policy. The visibility of the homeless issue in Atlanta was magnified by the fact that it was the home of several national news bureaus' regional offices; Atlanta's homeless problem quickly became "news," bringing "bad press" to a city fervently trying to revitalize its downtown neighborhoods.

Homeless coalitions and advocacy task forces. Local and state homeless coalitions were key in promoting public interest and involvement in this issue. In the absence of a strong city government response, the Atlanta Task Force for the Homeless took a leadership role in coordinating private agencies to provide much-needed homeless services. Although the Task Force could not force the city into human service action, it raised the level of public awareness of homeless issues considerably through the dissemination of materials, as well as the coordination of homeless services among private providers.

While Seattle and St. Louis had stronger involvement at the municipal government level, the homeless coalitions in those cities were no less active or important in promoting homeless services. Seattle's numerous coalitions worked in conjunction with the city's Department of Human Resources (DHR) to ensure a broad base of community support for homeless issues. And since its inception in 1985, the St. Louis Homeless Services Network, under the auspices of DHS, has represented an exemplary public-private collaboration.

Variations in homeless policy across cities reflect, in part, the different beliefs and strategies endorsed by local advocates. For example, the Atlanta Task Force for the Homeless took the position that homelessness is first and foremost a housing issue; thus, its emphasis was toward involvement with housing, not family support services. And since the city is not legally responsible for providing support services, this housing orientation makes strategic sense.

In contrast, the St. Louis Homeless Services Network Board supports a range of services reflecting varying philosophies on the causes and solutions to homelessness. Finally, in Seattle, while the individual styles of each provider vary, there is overall consensus that comprehensive homeless services, including economic and noneconomic support, should be provided by the city, with assistance and support from the private sector. This attitude is clearly reflected in DHR policy.

Visionaries. In each city there were people with a vision who were instrumental in policy formation. These individuals are described elsewhere as "political entrepreneurs"—actors who take strategic advantage of "windows of opportunity" in the political environment to further their efforts.[90] Informants in Seattle identified their mayor as one, due to his long-standing commitment to human services. In St. Louis, Atlanta, and Seattle, other actors within city government were identified as visionaries. Sam Spade, director of St. Louis CDA in the early 1970s, saw an opportunity for the city to get involved in homeless services through the awarding of CDBG funds. Connie Curry, former director of Atlanta's CDA and present director of OCCA, is said to have "single-handedly done the job" of promoting a response to homelessness within Atlanta's city government. Described as a "mover," Karen Dawson of Seattle's DHR has been actively involved in the city's response to homelessness since the late 1970s.

Homeless Family Policy

It appears that cities generate homeless family policy at some point *after* policies for the adult homeless population are in effect. That is, experience in dealing with homelessness in general is a necessary precursor to focusing attention on the needs of homeless families. In addition to assuming a developmental course to these policies, however, one must consider what political scientists call the "political culture" of a city in order to understand the particular character of these family policies.[91] While political culture generally refers to a wide range of attitudes and beliefs about the role of government and the responsibilities of citizens, I use it in this case to describe local attitudes about the apportionment of public (governmental) and private (nongovernmental and family) responsibility for the well-being of families and children. Thus, at a minimum, a city's relative developmental maturity *and* its political culture interact to produce homeless family policy.[92]

Developmental stages. Cross-site analyses yield evidence of a developmental course through which cities progress as they formulate homeless policy; the more advanced stage in this developmental sequence is the establishment of policy for homeless *families.*[93]

The first three developmental stages correspond to the factors noted earlier: public recognition of the homeless problem, advocacy activity to exert pressure on city government to respond, and key players who see a unique opportunity to promote policy formation. The fourth stage may well be the establishment of a mayoral task force to document the homeless problem, make policy recommendations, and designate a lead agency to coordinate the implementation of task force recommendations. In this four-stage developmental model, the designation of a lead agency to coordinate city involvement marks the final stage in developing policy for homeless *adults.*

A second round of planning occurs for policy regarding homeless *families.* This is the fifth step in the policy formation process: the recognition of homeless families as a distinct subgroup of the general homeless population, with special service needs. While each city had reached stage four—the designation of a lead agency—the cities were at different developmental points regarding homeless family policy. Two cities provide an example: Seattle, having been involved with general homeless service provision for almost a decade longer than other cities in this study, was working through the final stage of implementing policy recommendations specific to the support needs of homeless families. On the other hand, St. Louis, having been involved in the provision of general homeless services since the mid-1980s, was just beginning to discuss the merits of considering homeless families as a subgroup of the homeless population with a distinct set of service needs.

Public versus private responsibility for families. In his ground-breaking work on state political culture, David Elazar describes three basic orientations to political life: individualistic, moralistic, and traditional.[94] Within the individualistic political culture, the least government intervention is the best arrangement, with social needs being met through mutually obligating personal relationships. Public involvement in the community on behalf of the commonweal, including forays into "private" matters when they are deemed appropriate, is a hallmark of the moralistic political culture. And political life with a traditional orientation generally assumes some degree of public attention to social needs, but supports the existing arrangements.

This range of political culture is apparent in the cities under discussion here. Informants, city to city, often expressed dramatically different notions about the proper balance of public and private responsibilities for the well-being of homeless families. Programs and policies for homeless families, in turn, reflected these disparate orientations. So while in each city there was agreement that homelessness was a serious problem needing some manner of public solution, each offered an idiosyncratic definition of "public" and "solution." One sees these differences most clearly in answer to two fundamental questions regarding services for homeless families: Which sector, and which agencies, should provide them? and, What kinds of supports should be available?

Which sectors and which agencies should provide the services? Social policy analysts Grubb and Lazerson[95] argue that United States family policy has been characterized throughout our history by a tension between private needs and public obligations; this tension, apparent in this study, frames the national debate about solutions to family homelessness.[96] Informants in each city drew boundaries between public and private sector responsibility for providing housing and support services. Some flatly argued that government is responsible for the well-being of families, and a mix of local, state, and federal dollars is necessary. They believed, however, that the bulk of policy development and implementation should remain at the local level, where clients are known, and providers can negotiate with them and with each other. Other informants suggested that family matters are best left in the hands of the private sector—"private" here meaning a nongovernmental group, such as a church, charitable organization, or a private nonprofit service agency.

Seattle and Atlanta offer the most distinct contrasts on this issue. In Seattle, there is general agreement in both the public and private sectors that while the city should not be totally responsible for providing all homeless services, an agency such as DHR is the appropriate coordinator of citywide homeless services. "We [in Seattle city government] are grappling with what a *systemic* response to homeless families is."[97] There is recognition in Seattle that a comprehensive policy response to homeless families must incorporate both public and private sector efforts, and that these efforts must consider how the entire social service system behaves in relation to all families, including those considered high risk.

Seattle's largely public response to family homelessness is easily contrasted with the private, and even personal, response that has arisen in other communities, such as Atlanta. Atlanta's shelter system is predominantly comprised of church-sponsored facilities that provide minimal emergency services such as food, clothing, and shelter. Since the problem of family homelessness is viewed as stemming primarily from the lack of low-income housing, these emergency, instrumental supports, which private groups are adept at organizing, seem well-placed in the private sector.[98] In fact, this kind of service is considered a moral or religious imperative for many who work in family shelters and with homeless families. As one informant noted about this arrangement: "They [the churches] are small, they do it well, and if they truly believe in their faiths, they ought to do it."[99]

What kinds of support should be available? Key informant opinions on this issue were arrayed on a continuum that, at one end, considered housing services and emergency instrumental supports (food, clothing, immediate shelter) the only necessary ones, and at the other end, considered a mix of housing, other economic supports (broader income maintenance programs, employment training programs, child care, etc.), and noneconomic supports (for example, parent education, family counseling, supportive transitional housing) as critical to solving the family homelessness crisis. Those informants arguing for a comprehensive approach saw a central role for government in purveying that wide range of services; those promoting a more limited intervention into the problem consigned to government only the job of providing low-income housing. They felt, in essence, that government should not meddle in the private world of the family.

Both Seattle and St. Louis provide more comprehensive services, defining the root causes of family homelessness more broadly than the lack of affordable housing. In fact, Seattle's policies evolved in its Department of Human Resources, as opposed to an agency devoted to housing; as such, homelessness in Seattle always has been framed, first and foremost, as a human services issue. Since 1987, DHR has responded with emergency shelter, longer-term supportive housing, intensive case management, and homelessness prevention among poor, marginally housed families. The director of human resources maintains that these investments in both homeless and near-homeless families is the only sure way to alleviate current and future homelessness; housing alone is insufficient.[100]

The City of St. Louis requires homeless parents receiving permanent housing assistance through city auspices to participate in parent education and living skills programming. The Department of Human Services contracts with a large multiservice community center to provide these mandatory family support services in addition to transitional housing and permanent housing referrals. Some providers in St. Louis are uncomfortable with mandatory requirements for participation in family programming, but the city feels that once a family reaches a shelter, it has an unusual opportunity to help these families, no doubt living under great stress.[101]

Unlike Seattle and St. Louis, the prevailing attitude in Atlanta, clearly articulated by representatives of the Atlanta Task Force for the Homeless, is that homelessness is first and foremost a housing issue; beyond housing, homeless families likely need only limited emergency assistance, which is best provided by private groups. Explanations for this position are confounded by the city's lack of legal obligation to provide *any* human services; it may be that advocates have made a strategic decision to frame the problem so as to engage the city only on its obligations. However this has occurred, Atlanta's shelter system reflects this position: only limited family support services beyond emergency shelter are available. In fact, the city's efforts to provide these services have been criticized by several Task Force members who feel that they are not, and should not be, the responsibility of local government.[102]

CONCLUSIONS

Throughout this country, services for homeless families have been left primarily to municipalities to negotiate. Each of the cities in this study has developed a system of shelter and service that reflects its own political culture and character, and the length of time and degree of effort heretofore directed towards this problem. There is clearly no one best model to propose.

It does appear, however, that since the conduct of this research, housing advocates, many government administrators, programs personnel, and homeless families themselves have sought, productively, to *complicate,* rather than *simplify*, discussions about the causes of, and solutions to, family homelessness. Undeniably, increasing the affordable housing stock is the necessary first step; a recent report of American Housing Survey data collected by the U.S. Bureau of the Census demonstrates that, since 1970, when the number of low-rent units was somewhat higher than the number of low-income renters, a yawning gap in the opposite direction has grown between the two. By 1989, the low-rent housing stock had decreased almost 20%, while the number of low-income renters had increased 33%, leaving over four million potential renters without affordable housing.[103]

It seems likely, however, that in many cases family homelessness also bespeaks some family dysfunction, or at a minimum, seriously stressful experiences likely to cause future dysfunction. Despite a growing body of relevant developmental research, local key informants still stated that not enough is known about the correlates and consequences of family homelessness to design effective programs at the municipal level. As they stated, "We do not know enough about the population to know what 'works';"[104] "There is something really wrong when a girl chooses a shelter over her mother's house. . . . We have to find out what it is and remedy it before they end up homeless;"[105] "We need to know a lot more about how to support and promote services for *all* families."[106]

There are signs that this is beginning to occur. As other precipitants of family homelessness, for example wife battering, have become more widely documented and credited, acceptable approaches to serving these families and stabilizing their housing situations have broadened. It is likely that through the 1990s more comprehensive policies will emerge, crafted at the local level and reflective of each city's particular vision of proper public and private roles in supporting these, and other, families.

APPENDIX A: LIST OF INTERVIEWS

Unless otherwise noted, all interviews were conducted in person.

John Abercrombie: Co-Chair, Atlanta Task Force for the Homeless; Director of Charis Community Housing, August, 1988.

Anita Beaty: Director, Atlanta Task Force for the Homeless, telephone interview, July, 1988; group interview, August, 1988.

Nancy Boxill: Fulton County Commissioner, Atlanta, August, 1988.

Karen Clark: Deputy Director, Sacred Heart Shelter and Our Place Day Care Center, Seattle, July, 1988.

Carolyn Cohen: Transitional Housing Coordinator, St. Patrick's Center, St. Louis, September, 1988.

Barbara Conrad: Home Economist, Basic Living Skills Teacher, St. Patrick's Center, St. Louis, September, 1988.

Connie Curry: Director, Office of Community and Citizen Affairs, Atlanta, August, 1988.

Marty Curry: Human Services Strategic Planning Office, City of Seattle, July, 1988.

Dorothy Dailey: Homeless Services Coordinator, Department of Human Services, St. Louis, September, 1988.

David Davidson: Assistant to Anita Beaty, Atlanta Task Force for the Homeless, August, 1988.

Karen Dawson: Survival Services Coordinator, Seattle, Department of Human Resources; Co-Chair, Seattle Emergency Housing Coalition, July, 1988.

Martha Dilts: Executive Director, Seattle Emergency Housing Service, July, 1988.

Laurie Downs: Executive Director, Atlanta Children's Shelter, August, 1988.

George Eberle: Chair, Mayor's Task Force on the Homeless; Director, Consolidated Neighborhood Services, St. Louis, September, 1988.

Joan Haynes: Project Director, Robert Wood Johnson Health Care for the Homeless Project, Seattle, July, 1988.

Mary Hess: Program Coordinator, Broadview Transitional Housing, Seattle, July, 1988.

Loretta Horton: Director, Good Samaritan Service Center, St. Louis, September, 1988.

Ruthann Howell: Executive Director, Salvation Army Social Services Division; Co-Chair, Seattle Emergency Housing Coalition, Seattle, July, 1988.

Sylvie McGee: Director, Washington Coalition for the Homeless, Seattle, August, 1988.

Tina Narr: Assistant Director, YWCA, Seattle, July, 1988.

David Okimoto: Director, Department of Human Resources, Seattle, July, 1988.

Sue Taylor: Administrator, Salvation Army Hospitality House, St. Louis, September, 1988.

Judith Moll Weilepp: Project Director, Health Care for the Homeless Coalition, St. Louis, September, 1988.

APPENDIX B: HOMELESS FAMILIES AND THE SHELTER SYSTEMS ACROSS CITIES

At the time of this research, estimates of the homeless populations in the three study sites were as follows: 1,000 in St. Louis; 3,000–5,000 in Seattle; and 7,000–10,000 in Atlanta. The national average percentage of homeless *families* among the total homeless population was 40%. The range across these cities was 50% in Atlanta, 66% in Seattle, and 70% in St. Louis.[107] Two-parent homeless families are reported to be more prevalent in cities west of the Mississippi River,[108] accounting for approximately half the census in Seattle, compared to only 10–25% in Atlanta. Although minorities comprised 58% of the general homeless population nationally,[109] two of the study sites reflected a higher figure: in Atlanta and St. Louis it was estimated that over 70% of their cities' homeless family population were members of minority groups.

The shelter systems differ in character, structure, and funding. At the time of the study, Atlanta's system was comprised primarily of congregate, night-only shelters, funded predominantly through private sources. Many operated in the winter months only. In contrast, 70% (twenty-one) of the thirty-two shelters and transitional facilities in Seattle received city funding. Nineteen of those served homeless families; half of these serve homeless families exclusively. Further, they were predominantly year-round, 24-hour facilities. All residential facilities for homeless families excluded homeless single adult males.

Almost all the homeless shelters in St. Louis were year-round facilities; half operated on a 24-hour basis.[110] While many of the shelters served more than one subgroup of the homeless population, there were no overnight facilities that combine shelter for homeless families with shelter for single adult males. Shelters were supported by multiple funding sources; over 90% received some private support, and 41% received city funds.

NOTES

1. P. H. Rossi (1990). The old homeless and the new homeless in historical perspective. *American Psychologist, 45*,(8), 954–959; J. D. Wright (1989). *Address unknown: The homeless in America.* Hawthorne, NY: Aldine de Gruyter.

2. National Academy of Sciences, Institutes of Medicine: Committee on Health Care for the Homeless People (1988). *Homelessness, health, and human needs.* Washington, D.C.: National Academy Press.

3. U.S. General Accounting Office (1989). *Children and youths: About 68,000 homeless and 186,000 in shared housing at any given time* (GAO/PEMD–89–14). Washington, D.C.: U.S. Government Printing Office.

4. See, for example, B. Weitzman, J. Knickman, & M. Shinn (1990). Pathways to homelessness among New York City families. *Journal of Social Issues, 46*(4), 125–140; U.S. GAO (1989), *Children and youths*; Wright (1988), *Address unknown*; P. H. Rossi, J. D. Wright, G. A. Fisher, & G. Willis (1987). The urban homeless: Estimating composition and size. *Science, 235*, 1336–1341.

5. For discussions of the economic bases of family homelessness, see, for example, M. W. Edelman & L. Mihaly (1989). Homeless families and the housing crisis in the United States. *Children and Youth Services Review, 7*(1), 91–108; J. D. Wright (1989), *Address unknown*; K. Y. McChesney (August, 1988a). *Homeless families, homeless children: How family poverty leads to homelessness.* Paper presented at the meeting of the Society for the Study of Social Problems, Atlanta, GA; K. Y. McChesney, (August, 1988). *Policy implications of the low-income housing ratio for homeless families.* Paper presented at the meeting of the Society for the Study of Social Problems, Atlanta, GA; National Coalition for the Homeless (1988). *Summary: The Stewart B. McKinney Homeless Assistance Act.* Washington, D.C.: Author; K. Y. McChesney (1987). Paths to family homelessness. In U.S. House of Representatives, Select Committee on Children, Youth, and Families, *The crisis in homelessness*, 175–206. Washington, D.C.: U.S. Government Printing Office. *Necessary relief: The Stewart B. McKinney Homeless Assistance Act.* Washington, D.C.: Author; J. D. Wright & J. Lam (1986). The low income housing supply and the problem of homelessness. *Social Policy, 17*(4), 48–53.

6. See, for example, M. Shinn, J. Knickman, & B. Weitzman (1991). Social relationships and vulnerability to becoming homeless among poor families. *American Psychologist, 46*, 1180–1187; D. Wood, B. Valdez, T. Hayashi, & A. Shen (1990). Homeless and housed families in Los Angeles: A study comparing demographic, economic, and family function characteristics. *American Journal of Public Health, 80*, 1049–1052; L. J. Axelson & P. W. Dail (1988). The changing character of homelessness in the United States. *Family Relations, 37*, 463–469; E. Bassuk & L. Rosenberg (1988). Why does family homelessness occur?: A case

control study. *American Journal of Public Health, 78,* 783–788; McChesney (1987), Paths to family homelessness; E. Bassuk, L. Rubin, & A. Lauriat (1986). Characteristics of sheltered homeless families. *American Journal of Public Health, 76,* 1097–1101; Committee of Government Operations (1986). *Homeless families: A neglected crisis* (October, 1986). Sixty-third Report by the Committee on Governmental Operations. Washington, D.C.: U.S. Government Printing Office; E. Bassuk (June, 1985). *The feminization of homelessness: Homeless families in Boston shelters.* Keynote address given at Shelter, Inc., Cambridge, MA.

7. For a more extensive review, see, for example, A. L. Solarz (1988). Homelessness: Implications for children and youth. *Social Policy Report, 3*(4). Washington, D.C.: Society for Research in Child Development, Committee on Child Development and Social Policy; P. J. Acker, A. H. Fierman, & B. P. Dreyer (1987). An assessment of parameters of health care and nutrition in homeless children. *American Journal of Diseases of Children, 141*(4), 388; E. L. Bassuk & L. Rubin (1987). Homeless children: A neglected population. *American Journal of Orthopsychiatry, 57,* 279–286; National Coalition for the Homeless (1987). *Broken lives: Denial of education to homeless children.* Washington, D.C.: Author.

8. W. N. Grubb & M. Lazerson (1982). *Broken promises: How Americans fail their children.* New York: Basic Books.

9. At the federal level, see U.S. House of Representatives (1990). *Stewart B. McKinney Homeless Assistance Amendments Act of 1990* (Report 101–951). Washington, D.C.: U.S. Government Printing Office; U.S. House of Representatives (1987). *Stewart B. McKinney Homeless Assistance Act* (Report 100–174). Washington, D.C.: U.S. Government Printing Office.

10. By noneconomic needs, I mean those not directly satisfied by housing or income maintenance. Thus noneconomic supports include education, peer support, assistance managing daily living, and the like.

11. For the earlier, four-city investigation, see P.M.D. Little (1990). Local responses to homeless families in four cities: A multiple-site case study in policy formation. Unpublished Master's thesis, Tufts University, Medford, MA. Research for this larger study would not have been possible without the generous support of The Better Homes Foundation, Newton, MA. The majority of data for this study were collected through September, 1988. Since that time, there have been local mayoral elections, changes in staffing within city agencies, and the like. Unless noted otherwise, information in each case, including the title of key informants, reflects the state of homeless policy formation as of 1988.

12. The original investigation included forty-five telephone and field interviews; material in this chapter is presented based on a subset of twenty-three informants.

13. F. Jacobs & M. Davies (Winter, 1991). Rhetoric or reality? Child and family policy in the United States. *Social Policy Report, 5*(4), 1–25.

14. D. Wood et al. (1990). Homeless and housed families in Los Angeles; Children's Defense Fund (1989). *An agenda for the 1990s: A children's defense budget.* Washington, D.C.: Author; C. Mills & H. Ota (November, 1989). Homeless women with minor children in the Detroit metropolitan area. *Social Work, 346,* 485–489; M. H. Phillips, N. DeChillo, D. Kronenfeld, & V. Middleton-Jeter (1988). Homeless families: Services make a difference. *Social Casework: Journal of Contemporary Social Work, 69*(1), 48–53; P. L. Maza & J. A. Hall (1988). *Homeless children and their families: A preliminary study.* Washington, D.C.: Child Welfare League of America; Bassuk et al. (1986), Characteristics of sheltered homeless families.

15. L. Weinreb & P. H. Rossi (February, 1991). *Homeless families: Public policies, program responses, and evaluation strategies.* Paper presented at NIMH/NIAAA meeting

"Homeless families with children: Research perspectives," Boston, MA; L. Weinreb & E. L. Bassuk (1990). Substance abuse: A growing problem among homeless families. *Family and Community Health, 13*(1), 55–64; M. Comfort, T. E. Shipley, K. White, E. M. Griffith, & I. W. Shandler (1990). Family treatment for homeless alcohol/drug-addicted women and their children. *Alcoholism Treatment Quarterly, 7*(1), 129–147.

16. Shinn et al. (1991), Social relationships and vulnerability; Wood et al (1990), Homeless and housed families in Los Angeles; Bassuk & Rosenberg (1988), Why does family homelessness occur?; Maza & Hall (1988), *Homeless children and their families*; McChesney (1987), Paths to family homelessness.

17. Bassuk & Rosenberg (1988), Why does family homelessness occur?

18. Bassuk & Rubin (1987), Homeless children; Bassuk et al. (1986), Characteristics of sheltered homeless families.

19. McChesney (1987), Paths to family homelessness.

20. Maza & Hall (1988), *Homeless children and their families*, 13.

21. S. Parker, S. Greer, & B. Zuckerman (1988). Double jeopardy: The impact of poverty on early child development. *The Pediatric Clinics of North America, 35*, 1227–1240.

22. G. Alperstein, C. Rappaport, & J. Flanigan (1988). Health problems of homeless children in New York City. *American Journal of Public Health, 78*, 1232–1233; Acker et al. (1987), An assessment of parameters of health care and nutrition in homeless children; D. Miller & E. Lin (1987). Children in sheltered homeless families: Reported health status and use of health services. *Pediatrics, 81*, 668–673; J. D. Wright & E. Weber (1987). *Homelessness and health*. New York: McGraw-Hill.

23. T. Gross & M. Rosenberg (1988). Shelters for battered women and their children: An under-recognized source of communicable disease transmission. *American Journal of Public Health, 77*, 1198–1201.

24. L. D. Waxman & L. M. Reyes (1989). *A status report on hunger and homelessness in America's cities: 1988*. Washington, D.C.: U.S. Conference of Mayors; J. Molnar, T. Klein, J. Knitzer, & B. Ortis-Torres (1988). *Home is where the heart is: The crisis of homeless children and families in New York City*. New York: Bank Street College of Education; Solarz (1988), Homelessness: Implications for children and youth; Bassuk & Rubin (1987), Homeless children; E. Schmitt (November 16, 1987). Homeless students face long roads to school. *New York Times*, 15.

25. National Coalition for the Homeless (1987), *Broken lives*.

26. L. Rescorla, R. Parker, & P. Stolley (1991). Ability, achievement, and adjustment in homeless children. *American Journal of Orthopsychiatry, 61*, 210–220; Molnar et al. (1988), *Home is where the heart is*; Phillips et al. (1988), Homeless families; N. A. Boxill & A. L. Beaty (1987). An exploration of mother/child interaction among homeless women and their children using public night shelter in Atlanta, Georgia. In U.S. House of Representatives, Select Committee on Children, Youth, and Families, *The crisis in homelessness: Effects on children and their families*, 134–154. Washington, D.C.: U.S. Government Printing Office; Bassuk & Rubin (1987), Homeless children; Bassuk et al. (1986), Characteristics of sheltered homeless families.

27. Boxill & Beaty (1987), An exploration of mother/child interaction among homeless women.

28. Boxill & Beaty (1987), An exploration of mother/child interaction among homeless women, 151.

29. Wright (1989), *Address unknown*.

30. Solarz (1988), Homelessness: Implications for children and youth.

31.   F. H. Jacobs, P. M. D. Little, & C. Almeida (1993). Supporting family life: A survey of homeless shelters. *Journal of Social Distress and the Homeless;* 2(4), 269–288; Edelman & Mihaly (1989), Homeless families and the housing crisis in the United States; Waxman & Reyes (1989), *A status report on hunger and homelessness*; Solarz (1988), Homelessness: Implications for children and youth.

32.   Solarz (1988), Homelessness: Implications for children and youth.

33.   Interview with Nancy Boxill, Fulton County Commissioner, Atlanta, GA, August, 1988.

34.   Key informants were offered anonymity for any information they wished to keep confidential. A link-file system, which assigns numbers to each interview, was developed for that purpose. These interviews are reported by number and date. Interview #34, August, 1988.

35.   Interview with John Abercrombie, Co-Chairman, Atlanta Task Force for the Homeless, and Director, Charis Community Housing, Atlanta, GA, August, 1988.

36.   Interview with Abercrombie, August, 1988.

37.   See B. Shapiro (1985). *Homelessness in Atlanta: A 5-year plan.* Atlanta: Alliance for Human Services.

38.   Interview with Boxill, August, 1988.

39.   Atlanta Task Force for the Homeless (1987). *Homelessness in metro Atlanta: A working paper with recommendations.* Atlanta: Author.

40.   Boxill & Beaty (1987), An exploration of mother/child interaction.

41.   Interview with Abercrombie, August, 1988; Interview with Boxill, August, 1988.

42.   Atlanta Task Force for the Homeless (1987), *Homelessness in metro Atlanta.*

43.   Interview with Boxill, August, 1988.

44.   Interview with Abercrombie, August, 1988; Interview with Anita Beaty, Director, Atlanta Task Force for the Homeless, August, 1988; Interview with Boxill, August, 1988.

45.   Interview with Beaty, August, 1988; Interview with Boxill, August, 1988; Interview with Connie Curry, Director, Atlanta Office of Community and Citizen Affairs, August, 1988.

46.   Interview with Beaty, August, 1988.

47.   Selected key informants in each city were asked to review an earlier draft of this essay. Salient comments from their reviews are presented throughout this chapter, and cited as "during review." During review (February, 1990), this position was softened. Beaty and Curry both feel that the special needs of homeless families (privacy, child care, family support) necessitate some service segregation.

48.   Interview with Boxill, August, 1988.

49.   Night-only congregate shelters are not thought to be the best shelter structure for families. Family-oriented shelters tend to be small, 24-hour facilities, with individual living spaces for each family. See Jacobs, Little, & Almeida (in press), Supporting family life.

50.   Interview with Judith Moll Weilepp, Project Director, Health Care for the Homeless Coalition, St. Louis, September, 1988.

51.   Interview #1, September, 1988; Interview #4, September, 1988.

52.   Interview with Weilepp, September, 1988.

53.   The Relocation Clearinghouse data did not account for duplicate requests (the same family calling more than one shelter).

54.   Interview with Weilepp, September, 1988.

55.   J. J. Stretch, L. Krueger, & A. K. Johnson (1987). *Consent Decree enforcement and implementation.* St. Louis: Department of Human Services.

56.   Stretch et al. (1987), *Consent Degree enforcement and implementation.*

57.   Office of the Mayor (1985). *Mayor's Task Force on the Homeless report.* St. Louis:

Author.

58. Interview with George Eberle, Chair, Mayor's Task Force on the Homeless; Director, Consolidated Neighborhood Services, St. Louis, September, 1988.

59. Interview with Eberle, September, 1988.

60. Interview with Eberle, September, 1988.

61. Interview with Sue Taylor, Administrator, Salvation Army Hospitality House, St. Louis, September, 1988.

62. Interview with Dorothy Dailey, Homeless Services Coordinator, Department of Human Services, St. Louis, September, 1988.

63. Interview with Carolyn Cohen, Director, Transitional Housing Program, St. Patrick's Center, St. Louis, September, 1988.

64. Interview with Taylor, September, 1988.

65. Interview with Martha Dilts, Executive Director, Seattle Emergency Housing Service, July, 1988; Interview with Ruthann Howell, Executive Director, Salvation Army Social Services Division, and Co-Chair, Seattle Emergency Housing Coalition, Seattle, July, 1988.

66. During review, Dilts (January, 1990) emphasized that like all nonprofits, SEHS operates with patchwork funding from several sources (United Way, private donations, federal funds) in addition to city funds.

67. Interview #13, July, 1988; Interview #25, July, 1988; Interview #28, July, 1988.

68. Interview with Karen Dawson, Survival Services Coordinator, City of Seattle, Department of Human Resources, and Co-Chair, Seattle Emergency Housing Coalition, July, 1988.

69. Interview with Dilts, July, 1988.

70. Interview with Howell, July, 1988.

71. Department of Human Resources (1986). *Strategy for the downtown homeless.* Seattle: Author.

72. Interview with Dawson, July, 1988.

73. Interview with Marty Curry, Human Services Strategic Planning Office, City of Seattle, July, 1988; Interview with Dawson, July, 1988.

74. Interview with M. Curry, July, 1988.

75. During review Dawson (January, 1990) added the following: "Please include Tom Byers, staff to Mayor Royer, as one of the true 'visionary persons' in the world of homeless families." This endorsement by Dawson is the only time Byers was mentioned during the Seattle case preparation. Interview with Curry, July, 1988; Interview with Dawson, July, 1988; Interview with Joan Haynes, Project Director, Robert Wood Johnson Health Care for the Homeless Project, Seattle, July, 1988; Interview #13, July, 1988; Interview #25; July, 1988; Interview #28, July, 1988.

76. Department of Community Development & Health and Human Services Strategic Planning Office (1987). *Homeless family strategy.* Seattle: Author.

77. Interview with Dawson, July, 1988.

78. Interview with Sylvie McGee, Director, Washington Coalition for the Homeless, Seattle, August, 1988.

79. Interview #24, August, 1988.

80. Interview #8, July, 1988.

81. Interview #7, July, 1988.

82. Interview #17, July, 1988.

83. Interview #8, July, 1988.

84. Interview #13, July, 1988.

85. Interview with M. Curry, July, 1988.

86. Interview #8, July, 1988; Interview #17, July, 1988.

87. Interview with Haynes, July, 1988.

88. Interview with David Okimoto, Director, Department of Human Resources, Seattle, July, 1988.

89. C. D. Hayes (Ed.) (1982). *Making policies for children: A case study of the federal process*. Washington, D.C.: National Academy Press.

90. See, for example, B. Hausman [this volume]. Policy entrepreneurship and the emergence of family support programs; J. Kingdon (1984). *Agendas, alternatives, and public policies*, 188-193. Boston: Little Brown.

91. B. Hausman [this volume]. Policy entrepreneurship and the emergence of family support programs; S. Zimmerman (1992). *Family policies and family well-being: The role of political culture*. Newbury Park, CA: Sage Publications; D. Elazar (1986). Marketplace and commonwealth and the three political cultures. In M. Gittell (Ed.), *State politics and the new federalism*, 172–179. New York: Longman.

92. No doubt there are many factors that influence homeless family policy. These two are particularly prominent in this cross-site study.

93. Since Atlanta is not legally obligated to provide human services, it does not lend itself to analysis using this developmental model.

94. Elazar (1986), Marketplace and commonwealth.

95. Grubb & Lazerson (1982), *Broken promises*.

96. Axelson & Dail (1988), The changing character of homelessness.

97. Interview with Okimoto, July, 1988.

98. See Jacobs, Little, & Almeida, Supporting family life (1993), for a more detailed categorization of support services for homeless families.

99. Interview with Abercrombie, August, 1988.

100. Interview with Okimoto, July, 1988.

101. Interview with Dailey, September, 1988.

102. Interview #14, August, 1988; Interview #22, August, 1988; Interview #23, August, 1988.

103. Children's Defense Fund (1992). *The state of America's children: 1992*. Washington, D.C.: Author.

104. Interview with Boxill, August, 1988.

105. Interview with Taylor, September, 1988.

106. Interview with M. Curry, July, 1988.

107. U.S. Department of Housing and Urban Development, Office of Policy Development and Research (1989). *A report on the 1988 National Survey of Shelters for the Homeless*. Washington, D.C.: Author.

108. Molnar et al. (1988), *Home is where the heart is*.

109. U.S. Department of Housing and Urban Development, Office of Policy Development and Research (1989), *A report on the 1988 National Survey of Shelters for the Homeless*.

110. See A. K. Johnson (1988). A survey of the St. Louis area emergency shelters for the homeless. St. Louis: Homeless Services Network Board.

7

Selective Nontreatment of Handicapped Newborns: Implementation of the Baby Doe Laws of 1984

Martha Pott

On April 9, 1982, "Baby Doe" was born in Bloomington, Indiana. He had two surgically correctable birth defects that prevented food and water from reaching his stomach. He also had Down Syndrome, a chromosomal abnormality producing mild to severe retardation. Cardiac problems, common in children with Down Syndrome, were suspected but later turned out not to be present. His condition at birth was unstable: his heart was pumping ineffectively, making him limp and blue, and he required resuscitation at birth.[1]

The newborn's parents, acting on advice from their obstetrician, refused the corrective surgery, which would certainly have been performed had the baby not had Down Syndrome. The obstetrician told them that the surgery was difficult, accompanied by significant pain, and that the child's level of mental retardation would be such that he would not be able to enjoy a "minimally adequate quality of life."[2] The parents, both public school teachers, were familiar with Down Syndrome and believed it would be wrong to subject their child to what they considered an inferior life.[3] Furthermore, they believed a handicapped child would place a burden on the family, which would not be fair to their other two children. Although another couple offered to adopt the baby, the parents refused, stating that they had made their decision in their child's best interests, not to be free of the burden of caring for him.[4] The parents were told that without the surgery, their baby would develop pneumonia and die within a few days. To hasten that end, the medical orders stipulated keeping the baby as comfortable as possible, with sedation as necessary, but providing no intravenous food or water.[5]

Despite challenges by other physicians[6] and legal proceedings that reached the Indiana Supreme Court, the parents' right to make this decision was upheld, and the baby died after six days. This scenario could not happen legally today because of a federal statute, first passed in 1984, that mandates treatment in such cases. The legislation contains what are commonly known as the Baby Doe laws, for which the case just cited was the catalyst. The Baby Doe laws and regulations state that medical treatment cannot be withheld from a newborn except in extreme circumstances, and that an existing or potential handicapping condition cannot be a factor in making a treatment decision.[7]

The Baby Doe case posed two central conflicts between private and public rights and responsibilities. The first regards the private rights of parents to make decisions about their children and their responsibilities to make those decisions in their children's "best interests," versus public rights and responsibilities to protect those incapable of protecting themselves, and those who may be subject to discrimination. The Baby Doe laws represented the first attempt by the federal government to instruct parents how to make decisions about their child, outside the child protective service system. In fact, the Baby Doe laws eventually became amendments to the Child Abuse Prevention and Treatment Act. Does this mean that parents who make nontreatment decisions for their severely handicapped newborn, believing those decisions to be in the child's best interests, are child abusers because of medical neglect? Should parents be entrusted to make these determinations for their child? If not, then whose responsibility is it?

Secondly, the Baby Doe laws represented the first attempt by the federal government to regulate the medical profession's right and felt obligation to make treatment decisions on behalf of patients. Doctors and parents together historically have made treatment decisions about newborns, and this legislation can be seen as an attempt to take that control away from them. Should that be the government's right or responsibility?

This case study begins by presenting an overview of the circumstances leading to the current Baby Doe regulations, and then describes them. The major focus of this research, however, is on the implementation of Baby Doe laws. Have Baby Doe policies been implemented as intended by their authors and stipulated in the statute? What has been the impact of the Baby Doe laws on medical and hospital practices? How have treatment decisions for vulnerable newborns, or medical procedures, changed as a result of the Baby Doe legislation?

METHODOLOGY

This implementation case study relies on data from three sources. The first is interview data examining the beliefs and practices of those with a stake in treatment decisions for handicapped newborns. The second is archival data—official documents commissioned by the legislature to assess whether the requirements of the Baby Doe legislation were applied. The third is published survey data describing beliefs and practices of physicians.

Sixteen interviews[8] were conducted during 1989 with individuals closely involved with the treatment and decision-making process—parents, neonatologists, directors of neonatal intensive care units (NICUs), neonatal nurses, hospital social workers, and child protective service agency directors—and with those who have an interest in how these decisions are made—medical ethicists, disability rights activists, and representatives of the prolife movement. These semistructured interviews ranged from one to two hours in length, were tape-recorded and transcribed verbatim, then analyzed using Ethnograph, a program for analysis of qualitative data.[9] Content analysis was conducted in areas such as infants' rights, parents' rights, ethics of nontreatment, NICU technology, and the need for the legislation.

All interviews were conducted in the greater Boston area, with all NICUs in the area represented. Boston-area hospitals provide "state of the art" medical care for vulnerable newborns; the hospitals hold world-class reputations, and many are affiliated with excellent teaching institutions. While it is unclear how applicable are these findings to other regions of the country, they likely represent practice at other metropolitan teaching hospitals.[10]

SETTING THE STAGE FOR BABY DOE

At least five major factors brought the Baby Doe issue to public awareness,[11] setting the stage for an event that called into question both the "private" prerogatives of parents, families, and the medical profession to decide the fate of disabled infants, and the rightful extent of "public" governmental involvement. First, advances in medical technology over the previous fifteen years made it possible to repair serious birth defects and to keep alive very small, ill, or premature infants.[12] Second, the disability-rights movement came into full swing in the 1970s with two major pieces of legislation protecting the rights of the disabled.[13] Third, the 1970s saw a push toward deinstitutionalization of the handicapped. Fourth, women were entering the workforce in increasing numbers, and were not as available to care for children at home as before, particularly handicapped children who required so much more care. Fifth, the prolife[14] movement was gaining momentum; President Reagan had campaigned on a right-to-life ticket and he owed a debt to those supporters.[15]

The medical profession has never taken lightly possible governmental intrusion into its well-guarded domain of deciding medical care for newborns. Considerable discussion about Baby Doe issues took place in medical journals in the 1970s. In 1971, a leading journal published selection criteria used at a prominent hospital for deciding which children with myelomeningocele (a birth defect in which part of the spinal column is exposed, producing paralysis) could benefit from treatment and be assured a "reasonable quality of life."[16] Two years later, two well-known neonatologists reported that, from 1970 to 1972, 14% of deaths in the NICU at Yale-New Haven Hospital were due to discontinuance or withdrawal of treatment.[17] Three justifications for nontreatment were provided: to prevent ongoing suffering while waiting for an inevitable death; to escape "wrongful life," or a poor quality of life; and to uphold the right of parents to make such decisions.

Subsequently, a survey of 457 pediatricians reported that nontreatment decisions were indeed being made.[18] Doctors surveyed believed they did not have to maintain the life of a severely handicapped newborn even though they had the technology to do so; that the right to make these decisions is held by parents first, and physicians second; and that decisions should be made on the basis of medical predictions about longevity and quality of life. In the same journal, another survey of 230 pediatricians revealed that 80% of the respondents thought that parents should have the right to withhold consent for corrective surgery for a handicapped child, and 45% believed that consent for lifesaving procedures could be withheld for "psychosocial reasons," such as the probable impact on the marriage, family, or other siblings.[19]

The percentage of all babies who fall into the Baby Doe category is actually quite small; about 2.5% of all births involve a significant physical defect, although few of these are life threatening. Most do not require immediate medical intervention.[20] Children born with syndromes or conditions that affect cognitive and/or physical capacities (e.g., Down Syndrome) are much rarer.[21] For example, spina bifida occurs in 1 to 2 of every 1000 births, and is fatal in 5%–20% of those affected.[22]

Far more prevalent than birth defects, low birth weight babies (those weighing less than 5 1/2 pounds) are considered one of the most serious health problems in the United States.[23] Although low birth weight babies make up 7% of all births in the United States, they account for 60% of deaths within the first month of life.[24] More disturbing is the fact that every year proportionally more children fall into the "very low birth weight" category, weighing less than 1500 grams, or 3 pounds, 5 ounces. While these babies comprise only 1.2% of all births, this is 40,000 infants, and they account for 50% of all deaths before age one.[25] Among survivors, 16%–18% will have "lasting neurological impairment," that is, cerebral palsy or mental retardation.[26] Neonatal and perinatal care for these infants is extremely costly—over $2000 per day—with babies typically staying three to four months or longer in a NICU.[27]

The explosion in medical technology to sustain premature and low birth weight infants raises questions about the effectiveness of various therapies to lower mortality rates.[28] Longitudinal studies conducted during the 1980s have yielded conflicting findings, with most showing increasing survival rates over the decade,[29] although not for infants weighing less than 750 grams.[30] At this time, the lowest limits of viability appear to be about twenty-four to twenty-five weeks gestation and 600–750 grams birth weight.[31]

RESPONSE TO THE BIRTH OF BABY DOE

It was within this context of medical, social, and political forces that the stage was set for controversy surrounding the birth of Baby Doe. The medical orders prohibiting Baby Doe from receiving food or water caused an uproar in the hospital. In a series of attempts to force treatment and nourishment for the baby, two physicians, joined by prolife activists and attorneys, succeeded in having a guardian ad litem (a legal advocate who acts on behalf of an incompetent person) appointed to represent Baby Doe. However, all attempts at legal intervention, including an investigation by the county child abuse prevention service agency, failed and the parents' right to decide treatment on behalf of their baby was upheld.[32] Finally, an appeal to the Indiana Supreme Court was turned down without explanation. This might have been the end of the Baby Doe case, except for the fact that in the courthouse, a group of reporters who were waiting for another case to be called heard the proceedings on behalf of Baby Doe, and immediately sent the details of this volatile story to newspapers across the country.

Governmental Response to the Baby Doe Case

Members of disability rights and prolife organizations responded to the news of Baby Doe by going straight to Washington. They pushed for an application of Section 504 of the Rehabilitation Act of 1973, which prohibits discrimination by agencies receiving federal funds on the basis of handicap.[33] Under pressure to develop regulations with more authority, the administration, under the direction of C. Everett Koop, the then U.S. Surgeon General, issued an Interim Final Rule on March 2, 1983, which went into effect immediately.[34] These regulations were to be posted conspicuously in every delivery room, maternity ward, pediatric unit, and nursery in every hospital that received federal funds. The warning read, "Discriminatory failure to feed and care for handicapped infants in this facility is prohibited by federal law." Included in the posting was a notice of a "Handicapped Infant Hotline," a number to call and speak confidentially about suspected food or medical treatment being denied a disabled infant. It was anticipated that nurses in particular would be eager to report physicians who were letting disabled newborns die.

Six weeks after the regulations were put into effect, a suit was brought on behalf of the American Academy of Pediatrics, the National Association of Children's Hospitals, and the Children's Hospital National Medical Center in Washington, D.C. The case was heard by Judge Gerhard Gesell, who struck down the Baby Doe regulations on a technicality, and termed them "hasty and ill-considered."[35] In so doing, Judge Gesell expressed his opposition to the regulations, pointing out that they failed to address both the issue of suffering during a futile treatment attempt, and the possibility that they would prolong death rather than life. In late June, 1983, revised regulations were released, specifically stating that treatment was not mandatory if the purpose were to prolong a death. Almost 17,000 comments were received by Health and Human Services about the regulations; 97% backed the administration, probably reflecting a well-organized campaign of the prolife movement.

Baby Jane Doe: A Test Case for the Administration

Before the revised regulations could be released, a test case emerged: "Baby

Jane Doe" was born on Long Island in October, 1983. Her medical status was much more grave than the Bloomington Baby Doe: she had many disabling conditions, only some of which could be repaired surgically. While there was disagreement about the baby's future quality of life, everyone agreed she would be severely mentally retarded and physically impaired. Her parents refused surgery, and court challenges ensued. A lower court ruled that the child must undergo surgery, but the New York Court of Appeals affirmed the parents' right to make a nontreatment decision on behalf of their child. In addition, the justices sharply attacked the regulations that allowed third parties to interfere with what they determined to be private decisions that parents should make.[36]

The Reagan administration made this a test case for the Baby Doe regulations, and filed an appeal with the U.S. Court of Appeals. Surgeon General Koop stated the administration's view: "We're not just fighting for this baby, but for the principle of this country that every life is individually and uniquely sacred."[37] But the Court's decision, which was ultimately heard and upheld in June, 1986, by the U.S. Supreme Court, struck down the justification for the regulations, stating that Section 504 of the Rehabilitation Act was meant to prevent discrimination in employment and housing, and was never intended to apply to handicapped newborns.[38]

During this litigation, the American Academy of Pediatrics had sought a compromise with prolife and disability rights advocates, who held that treatment decisions should be based on medical criteria alone, not on the child's potential. However, the agreement dissolved because it contained too much "quality of life" language to suit disability rights representatives. In addition, the Academy refused to put a separate child advocate on the proposed hearing committee, asserting that there were plenty of child advocates within the medical profession. Disability rights activists had long advocated for an outside, impartial advocate, and this dispute derailed the compromise.[39]

Baby Doe Legislation

With the regulations thrown out, Congress embarked on legislation aimed at protecting the interests of vulnerable newborns. The House bill redefined child abuse to include the withholding of life-sustaining treatment and nutrition from disabled infants, and it ordered that states must protect these rights of disabled children in order to qualify for federal child abuse grants. While the bill passed almost unanimously (396 to 4) in February, 1984, those numbers did not reflect the intense debate and division among members of Congress, largely along liberal and conservative lines. Rather, it appeared that it was impossible for most to vote against such a politically and socially delicate topic in an election year. The Senate bill, which passed by a unanimous vote in July, 1984, proposed a similar redefinition of child abuse, but it listed a few exceptions to treatment, such as in cases where treatment would only prolong dying.

A compromise bill, Public Law (P.L.) 98–457, was passed on October 9, 1984, as an amendment to the Child Abuse Prevention and Treatment Act: the Child Abuse Amendments of 1984. On April 25, 1988, it was reauthorized for three years as P.L. 100–294: the Child Abuse Prevention, Adoption, and Family Services Act of 1988, and again on May 28, 1992, as part of the Child Abuse, Domestic Violence, Adoption, and Family Services Act of 1992.

THE BABY DOE STATUTE: AMENDMENTS TO THE CHILD ABUSE PREVENTION AND TREATMENT ACT

P.L. 100–294, The Child Abuse Prevention, Adoption, and Family Services Act of 1988, Sec. 8(b)(10), states that, in order for a state to qualify for federal funds to help establish and maintain child abuse and neglect prevention and treatment, it must have in place a state law "for the purpose of responding to the reporting of medical neglect (including instances of withholding of medically indicated treatment from disabled infants with life-threatening conditions), procedures or programs, or both (within the state child protective services system), [with] . . . authority . . . to pursue any legal remedies . . . necessary."[40] There are three allowable exceptions to this mandate:

- A) the infant is chronically and irreversibly comatose
- B) the provision of such treatment would
    - 1) merely prolong dying
    - 2) not be effective in ameliorating or correcting all of the infant's life-threatening conditions
    - 3) otherwise be futile in terms of the survival of the infant
- C) the provision of such treatment would be virtually futile in terms of the survival of the infant and the treatment itself under such circumstances would be inhumane.[41]

Food, hydration, and medication may not be withheld under any circumstances. One of the most important stipulations of the new law is that it does not "permit life and death treatment decisions to be made on the basis of subjective opinions regarding the future 'quality of life' of a retarded or disabled person."[42]

The child protective service system was selected as the arena for Baby Doe investigations because, according to the rules and regulations, its goal is preservation of the family within the context of protecting the child.

> The legislation represented a careful balance between the need to establish effective protection of the rights of disabled infants and the need to avoid unreasonable governmental intervention into . . . parental responsibilities. The decision to provide or withhold medically indicated treatment is, except in highly unusual circumstances, . . . the parents' right and responsibility. The parents' role as decision maker must be respected and supported unless they choose a course of action inconsistent with applicable standards established by law."[43]

There was considerable debate about several aspects of the bill. The exceptions to treatment were the result of compromises among various interest groups, with many advocating for treatment under all circumstances. Conservative members of Congress, supported by the disability-rights and prolife movements, wanted mandatory Infant Care Review Committees (ICRCs), which would oversee nontreatment decisions. The medical profession lobbied heavily against this proposal, believing it an unnecessary and unprecedented supervision of medical practice by an outside board. In the compromise legislation ICRCs, although strongly recommended, were made voluntary. There was also much discussion about definitions of key terms, such as "imminent" to characterize proximity of time at which death might occur, and "merely prolong dying."[44]

IMPLEMENTATION OF THE BABY DOE LAWS AND REGULATIONS

How well have the Baby Doe laws and regulations been implemented? By June, 1988, a congressional report found that Baby Doe procedures were in place across the country.[45] However, there has been no significant increase in the number of referrals received by child protective service agencies after the regulations went into effect as compared to before.[46] This discrepancy raises several interesting questions: How widespread are these cases? What is actually happening when a Baby Doe decision has to be made? How much attention is being paid to the Baby Doe laws? Does current practice represent an implementation success or an implementation failure? What accounts for the shape of this policy's implementation? Five major findings emerged from this implementation analysis.

1. Almost all states accepted funds for Baby Doe implementation. State child protective service agencies implemented procedures for educating hospital staff, establishing liaisons with hospitals, and receiving Baby Doe case referrals for investigation as stipulated by the law.[47] On the surface, the Baby Doe legislation appears to be successfully implemented.

2. Nonetheless, not much has changed within NICUs since the Baby Doe amendments and regulations were issued. All practitioners interviewed reported that their treatment practices remained substantially as they were.

3. Furthermore, despite the Baby Doe legislation and awareness of these issues, nontreatment decisions are being made that may be in violation of the Baby Doe laws, and that certainly are not in keeping with the original intent of the legislation. In these cases treatment may or may not be beneficial in terms of saving the child's life, and if the child survives, it is likely to have significant disabilities. Within this "gray" area, "quality of life" decisions are being made that may discriminate against the handicapped.

4. Overtreatment appears to be a significant problem in NICUs. This is most likely due to fear of litigation, but other factors such as inaccurate knowl-

edge of the requirements of the Baby Doe laws, and the compelling nature of neonatal technology, are also contributors.

5.   There is evidence that, despite good intentions, it is virtually impossible to legislate the behavior of parents and medical personnel in situations where the stakes are so high.

Why has implementation of the Baby Doe regulations taken its particular course? One way to understand the process is to measure it along the following three indices of successful implementation—indices that take into account both top-down and bottom-up implementation pathways:[48] (1) Is there agreement on the definition of the problem and its tractability? (2) Does the statute have the ability to structure implementation? and (3) Do the key players in the implementation process share a consonant value base?[49]

Defining the Problem

Was there a problem? In the case of Baby Doe, it is unclear that there was a problem in the first place. When the Bloomington Baby Doe was born, President Reagan and Surgeon General Koop immediately seized the issue as if nontreatment were widespread. Yet there is evidence that the Baby Doe case was not representative at that time, and would be much less so today. Every doctor or nurse interviewed stated that the Baby Doe case would not have happened in their hospitals within the last ten to fifteen years. As one NICU director stated, "I think there are very few physicians who would have taken the stand that that [Bloomington] physician took. . . . In this institution that case would never have arisen. . . . Here, [the baby] would have had an operation."[50]

To be sure, nontreatment on the basis of a handicap had been widespread before the mid-1970s,[51] but had declined steadily during the next ten years. A NICU director reported, "I can't imagine what happened in Indianapolis [sic] happening in any hospital in Boston in 1983. In '73 absolutely, but in '83, no."[52] A survey conducted just after Baby Doe was born revealed a consensus among physicians and ethicists that a baby with identical circumstances to Baby Doe should receive corrective surgery.[53]

Government evidence also indicated that Baby Doe situations were rare. In March, 1983, after the interim final rule was released by Health and Human Services, the 24-hour "hotline" established to receive Baby Doe reports had 572 calls, only 16 of which appeared to be valid complaints. Of these, seven cases were determined to be worthy of investigation, and none reported a violation of the regulations.[54] Even the official government report on compliance with the new Baby Doe requirements issued in 1987 concluded,

It is not clear what impact the federal legislation and increased state responsibility have had on the incidence or handling of Baby Doe cases. There has been no significant increase in the volume of reports received after October, 1985, and most states feel that existing child abuse and neglect procedures would have been adequate to respond to Baby Doe reports.[55]

The extreme response to the Bloomington Baby Doe case, which defined the issue as a problem, grew out of a number of factors. One was the growing strength of the disability-rights movement and the public's increasing awareness of the rights of the disabled. Second, to some the Baby Doe case appeared to be a short step away from abortion. President Reagan may have seized this opportunity to prove that he intended to take a vigilant stance on prolife issues. As the head of the Massachusetts prolife organization stated, "The prolife movement, from the beginning, had said the rationale for abortion on demand would lead to infanticide and euthanasia. In our minds these are all linked."[56] Surgeon General Koop shared Reagan's prolife views, and had treated disabled children in his pediatric surgery practice. He did not intend to shy away from challenging the medical profession, if necessary, on this issue about which he had such strong opinions.

Tractability of the problem. With regard to the manageability of a legislative solution to the Baby Doe problem, we look first at the degree to which the target group is required to change and the difficulty it may have in changing.[57] In the case of Baby Doe, it was physicians and hospitals that needed changing, and there was tremendous resistance. Lawsuits initiated by medical organizations after the first notices were posted indicated that the profession did not take lightly the idea that the federal government would control their medical practice, which they believed to be sound and ethical. After the final Baby Doe regulations were issued, the American Academy of Pediatrics began to mobilize to influence the application and interpretation of the bill. In a May, 1985, letter to members, the Academy declared the final Baby Doe rules "acceptable;"[58] however, the letter also contained strong recommendations to begin immediate negotiations with child protective service agencies about procedures for handling Baby Doe referrals, procedures that would place medical personnel in an active role. In addition, the letter pointed out two portions of the regulations that were neither mandatory nor legally binding: the definition of "withholding of medically indicated treatment," and procedures regarding "how to form Infant Care Review Committees." The letter asserted, "Neither states nor hospitals are under any requirement to adhere to these guidelines. Any attempt to use these to justify objectionable provisions either in regulation or state laws should be fought."[59]

According to the director of a large NICU, "When the initial laws came up, I think it made everybody in the nursery very angry, that people thought we weren't doing the proper thing."[60] Another neonatologist told a colleague assigned to a "Baby Doe squad" (an investigatory team), "This is the wrong thing; you shouldn't be part of something that's doing this to physicians."[61] National survey data supported this local interview data. A 1988 national survey found that neonatologists believed the current federal regulations were a mistake; 81% disagreed with the statement that the Baby Doe regulations would result in improved care for all infants, and over 75% disagreed with the statement that the regulations were needed to protect the rights of the handicapped.[62]

Medical social workers were also cautious about the need for the statute. In a letter from the National Association of Perinatal Social Workers to the National Center on Child Abuse and Neglect, a plea was issued for allowing hospital staff, particularly physicians, "to work effectively, thoughtfully, cooperatively, and non-defensively."[63] Without a perceived need for the legislation, and being resistant to the intrusion, physicians, nurses, and other professionals, the "street-level bureaucrats" of Baby Doe, were unlikely to be vigilant about enforcing it.

Finally, the highly specialized technology surrounding the treatment of vulnerable newborns makes it very difficult, if not impossible, to rely on legislated procedures.[64] Clinicians argued that the complexity of the issues requires decisions by those who are best able to understand both the limitations and expansiveness of this technology.[65]

Ability of the Statute to Structure Implementation

Several key elements of successful implementation pertain to the ability of the statute to structure its own implementation. These include the specificity of statute language, the appropriate choice and expertise of implementing actors and agencies, and the funding made available.[66] The Baby Doe legislation was found wanting here as well.

Statute language. Was the statute language specific in stating goals and objectives of the legislation? Despite much effort to specify and clearly define all relevant terms during the course of the statute's development, the final version of the laws and regulations still contained many terms and definitions that were open to interpretation, leaving wording that was loose and ambiguous.

Most of the terms finally agreed upon were the result of rancorous discussions and subsequent compromises among the authors, disability-rights advocates, prolife representatives, and the medical profession. The very fact that what was settled on was something most individuals and groups accepted meant that statute language was left somewhat ambiguous. This left room for each group to read into the language what it believed, or wanted, to be true. The very basis of Baby Doe treatment decisions, "reasonable medical judgment," assured a place for interpretation in making nontreatment choices.

There were other subjective terms in the Baby Doe regulations. For example, the phrase "merely prolong dying" was meant to refer to "situations where death is imminent,"[67] but a definition of "imminent" was not provided. Those interviewed disagreed as to what "merely prolong dying" and "imminent" meant. A representative of Massachusetts Citizens for Life said, "For most prolifers, the way we understand [imminent] . . . is that the process of death is already set in, not that [the child] . . . will die within a year."[68] A NICU director stated, "When I say a terminal condition, I don't necessarily mean tomorrow. They may live for six months or eight months, but they don't survive. . . . If a child has one of those lethal chromosomal abnormalities that results uniformly in death, like Trisomy 18, Trisomy 13, then treatment is prolonging death."[69] To a NICU nurse, a lethal condition "must be a newborn death, within the first month,"[70] whereas an official from the World Institute on Disability said, "To me, imminent means within the next few months."[71] These distinctions may have been trivial to some, but to others they were critical to ethical decision making.

There was also disagreement among those interviewed, among framers of the statute, and among physicians surveyed, as to what was meant by "inhumane treatment." There was even controversy about whether appropriate nutrition, hydration, and medication (mandated by the Baby Doe laws) could be defined as a form of medical treatment if delivered artificially (e.g., intravenously) and could therefore be withheld under certain circumstances.[72]

The ambiguous wording of the Baby Doe statute meant that such decisions were left to individuals closest to the specific cases. In those cases, those who implemented the law were, in a real sense, writing it.

Implementing actors and agencies: Street-level bureaucrats. Did the statute designate appropriate and effective agencies and individuals for overseeing the implementation of the laws and regulations? Physicians and NICU nurses were the individuals directly responsible for implementing Baby Doe legislation. Yet few medical personnel interviewed knew the specific requirements of the laws, particularly the three conditions for which nontreatment was allowed. This local finding was supported by a later national survey of neonatologists.[73] How could medical personnel implement laws about which they were uninformed?

There was disagreement as to the best public agency for implementing Baby Doe laws. The statute designated child protective service agencies as responsible for establishing procedures to assure prompt notification of suspected Baby Doe cases, communicate efficiently with hospitals, access medical files, and pursue legal remedies for suspected violations. The government's 1987 *Survey of State Baby Doe Programs*[74] reported that most child protective service agencies had accomplished these objectives. However, while 55% of responding states believed that these agencies were the proper arena to handle Baby Doe cases, 22% stated that they were not, because of the medical and ethical issues involved. An ethics committee member commented: "These problems . . . do not belong in child protective services. What is needed is increased sharing of information . . . , not regulation by child protective services. I find it philosophically, emotionally, and professionally repugnant to involve child protective services in the decision-making process."[75] A supervisor in a child protective service agency stated that the Baby Doe legislation "seemed like an unnecessary piece of business to us. . . . It seemed like we had a way to do this, and that if the questions were more technically medical, it was a Department of Public Health and child health issue."[76] Even though a disability-rights representative called nontreatment "the most extreme form of child abuse," she acknowledged, "I don't know what ability child protective service [has] to make decisions in a life and death issue, so bringing them in on a decision-making level [is not] appropriate."[77]

One thing is certain: There were very few referrals of Baby Doe cases nation-wide. Twenty-two Baby Doe reports were received from fifteen states before October, 1985, and nineteen reports in thirteen states during the next five years; by 1989, twenty-four states had never received a Baby Doe report, including Massachu-setts.[78] There are three factors that may explain these numbers: First, child protective service agencies were already overwhelmed with the burgeoning caseload of child abuse reports; they could not readily absorb the additional burden of Baby Doe cases. A neonatologist reported, "They're [child protective service agencies] so over-whelmed, you just don't get the services, the response, so that's not someone you'd go to on this issue."[79] Second, the level of medical expertise needed to understand many Baby Doe issues was not already present within the agencies. Third, there was a basic resistance by those working with parents of vulnerable newborns to call in a child abuse agency for an issue as sensitive as Baby Doe. A letter from the National Association of Perinatal Social Workers stated that "families almost invariably become alarmed, defensive, and anxious when there is even a hint that their situation might be dealt with by Child Protective Service."[80]

However, many disability-rights and prolife leaders believed that child protec-tive service agencies were the proper arena. And some physicians and hospitals also saw them as acceptable implementing agencies because they were the least interven-tionist of possible "watchdog" agencies. A medical social worker agreed, stating, "they're investigatory and facilitating; it's either Department of Social Services or the courts."[81] A NICU director said, "I suppose [Child Protective Service] is as good as any. I mean, I'm not very enamored of the Board of Registration in Medicine, so I'm not sure I'd ask them to do it."[82]

Funding. Requirements of the Baby Doe legislation were not binding upon states, but were tied to funding. By giving up federal child abuse funding, states could opt out of the Baby Doe rules. One informant stated that the Massachusetts Department of Social Services considered foregoing federal funds to avoid having to implement Baby Doe.[83] Federal contributions to child-abuse agencies were relatively insignificant given the size of some states' budgets,[84] so if the law proved to be too cumbersome, there was not much incentive to comply.

However, almost all jurisdictions[85] initially chose to participate. During fiscal year (FY) 1985, fifty-four of fifty-seven jurisdictions applied for funds to establish and implement the procedures and programs relating to the Baby Doe amendments, and a total of $2.7 million was awarded. In addition, most states applied for a one-time discretionary grant of $500,000 to support information and education programs for child protective service workers and medical personnel.[86]

A Consonant Value Base for the Policy?

Successful implementation is more likely when key players share the values inherent to the policy, that is, when the policy does not come into conflict with deeply held personal, cultural, or religious beliefs.[87] With regard to Baby Doe, there was no consonant value base for the policy. Issues such as Baby Doe lie at the center of belief systems about the rights of disabled individuals, parents, newborns, and doctors. Thus, many informants agreed with the statement of one: "You can't legislate these kinds of issues. That's the bottom line."[88]

A discussion of values relevant to Baby Doe takes place in three arenas. The first regards the right of parents to make important decisions about their children; a related issue is whether family needs should be weighed against the vulnerable newborn's rights. The second concerns whether the disabled are valued members of society, and whether the disabled and newborns have the same rights as other members. The third is the most volatile: whether and to what extent quality of life should be considered when making treatment decisions, and whether one person should, in fact, make such determinations for another.

Parents' rights and the role of the child in the family. Parents are held legally, socially, and morally responsible for their children's welfare, and normally give permission for their medical care.[89] Even before Baby Doe became a well-known term, nontreatment decisions were regularly being made for vulnerable newborns in newborn intensive care units.[90] Typically, these decisions were made by parents and physicians together, although usually with the awareness (and tacit approval) of others surrounding the baby—nurses, clergy, and social workers. Although child protective service agencies were occasionally called in to obtain a court order for treatment against parents' wishes, those occasions were rare.[91] In a review of the history of parent-child relationships, Silverman pointed out that the notion that all children should be rescued is a relatively recent one.[92]

Nationwide surveys of professionals close to the Baby Doe implementation process (pediatricians, pediatric surgeons, NICU nurses, and neonatologists) conducted before, during, and after passage of the legislation, revealed a strong bias that parents should have the right, and in fact are obligated, to make Baby Doe decisions.[93] Interviews with hospital personnel supported the belief that parents' wishes should be followed. As one informant, a neonatologist, described these decisions, "I now think we're at a time where we can still exercise, with the family's agreement . . . what seems appropriate for that particular baby. Always with the family's consent."[94] When informants were asked who should make nontreatment decisions in cases where it was determined that policies would allow a nontreatment choice, all those interviewed said medical personnel and parents together should decide; when asked who should have the ultimate decision, everyone, with the exception of a representative of a disability-rights agency, said "parents." A neonatal nurse-clinician described practice in her NICU: "I think parents have to make those judgments for themselves—all we can do is tell them what the choices are, and try not to put any favor on either one of the decisions."[95] And a medical ethicist, who is also a pediatrician, indicated that, while the standard for making a decision is the best interests of the infant, parents "should be making the decision . . . . [T]he burden of proof is on us as to why they should be disqualified as the surrogates, and a reason would be that they're clearly (underline that and put it in quotes) not speaking in the interest of the infant."[96]

Even those connected with the disability-rights movement believed that parents should have a strong, but not ultimate, voice in the decision-making process, but pointed out their need for professional consultation. One member said, "Parents really need support [and] . . . appropriate information, and should be able to talk to parents of children with those disabilities. Parents don't have a right to take away their child's life because they're ignorant."[97] The parent of a severely disabled child thought parents should have the "bottom line" decision-making power, but qualified that by saying, "I want to say the parents, but I'm not sure they always get the best support."[98]

To be sure, the role that physicians play is a powerful one. After all, they convey to parents much of the information about their child's medical condition, including its prognosis. The U.S. Civil Rights Commission concluded that these factors put physicians, rather than parents, in charge of such decisions.[99]

It was also the case that, in some circumstances, the legislation took considerable control away from parents, sometimes with grave consequences. One parent reported that her severely brain-damaged baby was further victimized by the Baby Doe laws; asphyxiated at birth and with reportedly less than 10% brain function, he was supported on a respirator and would have been kept alive that way indefinitely despite her wishes to remove life support, but the baby died within a week.[100] A NICU nurse reported a similar case: "We had a baby who was here for five days and . . . he was just at a point where we couldn't tell if he was going to die. . . . And on the fifth day his dad came over and said, 'I've had enough; take him off the respirator.' And we . . . had to get a court order to take custody of the baby. And that was the only time we've been on the opposite side from the parents—it felt awful."[101] Other parents reported being "steamrolled" by physicians when they requested that doctors stop providing "overzealous" care to their extremely premature infants.[102] Though the consequences could be catastrophic, the cases just described were probably relatively uncommon. Parents appeared to have considerable control in many circumstances. A parent informant said that she and her husband were told about potential disabilities in their very premature daughter and were told by the doctors, "You need to decide what to do."[103]

There is an interesting dilemma presented by the issue of parents' rights and abilities to make treatment or nontreatment decisions: Are parents, as those people closest to the situation, in the best place to make this decision, or are they in the worst position for the same reason? Is government, because it is not personally involved, a better arbiter of these decisions? This debate is sometimes referred to as one between "close-up" and "distant" ethics, as set forth by Raymond Duff, a well-known neonatologist who has written extensively on Baby Doe issues.[104] He believes decisions should be made by parents because "[they have] the strongest bonds of affection known to mankind. If we cannot trust these persons to do justice here, can anyone be trusted?"[105] But others worry that parents will make decisions for reasons other than the best interests of the child, such as the child's impact on the rest of the family, or future costs of medical care. Of those interviewed, the majority stated that costs of medical care and education should not be factors in making treatment decisions; however, some parents may find it difficult to overlook these factors.[106]

There is contradictory research evidence on the extent to which disabled children present a hardship to their family members. The majority of studies show adverse effects on parents, such as extreme stress, exhaustion, and financial problems.[107] At-home care costs for many of these children are staggering, and much of them are not covered by insurance.[108] Some studies show increased marital problems and divorce in families with handicapped children,[109] while others do not.[110] Some research finds that siblings of disabled children are at risk for adjustment problems themselves,[111] but other studies show no ill effects.[112] While more research is needed in this area, most parents cannot help but take those factors into account.[113] A NICU director stated the dilemma:

> Families should not be burdened by the decisions that we make for their children, and on the other hand, children should not be burdened by the decision that their family makes because of their family's own self-interest. I don't know the answer to that. We may say the child will destroy the family and then who have we helped? I don't know that one. The President's Commission says you can't look at the family, that it's the best interests of the child. That's pretty glib, especially if you destroy the family in the process, the best interests of that child will probably suffer as well.[114]

On the other hand, some would argue, if the child is allowed to die, her or his best interests are surely not served.

Rights of the disabled and quality of life: Deciding the "best interests" of the disabled infant. Baby Doe decisions often hinge on whether life is seen as intrinsically valuable, or valuable only if it holds some level of quality. As one informant framed it, "We are a . . . deeply divided society over whether it's sanctity of every human life, or some standard, some quality of life that has to be achieved by an individual member of the human race before you can grant them human status."[115] How can these determinations be made? Who should make them?

There is a well-established tradition of deciding medical care based upon the "best interests" of the patient; in Baby Doe cases, determining those best interests is usually difficult. Historically, best interests often included consideration of the child's long-term life with a disability, that is, the quality of life, and the pain and suffering that might be encountered along the way. Nontreatment decisions based upon quality of life judgments were part of medical practice before Baby Doe[116] and have been since.[117] The birth of Baby Doe stimulated arguments both in favor of quality of life decisions,[118] and opposed to it.[119]

The Baby Doe laws explicitly prohibited considering quality of life in making Baby Doe decisions. They did, however, allow nontreatment if it was "virtually futile" and "inhumane," and to many, consideration of these factors forced a quality of life discussion. While the regulations stated that "inhumane" cannot mean a life with a disability—the treatment *itself* must be inhumane, not the future life[120]—the laws were inconsistent. First, the rule permitted nontreatment of infants who were irreversibly comatose but not necessarily dying, indicating that quality of life could be a consideration. Second, nontreatment decisions could be made if the treatment would only prolong dying, but, according to a strict vitalist position, to prolong dying also prolongs life.[121]

A prolife representative stated, "Even if you're dealing with someone who is no longer functioning as a conscious, rational member of the human race, you are still dealing with a living member of the human race. . . . You never deprive a human being of life for social, economic, or personal reasons. The right to life is an intrinsic, inalienable right."[122] The Fourteenth Amendment to the U.S. Constitution ("no state shall deny the equal protection of the law") is often given as the basis of treating disabled newborns under standards of nondisability.[123]

Disability rights members were suspicious that unjustifiable nontreatment decisions were being made using unlawful quality of life criteria. They believed the child deserved and needed a separate advocate on decision-review boards. While physicians, nurses, social workers, or ethicists were often seen as filling that role, each may, in fact, have had his or her own agenda to promote. A representative from a disability-rights organization believed Baby Doe decisions should be made by a committee that "clearly has to have appropriate representation of people who feel very strongly about the rights of the disabled" and further stated that "it has to be an equal balance on the committee. It can't be one advocate against everyone else."[124]

When current NICU practices were examined for this case study, there was evidence of nontreatment decisions being made based on quality of life considerations, in violation of Baby Doe policy.[125] Because of the gray area within the law and the imprecise wording, it was hard to pinpoint views and practices on this issue. A NICU director stated: "Now, you'll get a lot of argument from people [about] what [futile] means—futile to maintain life or futile [to maintain] a reasonable quality of life, and it's not clear how quality of life fits in there."[126] A nurse-manager of a NICU said, "The Baby Doe regulations are somewhat contradictory in my opinion because they say quality of life should not be a determining factor, but it always plays a part in the decision."[127] A NICU nurse described a case where a quality of life decision was made about a baby who was born with full cognitive abilities but had no motor control from the neck down. He was resuscitated at birth and "when they had the diagnosis, the team felt like the family had two options—they could remove life support at this time, or they could go on to place the baby in some kind of nursing home so he could be on a ventilator. . . . And actually, [the parents] opted to discontinue life support."[128]

Similar controversy surrounds the concept of "pain and suffering," and its relationship to "quality of life." The prolife movement supported the Baby Doe regulations that stated that "inhumane treatment," or "pain and suffering" did not refer to living a life of any particular kind, but referred to the organic pain of the treatment, or the physical sensations, that were experienced during treatment.[129] According to a representative from the prolife movement, "The idea that life is a burden and that you're better off dead is anathema to our point of view."[130] But suffering was a real concern to those treating babies, particularly nurses on the front line. One NICU nurse said, "Suffering we equate with the best interests of the child—it's a very important factor for us. . . . It's also suffering of the family . . . [and] there is the family's interpretation of suffering for their child."[131]

Those interviewed for this study who spoke to the issues of quality of life and pain and suffering did so out of deep concern for what they believed to be the current and potential life of a vulnerable newborn. However, most neonatologists do not work directly in follow-up programs, and their understanding of the quality of life for disabled children may not have reflected what current technology and treatment practices could offer. Even if treating physicians were aware of such opportunities, it appears inevitable that there will be differences of opinion about the value of a life with a disability, and discrimination against the disabled may occur. Most people have some standard below which they consider the quality of life to be so poor that they would not want it lived that way. Yet, as advocates for the disabled pointed out, there are very few severely handicapped individuals who would rather be dead. A disability-rights activist, convinced that discrimination against the disabled took place in NICUs, stated: "The cold bottom line is that society is the way it is because nondisabled people have . . . not valued the participation of disabled people appropriately."[132]

IMPACT OF THE BABY DOE LEGISLATION

Despite the apparent failure of the Baby Doe laws to alter the treatment of newborns as the president, surgeon general, and legislators had hoped, the legislation had some impact on medical practice in NICUs. First, it caused hospitals to be more careful, to document what they do, to establish procedures where there had been none, and to document procedures that had been unwritten. When asked why no Baby Doe case had been referred to the Massachusetts child protective services agency receiving them since the legislation was passed, a supervisor for the agency responded:

I have a couple of very clear opinions about that. One, I think hospitals hopped to it and got their Infant Care Review Committees in place in anticipation. . . . It was a forum for people to learn and share in a kind of open way, some of those issues that [were] not otherwise happening in the hospital, so I think that was very healthy . . . . [It also] escalated the medical legal issues, it escalated the teaching issues for medical students, and hospitals looked at their own work more carefully."[133]

Although not required by the law, many hospitals established the recommended Infant Care Review Committees, or scrutinized the composition and operating procedures of their existing ethics committees to make sure they were responsive to requirements of the Baby Doe legislation.

Another, perhaps unfortunate, impact was overtreatment. Teaching hospitals had long been accused of overtreating, and there is evidence that the Baby Doe legislation caused medical personnel to be even more cautious about withdrawing life support. Fear of litigation was the primary motivator, but the uproar that accompanied the birth of the Bloomington Baby Doe and subsequent notices by Surgeon General Koop and President Reagan had the effect of making medical personnel believe it was the law to treat all babies under all circumstances. A national survey of neonatologists conducted in 1986 found that there was considerable uncertainty as to the requirements of the law, which they believed encouraged or required overtreatment;[134] this view was still held by many physicians five years later.[135]

Interview data supported this concern about overtreatment. A Department of Social Services official stated that there hadn't been any Baby Doe referrals in Massachusetts because, "in big urban teaching hospitals . . . we overtreat. I use that word thoughtfully, because I think that the atmosphere of concern about malpractice, the Baby Doe business, and just the general technically aggressive way medicine is practiced currently leads to children being treated and the discussion about whether to withhold treatment doesn't ever happen."[136] In the federal report on effectiveness of Infant Care Review Committees under the Baby Doe program, many comments were made about the problem of overtreatment, such as: "Fear of malpractice lawsuits has caused many hospitals and physicians to continue treatment for infants who have virtually no chance for survival. The treatment is often painful and only prolongs the infant's dying."[137] Parents often do not object to overtreatment, taking it as a sign that physicians are hopeful about their baby's prognosis.

A third impact of the Baby Doe legislation was increased awareness of the rights of the disabled. If implemented as intended and written, the Baby Doe legislation can be seen as another step toward increasing the public's awareness of the rightful place within society for those who are born with disabilities.

Finally, the Baby Doe legislation mobilized the resources of many groups in opposition to, or in support of, the statute. Medical, social work, disability-rights, and prolife organizations all took active roles in responding to the legislation, and continue to have an interest in it. This heightened the struggle between the public's perceived rights and responsibilities to protect vulnerable newborns, the rights and responsibilities of parents to make life and death decisions for their children, the rights and responsibilities of government to regulate the medical industry, and the rights and responsibilities of that industry to insist on practices in accord with its own professional standards.

SUMMARY AND CONCLUSIONS

What have we learned about implementation from the Baby Doe case? Legislation such as Baby Doe has many intended as well as unintended consequences. Politically, the legislation may have been a success even before it was enacted. For President Reagan, the outcome was quite positive. He was able to seize the opportunity of Baby Doe's birth to demonstrate a strong prolife stance. Although abortion was very controversial, virtually everyone could agree about responding to the needs of a vulnerable newborn. Liberal and conservative members of Congress compromised amid vitriolic debate to protect the rights of those perceived as totally helpless victims of discrimination, which won them constituent support in an election year. C. Everett Koop had the opportunity to act as a strong surgeon general who was not afraid to challenge the well-entrenched medical profession, and to champion a cause which was a political as well as a private crusade. In light of all this, what came later—implementation—may be less relevant.

In one sense, the Baby Doe legislation was effectively implemented as written. Following its enactment, almost all states applied for Baby Doe funds, and their child protective service agencies established programs to respond to Baby Doe cases. Yet almost no referrals were made to those agencies, and hospital practices appeared not to have been substantially altered since the legislation was passed. Thus, while implementation procedures were clearly in place, there was an apparent lack of impact. Several reasons account for this.

Despite massive publicity, there were, in fact, many fewer true "Babies Doe" than the initial publicity suggested, so there was less of a problem to fix than many had thought. Most hospital practitioners did not see the need for the legislation. Many NICUs already had procedures for deciding the care of vulnerable newborns—procedures the medical community believed to be ethical and medically sound—and thus they resisted government's intrusion. They succeeded in altering the laws and regulations to allow reasonable medical judgment to continue to govern decision making about such infants, and lobbied for language that was subject to interpretation. Rapidly changing technology made it imperative that medical personnel inform such decisions.

The Baby Doe legislation also did not have a substantial impact on medical practice because it went against deeply held beliefs that parents are in the best place to make "good faith" decisions about their children. There was strong resistance to interfering with the perceived right of parents to do so.

The American public is deeply divided over the meaning of life, the definition of personhood, and the role of disabled members of our society. These differences become salient when Baby Doe decisions have to be made. Despite specific wording in the legislation prohibiting quality of life decisions, many practitioners believed that quality of life is a valid and important consideration when making nontreatment decisions in the "best interests" of an infant, and that leading a life with a severe disability may be worse than no life at all. This view was vehemently rejected by the disabled and prolife communities. A disabled individual stated, "I feel very strongly that there are such biases within the medical profession about providing medical intervention for people that they conceive as having a life that is not qualitative."[138]

The nursing director of a leading NICU summed up these issues as follows:

> I question the intent [of the legislation]. You know, as a health care professional, I'm always suspicious of federal intervention—the attempt to regulate and label a situation that is unique in every instance. So I'm not quite certain that those legislators who wrote the legislation, the rules, had a real sense of the expansiveness of technology, the desires of families, and the quality of life issues that surround these babies.[139]

These clashes of ideology, then, perhaps presented the greatest barriers to implementation of the Baby Doe legislation as it was proposed. It was here that the rights and responsibilities of various groups—both public and private—came into conflict. Thus it may be impossible, despite good intentions, to legislate issues such as Baby Doe, which our society still seems to consider essentially private and which delve into the core of ethical beliefs.

APPENDIX: LIST OF INTERVIEWS

Supervisor, Child Protective Service Agency, Boston, MA, February, 1989.
Administrator, Child Protective Service Agency, Boston, MA, February, 1989.
Director, Neonatal Intensive Care Units, Boston, MA, February, 1989.
Hospital Social Work Director, Boston, MA, February, 1989.
Nurse Manager, Neonatal Intensive Care Unit, Boston, MA, March, 1989.
Director, Neonatal Intensive Care Unit, Boston, MA, March, 1989.
Parent of two handicapped children who were in Neonatal Intensive Care Units, Boston, MA, March, 1989.
Director, Disability advocacy organization, Boston, MA, March, 1989.
Medical ethicist, Boston, MA, March, 1989.
Researcher and writer on disability issues and parent of a child with a disability, Boston, MA, April, 1989.
Director, advocacy organization for parents of children with disabilities and hospitalized children, Boston, MA, June, 1989.
Neonatologist, Boston, MA, June, 1989.
Director, Neonatal Intensive Care Unit, Boston, MA, June, 1989.
Medical ethicist and professor of medical ethics, Boston, MA, June, 1989.
Nurse-clinician, Neonatal Intensive Care Unit, Boston, MA, June, 1989.
Administrator, state prolife organization, Boston, MA, July, 1989.

NOTES

1.   R. Gustaitis & E.W.D. Young (1986). *A time to be born, a time to die: Conflicts and ethics in an intensive care nursery.* Reading, MA: Addison-Wesley; J. Lyon (1985). *Playing God in the nursery.* New York: W.W. Norton; R. F. Weir (1984). *Selective nontreatment of handicapped newborns: Moral dilemmas in neonatal medicine.* New York: Oxford University Press.

2.   Infant Doe v. Bloomington Hospital, 104 S. Ct. 394 (1983).

3.   Much of the factual information about the Bloomington Baby Doe case is based upon information reported in *Playing God in the Nursery*, by Jeff Lyon (1985). Lyon writes extensively about medical issues, and personally compiled the details of the case from interviews conducted between June, 1983 and February, 1984 with key figures in the case. Those interviewed included physicians, hospital administrators, prosecutors, judges, and others with intimate first-hand knowledge of the case and circumstances surrounding it.

4.   Lyon (1985), *Playing God in the nursery.*

5.   J. Bopp, Jr. & T. J. Balch (1985). The child abuse amendments of 1984 and their implementing regulations: A summary. *Issues in Law and Medicine, 1*(2), 91–130.

6.   Ind. Cir. Ct. (April 12, 1982).

7.   The first Baby Doe legislation, P.L. 98–457, was reauthorized in 1988 as P.L. 100–294, and again in 1992 as P.L. 102–295. The current Baby Doe legislation is contained in the "Medical Neglect" section of the Child Abuse Prevention and Treatment Act, P.L. 102–295, passed on May 28, 1992.

8.   See Appendix: List of Interviews.

9.   Qualis Research Associates (1988). *The Ethnograph, 2.0: A software package for the analysis of qualitative data.* Littleton, CO: Author.

10.   Key informants were offered anonymity. A link-file system, which assigns numbers to each interview, was developed for that purpose. These interviews are reported by number and date. Interview #12, June, 1989; Interview #14, June, 1989.

11.   C. H. Weiss (1988). Ideology, interests, and information: The basis of policy positions. In D. Callahan and B. Jennings (Eds.), *Ethics, the social sciences, and policy analysis.* New York: Plenum Press; E. E. Maccoby, A. J. Kahn, & B. A. Everett (January, 1983). The role of psychological research in the formation of policies affecting children. *American Psychologist, 38*(1), 80–84; C. D. Hayes (Ed.) (1982). *Making policies for children: A study of the federal process.* Washington, D.C.: National Academy Press.

12.   J. B. Grogaard, D. P. Lindstrom, R. A. Parker, B. Culley, & M. T. Stahlman (1990). Increased survival rate in very low birth weight infants (1500 grams or less): No association with increased incidence of handicaps. *Journal of Pediatrics, 117*, 139–146; W. H. Kitchen, G. W. Ford, L. W. Doyle, A. L. Rickards, & E. A. Kelly (1990). Health and hospital readmissions of very-low-birth-weight and normal-birth-weight children. *American Journal of Diseases of Children, 114*, 213–218; Weir (1984), *Selective nontreatment of handicapped newborns.*

13.   Section 504 of the Rehabilitation Act of 1973; P.L. 94–142, The Education for All Handicapped Children Act.

14.   In most cases, the term "prolife" is used here, rather than "right-to-life" or "anti-abortion," as that is the term used by most informants for this chapter. Baby Doe issues are one of three arenas targeted for education and action by Massachusetts Citizens for Life, the prolife organization interviewed here.

15. Interview #9, March, 1989.

16. J. Lorber (1971). Results of treatment of myelomeningocele. *Developmental Medicine and Child Neurology, 13*, 279–303.

17. R. S. Duff & G. M. Campbell (1973). Moral and ethical dilemmas in the special-care nursery. *The New England Journal of Medicine, 289*, 890–894.

18. M. D. Shaw, J. G. Randolph, & B. Manard (1977). Ethical issues in pediatric surgery: A national survey of pediatricians and pediatric surgeons. *Pediatrics, 60*(4), 588–599.

19. I. D. Todres, D. Krane, M. C. Howell, & D. C. Shannon (1977). Pediatricians' attitudes affecting decision-making in defective newborns. *Pediatrics, 60*(2), 197–201.

20. *Federal Register, 50*(72) (April 15, 1985), Rules and Regulations, 14886.

21. *Federal Register, 50*(72) (April 15, 1985), Rules and Regulations, 14886.

22. Report to Congress: Infant mortality (April, 1989). National Institutes of Health: National Institute of Child Health and Human Development.

23. M. C. McCormick, J. C. Bernbaum, J. M. Eisenberg, S. L. Kustra, & E. Finnegan (1991). Costs incurred by parents of very low birth weight infants after the initial neonatal hospitalization. *Pediatrics, 88*(3), 533–541; P. J. McGauhey, B. Starfield, C. Alexander, & M. E. Ensminger (1991). Social environment and vulnerability of low birth weight children: A social-epidemiological perspective. *Pediatrics, 88*(5), 943–951.

24. Report to Congress: Infant mortality (April, 1989).

25. F. H. Jacobs & M. W. Davies (1991). Rhetoric or reality? Child and family policy in the United States. *Social Policy Report, 5*(4), 1–25. Society for Research in Child Development; Report to Congress: Infant mortality (April, 1989).

26. J. E. Brody (October 1, 1991). A quality of life determined by a baby's size. *New York Times*, 1.

27. *New York Times* (February 19, 1989), 1; *New York Times* (September 29, 1991), 1.

28. J. D. Lantos, S. H. Miles, M. D. Silverstein, & C. B. Stocking (1988). Survival after cardiopulmonary resuscitation in babies of very low birth weight: Is CPR futile therapy? *New England Journal of Medicine, 318*(2), 91–95; M. Lewis & M. Bendersky (1989). Cognitive and motor differences among low birth weight infants: Impact of intraventricular hemmorrhage, medical risk, and social class. *Pediatrics, 83*(2), 187–192.

29. E. L. Hoffman & F. C. Bennett (1990). Birth weight less than 800 grams: Changing outcomes and influences of gender and gestation number. *Pediatrics, 86*(1), 27–34; S. Saigal, P. Rosenbaum, B. Hattersley, & R. Milner (1989). Decreased disability rate among 3-year-old survivors weighing 501 to 1000 grams at birth and born to residents of a geographically defined region from 1981 to 1984 compared with 1977 to 1980. *Journal of Pediatrics, 114*(5), 839–846.

30. G. P. Aylward, S. I. Pfeiffer, A. Wright, & S. J. Verhulst (1989). Outcome studies of low birth weight infants published in the last decade: A metaanalysis. *Journal of Pediatrics, 115*(4), 515–520; Grogaard et al. (1990), Increased survival rate in very low birth weight infants (1500 grams or less); M. Hack & A. A. Fanaroff (1989). Outcomes of extremely-low-birth-weight infants between 1982 and 1988. *New England Journal of Medicine, 321*(4), 1642–1647.

31. Because many of these longitudinal studies had high attrition rates (e.g., 55% in Grogaard et al. [1990]), and because they compare different populations, different time periods, and break down categories of extreme, very, and low birth weight differently, any conclusions drawn from these data must be considered cautiously. In addition, since neonatal technology changes so rapidly, and one cannot know the actual development of such babies for at least 2–3 years, the outcome knowledge base is always outdated by technological

innovation by several years.

32. Lyon (1985), *Playing God in the nursery*; Ind. Cir. Ct. (April 12, 1982).

33. Lyon (1985), *Playing God in the nursery.*

34. *Federal Register, 48*(123) (March 7, 1983), 9630–9632.

35. American Academy of Pediatrics v. Heckler, No. 83-0774, U.S. District Court, Washington, D.C. (April 14, 1983).

36. Weber v. Stony Brook Hospital, 467 NYS 2d 685 (1983); Weber v. Stony Brook Hospital, 465 NE 2d 1186 (1983); U.S. v. University Hospital of N.Y. at Stony Brook (1983).

37. Koop, on CBS's "Face the Nation" (November 6, 1983).

38. U.S. v. University Hospital at Stony Brook, U.S. Court of Appeals for the Second Circuit, 83–6343 (1984).

39. Lyon (1985), *Playing God in the nursery.*

40. P.L. 100-294: Child Abuse Prevention, Adoption, and Family Services Act of 1988 (April 25, 1988). 102 Stat. 102–126.

41. P.L. 100-294: Child Abuse Prevention, Adoption, and Family Services Act of 1988 (April 25, 1988). 102 Stat. 102–126.

42. *Federal Register, 50*(72) (April 15, 1985), Rules and Regulations, 14879.

43. *Federal Register, 50*(72) (April 15, 1985), Rules and Regulations, 14880.

44. *Federal Register, 50*(72) (April 15, 1985), Rules and Regulations, 14880, 14889-91.

45. Report to Congress: Implementation of Child Abuse Amendments of 1984 relating to disabled infants with life-threatening conditions (Section 4(b)(2)(K) of P.L. 93–247) (June, 1988); R. P. Kusserow (September, 1987). *Survey of state Baby Doe programs*, Office of Inspector General, Office of Analysis and Inspections, Dept. of Health and Human Services, Document No. OAI-03-87-00018.

46. Kusserow (1987), *Survey of state Baby Doe programs.*

47. R. P. Kusserow (September, 1987). *Infant care review committees under the Baby Doe program*, Office of Inspector General, Office of Analysis and Inspections, Dept. of Health and Human Services; Document No. OAI-03-87-00018.

48. D. L. Calista (August, 1986). Linking policy intention and policy implementation: The role of the organization in the integration of human services. *Administration and Society, 18*(2), 263–286; E. G. Hargrove (1985). *The missing link: The study of the implementation of social policy.* Washington, D.C.: The Urban Institute Press; F. J. Thompson (1984). Policy implementation and overhead control. In G. C. Edwards III (Ed.), *Public policy implementation.* Greenwich, CT: JAI Press; D. A. Mazmanian & P. A. Sabatier (1981). *Effective policy implementation.* Lexington, MA: Lexington Books; R. F. Elmore (1980). Backward mapping: Implementation research and policy decisions. *Political Science Quarterly, 94*(4), 601–616; M. Lipsky (1980). *Street-level bureaucracy: Dilemmas of the individual in public services.* New York: Russell Sage Foundation; R. Weatherley & M. Lipsky (1977). Street-level bureaucrats and institutional innovation: Implementing special-education reform. *Harvard Educational Review, 47*(2), 171–197.

49. J. J. Gallagher (1981). Models for policy analysis: Child and family policy. In R. Haskins & J. J. Gallagher (Eds.), *Models for analysis of social policy.* Norwood, NJ: Ablex Publishing; J. J. Gallagher, P. L. Trohanis, & R. M. Clifford (1989). *Policy implementation and P.L. 99–457: Planning for young children with special needs.* Baltimore: Brookes Publishing.

50. Interview #6, March, 1989.

51. Shaw et al. (1977), Ethical issues in pediatric surgery; Duff & Campbell (1973),

Moral and ethical dilemmas in the special-care nursery; Lorber (1971), Results of treatment of myelomeningocele.

52. Interview #3, February, 1989.

53. B. W. Levin (1985). Consensus and controversy in the treatment of catastrophically ill newborns. In T. H. Murray & A. L. Caplan (Eds.), *Which babies shall live? Humanistic dimensions of the care of imperiled newborns.* Clifton, NJ: Humana Press.

54. Lyon (1985), *Playing God in the nursery.*

55. Kusserow (1987), *Survey of state Baby Doe programs.*

56. Interview #16, July, 1989.

57. Mazmanian & Sabatier (1981), *Effective policy implementation.*

58. R. J. Haggerty (May 2, 1985). Letter from President of the American Academy of Pediatrics to all members.

59. Haggerty (May 2, 1985), Letter from President of the American Academy of Pediatrics to all members.

60. Interview #13, June, 1989.

61. Interview #12, June, 1989.

62. L. M. Kopelman, T. G. Irons, & A. E. Kopelman (1988). Neonatologists judge the "Baby Doe" regulations. *New England Journal of Medicine, 318*(11), 677–726.

63. S. A. Mack, Chairperson, Social Action Committee of National Association of Perinatal Social Workers (February 7, 1985). Letter from National Association of Perinatal Social Workers to National Center on Child Abuse and Neglect.

64. Hargrove (1985), *The missing link.*

65. Interview #12, June, 1989; Interview #15, June, 1989.

66. D. A. Mazmanian & P. A. Sabatier (1983). *Implementation and public policy.* Glenview, IL: Scott, Foresman; Mazmanian & Sabatier (1981), *Effective policy implementation.*

67. *Federal Register, 50*(72) (April 15, 1985), Rules and Regulations, 14890.

68. Interview #16, July, 1989.

69. Interview #6, March, 1989.

70. Interview #15, June, 1989.

71. Interview #8, March, 1989.

72. M. H. Gerry & M. Nimz (1987). The federal role in protecting Babies Doe. *Issues in Law and Medicine, 2*(5), 339–377.

73. Kopelman et al. (1988), Neonatologists judge the "Baby Doe" regulations.

74. Kusserow (1987), *Survey of state Baby Doe programs.*

75. R. P. Kusserow (September, 1987), Infant care review committees under the Baby Doe program.

76. Interview #1, February, 1989.

77. Interview #8, March, 1989.

78. Kusserow (September, 1987), *Survey of state Baby Doe programs*; Interview #2, February, 1989.

79. Interview #12, June, 1989.

80. Mack (1985), Letter from National Association of Perinatal Social Workers.

81. Interview #4, February, 1989.

82. Interview #3, February, 1989.

83. Interview #2, February, 1989.

84. S. A. Newman (1989). Baby Doe, Congress, and the states: Challenging the federal treatment standard for impaired infants. *American Journal of Law and Medicine, 15*(1), 1–60;

Gerry & Nimz (1987), The federal role in protecting Babies Doe.

85. Jurisdictions include the 50 states, the District of Columbia, the Commonwealth of Puerto Rico, the Virgin Islands, Guam, American Samoa, the Commonwealth of the Northern Mariana Islands, and the Trust Territory of the Pacific Islands.

86. Report to congress: Implementation of child abuse amendments of 1984 relating to disabled infants with life-threatening conditions, (Section 4(b)B(2)(K) of P. L. 93–247, as amended) (1988); Kusserow (1987), *Survey of state Baby Doe programs.*

87. Gallagher et al. (1989), *Policy implementation and P.L. 99–457*; Gallagher (1981), Models for policy analysis.

88. Interview #14, June, 1989.

89. Newman (1989), Baby Doe, Congress, and the states.

90. Duff & Campbell (1973), Moral and ethical dilemmas in the special-care nursery.

91. Informants who spoke about this issue could only recall one Baby Doe case in which a court order had to be obtained to provide treatment against parents' wishes: Interview #3, February, 1989; Interview #5, March, 1989. However, court orders are routinely obtained to provide treatment in the case of Jehovah's Witnesses, whose religion prohibits medical treatment: Interview #2, February, 1989; Interview #3, February, 1989.

92. W. A. Silverman (December, 1981). Mismatched attitudes about neonatal death. *Hastings Center Report, 11*(6), 12–16.

93. Kopelman et al. (1988), Neonatologists judge the "Baby Doe" regulations; T. A. Savage, D. L. Cullen, K. T. Kirchhoff, E. J. Pugh, & M. D. Foreman (1987). Nurses' responses to do-not-resuscitate orders in the neonatal intensive care unit. *Nursing Research, 36*(6), 370–373; Murray & Caplan (Eds.) (1985), *Which babies shall live?*; Shaw et al. (1977), Ethical issues in pediatric surgery; Todres et al. (1977), Pediatricians' attitudes affecting decision-making in defective newborns.

94. Interview #12, June, 1989.

95. Interview #15, June, 1989.

96. Interview #14, June, 1989.

97. Interview #8, March, 1989.

98. Interview #7, March, 1989.

99. American Medical Association News (December 2, 1988).

100. Personal communication (August, 1985).

101. Interview #15, June, 1989.

102. *New York Times* (September 30, 1991), 1.

103. Interview #7, March, 1989.

104. R. S. Duff (1987). Close-up versus distant ethics: Deciding the care of infants with poor prognosis. *Seminars in Perinatology, 11*(3), 244–253.

105. Duff (1987), Close-up versus distant ethics.

106. E.g., Interview #4, February, 1989; Interview #5, March, 1989; Interview #7, March, 1989.

107. N. Hobbs, A. Perrin, & S. Ireys (1986). *Chronically ill children and their families.* San Francisco: Jossey-Bass; M. J. McCracken (1984). Cystic fibrosis in adolescence. In R. W. Blum (Ed.), *Chronic illness and disabilities in childhood and adolescence.* Orlando, FL: Grune & Stratton; K. A. Crnic, W. N. Friedrich, & M. T. Greenberg (1983). Adaptation of families with mentally retarded children: A model of stress, coping, and family ecology. *American Journal of Mental Deficiency, 88*, 125–138.

108. *Boston Globe* (November 11, 1988), 19; McCormick et al. (1991), Costs incurred by parents of very low birth weight infants after the initial neonatal hospitalization.

109. H. Gabel, J. McDowell, & M. C. Cerreto (1983). Family adaptation to the handicapped infant. In S. G. Garwood & R. R. Fewell (Eds.), *Educating handicapped infants.* Rockville, MD: Aspen; A. Gath (1974). Sibling reactions to mental handicap: A comparison of the brothers and sisters of mongol children. *Journal of Child Psychology and Psychiatry, 15,* 187–198.

110. S. K. Lee, P. L. Penner, & M. Cox (1991). Impact of very low birth weight infants on the family and its relationship to parental attitudes. *Pediatrics, 88*(1), 105-109; S. E. Waisbren (1980). Parents' reactions after the birth of a developmentally disabled child. *American Journal of Mental Deficiency, 84*(3), 345–351.

111. S. M. McHale & W. C. Gamble (1989). Sibling relationships of children with disabled and nondisabled brothers and sisters. *Developmental Psychology, 25*(3), 421–429; N. Breslau, M. Weitzman, & K. Messenger (1981). Psychologic functioning of siblings of disabled children. *Pediatrics, 67,* 344–353; F. Trevino (1979). Siblings of handicapped children: Identifying those at risk. *Social Casework, 60,* 488–493.

112. S. G. Tritt & L. M. Esses (1988). Psychosocial adaptation of siblings of children with chronic medical illness. *American Journal of Orthopsychiatry, 58*(2), 211–220.

113. For a review of these factors, see M. Seligman & R. B. Darling (1989). *Ordinary families, special children: A systems approach to childhood disability.* New York: Guilford Press; and Crnic et al. (1983), Adaptation of families with mentally retarded children.

114. Interview #3, February, 1989.

115. Interview #16, July, 1989.

116. Shaw et al. (1977), Ethical issues in pediatric surgery; Duff & Campbell (1973), Moral and ethical dilemmas in the special-care nursery; Lorber (1971), Results of treatment of myelomeningocele.

117. Otis Bowen v. American Hospital Association, et al., (June 9, 1986). 106 S. Ct. 2101, 90 L. Ed., 2d 584, 54 U.S.C.W. 4579.

118. E.g., L. Gostin (1985). A moment in human development: Legal protection, ethical standards and social policy on the selective non-treatment of handicapped neonates. *American Journal of Law and Medicine, 11*(1), 31–78.

119. E.g., N. Lund (1985). Infanticide, physicians, and the law: The "Baby Doe" amendments to the child abuse prevention and treatment act. *American Journal of Law and Medicine, 11*(1), 1–29.

120. *Federal Register, 50*(72) (April 15, 1985), Rules and Regulations, 14892.

121. See, e.g., A. Goldworth & D. K. Stevenson (1989). The real challenge of "Baby Doe": Considering the sanctity and quality of life. *Clinical Pediatrics, 28*(3), 119–122.

122. Interview #16, July, 1989.

123. R. Turnbull, D. Guess, & A. P. Turnbull (1988). Vox populi and Baby Doe. *Mental Retardation, 26*(3), 127–132.

124. Interview #8, March, 1989.

125. *New York Times* (January 30, 1991), 1.

126. Interview #3, February, 1989.

127. Interview #5, March, 1989.

128. Interview #15, June, 1989.

129. *Federal Register, 50*(72) (April 15, 1985), Rules and Regulations, 14892; Interview #16, July, 1989.

130. Interview #16, July, 1989.

131. Interview #5, March, 1989.

132. Interview #8, March, 1989.

133. Interview #2, February, 1989.

134. Kopelman et al. (1988), Neonatologists judge the "Baby Doe" regulations.

135. *New York Times* (September 29, 1991, September 30, 1991, & October 1, 1991).

136. Interview #1, February, 1989.

137. Kusserow (September, 1987), *Infant care review committees under the Baby Doe program.*

138. Interview #8, March, 1989.

139. Interview #5, March, 1989.

8

AIDS Education in the Cambridge Public Schools: An Implementation Study

Robert B. Griffith

Human Immunodeficiency Virus (HIV), the virus which causes AIDS, is most commonly spread when an infected individual either engages in unprotected sexual intercourse or shares a used needle with other intravenous drug users. Although the Centers for Disease Control (CDC) estimates that approximately 1.5 million people are infected with HIV in the United States alone,[1] by eliminating or changing these behaviors it is possible to contain the spread of this epidemic. Health officials argue that students should be among the groups targeted to receive information regarding HIV infection, for two reasons: (1) The high rates of sexually transmitted diseases (STD), pregnancy, and drug use among teenagers indicate that many are already engaging in these high-risk behaviors; and (2) getting information in school is likely the most efficient way to curtail or prevent these behaviors.[2]

Comprehensive public school AIDS and sexuality education, which was first advocated by then Surgeon General C. Everett Koop in 1986, is not universally available in the United States (see appendix A).[3] The Reagan and Bush administrations left the decision of whether or not to mandate AIDS education in the public schools to policy makers at the state level.[4] As of 1989, twenty-eight states and the District of Columbia mandated the provision of some type of AIDS education in the schools; a majority of those do not provide local public schools with specific details regarding the content of such education.[5] As a result, most AIDS education policies are determined at the local level, which has led to a wide variety of AIDS education programs.[6] Some school districts—for example, Irvington, NJ; St. Paul, MN; Houston, TX; Fort Meyers, FL—offer detailed curricula about HIV transmission, including information concerning the effectiveness of condom use in preventing the spread of AIDS.[7] Some, like Jacksonville, Florida,[8] offer a quick, "stop-gap" type of instruction that merely stresses abstinence; many provide no AIDS education at all.[9]

How are local school districts reacting to the call for AIDS education? What type of AIDS education programs are being provided? Are they being offered within the context of comprehensive health education? The answers to questions like these are vital to our understanding of this issue. If local school districts are experiencing difficulty providing such programs, identifying the barriers to implementation would be necessary before such problems could be rectified.

THE PRESENT STUDY

The main purpose of this study, therefore, was to investigate how AIDS education was actually being implemented at the local level in an inner-city school district (Cambridge, Massachusetts) by asking the following questions:

1. What is Cambridge's public school AIDS education policy?
2. To what extent and in what ways has this policy been translated into the city's programs?
3. How did these AIDS education programs develop, and who played a major role in their formation?
4. What factors have had the greatest impact on Cambridge's AIDS education policy and programs?

A number of data collection strategies were utilized for this investigation, including twenty-seven key-informant interviews, an extensive review of pertinent documents and records, and observations. The semistructured key-informant interviews, which averaged seventy-five minutes in length, were conducted between May, 1989, and March, 1991, with various experts in the field of AIDS and sexuality education and select members of the Cambridge community (see appendix B). Materials produced by students, textbooks, letters to and from parents, newspaper articles, curricula outlines, and the minutes from various AIDS Task Force meetings also provided valuable insight as to how Cambridge developed and implemented its AIDS education policy. Other documents—particularly various AIDS curricula— were examined as part of an extensive literature review.

One might predict that this school district would have a particularly good AIDS education program, for the following reasons:

1. Cambridge built the first full-service, school-based health center in the state.
2. At the time of this investigation Cambridge had the third highest incidence of AIDS in the state, behind Boston and Provincetown.[10]
3. Cambridge has potential access to a number of business and intellectual resources located in the city, including Harvard University, Massachusetts Institute of Technology, and Lesley College. The home offices of Polaroid; Arthur D. Little Company; Lotus, Inc.; and Draper Laboratories are also found within the city's 6.2 square miles.[11]
4. Cambridge's reputation of being one of the most liberal congressional districts in the country further heightened such expectations. The home district of former Speaker of the House Tip O'Neill and the site of a large amount of student activism in the 1960s, Cambridge was also one of the first

cities in the nation to implement a voluntary school desegregation pro-gram.[12] One might therefore expect a "liberal" city such as Cambridge to have an effective AIDS education policy in place.

These factors call into question the representativeness of Cambridge in compari-son to other urban school districts. One could argue that even if Cambridge's AIDS education policy were shown to possess all the attributes of a successful program, any attempts to generalize the findings of this study to other communities would be meaningless. However, according to the "bedrock" or "best case" method of site selection, Cambridge is a good choice. If further analysis reveals that Cambridge's AIDS education policy falls short of this expectation, its experiences likely would have great relevance to less advantaged communities.[13]

CAMBRIDGE'S AIDS EDUCATION POLICY: BACKGROUND AND BEGINNINGS

Health Education Coordinator Bill Bates, whom one informant[14] considered "the main proponent of comprehensive health education within the school adminis-tration," described Cambridge's approach to the provision of health education in this way: "Health education in Cambridge is viewed as a social responsibility, because serious health problems are, in effect, social problems."[15] By fostering a collabora-tion between the schools and the various health, counseling and guidance, and human service agencies available within the community, Bates explained, the school system is able to provide both health education and services to students. The school system's AIDS education policy mirrored the health education policy. Outside agencies, in collaboration with the schools, were therefore expected to provide most of the AIDS education programs offered in the district.

Cambridge's AIDS Education Policy

As a result of this philosophy, no formal plan for the provision of AIDS education existed within the school system from 1987–1990. No formal written goals were established, no specific curriculum had been adopted, and there were no signs that the administration planned to alter this policy approach anytime in the near future.[16] Even though the school department had not yet developed any specific goals for AIDS education, it was apparent that some informal goals did exist. Bates mentioned that "kids already know a lot about AIDS—and not just in this district. The real challenge for AIDS education lies in getting students to change their behavior."[17]

Bill Timmins—one of the two staff developers who worked with teachers to integrate health education into their curricula—expanded upon this philosophy. One of the most important aspects of AIDS education is to "challenge the student's attitudes about this disease and get them to think about their attitudes," he explained. "This is important because most kids think they are invincible. If they are not gay or sticking a needle in their arm, they aren't concerned about AIDS affecting them. And they aren't concerned about their partner's past sexual history."[18] Three major health programs which developed as a result of Cambridge's "collaborative" approach to health education set both context and precedent for AIDS education.

Health Education in Cambridge Prior to AIDS Education

Despite the fact that many elected officials in Cambridge were social conservatives in a state that did not mandate comprehensive health education, Cambridge public school students did benefit from two health-related initiatives begun prior to the release of the *Surgeon General's Report on AIDS* in September of 1986: The Know Your Body sexuality education course and the Teen Health Center. In addition, a task force designed to investigate the feasibility of providing comprehensive health education was also formed while these two programs were being established.

The Know Your Body program. The Know Your Body (KYB) program is a ten-session sexuality education curriculum that first became available to every eighth-grade student in the Cambridge school system during the fall of 1985. In the fall of 1986, a slightly revised version of Know Your Body was also offered to all fifth-graders in the system. This program covers a variety of topics related to human sexuality, including male and female reproductive anatomy and physiology, puberty, sex roles, pregnancy and families, teen pregnancy and pregnancy alternatives, birth control, AIDS and sexually transmitted diseases, decision making and peer pressure, sexual abuse prevention, and sex role stereotypes.

According to instructors Tina Alu and Kim DeAndrade, there are two major goals to KYB: (1) to foster an environment that allows children to feel comfortable enough to ask questions, and (2) to encourage students to talk about the issues discussed in class with their parents.[19] Getting this program established in the schools was a long process, beginning in the fall, 1976. DeAndrade, a birth control counselor for Cambridge Family Planning, noticed that many of her teenage women clients first came in for pregnancy testing and then inquired about birth control. "I realized there was something wrong with this," she stated. "Waiting for the kids to come in wasn't prevention."[20] DeAndrade gradually began devoting more of her time to giving workshops and was eventually named education coordinator for Cambridge Family Planning.

In 1982, some of DeAndrade's former pupils who attended an after-school workshop asked their principal if she could speak at their school. The principal agreed, and DeAndrade came in and talked about sexuality to the eighth graders later that year.[21] Through word-of-mouth, the program gradually expanded, and

DeAndrade was invited to speak at other city schools. By 1984, eleven of the district's thirteen elementary schools offered KYB in the eighth grade, and four offered it in the fifth grade. Teaching Know Your Body had become DeAndrade's full-time job, although Cambridge Family Planning continued to fund the entire program.

In 1985, the school committee decided, by a four-to-three margin, to offer KYB to each eighth grader in the system and allocated $4,800 to the program. One year later, in 1986, the administration asked DeAndrade to offer KYB to all fifth graders, and the stipend was increased to $11,000. The Know Your Body program had become a fixture in the Cambridge school system.

Tina Alu, the instructor who replaced DeAndrade in 1987, offered four reasons why KYB was so successful: First, all parents are invited to attend a parent information night—held at their child's particular elementary school—so they can meet the teacher, ask questions, and learn about the program. Second, parental permission is required in writing before a student is allowed to participate in the program. Third, teachers are invited to sit in on any or all of the classes, provided a majority of the students agree. Fourth, evaluation forms are given to all teachers, parents, and students involved in the program.[22]

Establishment of the Teen Health Center. Before the surgeon general's report on AIDS was released in 1986, plans for the construction of a school-based health clinic were underway in Cambridge. Nancy Ryan, who helped to found the center, explained that even though five neighborhood clinics existed in the city of Cambridge at the time, "many of the poorer families in Cambridge were not utilizing these clinics. So it became clear that a school-based health clinic might make it easier for younger members of the community to receive adequate medical attention if needed." An "informed group of people," including a number of concerned individuals in the community and "several progressive city councillors," got together to discuss the possibility of building such a facility.[23] A community-based coalition of "parents, teachers, teens, health, and social service professionals and other interested people" also became involved, and organized community forums and a petition drive, attended "innumerable community meetings," and applied for and received a $60,000 grant from the United Way.[24] In September, 1987, the Teen Health Center at Cambridge Rindge and Latin School (CRLS) opened to students.

The school department provided the space for the center, and the city provided monies for the renovation. Health services include preemployment and preparticipation physicals, lab tests, psychiatric evaluations and treatment, and gynecologic exams. Family-planning counseling, prenatal and postpartum care, primary care for teen parents and their infants, drug and alcohol counseling, social services, and home visitation are also available. Health education, nutritional counseling, smoking prevention groups, and AIDS education, among other topics, are also offered.[25] Significantly, the School Committee refused to allow the center to be built if birth control devices were distributed. As a result, the center originally only provided interested students with information and counseling on birth control.

Those seeking birth control samples were referred to one of the five neighborhood centers, which were allowed to dispense birth control devices.[26]

The school health task force. Before AIDS education was first provided in Cambridge, a third project—designed to introduce comprehensive health education in the schools—was initiated. This project had less impact than the Know Your Body program and the Teen Health Center initiatives, however, perhaps because the goal of this initiative was targeted at the entire school system (as opposed to introducing one new program in a particular grade).[27] In early 1987, Bill Bates encouraged a number of parents, teachers, administrators, health professionals, and other concerned members of the community to investigate the possibility of providing comprehensive health education in the Cambridge schools.[28] The Comprehensive Health Education Task Force (CHETF) sent its recommendations to the school committee in June, 1987, but the report "never found its way onto the school committee's agenda as an action item."[29]

Two AIDS Education Initiatives

The school department decided to offer the first AIDS education program in Cambridge in 1987. On May 19, approximately 400 high-school juniors and seniors attended a lecture by doctors, health professionals, and school administrators in the high-school auditorium. Students were given facts about AIDS and also shown a film, which urged the "use of condoms and avoidance of intravenous drugs as the two most effective methods of avoiding AIDS."[30] When students were informed that condoms and other birth control devices would not be dispensed at the Teen Health Center—scheduled to open that fall—some of them became angry and questioned this decision, igniting substantial controversy.[31] It would not be the last time that students voiced their opinions regarding the provision of condoms and the district's AIDS education policy.

Although the CHETF report did not radically affect Cambridge's AIDS education policy, school administrators did become more involved in the area of AIDS education in 1987.[32] In the fall of that year, Cambridge was invited to attend the first AIDS training session offered jointly by the State Department of Education (DOE) and the State Department of Public Health (DPH). Cambridge accepted, and five representatives from the school system attended the three-day session.[33] The overall strategy of the training was to help make administrators aware of the importance of AIDS education, in hopes that it would trickle down throughout the system.[34]

The Cambridge AIDS Task Force

Coincidentally, at the same time that the school administration began to get involved in the area of AIDS education, another community group—the Cambridge

AIDS Task Force (ATF)—was formed in July, 1987. Eventually this group did collaborate with the school system, and was identified by Bill Bates as "a prime source in helping get AIDS education done in the high school, in the elementary schools, and in parent and teacher training."[35] Cathy Hoffman, the outspoken chair of the AIDS Education Subcommittee of the ATF, agreed: "The AIDS Task Force has done most of the work in getting AIDS education taught in the schools."[36]

City Council Member Alice Wolf, who was also one of the "several progressive City Councillors" responsible for helping establish the Teen Health Center,[37] first came up with the idea for an AIDS Task Force after attending a national meeting about AIDS and the need for cities to prepare for its impact.[38] She consulted with Dr. Paul Epstein of the Cambridge Hospital soon after attending this meeting, and was informed that by 1991 roughly twenty-three hospital beds would be needed on a continual basis to care for persons with AIDS (PWAs) if infection rates progressed as predicted. Although relatively few AIDS cases had been reported in Cambridge at the time, it was clear that within a few years the community would not have sufficient resources to provide adequate care for PWAs. "We realized that we would soon have very sick people in the community, with no one available to them," Wolf explained.[39]

Wolf then asked Councillor Francis Duehay, chair of the Committee on Health and Hospitals, for his support. Together they convinced the rest of the City Council to authorize the formation of a citywide AIDS Task Force (ATF).[40] Dr. Melvin Chalfen, the commissioner of Health and Hospitals, became responsible to the City Council for the actions of the Task Force, and Dr. Epstein—whom Cathy Hoffman described as "the leading progressive person for health issues in Cambridge"—was named chairperson of the twenty-eight-member force.

The goal of the AIDS Task Force was to get as many community groups, agencies, and people involved as possible.[41] Numerous representatives from various community groups can be found on the ATF, including the police and fire departments, funeral homes, health clinics, the schools, public housing, the Women's Commission, the Peace Commission, community organizations representing various ethnic groups, public and private hospitals, and private industry.

At the first meeting, members chose four areas of the AIDS crisis to address, and formed a subcommittee for each. They included education, public policy, services and resources, and a steering committee, which would determine the direction of the Task Force. A "coordinator" position to oversee educational and care-providing efforts, and to fund raise, was also recommended;[42] eight months later, Jennifer Burgess Wolfrum, M.Ed., was hired as the City AIDS Task Force coordinator.

According to Chalfen, once the AIDS Education Subcommittee was formed, it "looked to where the risks were and where the needs were greatest, and that included reaching the young people attending school." Chalfen remarked that "what the schools were doing did not seem sufficient. There should have been an ongoing, regular health program in place." Since there was not, the members of the Education

Subcommittee planned to "get things going and encourage more [AIDS education]."[43]

In September, 1988—fifteen months after the AIDS Task Force first convened and five months after the coordinator was hired—the members of the Education Subcommittee sent a memo offering to work with the members of the School Committee regarding AIDS education in the Cambridge schools. Although the School Committee did not formally respond,[44] this action marked the beginning of the Education Subcommittee's involvement in AIDS education in Cambridge.

INITIAL AIDS EDUCATION PROGRAMS

From fall, 1987 through spring, 1990, several major AIDS education programs resulted from collaborations between the school system and outside agencies.

AIDS Awareness Week

The first AIDS program geared toward all high-school students in Cambridge was AIDS Awareness Week, which was first held in April, 1988. Since then, it has become an annual event at Cambridge Rindge and Latin School (CRLS)—the city's only public high school. During this week, students attend one 45-minute assembly about AIDS. The assembly meets in the high-school gymnasium in place of a regular physical education class. Although initially sponsored by the AIDS subcommittee of the Comprehensive Health Education Task Force, in subsequent years this program has been provided by the AIDS Education Subcommittee of the ATF. Even though this function is "coordinated by the school department," one informant estimated that the subcommittee did "about 95% of the work necessary to get this program in the high school."[45]

The basic format is a presentation of the facts about AIDS by speakers, sometimes accompanied by video tapes. In addition, people who are HIV-positive or have AIDS have spoken about their personal experiences. At the second AIDS Awareness Week, Michael Razzino, who is HIV-positive and a member of both the Education Subcommittee and the Steering Committee of the ATF, talked about what it was like living with the prospect of developing AIDS, and also answered students' questions. He recalled that the big groups hindered the format. If the questions were appropriate from the start, things "went okay," he said. "If they asked really strange and horrible questions, though, it didn't go well."[46]

The third AIDS Awareness Week was presented by the AIDS peer leaders in early 1990. The question and answer format utilized the year before was eliminated because it did not work well in a large group setting. Instead, video tapes about AIDS were shown, and the Education Subcommittee provided speakers from various minority populations in the community to speak to individual classrooms as a follow-up. Teachers could sign up to have a speaker come into their classrooms, although less than 50% did so.[47]

A number of additional programs were introduced into the Cambridge schools during the 1988–1989 academic year. Besides AIDS Awareness Week, AIDS was discussed in the ninth-grade health class and in the Know Your Body program. In addition, an AIDS peer leadership program was introduced, and a number of AIDS assemblies were presented to students in grades five through eight as part of a kite-making contest.

Know Your Body

A session on AIDS was first added to the Know Your Body curriculum during the 1988–1989 school year. In both the fifth and eighth grades, students are briefly presented with the facts about AIDS. Tina Alu solicits "facts" from each student, uncovering "a lot of misinformation" in the process.[48] She recalled how a fifth grader asked what would happen if two students, each with cuts on their arms, walked into each other in the hall and accidently rubbed their cuts together. Could one of them get AIDS? Alu works to provide correct information, hoping to alleviate some of the students' fears regarding HIV as a result. Shelly Mains, a part-time KYB instructor at the time, observed that "one of the aspects I'll focus on more is dealing with people with AIDS, instead of just information. I kind of see attitudes are lagging behind."[49]

Ninth-Grade Health Instruction

Ninth-grade health class is a requirement in CRLS. The textbook used was *Understanding Health*,[50] but there was no standard, written curriculum used at the time this study was conducted. Instead, each teacher determined the course's topics, sequence, and emphasis.[51] Nevertheless, all ninth-grade health classes covered a wide range of topics, including families, emotions, nutrition, diseases (such as cancer), death and dying, smoking, alcohol and drug abuse, sexuality, and AIDS. In the informant's class, the unit on sexuality covered marriage, the reproductive system, pregnancy, STDs, and contraceptives—including the use of condoms. In addition, an instructor from the Know Your Body curriculum visited each of the informant's classes during the semester, brought in various birth control samples, and explained how each contraceptive device works.[52]

None of the ninth-grade health teachers were trained by the school department to teach about AIDS.[53] Although the informant attended an all-day workshop on AIDS at Suffolk University—on a voluntary basis—and incorporated AIDS education into her classes, she was unaware of how much time the other teachers spent on the topic.[54] Surprisingly, the textbook did not have a chapter on AIDS, and the term "AIDS" was only mentioned on four different pages.

Therefore, the AIDS curriculum used in class was developed by the instructor.

Six of this teacher's classes (two weeks' worth) were devoted entirely to AIDS. This topic also came up in other units, including drug abuse, STDs, and birth control, so it was discussed in ten classes altogether. When asked how much students knew about AIDS before taking the class, the informant replied, "Not much, especially on prevention. Most of them can just come up with 'use a condom.'"[55]

AIDS Peer Leadership Program

The AIDS peer leadership training program used in Cambridge was designed by the Medical Foundation, Inc., of Boston, and prepares selected adolescents to address groups of their peers in schools and community settings about AIDS and AIDS prevention. Decision making, peer pressure, communication skills, and values clarification exercises are built into this program. Peer leadership began at CRLS in 1984 as a way to disseminate information about drug and alcohol abuse prevention. In 1988, soon after the ATF was formed in Cambridge, Dr. Paul Epstein suggested that the peer leadership program be expanded to offer information on AIDS as well.[56] After several meetings with the school department, the program was approved— although participants would not be given school credit. Nevertheless, a number of students were recruited by Bill Timmins.[57]

The Medical Foundation received a state grant to pilot AIDS peer leadership training, and was able to pick up the cost of training the first year the program was offered. Since then, the funds needed to pay for this program have been made available by a federal grant entitled "Drug Free Schools," thus minimizing the cost to the Cambridge school system.[58]

Most students who participate in the outreach are eleventh and twelfth graders, according to Timmins. After twenty hours of extensive training, the peer leaders go into the classroom and talk to small groups, usually in pairs. They provide information about AIDS, and try to get students talking about their attitudes. Fifteen students trained to become AIDS peer leaders in the first year the program was offered. That year, some of the AIDS peer leaders provided public service announcements to students, and a group of five went to a TV station in a neighboring town to speak about AIDS with student representatives from other schools. A number of presentations were made in various elementary school classrooms as well.[59]

Providing AIDS peer leadership to all the elementary schools proved difficult for logistical reasons, however, and after the first year AIDS peer leaders stopped visiting elementary schools. Focusing their energy in the high school instead, they planned strategies to promote AIDS awareness within CRLS and offered classroom presentations. They were also responsible for running the third AIDS Awareness Week.[60]

AIDS Assemblies in the Elementary Schools

In early 1989, the AIDS Education Subcommittee of the ATF planned a kite contest designed to raise the level of awareness of AIDS among students in grades five through eight. Each kite produced was either to represent a local resident who died of AIDS, or to be tied in to some other AIDS-related theme. Subcommittee members visited the elementary schools and conducted AIDS education assemblies to present this idea to students. Cambridge Schools Superintendent Mary Lou McGrath approved this initiative, but due to a reluctance on the part of both elementary school principals and art teachers, only four of the district's elementary schools participated fully.[61]

The members of the subcommittee who conducted the assemblies quickly found that a majority of "kids know most of the facts [about AIDS], even in these grades."[62] Nevertheless, "it was striking how thirsty kids were to ask questions about AIDS."[63] As a result, most of the assemblies ended before all of the questions raised by students could be answered.[64] Although a majority of the questions asked by students were fairly straightforward, many questions were very sophisticated and often quite graphic. In fact, the fifth through eighth graders asked many of the same questions raised by those in high school.[65] "My personal opinion is that the lower grades feel more comfortable talking about things. There wasn't the laughing or joking or anything like that," reported Razzino. "Students in grades five through seven were pretty similar in this way," he stated, perhaps because many of these kids probably had not become sexually active yet. In the eighth grade, however, "the kids acted almost the same as the high schoolers," and were not as mature dealing with the issues surrounding AIDS as the fifth through seventh graders. "I expected it the other way around." Part of this discrepancy could have been due to the size of the groups, Razzino reasoned. "The high school groups were much larger."[66]

SOME CRUCIAL TURNING POINTS

A number of events critical to the implementation of Cambridge's AIDS education policy occurred during the 1989–1990 school year: AIDS workshops were provided by the AIDS Education Subcommittee to every teacher and principal in the district;[67] a survey conducted at the Teen Health Center indicated that a large number of students were engaging in unprotected sexual intercourse;[68] and students at CRLS petitioned the School Committee to allow condoms to be distributed at the health center.[69] These events forced the School Department and the AIDS Education Subcommittee to examine the district's programmatic response to the HIV epidemic.

In the fall of 1989, the AIDS Education Subcommittee was granted permission by Superintendent Mary Lou McGrath to provide mandatory teacher training to every teacher and principal in the school system. Rather than offering one "massive" training session, the subcommittee provided the workshops to teachers in small groups—a strategy which encouraged teachers to ask questions and to examine their own attitudes toward the disease. In addition, two or three teachers were recruited to act as resource people in each school.[70]

At the same time, local elections were held for both City Council and the School Committee in 1989. The City Council, which consisted of "a solidly progressive majority" for the first time in eighteen years, chose, by a vote of six to three, progressive Councillor Alice Wolf as the new mayor of Cambridge.[71] Since the mayor is also the chairperson and a voting member of the School Committee, progressives held a majority of School Committee seats for only the second time in eighteen years.[72]

It did not take long before the new School Committee was forced to examine the district's AIDS education policy. In March, 1990, it held a public hearing on condom distribution, raising the question of whether or not condoms should be made accessible to students through the high school's Teen Health Center. The hearing, which created a forum for parents and the community to express views on the issue of AIDS prevention, was precipitated by two crucial events: AIDS peer leaders had already begun to distribute condoms in the high school, and a petition supporting distribution signed by over 350 parents and students had been delivered to the School Committee.[73]

Earlier, in January of that year, six AIDS peer leaders began passing out envelopes containing condoms and printed information on AIDS prevention, teen pregnancy, and condom use to fellow students.[74] Marjorie Decker, one of the peer leaders, related the group's rationale:

> We came to the conclusion that with all that we had learned . . . condoms were the best prevention against the spread of AIDS. But beyond this we were very concerned with the statistics concerning the rise of infection among our own population. We also knew that to distribute condoms was going to be difficult through the already-established teen clinic. If the school was not going to distribute the condoms, then we were.[75]

The actions of the peer leaders, which occurred days after the petition had been presented, made local headlines—and gained the immediate attention of community leaders.

On March 12, 1990, one day prior to the School Committee hearing on the condom distribution ordinance, school officials made public the results of a March, 1989, Teen Health Center survey which indicated that over half of all CRLS students had engaged in sexual intercourse, and over half of these (57%) had initiated sexual activity between the ages of ten and fourteen. In addition, only 46% of the sexually active students stated that they used contraception "all of the time," while 11% stated they "usually" used contraception. The remaining 43% of sexually active students rarely or never used contraception.[76] Although the survey was only completed by 75% of CRLS students,[77] Teen Health Center Director Lynn Schoeff maintained that the results were nonetheless instructive. "Kids who didn't take it are seniors and kids who didn't come to school to take their mid-term exams," she reasoned. "What that says to me is that in some ways those kids who were more likely to be sexually active were not here."[78]

The atmosphere in the high-school auditorium prior to the start of the hearing was one of genuine excitement, since none of the approximately 150 persons present could predict how the seven-member School Committee would vote on the issue. During the course of the four-hour hearing, forty-three people (six health experts and thirty-seven citizens) testified, discussing condom distribution from two basic perspectives: Opponents argued from a moral and ethical standpoint (i.e., providing condoms and education about AIDS promotes sexual promiscuity), while proponents maintained that the issue was primarily one of public health. Thus, making condoms available on school grounds offered students the means to obtain them at a minimal price, without having to deal with the embarrassment of purchasing them in drug stores, which would lead to a reduction in the spread of HIV.[79]

Thirty-five of the forty-three people who testified that evening were in favor of providing condoms at the center.[80] In addition, many who testified—including all six health experts—also stressed the important role that education can play in the prevention of AIDS, teen pregnancy, and sexually transmitted disease. Dr. Chalfen, in fact, began the proceedings by stating that the district needs to provide a comprehensive K-12 health education curriculum that specifically includes topics like AIDS—a call that was often repeated throughout the evening.[81] However, despite the fact that a majority of those who testified that evening supported both condom distribution and an increase in sexuality education, none of the School Committee members disclosed how he or she would vote. The vote, scheduled for the following week, promised to be a close one.[82]

In a four to three vote, the School Committee decided to allow condoms to be dispensed to adolescents as a means of preventing the spread of HIV.[83] The committee's decision, which also stipulated that individuals requesting condoms receive counseling at the center, made Cambridge the first community in the state to allow a public high-school health clinic to dispense condoms.[84] The committee went further, and unanimously "agreed to take up a proposal to institute a comprehensive, kindergarten through twelfth-grade health curriculum" as a result of the many questions regarding the adequacy of the sexuality education being offered in the schools.[85]

Schoeff was unable to quantify how many students actually obtained counseling and condoms at the Teen Health Center in the six months following the School Committee's vote. However, she did explain how students go about obtaining condoms at the center:

[S]ometimes kids come in and they say very directly what it is that they want. Other times, however, they come in for what appears to be a regular, ordinary physical exam or sick visit and then in the course of the visit let the provider know that what they are really interested in is information about birth control or condoms.[86]

In cases such as this, students sometimes are asked to make another appointment:

> If the family planning counselor is here, we just kind of shuttle the kid in to see her. If the nurse practitioner has the time, which is often the case, she will actually sit with the kid and spend some time educating the young person. And sometimes we'll make an appointment, if we think the kid is going to come back. We get a sense of how the kids are. If it's a kid who we think is not going to come back, we do everything that we can right then and there. If it's a kid who we know and who we think we can get back here, then we'll make an appointment for them to return.[87]

Schoeff explained that these counseling sessions "are really substantial," often beginning by helping students examine the decisions they have made about sexual activity.

> There are a lot of kids who come in here who are ambivalent about sexual activity, who are engaging in sex or are thinking about engaging in sex but don't really want to. And we've been able to help support the abstinence side of their ambivalence— help the kids make decisions that are more congruent with what they really feel and believe. Help them sort of learn to resist the pressure that they're getting, whether it's internally or externally.[88]

The student's past and present sexual activity is then discussed, and the risks associated with those activities are assessed. "To those who are sexually active and are determined to remain sexually active—actually for all of them—we talk about various forms of contraception and disease prevention."[89] Regardless of the form of contraception chosen, however, the imperative to use condoms is stressed. Students are also coached on how to buy condoms, if necessary, and AIDS is also discussed.[90]

THE IMPLEMENTATION OF AIDS EDUCATION PROGRAMS IN CAMBRIDGE: AN ANALYSIS

To what extent did the Cambridge school department implement AIDS education as it had intended? This implementation question, necessarily posed for all interventions, is critical in this case. School systems failing to implement quality AIDS education programs effectively present two problems: First, students are deprived of information that could literally save their lives. Second, by giving the impression that they are providing students with important information, such school systems unwittingly lull the community into believing that an important service is being provided when in fact it is not. School systems giving such an impression would be less likely to draw the attention of proponents of AIDS education, who tend to spend their limited resources in districts where they believe no AIDS education policies are in place. The AIDS training sessions offered by the state to various school districts operated in this way, for example. Each year new school systems were invited to send representatives to the training, but there was no follow-up on the districts that had already attended.[91]

The desired outcome of a particular policy can be significantly altered during the implementation phase of the policy process, creating a situation where the services proposed in a particular policy are not provided as intended—if at all.[92] Mazmanian and Sabatier have argued that any policy or statute "seeking a substantial departure from the status quo will achieve its desired goals" if it meets six specific conditions.[93]

Condition #1

The policy objectives are clear and consistent or at least provide substantive criteria for resolving goal conflicts.[94]

When Cambridge began providing AIDS education to public school students in early 1987, the AIDS education policy in place at the time was not highly developed: Cambridge's policy for providing AIDS education basically stated that the schools and community agencies would collaborate in the effort to provide health and AIDS education. However, the policy did not contain any specific guidelines or goals for the provision of AIDS education, and there was no set curriculum in place.[95]

Furthermore, the confusion which resulted after the AIDS Education Subcommittee decided to sponsor the kite contest—which was approved for *all* the district's elementary schools—illustrates that criteria for resolving goal conflicts between the schools and assisting agencies were also never established.[96] At a meeting with the education subcommittee chair just prior to the event, many art teachers reported that their respective principals told them they did not have to participate in the project if they were uncomfortable, while others reported being told that their schools would not be participating at all. Despite last-minute support from Bill Bates, only four of thirteen elementary schools participated in the kite contest.[97] Had policy objectives been clear and consistent or provided criteria for resolving goal conflicts, this situation could have been avoided.

Condition #2

The policy incorporates a sound theory identifying the principal factors and causal linkages affecting objectives, and gives implementing officials sufficient jurisdiction over target groups and other points of leverage to attain, at least potentially, the desired goals.[98]

There is evidence to suggest that comprehensive and effective health education could help reduce the incidence of high-risk sexual behaviors among adolescents.[99] By focusing on skill development (i.e., coaching adolescents who choose not to have sex how to say "no" to their partners, and coaching those who do where to buy condoms, how to use them, etc.) these programs could help reduce the growing rates of unwanted pregnancy, infection with HIV, and other STD infections among teens. Cambridge's "collaborative" AIDS education policy, which was very broad and ambiguous, was not driven by the "skill development" theory, or any other explicit philosophy.[100] It basically stated that AIDS education programs were a community responsibility and left program design and implementation to the agents providing this education.

These agencies, however, *did* base their health education programs on skill development. Most of Cambridge's AIDS education programs attempted to help students make informed choices regarding their sexual behaviors, and in many cases students were given the opportunity to learn behaviors that allowed them to act on those choices. Thus, although Cambridge's AIDS education policy was not based explicitly on its own theoretical framework, the philosophy incorporated by most implementing agents corresponded with the tenets of "quality" AIDS education.

Were officials given sufficient jurisdiction and leverage over the schools to attain the desired goal of reducing high-risk behaviors among students? For the most part, yes. The Know Your Body class, for example, was offered to all fifth and eighth graders in the school system, and the curriculum was allowed to be explicit in the information transmitted. In addition, AIDS Awareness Week was offered to all students in grades ten through twelve, ninth-grade health was required of all students, and counseling was available to every teenager at the Teen Health Center. Later, in 1990, all teachers and principals were also required to attend an in-house AIDS training.

Condition #3

The policy structures the implementation process so as to maximize the probability that implementing officials and target groups will perform as desired. This involves assignment to sympathetic agencies or agents with sufficient financial resources, adequate access to supporters, adequate hierarchical integration, and supportive decision rules.[101]

Ensuring that the service providers are sympathetic to policy goals and procedures is crucial to successful implementation, because their collective actions become, or add up to, agency policy.[102] One could predict that no AIDS education policy could succeed if the teachers responsible for delivering this service were not supportive of the policy. Cambridge did not experience this implementation problem, for the most part. Agencies such as Cambridge Family Planning or implementing agents from the AIDS Education Subcommittee were far from hostile to the provision of AIDS education: The street-level bureaucrats delivering school-based AIDS education in Cambridge not only supported this cause, they were also highly committed to providing as comprehensive services as possible.

In fact, rather than use the substantial amount of discretion that Cambridge's broad AIDS education policy offered to inhibit the delivery of services, health educators in Cambridge used this discretion to design and implement new programs. The fact that there were no procedural guidelines that dictated how AIDS education programs should be provided simply made it *easier* for implementing agents: they were not subjected to unrealistic deadlines, could work at their own pace, and were never placed in a position to deliver services beyond their capabilities. As a result, a number of AIDS education programs were provided to students that might not have been delivered otherwise.

The vast majority of implementing agents were sympathetic to the issue.[103] They also appeared extremely dedicated to their work, and logged many additional hours to see that Cambridge offered as comprehensive a program as possible. The Education Subcommittee's approach to training teachers is illustrative:

> We had to have meetings with the principals, then we had to plan what type of training we were going to do, and then we had to get the people to do it. [Since] we really wanted to get the teachers into small groups, that meant we had to have five or six AIDS educators at every presentation. That's a lot of time commitment to ask of people who are doing this sort of as somewhat part of their jobs, somewhat above and beyond the call of their jobs. By the end of the spring we were looking cross-eyed, because we had other projects going all at the same time.[104]

Although these outside implementors were able to offer AIDS programs in the schools, insufficient resources restricted the type of programs that they were able to provide. In fact, of the twenty informants asked to name major barriers to AIDS education in Cambridge, nine mentioned a lack of funds to hire specialists and purchase materials for a new health/AIDS program.[105]

Condition #4

The leaders of the implementing agency or the agents themselves possess substantial managerial and political skill, and are committed to statutory goals.[106]

A high level of commitment among implementing agents was evident. When Alu was asked whether she enjoyed her work, for instance, she said, "I can't imagine anything I would rather do more." This attitude was shared by virtually all the implementing officials interviewed for this project, including Schoeff, Wolfrum, and others. The marked increase in AIDS education programs offered over the course of four years readily attests to the impact of such dedication, as does the fact that representatives from both the DPH[107] and DOE[108] described Cambridge's AIDS education programs as among the best in the state. This was an impressive achievement, especially considering the fact that the same relatively small number of individuals both developed *and* implemented these programs.

Assessing the managerial and political skill of implementing officials in Cambridge is much more difficult. But the fact that people from community groups and other outside agencies were welcome to operate within the schools is testament itself to their political acumen.

Condition #5

The program is actively supported by organized constituency groups and by a sufficient number of school officals throughout the implementation process.[109]

Without question, this particular condition was the most difficult for Cambridge to meet. The AIDS Task Force was the only constituency to actively support AIDS education in Cambridge until 1990, and active support from key legislators or administrators (excepting Bill Bates) was also minimal.

Lack of support from organized constituency groups. Although AIDS education was supported by the AIDS Task Force, the Education Subcommittee of that organization was also largely responsible for the provision of AIDS education in Cambridge. There were no other organized constituencies actively supporting this policy.

Parents, for example, played an important role in establishing the Teen Health Center and the Know Your Body program, but were not actively involved in AIDS education. Twelve informants stated that parental involvement in Cambridge's AIDS education policy has been "practically nonexistent,"[110] and six mentioned the lack of parental involvement as a major barrier to the provision of AIDS education. A typical illustration of the lack of parental involvement was a parent workshop held in 1988. After the decision to hold an AIDS Awareness Week in the high school was made, a parent information workshop was planned. Over 6,500 letters announcing the workshop were sent out with report cards to every parent in the school system, and it was publicized in the local newspaper. On the evening of the workshop, however, only two parents attended. Similar training sessions for parents held by the AIDS Education Subcommittee also drew very few parents between 1988 and 1989. Four separate training sessions were held by the Education Subcommittee during this period, and a total of four parents attended.[111]

Quite simply, very few parents were involved with AIDS education issues in Cambridge.[112] One ATF member openly admitted her frustration with this fact. She even wished there was a vocal group that was opposed to AIDS education or the distribution of condoms in the school, just so that the AIDS Task Force would be able to engage the community and parents in a debate about this issue and "get it out in the open."[113] No such minority came forward, however.

Many informants felt that pressure from a large segment of the community was the only way to get the School Committee actively involved in the AIDS education issue.[114] One School Committee member explained that if enough parents organized, "they could then appeal to the School Committee or [the] appropriate politician.... The best way to impact the School Committee is to approach them full force, with a lot of people. Not just two or three."[115] A second School Committee member pointed out that it was very difficult for any School Committee member to influence other committee members. The most effective way to get the school board to examine an issue like AIDS education was for "constituents to step forward and oblige us to set up an open public forum."[116]

Lack of active support from either the School Committee or the school administration. The second most common barrier to the provision of AIDS education—cited by half the informants—was the perceived reluctance of the school administration to mandate such education. Examples of this reluctance include:

- The report of the Comprehensive Health Education Task Force, submitted to the School Committee in June of 1987, never found its way onto the committee's agenda as an action item and was more or less forgotten.[117]
- The school administration took months to send out a parent survey regarding AIDS.[118] In March, 1988, a letter to all high school parents was drafted by Jennifer Burgess Wolfrum and the rest of the Education Subcommittee to present what students learned during the first AIDS Awareness Week. It also contained a survey which asked parents if they had any questions of their own and if they would be interested in a workshop about AIDS. However, because the first draft submitted to the School Department had contained the word "condom," Superintendent McGrath requested that the letter be revised—with the word "condom" taken out. The letter then had to be translated into nine different languages.[119] Eventually in May of 1989, fourteen months later, the letter went out. "It took fourteen months to get a two-page mailing out to all CRLS parents," one subcommittee member explained. "This sort of red tape and bureaucracy makes it so hard to [continue our efforts]."[120]
- The administration did not fully support the kite contest. Although permission to have the contest was obtained from McGrath, Foley, and Bates, when a majority of principals balked at this initiative the school administration did not insist the plan go forward as scheduled. Had the administration supported this initiative more forcefully, more than four of thirteen elementary schools probably would have participated.
- The administration did not allocate any funds or personnel to help provide AIDS education within the schools, and the policy itself was never restructured—until after the condom distribution vote.
- The School Committee and the administration were not involved in the area of AIDS education. Due to the conservative nature of the committee prior to the 1989 elections, AIDS education was not a top priority.[121]

Administrators who could have had a major impact on AIDS education in Cambridge—like the superintendent or the director of elementary education—also did not urge AIDS and health education. To do so, even if they were so inclined, would probably have had little effect on the conservative School Committee, and may have alienated them. In any event, a sufficient number of key school officials did not actively support AIDS education in Cambridge.

Condition #6

The relative priority of statutory objectives is not undermined over time by the emergence of conflicting public policies or by changes in relevant socioeconomic conditions which weaken the statute's causal theory or political support.[122]

Although there were never any clear-cut objectives for AIDS education in Cambridge, AIDS education programs became more entrenched over time. Political support for this initiative increased substantially after the policy was first implemented, especially within the School Committee after the 1989 elections. This increase in support helped lead to plans for the development of a comprehensive health education curriculum.

CONCLUSION

Cambridge met several, but not all, of the conditions noted above: it lacked a comprehensive plan for delivering services, adequate resources, and the support of major constituencies and high-ranking school officials. Nonetheless, it implemented a fairly effective policy from 1986–1990, suggesting a modification of the Mazmanian and Sabatier framework.

There were, in fact, advantages to the manner in which Cambridge implemented its original AIDS education policy. First, Cambridge turned its lack of clear and consistent policy objectives or goals to its advantage; this situation allowed for Cambridge's AIDS education programs to grow and expand over time, making good use of the outside experts who had "infiltrated" the system. As AIDS education became more of an issue both in society and in Cambridge, these programs became more ambitious and a number of AIDS education programs that would not otherwise have been offered were successfully implemented.

Although this broad approach provided implementing agents with a great deal of discretion, it was advantageous because it allowed them to remain on the fringes of a politically delicate issue. By choosing not to stipulate a number of policy objectives and goals, officials in Cambridge were able to sit back and let this policy unfold on its own—without becoming directly involved. By contrast, if clear and consistent policy objectives for the provision of AIDS education had been formulated by the School Committee, committee members would have been obligated to explain and probably defend their positions to constituents. Such a scenario would obviously place committee members in a rather delicate political position—by remaining "neutral," they avoided some potentially unfavorable publicity.

Members of the school administration—particularly Superintendent McGrath—also stood to gain from this approach. By remaining outside this potentially sensitive policy issue, McGrath lessened her chances of alienating either the School Committee or parents. Considering the furor that erupted when the neighboring Boston school system announced its AIDS education policy, it is easy to understand why key school officials would favor this approach.

That a sufficient number of key school officials did not actively support the policy, on the face of it a drawback, also appeared to benefit the cause: it placed key school officials in a win-win situation. If the policy worked and outside agencies were able to implement a satisfactory AIDS education policy, school officials would be able to share the credit. (After all, they had the foresight and vision to see the benefits of such an approach.) If it failed, however, a significant portion of the blame could be attributed to those same outside agencies (who, one could argue, should have been able to provide adequate AIDS education). In either case, the integrity of the School Committee remains intact, and members are spared the burden of dealing with a potentially difficult issue.

Finally, although the "usual" implementors—the teachers—were not overwhelmingly in support of AIDS and sexuality education, the Cambridge school system allowed implementing agents who were sympathetic to AIDS education to deliver these services in the schools. In this case, then, the "outsiders" became the "street-level bureaucrats," and they facilitated the policies' implementation.[123] These committed, knowledgeable service providers were given a great degree of discretionary power, and were therefore able to design and deliver AIDS education programs without needing to convert classroom teachers or principals. This no doubt hastened and strengthened AIDS education programming in the schools.

So although implementing agents encountered very little support from key officials, the fact was that key officials also did very little to stop implementing agents from providing AIDS education. The School Committee, for example, could have voted to forbid the participation of outside agencies in the provision of AIDS education in Cambridge. It also could have withdrawn funding for the Know Your Body program. The committee did not do this, however, and instead chose to avoid the area of AIDS education—for the most part. This only added to the discretionary power of implementing agents.

Mazmanian and Sabatier have identified three basic phases of the policy process: (1) policy formulation, (2) policy implementation, and (3) the reformulation of the policy by the original policy maker.[124] The events chronicled in this case study end at the beginning of this reformulation phase—at the time when the Cambridge School Department was just starting to develop and implement AIDS education in the context of comprehensive health education. Cambridge's plan to implement its new comprehensive health education policy relies heavily on nonspecialists (regular classroom teachers) to deliver health and sexuality education services. This policy calls for the formation of a "health team" in every elementary school. Consisting of the principal, the assistant principal, a parent liaison, the school nurse, a school psychologist, a physical education teacher, and three classroom teachers (one each from grades K-4, 5-6, and 7-8), this "health team" would first undergo health education training. After this training, the team would be responsible for "implementing the . . . program with advisory assistance from the Health Education and Human Development staff."[125]

The reliance on classroom teachers rather than specialists to deliver a significant portion of health and sexuality education presents Cambridge with a potentially serious implementation problem: Some instructors may be reluctant or even opposed to teaching AIDS and sexuality education—even after participating in the health team training. As responsibility for providing AIDS education moves from outside agencies to "internal" personnel, the Cambridge School Department will need to watch closely to see if comprehensive health education is actually being implemented. It is at this point that the behavior of street-level bureaucrats could adversely affect the delivery of this policy, and bear out traditional concerns.[126]

And, of course, the inevitable question of whether or not comprehensive health education "works," must be posed and answered systematically, in the near future. In short, how effective is comprehensive health education, combined with the accessibility of counseling and condoms at the Teen Health Center, in reducing the rates of unwanted pregnancy, sexually transmitted disease, abortion, and HIV infection among teenagers in Cambridge? A comparison of the behaviors reported in the 1989 survey with those reported in a more recent, 1992, survey (completed by 72% of the high-school students at CRLS) suggests that the combination of these two services does not lead to an increase in sexual activity among teenagers, while those who are sexually active are more likely to use condoms. In the 1989 survey, for example, 51% of participating students indicated that they had sexual intercourse, as compared with 49.4% in 1992. In 1989, 53.6% of sexually active students reported that they or their partners used condoms, compared with 57% who reported they "always" used condoms in 1992.[127] Hopefully, this promising preliminary data will encourage the district to continue its efforts.

In the meantime, it is only proper to question whether Cambridge's attempt to provide AIDS education is generalizable to other urban school districts. Earlier it was argued that Cambridge is likely not representative of cities its size. Yet, despite its advantages, providing quality AIDS education in Cambridge was a sometimes daunting challenge, and implementing comprehensive health education with its own personnel may present new problems as well. In the end, it took a combined effort from parents, students, the medical community, and key school officials to get this policy in place—a difficult task to be sure.

In fact, because it was so difficult for Cambridge to come to provide comprehensive health education, the "bedrock" or "best case" method of site selection suggests that other urban school districts may also be experiencing difficulty offering comparable programs. If this is the case, then one can assume that teenagers in many urban school districts are still not receiving the kind of instruction that experts believe can help them avoid HIV infection. In the meantime, however, a deadly epidemic rages on.

APPENDIX A: EFFECTIVE SEXUALITY EDUCATION STRATEGIES

Although local control of AIDS education policy allows a program to reflect local values and resources,[128] research indicates that effective sexuality education programs incorporate a number of similar strategies.[129] Researchers agree that simply providing students with information about AIDS and how it is transmitted does little to alter teenage sexual behavior.[130] This is not surprising, as information alone is rarely sufficient to change unhealthy behaviors; for example, millions of Americans smoke, even though the adverse health effects are well known.[131]

Although there are no studies to date which show that AIDS education can be done effectively[132]—the problem is still too new—an emerging body of sexuality education research indicates that some intervention strategies effectively alter high-risk sexual behavior in teenagers.[133] Comprehensive health education, combined with substantial teacher training, is one such strategy.[134] The use of peer leaders to get students to discuss the various social and peer pressures they encounter to become sexually active has also been effective.[135] Providing students with sexuality and contraceptive information, individual and group counseling, and medical and contraceptive services, either in school or at a neighborhood health clinic, has led teens to alter their high-risk sexual behaviors.[136]

Experts agree that providing AIDS education in the context of comprehensive health education is the best approach.[137] The philosophy guiding comprehensive health education is relatively simple: "Begin young if the aim is to promote good health and exercise; and teach health, not disease, if you wish to prevent problems such as smoking, drug abuse, and early pregnancy."[138]

When teaching about AIDS in this context, it is extremely important for the curriculum to be appropriate to the chronological and developmental age of the students.[139] In grades K-3, for example, some of the health issues students should be learning about include germs and their role in disease.[140] Teaching children to wash their hands before eating, to care for their teeth and gums, and not to eat food that has fallen on the floor is AIDS education, because it "communicates some important concepts about health and disease."[141] Specific AIDS education at this level is very basic, and should "be defined simply as a disease that some adults and teenagers get."[142] Allaying children's fears about the disease is the primary goal.[143]

In grades four to five, the same approach used in grades K-3 is appropriate, although an increased emphasis should be placed on the fact that bodies have natural sexual feelings. Students should also be encouraged to examine and affirm their own and their families' values about relationships.[144] Finally, in grades six to twelve, before they begin to have sex, students should gradually be taught the information and skills they will need to protect themselves from HIV infection and unplanned pregnancy: Helping them develop responsible decision-making skills about sex is an important part of this process.[145] Students "who choose to remain abstinent should be taught skills they can use to resist pressure to engage in intercourse. Students who choose to be sexually active need to learn how to acquire condoms and spermicide and how to use them effectively."[146]

APPENDIX B: LIST OF INTERVIEWS

Tina Alu: Instructor of sexuality curriculum taught in the fifth and eighth grades, Cambridge Family Planning; Member of the AIDS Education Subcommittee of the Cambridge AIDS Task Force, June, 1989.

Bill Bates: Grant Manager and Coordinator for Comprehensive Health and Human Services, Cambridge Public Schools. Also a member of the AIDS Education Subcommittee of the Cambridge AIDS Task Force, May, 1989.

Melvin Chalfen, M.D.: Commissioner of Health and Hospitals, City of Cambridge, and member of the AIDS Education Subcommittee of the Cambridge AIDS Task Force, July, 1989.

Fran Cooper: Cambridge School Committee member, parent of four children enrolled in the Cambridge Public Schools, June, 1989.

Kevin Cranston: AIDS and Health Education Consultant for the Massachusetts State Department of Education, June, 1989.

Devon Davidson: Specialist on AIDS education for the National Coalition of Advocates for Students (NCAS); parent of two children currently enrolled in the Cambridge Public Schools, October, 1989. Note: Devon Davidson was originally contacted as a parent.

Kim DeAndrade: Founder, developer, and former instructor of the sexuality education curriculum currently taught in the Cambridge Public Schools, November, 1989.

Paul Epstein, M.D.: Chairman of the Cambridge AIDS Task Force and a physician who works with AIDS patients, July, 1989.

Francis X. Foley: Director of Elementary Education, former principal and teacher in the Cambridge Public Schools, October, 1989.

Cathy Hoffman: Chair of the AIDS Education Subcommittee of the Cambridge AIDS Task Force, and a speaker at most of the student assemblies organized by the AIDS Task Force, June, 1989, and October, 1990.

Terry Leveritch: One of three instructors at the Brookline, Massachusetts, High School teaching a comprehensive course on the world AIDS pandemic, June, 1988.

Shelly Mains: Sexuality education instructor, Cambridge Family Planning, June, 1989.

Dorothy Martin: Parent of Cambridge Rindge and Latin School student, member of the AIDS Education Subcommittee of the Cambridge AIDS Task Force, and AIDS Coordinator in the Cambridge Visiting Nurses program, June, 1989.

Mary Mroz: Principal of R. F. Kennedy Elementary School in Cambridge, former teacher, October, 1989.

Ninth-grade health instructor: One of the Cambridge Rindge and Latin School's three ninth-grade health instructors, June, 1989.

Michael Razzino: Member of the AIDS Education Subcommittee of the Cambridge AIDS Task Force, and an HIV-positive individual who speaks at most of the student assemblies organized by the AIDS Task Force, June, 1989.

Shoshana Rosenfeld, R.N.: Adolescent AIDS Prevention Coordinator for the Massachusetts Department of Public Health, June, 1989.

Nancy Ryan: Member of the Public Policy Subcommittee of the Cambridge AIDS Task Force; also instrumental in getting Teen Health Center constructed, June, 1989.

Lynn Schoeff: Director of Cambridge Teen Health Center and member of the AIDS Education Subcomittee of the Cambridge AIDS Task Force, October, 1990.

Bill Timmins: Staff Developer and health instructor, Cambridge Public Schools, June, 1989, and October, 1989.

Larry Weinstein: Member of Cambridge School Committee, October, 1989.

Alice Wolf: Cambridge City Council Member, former Mayor of Cambridge and Chair of the Cambridge School Committee, October, 1990.

Jennifer Burgess Wolfrum: Community Health Coordinator for the City of Cambridge charged with working with the Cambridge AIDS Task Force, June, 1989, and October, 1990.

NOTES

1. D. Kong (June 8, 1992). Bold global AIDS strategy urged. *Boston Globe*, 25, 29.

2. Institute of Medicine/National Academy of Sciences (1989). *Mobilizing against AIDS*. Cambridge, MA: Harvard University Press; C. E. Koop (1986). *Surgeon General's report on Acquired Immune Deficiency Syndrome*. Washington, D.C.: U.S. Department of Health and Human Services.

3. National Association of State Boards of Education (1988). *Survey of state actions to promote AIDS education: Update*. Alexandria, VA: Author.

4. President's Domestic Policy Council (1987). *Principles for AIDS education*. Washington, D.C.: Author.

5. National Association of State Boards of Education (1988), *Survey of state actions to promote AIDS education*.

6. National Research Council (1989). *AIDS: Sexual behavior and intravenous drug use*. Washington, D.C.: National Academy Press; D. K. Lohrmann (1988). AIDS education at the local level: The pragmatic issues. *Journal of School Health*, 58(8), 330–334; National Association of State Boards of Education (1988), *Survey of state actions to promote AIDS education*; President's Domestic Policy Council (1987), *Principles for AIDS education*; U.S. Conference of Mayors (1987). Local school districts active in AIDS education. *AIDS Information Exchange*, 4(1), 1–10; J. Leo (November 24, 1986). Sex and schools. *Time*, 54–63.

7. Leo (November 24, 1986), Sex and schools.

8. NBC News (May 12, 1992).

9. National Research Council (1989), *AIDS: Sexual behavior and intravenous drug use*; Lohrmann (1988), AIDS education at the local level; U.S. Conference of Mayors (1987), Local school districts active in AIDS education; Leo (November 24, 1986), Sex and schools.

10. This high rate of HIV infection may in part be explained by the fact that Cambridge

has a very diverse cross section of ethnic groups and cultures found among its citizens. For example, minority groups comprise 50.1% of the student population, with African-American students accounting for 31.5%, Hispanics 12.3%, and Asians 6.2% (Cambridge School Department, *General Information Fact Sheet*, 1989). Since African-Americans and Hispanics have been hit disproportionately hard by the HIV epidemic, it is reasonable to expect that Cambridge would have a high incidence of AIDS.

11.   Cambridge School Department (1989). *General Information Fact Sheet*. Cambridge, MA: Author.

12.   Cambridge School Department (1989), *General Information Fact Sheet*; J. Hart (December 26, 1988). Cambridge turns to one of its own. *Boston Globe*, 29, 32.

13.   Jacobs, (1979). *The identification of preschool children with handicaps: A community approach*. Doctoral dissertation. Cambridge, MA: Harvard University Graduate School of Education; J. L. Pressman & A. Wildavsky (1973). *Implementation*. Berkeley, CA: University of California Press.

14.   Interview with Cathy Hoffman, Chair of the AIDS Education Subcommittee of the Cambridge AIDS Task Force, June, 1989. The author wishes to thank the Cambridge School Department and all the people who generously agreed to be interviewed for this study.

15.   Interview with Bill Bates, Grant Manager and Coordinator for Comprehensive Health and Human Services, Cambridge Public Schools, May, 1989.

16.   Interview #7; #9; #13; #17; #22; #25. Key informants were offered anonymity. A link-file system, which assigns numbers to each interview, was developed for that purpose.

17.   Interview with Bates, May, 1989.

18.   Interview with Bill Timmins, Staff Developer and Health Instructor, Cambridge Public Schools, June, 1989.

19.   Interviews with Tina Alu, Cambridge Family Planning, Know Your Body curriculum instructor, June, 1989; and Kim DeAndrade, founder, developer, and former instructor of Know Your Body curriculum, November, 1989.

20.   Interview with DeAndrade, November, 1989.

21.   Interview with DeAndrade, November, 1989.

22.   Interview with Alu, June, 1989.

23.   Interview with Nancy Ryan, member of the Public Policy Subcommittee, Cambridge AIDS Task Force, June, 1989.

24.   Teen Health Center, Cambridge Rindge and Latin School (1987). *Information Fact Sheet*. Cambridge, MA: Author.

25.   Interview with Lynn Schoeff, Director of Cambridge Teen Health Center and member of the AIDS Education Subcommittee of the Cambridge AIDS Task Force, October, 1990; Teen Health Center (1987), *Information Fact Sheet*.

26.   Interview with Ryan, June, 1989.

27.   Interview with Bates, May, 1989; Interview with Jennifer Burgess Wolfrum, Community Health Coordinator for the City of Cambridge, June, 1989; Interview with Devon Davidson, specialist on AIDS education for the National Coalition of Advocates for Students, October, 1989.

28.   Interview with Bates, May, 1989.

29.   Interview with Davidson, October, 1989.

30.   P. Hirshson (May 19, 1987). Students question condom dispensing ban. *Boston Globe*, 20.

31.   Hirshson (May 19, 1987), Students question condom dispensing ban.

32.   Interviews #9; #11; #21; #23; #25.

33. Interview #9.

34. Interview with Kevin Cranston, AIDS/Health Education consultant for the Massachusetts State Department of Education, June, 1989.

35. Interview with Bates, May, 1989.

36. Interview with Hoffman, June, 1989.

37. Interview with Ryan, June, 1989.

38. Interview with Alice Wolf, Cambridge City Council member, October, 1990; Interview with Paul Epstein, Chairman of the Cambridge AIDS Task Force and a physician who works with AIDS patients, July, 1989.

39. Interview with Wolf, October, 1990.

40. Interview with Wolf, October, 1990; Interview with Epstein, July, 1989.

41. Interview with Epstein, July, 1989.

42. Cambridge AIDS Task Force (July 7, 1987). Meeting Minutes.

43. Interview with Melvin Chalfen, M.D., Commissioner of Health and Hospitals, City of Cambridge, and member of the AIDS Education Subcommittee, July, 1989.

44. Interview with Wolfrum, June, 1989.

45. Interview with Hoffman, June, 1989.

46. Interview with Michael Razzino, member of the AIDS Education Subcommittee, Cambridge AIDS Task Force, June, 1989.

47. Interview with Hoffman, October, 1990.

48. Interview with Alu, June, 1989.

49. Interview with Shelly Mains, Cambridge Family Planning, sexuality education instructor, June, 1989.

50. Kane, 1987

51. Interview #24.

52. Interview #24.

53. Interview #24.

54. Interview #24.

55. Interview #24.

56. Interview with Epstein, July, 1989.

57. Interview with Wolfrum, October, 1990; Interview with Epstein, July, 1989; Interview with Timmins, June, 1989.

58. Interview with Wolfrum, October, 1990.

59. Interview with Timmins, October, 1989.

60. Interview with Timmins, October, 1990.

61. Interviews #6; #12; #14; #16.

62. Interview with Razzino, June, 1989.

63. Interview with Hoffman, October, 1990.

64. Interviews #6; #12; #14; #16.

65. Interview with Razzino, June, 1989.

66. Interview with Razzino, June, 1989.

67. Interview with Wolfrum, October, 1990.

68. Z. Gaulkin (March 15, 1990). Survey finds half of students sexually active. *Cambridge Chronicle*, 1, 9.

69. Interview with Wolfrum, October, 1990; Interview with Schoeff, October, 1990; Z. Gaulkin (March 15, 1990). Support grows for condoms at school. *Cambridge Chronicle*, 1, 9.

70. Interview with Wolfrum, October, 1990.

71. E. M. Stahl (January 4, 1990). New council picks Wolf as mayor. *Cambridge*

Chronicle, 1, 3.

72. Interview with Fran Cooper, Cambridge School Committee member and parent of four children enrolled in the Cambridge Public Schools, June, 1989.

73. D. Lewis (February 3, 1990). Students dispense condoms at Rindge and Latin School. *Boston Globe*, 30; Public Hearing of the Cambridge School Committee, March 13, 1990.

74. J. Roberts (March 19, 1991). Seminar held by Massachusetts Chapter of the American Civil Liberties Union. University of Massachusetts at Boston; Public Hearing of the Cambridge School Committee, March 13, 1990; S. Rockwell (September–November, 1990). CCAA interviews peer leaders from Rindge and Latin about distribution of condoms. *Care Notes*, 4–5. Cambridge Cares About AIDS, Inc.

75. Rockwell (September-November, 1990), CCAA interviews peer leaders from Rindge and Latin about distribution of condoms.

76. Gaulkin (March 15, 1990), Survey finds half of students sexually active.

77. Gaulkin (March 15, 1990), Survey finds half of students sexually active.

78. Interview with Schoeff, October, 1990.

79. Alderidge (March 13, 1990). Cambridge School Commitee Hearing.

80. Cambridge School Committee Hearing (March 13, 1990).

81. Cambridge School Committee Hearing (March 13, 1990).

82. Gaulkin (March 15, 1990), Support grows for condoms at school.

83. Cambridge School Committee Vote (March 20, 1990).

84. Z. Gaulkin (March 22, 1990). City becomes first in state with such a policy. *Cambridge Chronicle*, pp. 1, 9.

85. Z. Gaulkin (March 22, 1990). Committee approves condoms in school clinic. *Cambridge Chronicle*, 1, 9.

86. Interview with Schoeff, October, 1990.

87. Interview with Schoeff, October, 1990.

88. Interview with Schoeff, October, 1990.

89. Interview with Schoeff, October, 1990.

90. Interview with Schoeff, October, 1990.

91. Interview with Cranston, June, 1989; Interview with Shoshana Rosenfeld, R.N., Adolescent AIDS Prevention Coordinator for the Massachusetts Department of Public Health, June, 1989.

92. D. Mazmanian & P. Sabatier (1983). *Implementation and public policy.* Glenview, IL: Scott, Foresman; R. Weatherley & M. Lipsky (1977). Street-level bureaucrats and institutional innovation: Implementing special education reform. *Harvard Educational Review, 47*(2), 171–197; Pressman & Wildavsky (1973), *Implementation.*

93. Mazmanian & Sabatier (1983), *Implementation and public policy,* 41.

94. Mazmanian & Sabatier (1983), *Implementation and public policy,* 41.

95. Interview with Bates, May, 1989.

96. Interview with Hoffman, June, 1989; Interview with Bates, May, 1989.

97. Interview with Hoffman, June, 1989.

98. Mazmanian & Sabatier (1983), *Implementation and public policy,* 41.

99. S. Gordon (1990). Sexuality education in the 1990's. *Health Education, 21*(1), 4–5; M. Howard & J. McCabe (1990). Helping teenagers postpone sexual involvement. *Family Planning Perspectives, 22*(1), 21–26; National Research Council (1989). *AIDS: Sexual behavior and intravenous drug use.* Washington, D.C.: National Academy Press; Lohrmann (1988), AIDS education at the local level; M. Vincent, A. Clearie, & M. Schluchter (1987).

Reducing adolescent pregnancy through school and community-based education. *Journal of the American Medical Association, 257*(24), 3382–3386; L. Zabin, M. Hirsch, E. Smith, R. Streett, & J. Hardy (1986). Evaluation of a pregnancy prevention program for urban teenagers. *Family Planning Perspectives, 18*(3), 119–126.

100. See Appendix A.

101. Mazmanian & Sabatier (1983), *Implementation and public policy*, 41.

102. Mazmanian & Sabatier (1983), *Implementation and public policy*; M. Lipsky (1980). *Street-level bureaucracy.* New York: Russell Sage Foundation; Weatherley & Lipsky (1977), Street-level bureaucrats and institutional innovation; M. Lipsky (1976). Toward a theory of street-level bureaucracy. In W. D. Hawley & M. Lipsky (Eds.) *Theoretical perspectives on urban politics*, 196-213. Englewood Cliffs, NJ: Prentice- Hall.

103. A number of informants indicated that one health teacher was uncomfortable teaching about AIDS.

104. Interview with Wolfrum, October, 1990.

105. The lack of adequate funding was the third most frequently mentioned barrier by informants, behind the beliefs that teachers do not want to provide AIDS instruction because they are uncomfortable discussing this topic and/or because they lack training (75%), and a reluctance within the school administration to mandate AIDS education (50%).

106. Mazmanian & Sabatier (1983), *Implementation and public policy*, 41.

107. Interview with Rosenfeld, June, 1989.

108. Interview with Cranston, June, 1989.

109. Mazmanian & Sabatier (1983), *Implementation and public policy*, 41.

110. Interview with Hoffman, June, 1989.

111. Interview with Wolfrum, June, 1989.

112. Interviews #179; #22; #16; and #6.

113. Interview with Hoffman, June, 1989.

114. Interviews #7; #17; #22; and #25.

115. Interview with Cooper, June, 1989.

116. Interview with Larry Weinstein, member of the Cambridge School Committee, October, 1989.

117. Interview #20.

118. Interview with Hoffman, June, 1989; Interview with Wolfrum, June, 1989.

119. Interviews #6 and #16.

120. Interview #16.

121. Interview with Cooper, June, 1989; Interview with Weinstein, October, 1989.

122. Mazmanian & Sabatier (1983), *Implementation and public policy*, 41–42.

123. Weatherley & Lipsky (1977), Street-level bureaucrats and institutional innovation.

124. Mazmanian & Sabatier (1983), *Implementation and public policy*.

125. Cambridge health education policy (1990). *Recommendation for Health Teams.* Cambridge, MA: Cambridge School Department.

126. Mazmanian & Sabatier (1983), *Implementation and public policy*; Lipsky (1980), *Street-level bureaucracy*; Weatherley & Lipsky (1977), Street-level bureaucrats and institutional innovation; Lipsky (1976), Toward a theory of street-level bureaucracy.

127. B. Rawson (October 22, 1992). Survey yields snapshot of student health. *Cambridge Chronicle*, 10.

128. National Research Council (1989), *AIDS: Sexual behavior and intravenous drug use.*

129. Gordon (1990), *Sexuality education in the 1990's*; National Research Council

(1989), *AIDS: Sexual behavior and intravenous drug use*; B. Bock & L. Hoch (September, 1988). Teaching about AIDS. *Science and Children*, 22–25; National Coalition of Advocates for Students (1987). *Criteria for evaluating an AIDS curriculum*. Boston, MA: Author; National Professional School Health Education Organizations (1984). Comprehensive school health education. *Journal of School Health, 54*(8), 312–315.

130.   Howard & McCabe (1990). Helping teenagers postpone sexual involvement; T. Edgar, V. Freimuth, & S. Hammond (1988). Communicating the AIDS risk to college students: The problem of motivating change. *Health Education Research, 3*(1), 59–65; L. Strunin & R. Hingson (1987). Acquired Immunodeficiency Syndrome and adolescents: Knowledge, beliefs, attitudes, and behaviors. *Pediatrics, 79*(5), 825–828.

131.   National Research Council (1989), *AIDS: Sexual behavior and intravenous drug use*.

132.   Institute of Medicine/National Academy of Sciences (1989). *Mobilizing against AIDS*. Cambridge, MA: Harvard University Press; National Research Council (1989), *AIDS: Sexual behavior and intravenous drug use*.

133.   Howard & McCabe (1990), Helping teenagers postpone sexual involvement; J. Dryfoos (1987). School-based health clinics: A new approach to preventing adolescent pregnancy? *Family Planning Perspectives, 17*(2), 70–75; Vincent et al. (1987), Reducing adolescent pregnancy through school and community-based education; Zabin et al. (1986), Evaluation of a pregnancy prevention program for urban teenagers.

134.   Vincent et al. (1987), Reducing adolescent pregnancy through school and community-based education.

135.   Howard & McCabe (1990), Helping teenagers postpone sexual involvement.

136.   Zabin et al. (1986), Evaluation of a pregnancy prevention program for urban teenagers.

137.   Gordon (1990), Sexuality education in the 1990's; National Research Council (1989), *AIDS: Sexual behavior and intravenous drug use*; Lohrmann (1988), AIDS education at the local level; National Coalition of Advocates for Students (1987), *Criteria for evaluating an AIDS curriculum*; National Professional School Health Education Organizations (1984), Comprehensive school health education.

138.   T. Kirn (1988). Prevention starts in kindergarten in New York City. *Journal of the American Medical Association, 259*(17), 2516–2517.

139.   J. Hepworth & M. Shernoff (1989). Strategies for AIDS education and prevention. In E. D. Macklin (Ed.) *AIDS and families*, 39-80. Binghamton, NY: Hawthorn Press; National Research Council (1989), *AIDS: Sexual behavior and intravenous drug use*; Bock & Hoch (1988), Teaching about AIDS; Kirn (1988), Prevention starts in kindergarten in New York City; M. Quackenbush, M. Nelson, & K. Clark (Eds.) (1988). *The AIDS challenge: Prevention education for young people*. Santa Cruz, CA: Network Publications; National Coalition of Advocates for Students (1987), *Criteria for evaluating an AIDS curriculum*.

140.   Kirn (1988), Prevention starts in kindergarten in New York City; Quackenbush et al. (Eds.) (1988), *The AIDS challenge*.

141.   Quackenbush et al. (Eds.) (1988), *The AIDS challenge*, 172.

142.   National Coalition of Advocates for Students (1987), *Criteria for evaluating an AIDS curriculum*, 2.

143.   Hepworth & Shernoff (1989), Strategies for AIDS education and prevention; Bock & Hoch (1988), Teaching about AIDS; National Coalition of Advocates for Students (1987), *Criteria for evaluating an AIDS curriculum*.

144.   Hepworth & Shernoff (1989), Strategies for AIDS education and prevention;

National Coalition of Advocates for Students (1987), *Criteria for evaluating an AIDS curriculum.*

145. Hepworth & Shernoff (1989), Strategies for AIDS education and prevention; National Coalition of Advocates for Students (1987), *Criteria for evaluating an AIDS curriculum.*

146. Lohrmann (1988), AIDS education at the local level, 332.

9

A Season in the Sun: The Massachusetts Day Care Partnership Project

Lucy Hudson and Susan Latts Vlodaver

During the 1980s child care leapt from relative obscurity into the bright light of public policy. Demographic predictions of a dwindling American workforce focused attention on underemployed groups. Women of childbearing age and those with very young children were identified as a promising pool of new workers, critical to a healthy and growing economy. As increasing numbers of these women entered the labor force, family concerns, including issues of child care, came to the fore.

Nationally, 60% of mothers with children under age six are in the workforce,[1] compared to only 12% in 1950.[2] If current trends persist, by 1995 two-thirds of preschool-age children and over three-quarters of school-age children will have working mothers.[3] These mothers are working for a variety of reasons, including largely downward shifts in the economy, and changes in the structure of the American family. Indeed, conservative estimates suggest that less than 25% of the families in the United States now fit the traditional model in which the father works outside the home and the mother stays home to care for the children;[4] close to 26% of all children live in single-parent families,[5] and many two-parent families need the second income to remain financially self-sufficient.

In a 1990 study of child care arrangements made by working families,[6] an estimated 37% of the children were cared for by their parents with no additional help. When parents were not available, 22% of the children under age thirteen were cared for by relatives, 21% attended child care centers, 13% attended family child care, 3% received care from babysitters in their own homes, and 4% utilized other arrangements. As many parents have shifted, by necessity, from questioning whether they should work to evaluating the child care arrangements available to them while they do, they are often faced with a set of poor choices, sacrificing quality care for affordability or accessibility.

Looking towards a future in which the lack of adequate child care would prevent women from entering the workforce, Massachusetts leaders in the 1980s developed the blueprint for an ambitious child care system for working families. This plan transformed the state's child care landscape.

CHILD CARE IN MASSACHUSETTS

In 1984, Massachusetts Governor Michael Dukakis convened the Governor's Day Care Partnership Project, a group of public employees and private citizens, to investigate the problems of families needing child care and to propose statewide solutions. With significant commitment from the governor and his cabinet, persuasive advocacy from the child care community, and substantial investment from employers, philanthropies, unions, and the academic community, the Project brought widespread attention to the state of child care in Massachusetts. It also became a national model for public-private collaboration on the issue.

Almost ten years have passed since the spring of 1984, when Governor Dukakis charged the members of the Partnership Project with their tasks. In the analysis that follows, the authors discuss the immediate and longer-term impact of the Governor's Day Care Partnership Project, identifying the ways that the state child care system changed in the process. This chapter also offers an opportunity to consider the inevitable limits to costly state innovations, regardless of their merits; this case study suggests that without support from the federal government, the long-term success of ambitious state child care policies is doubtful.

The primary data source for this analysis is fourteen semistructured key informant interviews, conducted in 1988 and 1989, with state agency officials, child care providers, child care resource and referral agency staff, and advocates (see Appendix).[7] Follow-up conversations with these and other informants transpired in 1992 and 1993. In addition, archival materials, including memoranda and other reports from the Partnership Project, were gathered and analyzed, as were national data on child care utilization, quality, and affordability.

This case study begins with a brief history of the Governor's Day Care Partnership Project and a summary of the policy plan proposed in the Project's *Final Report*.[8] An overview of recommendations in the four major substantive areas— resource development, child care quality, affordability, and policy coordination and implementation—follows, with an assessment of the Project's success in implementing the recommendations in each area. The last section discusses the Partnership Project's overall impact on child care in Massachusetts.

The Foundations of the Governor's Day Care Partnership Project

The Massachusetts Day Care Partnership Project developed in response to state and federal child care policy upheavals in the early 1980s. Governor Edward King appeared bent on stemming the budding state interest in child care that had developed in the 1970s.[9] The federal government in President Reagan's first term reduced Title XX monies to support child care for children in low-income families.[10] As a result, although the demand for child care was growing, programs were forced to cut staff and services, and the state system fell into disarray.[11]

Frustrated both by the lack of general support for child care and the absence of a coherent plan for whatever services were to remain, representatives of the child care community developed their own comprehensive plan for state child care policy. Their 1982 report, *Caring about Children in Massachusetts: Feasible Day Care Policy for the 1980s*,[12] stressed the importance of child care affordability, availability, and quality, highlighting the need for coordination among the eleven different state agencies involved in child care policy at that time. According to this report:

> The values and benefits of child daycare are of interest to many fields of practice, especially health, education and social service, but each focusses on one value to the exclusion of the others. These narrow, specialized views are reflected in different bureaucracies of government. Nowhere in government is there a single overarching goal and a system for decision making to assure that one agency, in pursuit of its goal, does not inadvertently defeat the goal of a sister agency.[13]

Child care advocates also became involved in the gubernatorial election process. In May, 1982, they held a mock election debate for all gubernatorial candidates; Michael Dukakis won, and was then endorsed by the child care community. In fact, throughout his reelection campaign, Governor Dukakis promised to develop sound, enduring day care policy.[14]

In July, 1982, the Massachusetts legislature directed the Department of Social Services (DSS), the agency responsible for administering Title XX, "to develop a long-range comprehensive day care plan."[15] The DSS report, *A Comprehensive Child Day Care Delivery System: A Working Plan*,[16] echoed many of the recommendations in *Caring about Children in Massachusetts*. For example, it recognized the need for a new statewide delivery system that included child care resource and referral agencies (CCR&Rs) at the local level, and a child care policy unit at the state level.

Once elected, Governor Dukakis followed through on his campaign promise by constituting the Governor's Day Care Partnership Project (DCPP) in March, 1984. Dukakis charged the DCPP with making policy recommendations that would lead to high quality, affordable child care, accessible to families throughout the Commonwealth.[17] He also stressed the need for a coordinated state delivery system and state policies that would encourage the involvement of other sectors. The term "partnership" was chosen to symbolize "the importance of bringing together and coordinating private and public sector resources to best meet Massachusetts families' and children's needs."[18] The Project was cochaired by the governor's advisor on women's issues and a state senator. Because the recommendations were expected to be reflected in the Governor's budget request for the 1985–1986 fiscal year, the DCPP was given an October, 1984, deadline for its final report.

Over fifty representatives of state and local government, educators, child care providers and advocates, consumers, and business leaders met in five working groups (state government, private sector, local government and school systems, higher education, and state-as-employer) to prepare preliminary recommendations.

Each working group's recommendations received public scrutiny from several hundred people who attended twelve forums across the state; their comments were reviewed and incorporated into "prefinal recommendations." After an editing period of two months, a summary of recommendations was sent for final comments to members of the child care community. According to a DCPP member who was the executive director of a large child care agency, the forums "involved anyone who wanted to be involved in the process. Everyone could see his signature in the Partnership Project and was invested in it."[19]

The Final Report of the Partnership Project

The Final Report of the Governor's Day Care Partnership Project was published in January, 1985. The thirty recommendations were divided into four substantive areas: resource development, quality, affordability, and policy coordination and implementation. To oversee the enactment of these recommendations, Governor Dukakis established the Governor's Day Care Partnership Initiative. Its two-year charter was "to increase the supply, and improve the quality, of affordable day care for the families of the Commonwealth, based on the recommendations made by the Day Care Partnership Project."[20] In the sections below, we set the context for these recommendations within each area, detail the recommendations themselves, and assess the state's response.

Resource development. The *Final Report* found that only about one-third of Massachusetts parents could locate affordable, quality care. Shortages appeared particularly acute for infants, and for children, five to ten years of age, who needed before- and after-school care. Thus the Project considered two dimensions of resource development: increasing the supply of child care, and developing a dependable mechanism for informing parents about whatever child care was available.

The central recommendation in this area, and arguably for the Partnership Project as a whole, was to establish a statewide network of regionally based child care resource and referral agencies (CCR&Rs), with each acting as the community's hub of child care activity. The CCR&Rs were to be jointly supported by public and private funds: The state would pay the start-up costs and would provide a percentage of ongoing funds based on a local matching formula; local governments, the United Way, and other community groups were expected to contribute as well.

The *Final Report* charged the CCR&Rs with seven key tasks:
1. collecting and analyzing data on community child care resources
2. creating innovative partnerships to expand supply
3. providing technical assistance to groups interested in starting or expanding child care programs
4. offering consumer education to parents selecting a child care provider
5. handling voucher management to facilitate employer contributions and to

provide local sites where welfare recipients participating in the state's work and training program could transact their child care business

6. coordinating and purveying training to the entire spectrum of child care workers

7. assisting programs so that they could coordinate resources (for example, sharing transportation, or a toy lending library)

Other related initiatives were proposed to expand the supply of child care in communities, public schools, workplaces, and public housing projects. In keeping with the partnership model of the Project, innovations to stimulate supply were sought from five sets of collaborators: employers and state government; the Commonwealth and its employees with families; the state Department of Education and local school districts; the Executive Office of Communities and Development and local housing authorities; and the Executive Offices of Human Services, Communities and Development, Economic Affairs, the Department of Education, and the Governor's Office of Human Resources.

Did the Partnership Project result in the development of additional resources? As a direct result of the DCPP, eleven new CCR&Rs were established across the Commonwealth between 1985 and 1987; they joined with the Child Care Resource Center of Cambridge, one of the first in the country, to form a statewide network. The CCR&Rs were independent organizations funded by public and private dollars; all but one operated on a not-for-profit basis. The state's Office for Children contracted for core services, requiring the CCR&Rs to find additional private support that would allow them to offer comprehensive services. During the Project years, the CCR&Rs began to set their priorities and to develop services. The broad charter of the CCR&Rs also made successful implementation of all their responsibilities a daunting challenge. Those with sophisticated and creative leadership and staff—located in supportive communities—operated as was hoped, becoming central, trusted members of the local child care community with important relationships to local employers, city governments, and public school systems. Other agencies, either because they were located in resource-poor areas of the state, or because the child care resource and referral functions were not easily integrated into the services they already provided, had more difficulty.

One of the goals of the CCR&Rs was to improve quality by providing information to parents. It was thought that offering counseling would lead to better educated consumers who would demand higher quality child care; eventually, programs that did not meet minimum levels of quality would be forced to improve or to close. According to one CCR&R director, "The information we give to parents helps them feel confident about looking for quality child care. It helps to improve the quality of child care programs when people are demanding characteristics of quality."[21]

There has been no systematic evaluation of the parent education component. Parents who utilized CCR&R counseling services represented a small proportion of the adults seeking care for their children in Massachusetts. In fiscal year (FY) 1988

(July, 1987–June, 1988), the first year all twelve CCR&Rs were in operation, roughly 35,000 parents received information about finding child care;[22] during that time approximately 550,000 children were in child care programs. In FY 1990, the last year for which the state kept such statistics, the CCR&R network had served 25,879 parents in their search for child care.[23] Because the CCR&Rs could only advise parents on current supply, they could not provide workable solutions for many families. Such parents were often confounded by child care choices that were too expensive.

In 1989, Executive Office of Human Services (EOHS) Secretary Philip Johnston announced plans to establish a thirteenth state-funded CCR&R to serve Cape Cod.[24] Because the overall funding for CCR&Rs had not been increased, introducing this agency meant smaller state contracts for the others. This relatively minimal reduction of funding for the CCR&Rs presaged a far worse financial situation: in 1991, with the state's economy in a tailspin, all state funding was withdrawn.

As the state's budget problems have begun to resolve, child care funding has increased somewhat; for FY 1993, CCR&R services were allocated $200,000. While a far cry from the million dollar investment of the late 1980s, it gave encouragement to the struggling CCR&Rs. At present, it is unclear what the CCR&R system will look like in the next few years. It is likely that the larger and more established CCR&Rs will adapt more readily to diminished state support, since their funding sources are more diverse; the future of smaller, newer agencies is in question.[25]

Overall, the supply of licensed child care increased by 15% during the two years of the DCPP.[26] Additional providers of child care appeared in every arena the DCPP had specified; some of this activity no doubt resulted from CCR&R local campaigns to recruit family child care providers, and to support the development of other child care programming that would, in particular, serve infants and school-age children. Following the Governor's Day Care Partnership Initiative, from 1987 to 1991, 217 new child care centers opened and 3,685 additional family child care providers entered the field, representing 12% and 37% net increases respectively.[27]

In the early 1990s, people interested in child care policy began to question whether there continued to be a systemwide need for additional slots,[28] and in fact, by 1992, this overall growth trend had reversed itself. In that year 25 fewer centers and 127 fewer family child care providers held valid licenses to operate.[29] The concern in the area of supply then shifted to the availability of child care slots for children in specific age groups. In Boston, for example, the Boston Foundation Carol R. Goldberg Seminar on Child Care in Boston found an overabundance of licensed child care for preschoolers (three-to five-year-olds), and shortages for the rest: In 1991, while there were only 8,520 three- and four- year-olds to fill 10,456 slots, there were 13,832 children under three competing for 3,349 licensed slots, and 20,156 young school-age children for 2,446 places.[30] Concern also turned to focus on the supply of affordable, high quality care, which, even for three-and four-year-olds, was not thought to be sufficient.

Child Care Quality

Citing several studies linking quality early childhood education with both short-and long-term benefits for children,[31] the *Final Report* focused considerable attention on child care quality—an issue of growing interest to developmental researchers, child care providers, and parents across the country. It noted with alarm the many barriers to attaining and maintaining a high quality child care system: low wages and limited benefits, yielding high staff turnover rates, low professional esteem, and serious difficulty recruiting trained staff; insufficient public funding to fully underwrite the state's regulatory responsibilities; and too few opportunities for training and career advancement.

Over the past twenty years, researchers have identified the critical components of high quality child care programs. Now canonized by the National Association for the Education of Young Children into a generally accepted set of criteria, these components include positive teacher-child interactions; developmentally appropriate curriculum; active parent involvement; high staff qualifications and consistent staffing patterns; respectable wages; and systematic, continuous program evaluation.[32]

Teacher-child interactions. Teachers play a critical role in the education, socialization, and physical well-being of the children in their care. It is, in part, these interactions that enable children to explore the world around them, learning problem-solving approaches and developing self-esteem. In the context of this relationship, children learn to express themselves and communicate more fully with adults and peers. Recent research suggests that the amount of verbal interaction between caregiver and child is among the strongest predictor of quality care.[33]

Curriculum. Developmentally appropriate curricula seek to match teaching techniques and activity content with children's capacities and interests at different developmental stages. A developmental approach requires teachers to be aware of each child's developmental status and particular developmental trajectory. Teachers facilitate children's learning by observing, asking questions, making suggestions, and increasing the complexity of the activity as children become more competent.[34]

Parent involvement. Quality child care programs recognize the primary position parents hold in their children's lives. Caregivers have frequent contact with parents in order to share information about their children's daily activities, interests, and development; parents are seen as experts on their children and their family. Parents and caregivers become partners in caring for, and educating, children. Families also benefit from quality programming, since it offers a supportive social network to parents, and can help parents improve childrearing skills and feel more competent in that role.[35]

Staff qualifications and staffing patterns. Each of the above components of quality are dependent on the child care staff—their qualifications and the ways in which programs deploy them. Teachers set the overall tone of the program by structuring the environment, determining the curriculum, and interacting with children and parents; the better prepared teachers are, the stronger the program.

The 1989 National Child Care Staffing Study (NCCSS), a survey of teachers and their working conditions in center-based child care programs, clearly documented the relationship between training and the quality of care delivered.[36] It demonstrated that training—specifically college-level education—was a far greater predictor of quality than was experience. Other studies support this finding that caregivers with more education, particularly child development training, provided better quality care.[37]

Staffing stability is another crucial element of quality child care. Frequent turnover in caregivers confuses young children and slows development across domains; the NCCSS found children in programs with high staff turnover rates to be less proficient in language and social skills than those who had the benefit of more consistent care.[38] Children with stable caregivers also demonstrated more positive affect when arriving at the child care program.[39]

Finally, child care providers can only provide adequate supervision and individualized instruction for a limited number of children. Research has found that both the total group size and the adult-to-child ratio are critical to maintaining a safe and healthy environment.[40] Small groups in which each staff member is only responsible for a small number of children result in more interactions with children and adults, less aggressive behavior, more cooperation among children, and more elaborate and focused play.[41]

Wages. Among adult work environment variables, wages appear the primary determinant of quality.[42] Child care providers earn remarkably low wages, given their level of education. In Boston, for example, these professionals earn roughly half the salaries of comparably educated women professionals in other fields;[43] national data suggest they earn even less than nonprofessionals such as parking lot attendants.[44] According to the NCCSS, teachers earning the lowest wages were almost twice as likely to leave their jobs as those earning the highest wages.[45] Family day care providers generally earn less than staff in centers.[46]

Limited benefits and stressful working conditions also compromise child care quality. The NCCSS found that only 61% of the teachers working in nonprofit centers, and 16% of those in for-profit centers, received health benefits.[47] Despite their often minimal salaries and benefits, the NCCSS found many providers working long hours—even overtime—without compensation. And while by law, employees are entitled to a break after specific intervals of work, at least one study suggests that child care providers rarely receive them.[48]

Program evaluation. Systematic, periodic, program evaluation is critical to developing and maintaining quality early childhood programming. These evaluations, undertaken either by the programs themselves or by an independent evaluator, generate useful feedback on program operations for administrators, parents, and teachers.[49]

Partnership Project Recommendations on Quality

The Partnership Project's recommendations in the area of child care quality fell into three categories: wages and fringe benefits, training, and program standards.

Wages and fringe benefits. During the early 1980s, many child care programs in Massachusetts reported staff vacancies they were unable to fill. The DCPP recognized that low wages discouraged young people from entering the field, and were primarily responsible for the resulting high staff turnover. It also acknowledged that, in response, some programs had hired unqualified staff, violating the terms of their state license. The *Final Report* asked, "Without substantial wage increases, who will mind our children?"[50] The Salary Upgrading Initiative was designed to alleviate these staff recruitment and retention difficulties by increasing the wages of child care providers in programs with state contracts, roughly 20% of the state's child care providers.[51]

The DCPP established salary guidelines and recommended that over a two-year period the Department of Social Services increase reimbursement rates for contracted programs so that wages would fall within these salary guidelines by the end of the Initiative. The proposed salary range represented an ambitious jump from the average 1985 salaries, which were approximately $10,500 for teachers and $11,800 for head teachers. For a teacher earning an average 1985 wage, attaining the bottom of the guidelines' salary range represented a 19% wage increase; attaining the top of the range yielded a 47% boost in pay.[52]

Training. Prior to the DCPP, providers often did not obtain training, either because their low salaries precluded its purchase, or because there was little monetary incentive to improve their skills. The DCPP recognized that staff training was vital if children were to receive good care.

The *Final Report* offered implementation guidelines for a statewide training program. CCR&Rs were to be allocated funds to determine the training needs of child care providers in their communities, and then to develop the necessary training programs. Several state agencies were designated as partners in the coordination of the statewide plan. Among the requirements for gaining access to these funds, the training had to address the needs of providers from both child care centers and family day care homes, incorporate a counseling and career development component, and be financially and linguistically available to all child care workers.

Program standards. The Massachusetts Office for Children holds the statutory responsibility for licensing both center-based and family child care facilities. Funding for the Office for Children had not kept pace with increasing licensing caseloads. The *Final Report* recommended funding for the Office for Children commensurate with its regulatory and technical assistance tasks.

How successful was the Partnership Project in improving the quality of child care programs? The quality of child care programs in Massachusetts, per se, was not evaluated—either before the Project began or after its termination. However, the findings of the 1989 National Child Care Staffing Study, which examined forty-five child care programs in each of five cities, indicated that the quality of care offered to three- and four-year-olds in Boston was higher than in any of the other cities studied.[53]   The data that follow, then, do not directly assess the effects of the Partnership Project on child care quality; instead, they document the extent to which the recommendations were implemented, particularly as they pertain to wage upgrading and access to staff training, potentially the most significant mediators of quality programming.

   The Wage Upgrading Initiative. The Wage Upgrading Initiative of the DCPP produced significant increases in wages: between 1985 and 1987, Massachusetts appropriated $8 million for increases in child care salaries. Salary upgrading funds were distributed to child care programs that received state funds, with a specific contractual agreement that the money be used only to raise wages. Roughly 75% of all contracted programs participated in the Initiative.[54] Thus, average wages for staff in contracted programs increased by 32%, and family day care providers received a 41% increase in their reimbursement rates. By 1988, salaries fell within a few percentage points of the midpoint of the guidelines established by the DCPP.[55]

   This Initiative appeared to have had some effect on wages across the field, even though only programs with DSS contracts were eligible for the funds. In fact, a survey of contracted and noncontracted child care programs in metropolitan Boston found that comparable salary increases occurred in both types of programs.[56] This was true, perhaps, because the state, as the largest purchaser of child care, influenced the wages that an applicant for any position would accept. Some programs without state contracts were unable to offer competitive salaries, and so lost valued staff to programs holding contracts; this disparity generated some hard feelings.[57]

   The Wage Upgrading Initiative also appeared to have had a positive effect on staff recruitment and retention. Two large day care centers compiled data on the turnover rate in their programs, and found that between 1985 and 1988 the turnover rate fell from 37% to 27% in one program and from 29% to 15% in the other.[58] As one director remarked, "Salaries are still lower than other jobs, but the increases have begun to make people feel good about their job and, perhaps, stay in the field longer."[59] Family day care providers also reported positive effects from the wage upgrading.   "We saw dramatic changes in terms of attracting family day care providers. Several years back it was very difficult to attract anyone to the family day care program."[60] The consensus among providers, advocates, and government officials was that the incremental increases in salaries were beginning to stabilize the child care field.[61] Salary upgrading was read by child care providers as a signal that society was starting to place more value on their work; they were more hopeful about earning a "living wage," and thus remaining in child care. By 1988, there was still a crisis in recruiting and keeping qualified staff, but it had lessened some.[62] Since 1989, however, staff in DSS contracted programs have not received any salary increases, including cost-of-living raises.[63]

   Ironically, parents' ability to afford tuition was the most frequently cited negative result of this Initiative. Twenty-five percent of the programs holding DSS contracts did not request these monies, in part because the Initiative required programs serving a mixed clientele of DSS and non-DSS supported families to charge private-paying families no less than the rate DSS paid for its slots. These programs suspected that these tuition increases would price many low-and moderate-income families out of the child care market, and elected to forego participation.

Training. As a result of the DCPP, the CCR&Rs received funding for training. Each CCR&R developed an individualized training program to meet the needs of community providers. Workshops on a wide spectrum of issues were offered for a modest fee; many were offered in a range of languages. Much of the training was designed for entry-level providers, although some was offered to meet the needs of experienced teachers. In FY 1988, 13,000 child care providers attended courses, workshops, conferences, and seminars funded by the Office for Children; over 9,600 of these staff attended training organized by a local CCR&R.[64]

In addition, many of the CCR&Rs developed training materials for repeated use, such as manuals and videotapes. In FY 1988, the CCR&Rs also fielded roughly 25,000 requests for technical assistance, offering support groups for new administrators and family day care providers, advice to individuals opening centers, and assistance to administrators on program management.[65]

The Department of Social Services had offered training to child care workers since 1983, but prior to the Project, eligibility for the free conferences and college accredited courses was restricted to staff in programs holding DSS contracts. The DCPP transferred the program to the Office for Children (OFC) in FY 1987, and expanded eligibility to all staff in licensed child care centers and family day care homes. The result of this policy shift was a four-fold increase in the number of eligible providers, without any comparable increase in the number of courses offered. In 1988, for example, the Office turned away between 600 and 700 eligible providers each semester.[66] Further, since OFC wanted to ensure that all teaching staff were able to meet the basic staff qualification regulations, training was targeted primarily at entry-level staff, and to a lesser degree, at first-time program administrators. Few courses were offered to more experienced personnel.[67]

Many child care staff could not find appropriate courses that they could afford. Novice teachers needing introductory courses were turned away because space was so limited. More experienced staff who wanted training for continued professional development could not enroll in suitably challenging courses. Overall, the training initiative lacked sufficient funds to serve the number and range of providers desiring training. In addition, it lacked a coherent, sequential system.

The Partnership Project's limited training efforts did, however, lay the groundwork for a statewide Early Childhood Career Development Center, eventually funded by foundations, corporations, and private individuals. As envisioned by child care advocates and early childhood educators, it was to identify training needs, replicate successful models, and develop new approaches in underappreciated content areas or with underserved groups. Training opportunities would be thoughtfully sequenced so that skilled teachers would be able to progress up a career ladder, receiving the financial recognition for advancing their educations that would encourage them to continue teaching. In 1987, these planning efforts bore fruit in the form of the Child Care Careers Institute, supported by a funding consortium led by the Massachusetts Bay United Way. In 1989, with funding from several national foundations, the Center for Career Development in Early Care and Education was launched. Housed at Wheelock College, this center operates with a national training mandate.[68]

In 1990, state funding for child care training was wholly eliminated from the state's budget. The CCR&Rs have continued to sponsor some workshops and courses as part of their general operating mandate. Since then, the Child Care Careers Institute has taken the lead by creating a consortium of Boston-area colleges and universities that offer courses in early childhood education, hoping to develop a coordinated and accessible system of training opportunities for child care staff. An important initiative, its primary limitation is that it only serves Boston and eighty other neighboring communities.

While attending to two of the major sources of compromised quality in child care—wages and training—the Partnership Project did not address other factors that are associated with staff retention difficulties: the lack of fringe benefits, stressful working conditions, and the poor societal image of child care providers.[69] Furthermore, though wages were increased substantially during the years of the Project, they have remained stagnant since. Thus despite its efforts, serious dissatisfaction remains among professionals in the field.

Program standards. During the DCPP's tenure, the state Office for Children convened task forces to assist in the promulgation of school-age child care regulations, and to amend the group day care regulations to include sections on teacher qualifications and pilot or demonstration projects. The family day care licensing staff was expanded by twenty-one licensors to allow for speedier site visits and processing of licensing applications.[70] OFC has striven to maintain its commitment to comprehensive regulations in the face of a shrinking workforce and staff members' anxiety about the future of the agency.

Child Care Affordability

Although there is a range of child care arrangements available to families, child care costs limit parents' choices. Child care is a labor-intensive field; on average, over three-quarters (76%) of a child care center's budget is devoted to staff wages and benefits.[71] Child care is typically a family's fourth largest expense (after food, housing, and taxes); low-income families spend up to one-third of their incomes on child care.[72] And unlike public schools, or even higher education, where tuition accounts for only 30% of total revenues, parents of young children pay 83% of the total bill.[73]

Recent national figures indicate that the average tuition in centers is $1.59 per hour—$80 for a fifty-hour week, or roughly $4,100 per year.[74] In the Boston area, however, costs are significantly higher, with average weekly fees of $200 for infants and $150 for preschoolers in center-based care.[75] Family child care costs vary by provider and by neighborhood, and range from $65 to $225 per week.[76] Because quality care is usually more expensive, access to these programs is often determined by family income.

Attempting to tackle the affordability dilemma creates a conundrum first described by Gwen Morgan in the early 1980s as the "child care trilemma." Three factors (staff wages, adult-to-child ratios, and parent fees) coexist in an uneasy truce. Any attempt to improve one element produces negative consequences for one or both of the other elements: To improve wages, parent fees must increase or the adult-to-child ratio must suffer. To make the program more affordable to parents, adult-to-child ratios must increase or wages must decrease. Quality only improves at the parents' financial expense. Acknowledgment of this conundrum was evident in the Project's *Final Report*, which noted that, "Raising wages to assure quality could increase program rates to a level some moderate income families would be unable to afford."[77]

Partnership Project Recommendations on Child Care Affordability

The affordability recommendations were straightforward: three proposed increased funding for state-subsidized child care for low- and moderate-income parents, and two others focused on making state and federal child care tax policy more progressive.

Two principles guided these recommendations:

Continuity of care. Because children enter the system of state-subsidized care through any one of several doors, a change in parental employment status could terminate the child's eligibility for a particular program, even though the family continued to need subsidized child care. In particular, the *Final Report* cautioned against the unchecked expansion of child care vouchers. Vouchers are attractive because they allow parents more immediate access to subsidized care, since a parent does not need to wait for an opening in a center with a contract. However, if there is no long-term care available when a voucher expires, the family could find itself without child care altogether.

Socioeconomic mix. Many programs enrolling low-income families found themselves serving *only* this population; other programs served middle- and upper-income families exclusively. Socioeconomic segregation, the *Final Report* suggested, compromises the potentially rich environment that child care centers can provide when children of all incomes learn about, and from, one another. Such social isolation "would be harmful to all of our children."[78] As a result, recommendations in the *Final Report* were framed in a manner that encouraged economic integration.

How successful were the Partnership Project's affordability initiatives? In the state's FY 1987 budget, an Affordability Task Force was created to document the stressful impact child care fees had on family budgets, and to propose solutions. In 1987, the Task Force, chaired by the commissioner of the Office for Children, conducted a survey of 750 parents. The survey results were published in *Caring for Our Common Wealth: The Economics of Child Care in Massachusetts*, released in June, 1988. The report documented both the high cost of care to parents, and the programs' tight operating budgets. It also found that 41% of parents surveyed who were not employed said they would go to work or enter a training program if satisfactory, affordable child care were available to them. Finally, it noted that even with the significant investment already forthcoming from state government, only 42% of low-income children in care were receiving the subsidies for which they were eligible.[79]

Between 1985 and 1989, the number of subsidized child care placements increased substantially, from 20,000 to 32,000.[80] The operating principles that governed the subsidized child care system centered on providing dependable child care for children so their parents could work, further their work-related education, or attempt to cope with personal problems that were putting their children at risk for abuse or neglect.

As the state continued to increase its investment in subsidized child care, the Task Force set about proposing additional solutions to the problem. Released in 1989, *Cooperative Solutions to the High Cost of Child Care: Recommendations of the Child Care Affordability Task Force*[81] proposed significant involvement from federal, state, and municipal government, as well as from employers, philanthropies, and child care providers. These recommendations went largely unheeded, since by the time it was published, the state's serious economic downturn had begun. Additional state funding—indeed anything short of budget cuts—could not be considered. Efforts by the Task Force consequently centered on marketing the concept of child care tuition assistance to private employers.

The combination of a deepening recession, an unprecedented state deficit, and a new Republican administration under Governor William Weld yielded drastic cuts in subsidized child care. By 1992, only 22,000 subsidies remained, virtually eliminating the growth that had occurred during the Partnership Project's tenure and immediately afterwards.[82] On the other hand, the DCPP model of public-private partnership approaches to affordability problems has endured. For example, many credit the Project as the breeding ground for the recently completed Boston Foundation Goldberg Seminar recommendations on child care affordability in Boston.[83]

Policy Coordination and Development

At the time of the Partnership Project, eleven state agencies, scattered across five Secretariats, had some investment in child care policy and services. This diffusion of child care interests created confusion among constituencies and promoted competition among the agencies. As the *Final Report* noted, "Conflicting priorities and lack of coordination of resources and leadership by any one agency has been a continual problem."[84]

Partnership Project recommendations on policy coordination and development. The key recommendations in this area focused on defining a single office within the Executive Branch—the *Final Report* recommended the Governor's Office of Human Resources—in which child care policy would be made. Two policy-making bodies were also recommended: a Day Care Cabinet within state government comprised of representatives from all the state agencies that contributed to the state's child care policies, and a Day Care Advisory Committee composed of interested private citizens.

Did the Partnership Project achieve its goals of policy coordination and development? In 1985, Governor Dukakis made a personal commitment to implement the recommendations of the DCPP, and announced the creation of the Governor's Day Care Partnership Initiative for this purpose. The Initiative was a two-year project, administered through the Governor's Office of Human Resources under the direction of the governor's new day care coordinator. The coordinator was responsible for intersecretariat and interagency collaboration, and for developing further plans for the improvement of child care availability, affordability, and quality. She organized and staffed both the Day Care Cabinet, consisting of cabinet secretaries, and an Interagency Working Group, which brought together agency representatives to discuss child care issues. As the Initiative drew to a close, those involved appeared pleased with the fruits of their labor: Eleven of the seventeen major recommendations had been implemented in full, and progress had been made on the rest. Strategies for institutionalizing child care policy development within the permanent structure of state government were explored by the advisory committee, comprised of DCPP participants and other concerned citizens, and members of the Dukakis administration. In 1987, a Day Care Policy Unit was created within the Executive Office of Human Services (EOHS). Over the next three years, it produced periodic reports on both the continuing accomplishments of the DCPP, and on the general status of child care in the Commonwealth. These reports, and the other activities of the Unit appeared to help sustain public interest in child care.

Moving the Day Care Policy Unit to EOHS, rather than keeping it in the governor's office, rendered it a less powerful entity. EOHS was only one of five secretariats contributing to the state's child care policy. Its policy unit could largely dictate the activities of the Departments of Social Services, Public Health and Public Welfare, and the Office for Children, but it could not exact compliance, for example, from the Department of Education, or from the other three secretariats. And in fact, even within EOHS' boundaries, policy unit staff had to negotiate carefully within and across each agency's child care "territory."[85]

A major flaw of the Policy Unit's operation was its failure to integrate the multiple streams of federal and state funding dedicated to child care. These funding streams, each with a specific mission and target population, also have individual eligibility and reporting requirements. Because the DCPP occurred in a period of economic prosperity, and some additional funds were available for specifically targeted programs, the Policy Unit did not appear to feel pressured to establish consensual agreements among funders.

The advisory committee met well into Governor Weld's tenure. However, as the Weld administration took control of child care policy development, original committee members were replaced by Weld appointees. The Day Care Policy Unit ceased to exist, replaced by a single child care policy person who provided expertise and recommendations to the assistant secretary for Human Services in the Executive Office of Health and Human Services (EOHHS).[86] The easy working relationships between advocates and state employees began to disintegrate as funds became scarce, and many committed Dukakis staff left state government. Many of those remaining came to be viewed by some as representatives of an unsympathetic governor; some long-time spokespersons for child care noted that they did not feel well-received by the new administration.[87]

At the same time, a new advocacy group was constituted: the Massachusetts Independent Child Care Organization (MICCO). Its mission was to represent proprietary (for-profit) child care providers, a group largely without state contracts who had felt discriminated against by the referral policies of the CCR&Rs. Historically on the fringe of the policy process, they now seemed to have easier access to Weld officials than did the more established voices for child care.[88] This challenge came at a particularly difficult time, with the state's child care budget shrinking and Governor Weld's avowed support for the privatization of many services that had been managed by state government.[89]

Sympathetic state legislators developed an aggressive legislative strategy to define the state's role. During the development of the 1992–1993 state budget, amendments were introduced that would have moved child care from its home in EOHHS to the Department of Education.[90] While that move failed, it highlighted a growing adversarial climate between the executive and legislative branches of state government on issues of child care policy.

CONCLUSIONS

Was the Governor's Day Care Partnership Project a Success?

The Day Care Partnership Project yielded an immediate increase in the supply of child care and in child care wages; a public commitment to improving quality; substantially increased state spending, primarily in the area of subsidies; and visible, forceful leadership from the Day Care Policy Unit. It also built a coalition of people, representing a wide spectrum of interests, that envisioned and proposed a coherent child care delivery system. The more child care providers and advocates were brought into the policy-making arena, the more strongly they felt the possibility of exerting influence on the future course of child care. The years of the Partnership Project are recalled as a time when government really listened to voices in the child care community.[91] As Heidi Urich, the former coordinator of the Governor's Day Care Partnership Initiative, notes, "Massachusetts was unique among the states in committing itself at that time to a comprehensive program to tackle *all* the problems confronting child care, and in recognizing that this could only be done by mobilizing the highest levels of government and reaching out for partners in the private sector."[92]

To the poor second cousin that was child care, the Partnership Project's considerable monetary investment promoted an increased sense of professionalism and a growing optimism within the field. To many on the outside, however, child care remained undervalued. As one teacher remarked, "My sister-in-law asked me why I spent so much money getting my bachelor's degree just to be a babysitter."[93] Indeed, many parents still do not understand either the components of quality in early childhood programs, or the influences such programs can have on the lives of their children. Unlike other educational institutions—the public schools and institutions of higher education—child care has not yet achieved the public commitment it will need in order to reach its potential as a resource to families and to society as a whole. Despite its putative benefits, child care remains overwhelmingly a private family expense.[94]

The DCPP brought broad attention to the child care field, making child care a visible issue on the public agenda. It likely encouraged foundations to invest in child care-related policy and programming. For example, in 1988—the year after the Partnership Project ended—a consortium of grantors led by the United Way of Massachusetts Bay announced a million-dollar child care initiative; that same year, the Boston Foundation selected child care as the topic of its third Carol R. Goldberg Seminar, a three-year community planning effort. In 1992, the Boston Foundation released the Seminar's final report, *Embracing Our Future: A Child Care Action Agenda*. While the economic and political climate had changed dramatically, the Seminar's composition and recommendations reflected the concerns and intentions of the Partnership Project.[95]

The DCPP also appears to have cast its shadow on national child care policy development. The Act for Better Child Care (ABC), introduced in the U.S. Congress in 1987, is said to have borrowed generously from the DCPP.[96] Finally passed as the Child Care and Development Block Grant in 1990, by 1992 it had brought Massachusetts approximately $10 million to extend Partnership Project activities in child care quality and affordability. More locally, however, as the tenure of Governor Dukakis drew to a close, budget constraints and a political shift away from his priorities dampened, and in some cases, virtually extinguished, the effects of the Partnership.

Effects of the recession on state child care policy. The Governor's Day Care Partnership Project transpired at the end of a bullish period in the state's economic life. A remarkable economic turnaround had occurred between 1975 and 1987: Unemployment dropped from near-Depression levels—12.3% in 1975, to near full employment—3.2% in 1987. State fiscal stability replaced the record deficits of the previous decade.[97]

The serious economic problems that developed in Massachusetts in 1988 no doubt blunted the Partnership Project's impact. Ultimately, public mistrust of the Dukakis administration contributed to the election of the first Republican governor in two decades. From 1988 to 1991, the economy of Massachusetts declined rapidly. The high technology industry faltered, commercial real estate dried up, and housing values fell. The state lost approximately 175,000 jobs in 1991, for a total of 313,000 jobs lost over the prior two-year period.[98] The unemployment rate by 1991 was 9%, almost three times what it had been in 1987.[99] This recession ushered in an era of disinvestment in child care at the state level.

Thus both the success of the DCPP and its undoing must be seen in the context of the state's economic health. A buoyant economy puts people to work, increases competition for workers, and boosts the need for child care; a depressed economy relies on fewer workers and has less need for the "frills" that employers in a competitive labor market might offer to recruit and retain employees. Driven by a prosperous economy's need for productive workers, state government responds with programs, such as subsidized child care, that bring marginal adults into the labor force. When the labor shortage is replaced by large-scale layoffs, government no longer needs to place such a high priority on training potential workers.

It is impossible to determine what Governor Weld's approach to child care would have been had the state been on more secure financial footing. Nor is it possible to ascertain how the Dukakis administration would have handled the budget crisis had he remained in office. Indeed, many Massachusetts citizens felt that Governor Dukakis had denied the state's impending (and some say, predictable) economic downturn during his presidential bid in 1988, making the effects in all arenas, including child care, that much more severe.[100] On the other hand, Dukakis clearly believed in child care's potential benefits to families and children, and moved the issue partly out of personal conviction.

From his actions so far, it does not appear that Governor Weld shares this belief. As the recession deepened in 1990 and 1991, the painstakingly built child care system unraveled. Reductions in subsidized child care slots, discontinuation of the state-funded training program and of child care resource and referral services, decision-making that excluded most child care advocates, and repeated attempts to dismantle the Office for Children fueled the system's disintegration. At first the budget cuts were arguably necessary given the state's deficit. Eventually, however, it seemed to the child care community that the new governor's agenda did not include a priority commitment to quality, affordable child care. For example, during the development of the FY 1993 budget, Governor Weld proposed "privatizing" the Office for Children's child care licensing functions as a cost-saving measure.[101] Massachusetts' stature as a state with better than average child care rests, in part, on sound child care regulations coupled with strong enforcement; removing that function from OFC would likely have compromised the licensing process. The proposal ultimately was defeated by a Democratic legislature and very vocal opposition from parents and providers, but the situation illustrates why those concerned about child care worry about Governor Weld's commitment to the issue.

A Tall Order

The Governor's Day Care Partnership experience suggests that however divergent constituent interests may be, broad coalitions on behalf of child care can yield coherent public policy and significant improvements in practice. That's the good news. The Partnership Project also demonstrated, however, that policy innovations at the state level of government—especially those requiring additional resources— are rarely able to endure serious economic downturns.

Parents cannot afford to bear the full cost of child care, nor should child care providers continue to subsidize these costs through the acceptance of low wages. Public child care cannot realistically be considered wholly, or even primarily, a state's responsibility. The Project's case suggests that federal, state, and local government, the private sector, and parents need to join together to harness the political will and the economic resources necessary for the task.

In the language of economists, child care is both a "merit good" and a "social good." A merit good is "any good or service which provides more benefits to the consumer than the consumer recognizes, so that she or he tends to buy less of it than she or he would with full information about its benefits."[102] A social good is one that "in addition to benefiting the purchaser . . . also provides benefits to the wider community."[103]

Because child care is so expensive, parents must often settle for less costly care—care that is likely to offer fewer developmental benefits to children and which may, in fact, be harmful to their development. The negative consequences of such decisions may not be evident for years, but are likely to have far-reaching impacts on society as a whole. Therefore, it is only with the acceptance of child care as a social good—one that prepares socially responsible citizens and quality workers—that enduring progress in child care policy at all levels of government will occur.

APPENDIX: LIST OF INTERVIEWS

Douglas Baird: President, Associated Day Care Services, Boston, MA, June, 1989.
Kathi Carrales-Thomas: Executive Director, Child Care Project, Dorchester, MA, July, 1988.
Pat Cronin: Director, Day Care Services, Catholic Charities, Somerville, MA, June,

1989.

Nomi Davidson: Technical Assistance Manager, Child Care Resource Center, Cambridge, MA, June, 1989.

Nancy DeProsse: Organizer, District 65, Boston, MA, April, 1989.

Andrea Genser: Director, Child Care Resource Center, Cambridge, MA, June, 1989.

Patty Hnatiuk: Administrator, Special Legislative Commission on Early Childhood Programs, April, 1989.

Francine Jacobs: Co-convener, The Boston Foundation Carol R. Goldberg Seminar on Child Care in Boston, Boston, MA, February, 1993.

Merle Leak: Training Coordinator, Massachusetts Office for Children, Boston, MA, July, 1989.

Jackie Lowe: Executive Director, Massachusetts Association of Day Care Administrators (MADCA), Boston, MA, August, 1988.

Gale Moreno: Director, Open Center for Children, Somerville, MA, July, 1989.

Gwen Morgan: Lecturer, Wheelock College, Boston, MA, July, 1989.

Alice Sajdera: Head Teacher, Open Center for Children, Somerville, MA, May, 1989.

Joyce Sebian: Assistant Director, Day Care Policy Unit, Executive Office of Human Services, Commonwealth of Massachusetts, July, 1988.

Jack Wertheimer: Executive Director, Great Brook Valley Child Care, Worcester, MA, May, 1989.

NOTES

1. Children's Defense Fund (1992). *The state of America's children 1992*. Washington, D.C.: Author.

2. B. Reisman, A. J. Moore, & K. Fitzgerald (1988). *Child care: The bottom line: An economic and child care policy paper*. New York: Child Care Action Campaign.

3. N. L. Marshall, A. D. Witte, L. M. Nichols, F. Marx, M. E. Colten, & W. Miller (1988). *Caring for our common wealth: The economics of child care in Massachusetts*. Boston: Commonwealth of Massachusetts, Office for Children and United Way of Massachusetts Bay.

4. U.S. Department of Commerce: Bureau of the Census (March, 1992). *Household and family characteristics: March 1991* (Current Population Reports: Population Characteristics, Series P–20, No. 458). Washington, D.C.: U.S. Government Printing Office.

5. U.S. Department of Commerce: Bureau of the Census (1990). *1990 census of population and housing* (Summary tape file 1C). Washington, D.C.: U.S. Government Printing Office.

6. B. Willer, S. L. Hofferth, E. E. Kisker, P. Divine-Hawkins, E. Farquar, & F. B. Glantz (1991). *The demand and supply of child care in 1990*. Washington, D.C.: National Association for the Education of Young Children.

7. Unless otherwise indicated, informants are identified by the titles they held at the time of their interviews.

8. Commonwealth of Massachusetts: Governor's Day Care Partnership Project (1985). *Final report of the Governor's Day Care Partnership Project.* Boston: Author.

9. Child Care Resource Center (1981). Coping with cutbacks and planning for the future. *Child Care News, 8*(4), 1.

10. S. G. Garwood, D. Phillips, A. Hartman, & E. F. Zigler (February, 1989). As the pendulum swings: Federal agency programs for children. *American Psychologist, 44*(2), 434–440; U.S. Congress (1981). P.L. 97–35: *The Omnibus Budget Reconciliation Act of 1981.* Washington, D.C.

11. Child Care Resource Center (1981), Coping with cutbacks.

12. G. Morgan (1982). *Caring about children in Massachusetts: Feasible day care policy for the 1980s.* Boston: Boston University School of Social Work.

13. Morgan (1982), *Caring about children in Massachusetts,* 4.

14. Interview with Jack Wertheimer, Executive Director, Great Brook Valley Child Care, Worcester, MA, May, 1989.

15. Massachusetts Department of Social Services. (1983). *A comprehensive child day care delivery system: A working plan.* Boston: Author, 1.

16. Massachusetts Department of Social Services (1983). *A comprehensive child day care delivery system.*

17. Commonwealth of Massachusetts: Governor's Day Care Partnership Project (1985), *Final report.*

18. Commonwealth of Massachusetts: Governor's Day Care Partnership Project (1985), *Final report,* 8.

19. Interview with Wertheimer, May, 1989.

20. Commonwealth of Massachusetts: Governor's Day Care Partnership Initiative (1987). *Partnerships for day care.* Boston: Author, i.

21. Interview with Andrea Genser, Director, Child Care Resource Center, Cambridge, MA, June, 1989.

22. Massachusetts Office for Children (1989). *Child care in Massachusetts: Facts and figures FY '88.* Boston: Author.

23. Massachusetts Office for Children (1991). *Child care resource and referral agencies: FY '90 annual report.* Boston: Author.

24. Karen Sheaffer, Program Manager, Resources and Training, Massachusetts Office for Children, Boston, personal communication, December, 1992.

25. There has been concern for the less established CCR&Rs for several years, as Genser voiced in her June, 1989, interview.

26. Commonwealth of Massachusetts: Governor's Day Care Partnership Initiative (1987), *Partnerships for day care.*

27. Joan Clarke, Manager, Systems Unit, Massachusetts Office for Children, personal communication, December, 1992.

28. Douglas Baird, President, Associated Day Care Services, Boston, personal communication, January, 1993.

29. Personal communication with Clarke, December, 1992.

30. The Boston Foundation Carol R. Goldberg Seminar on Child Care in Boston (1992). *Embracing our future: A child care action agenda.* Boston: Author.

31. J. Berrueta-Clement, L. Schweinhart, W. Barnett, A. Epstein, & D. Weikart (1984). *Changed lives: The effects of the Perry Preschool Program on youth through age 19.* Ypsilanti, MI: High Scope Press; Consortium for Longitudinal Studies (1978). *Lasting effects after preschool.* Washington, D.C.: U.S. Government Printing Office. For a more recent

discussion, see C. D. Hayes, J. L. Palmer, & M. J. Zaslow (1990). The effects of child care. In C. D. Hayes, J. L. Palmer, & M. J. Zaslow (Eds.). *Who cares for America's children?*, 45–83. Washington, D.C.: National Academy Press.

32. S. Bredekamp (Ed.) (1987). *Accreditation criteria and procedures: Position statement of the National Academy of Early Childhood Programs.* Washington, D.C.: National Association for the Education of Young Children.

33. D. Phillips, K. McCartney, & S. Scarr (1987). Child care quality and children's social development. *Developmental Psychology, 23*, 537–543.

34. S. Bredekamp (Ed.) (1986). *Developmentally appropriate practice in early childhood programs serving children from birth through age 8.* Washington, D.C.: National Association for the Education of Young Children.

35. National Association for the Education of Young Children; *Families and early childhood programs.* Washington, D.C.: Author; E. Galinsky (1977). *The new extended family: Day care that works.* Boston: Houghton Mifflin; D. Powell (1987). Day care as a family support system. In S. L. Kagan, D. R. Powell, B. Weissbourd, & E. F. Zigler (Eds.). *America's family support programs*, 115–132, New Haven, CT: Yale University Press.

36. M. Whitebook, C. Howes, & D. Phillips (1989). *Who cares? Child care teachers and the quality of child care in America: Executive summary, National Child Care Staffing Study.* Oakland, CA: Child Care Employee Project.

37. A. Clarke-Stewart & C. Gruber (1984). Day care forms and features. In R. C. Ainslie (Ed.), *The child and the day care setting: Quality variations in day care*, 35–62. New York: Praeger; C. Howes (1983). Caregiver behavior in center and family day care. *Journal of Applied Developmental Psychology, 4*, 99–107; J. Stallings & A. Porter (1980). *National Daycare Home Study.* Palo Alto, CA: SRI International; P. Divine-Hawkins (1981). *Family day care in the United States.* Washington, D.C.: U.S. Department of Health and Human Services; R. Ruopp, J. Travers, F. Glantz, & C. Coelen (1979). *Children at the center: Final report of the National Day Care Study.* Cambridge, MA: Abt Associates; L. Berk (1971). Effects of variations in the nursery school setting on environmental constraints and children's modes of adaptation. *Child Development, 42*, 834–869;

38. Whitebook et al. (1989), *Who cares?*.

39. E. Cummings (1980). Caregiver stability and day care. *Developmental Psychology, 16*, 31–37.

40. American Academy of Pediatrics: Committee on Early Childhood, Adoption, and Dependent Care (1987). *Health in day care: A manual for health professionals.* Elk Grove Village, IL: Author.

41. C. Howes & J. Rubenstein (1985). Determination of toddlers' experience in day care: Age of entry and quality of setting. *Child Care Quarterly, 14*, 140–151; Clarke-Stewart & Gruber (1984), Day care forms and features; M. Cummings & J. Beagles-Ross (1984). Toward a model of infant day care: Studies of factors influencing responding to separation in day care. In R. C. Ainslie (Ed.), *The child and the day care setting*; Howes (1984), Caregiver behavior in center and family day care; Ruopp et al. (1979), *Children at the center*; Stallings & Porter (1980), *National Daycare Home Study.*

42. Whitebook et al. (1989), *Who cares?*.

43. The Boston Foundation Carol R. Goldberg Seminar on Child Care in Boston (1992), *Embracing our future.*

44. K. Modigliani (1988). Twelve reasons for the low wages in child care. *Young Children, 43*, 14–15.

45. Whitebook et al. (1989), *Who cares?*.

46. Willer et al. (1991), *The demand and supply of child care in 1990*.

47. Whitebook et al. (1989), *Who cares?*.

48. M. Whitebook, C. Howes, R. Darrah, & J. Friedman (1982). Caring for the caregivers: Staff burnout in child care. In L. G. Katz (Ed.), *Current topics in early childhood education 4*, 211-235, Norwood, NJ: Ablex Publishing.

49. Bredekamp (1987), *Accreditation criteria and procedures*.

50. Commonwealth of Massachusetts: Governor's Day Care Partnership Project (1985), *Final report*, 29.

51. Only child care programs providing services to children in low-income, working families, those at risk of being abuse or neglected, and those with special needs (including developmental delays and environmental risks) are eligible for contracts with the state's Department of Social Services. And only a minority of those eligible, in fact, secure contracts.

52. Commonwealth of Massachusetts: Governor's Day Care Partnership Initiative (1987), *Partnerships for day care*.

53. M. Whitebook, C. Howes, & D. Phillips (1989). *National Child Care Staffing Study Boston report*. Oakland, CA: Child Care Employee Project.

54. Interview with Joyce Sebian, Assistant Director, Day Care Policy Unit, Executive Office of Human Services, Commonwealth of Massachusetts, Boston, July, 1988.

55. Interview with Sebian, July, 1988.

56. Child Care Resource Center (1986). *Child care salaries and benefits, 1986*. Cambridge, MA: Author.

57. Personal communication with Baird, December, 1992.

58. Interview with Baird, June, 1989.

59. Interview with Gale Moreno, Director, Open Center for Children, Somerville, MA, July, 1989.

60. Interview with Pat Cronin, Director, Day Care Services, Catholic Charities, Somerville, MA, June, 1989.

61. Interview with Sebian, July, 1988.

62. Interview with Sebian, July, 1988.

63. Massachusetts Office for Children: Statewide Advisory Council (1991). *Children's Budget FY '92: Our forgotten commitment to children*. Boston: Author.

64. Massachusetts Office for Children (1989), *Child care in Massachusetts*.

65. Massachusetts Office for Children (1989), *Child care in Massachusetts*.

66. Interview with Merle Leak, Training Coordinator, Massachusetts Office for Children, Boston, MA, July, 1989.

67. Personal communication with Sheaffer, December, 1992.

68. Center for Career Development in Early Care and Education (1993). About the Center. Unpublished document. Boston: Author.

69. Modigliani (1988), Twelve reasons for the low wages in child care.

70. Commonwealth of Massachusetts: Governor's Day Care Partnership Initiative (1987), *Partnerships for day care*.

71. Marshall et al. (1988), *Caring for our common wealth*.

72. The Boston Foundation Carol R. Goldberg Seminar on Child Care in Boston (1992), *Embracing our future*.

73. The Boston Foundation Carol R. Goldberg Seminar on Child Care in Boston (1992), *Embracing our future*.

74. Willer et al. (1991), *The demand and supply of child care in 1990*.

75. The Boston Foundation Carol R. Goldberg Seminar on Child Care in Boston (1992),

Embracing our future.

76. Annajean McMahon, Child Care Choices of Boston, personal communication, September, 1991.

77. Commonwealth of Massachusetts: Governor's Day Care Partnership Project (1985), *Final report*, 39.

78. Commonwealth of Massachusetts: Governor's Day Care Partnership Project (1985), *Final report*, 39.

79. Marshall et al. (1988), *Caring for our common wealth.*

80. Massachusetts Office for Children (1989), *Child care in Massachusetts.*

81. Massachusetts Child Care Affordability Task Force (1989). *Cooperative solutions to the high cost of child care: Recommendations of the Child Care Affordability Task Force.* Boston: Commonwealth of Massachusetts.

82. J. Shortt (March, 1992). Unpublished data, Massachusetts Executive Office for Health and Human Services.

83. See The Boston Foundation Carol R. Goldberg Seminar on Child Care in Boston (1992), *Embracing our future.*

84. Commonwealth of Massachusetts: Governor's Day Care Partnership Project (1985), *Final report*, 42.

85. Personal communication with Sheaffer, December, 1992.

86. When Governor Weld took office, his first EOHS secretary changed the name to the Executive Office of Health and Human Services to correspond to the parallel federal agency.

87. Personal communication with Baird, January, 1993.

88. Personal communication with Baird, January, 1993.

89. "Privatization" would be far-reaching; Weld plan for companies to take over programs could reshape government (April 29, 1991). *Boston Globe*, 1.

90. F. E. Berry, D. B. Cohen, & K. W. Fitzgerald. Early Care and Education Initiative. Unpublished draft. Boston: Massachusetts Children's Legislative Caucus.

91. Interview with Wertheimer, May, 1989.

92. Heidi Urich, former coordinator of the Governor's Day Care Partnership Initiative, personal communication, February, 1993.

93. K. Harrington (May, 1989). As I see it . . . it's more than babysitting. *A Common Ground,* 4(5), 3.

94. The Boston Foundation Carol R. Goldberg Seminar on Child Care in Boston (1992), *Embracing our future.*

95. Interview with Francine Jacobs, Co-convener, The Boston Foundation Carol R. Goldberg Seminar on Child Care in Boston, February, 1993.

96. Personal communication with Baird, January, 1993.

97. Hurting Massachusetts is ready for a new leader (October 21, 1990). *Minneapolis Star and Tribune*, 1A.

98. Massachusetts' job losses continue to break records (August 4, 1991). *The Boston Globe*, A89.

99. L. Rivera-Torres (March, 1993). Economic conversion and community development in New England. Unpublished paper presented at Department of Urban and Environmental Policy Seminar, Tufts University, Medford, MA.

100. Dukakis approval rating plunges to low of 19%, poll shows (March 12, 1989). *Boston Globe*, 25.

101. Children's office cut is criticized (February 5, 1992). *Boston Globe*, 21.

102. M. Culkin, S. W. Helburn, & J. R. Morris (1990). Current price versus full cost: An

economic perspective. In B. Willer (Ed.), *Reaching the full cost of quality in early childhood programs*, 9–26. Washington, D.C.: National Association for the Education of Young Children, 13.

103. Culkin et al. (1990), Current price versus full cost, 13.

10

Considering Race, Class, and Gender in Child and Family Policy

Margery W. Davies and Francine H. Jacobs

Tolstoy declared "all happy families are alike," while Nabokov offered the opposite observation—that "all happy families are more or less dissimilar." In this volume, we have spoken of children and families as though they were unitary entities—all children and families, happy or unhappy, more or less alike. This chapter is meant to correct that impression. The United States, a country with many traditions and cultures, has been portrayed, and has chosen to portray itself, as monolithic—common values, common history, common experiences. But the experiences of poor, female-headed families are not the same as those of two-parent, multigenerational Cambodian immigrant families, or as those of middle-class divorced families in Marin County, California. Mothers experience the world differently than do fathers, wealthy children differently than working-class children, white Protestant families differently than Muslim families. One's racial, ethnic, and religious identity, class affiliation and interests, and gender all profoundly affect daily life. As the United States becomes more diverse,[1] and family forms increasingly depart from the modern nuclear family,[2] students of policy must consider how these differences affect children, families, and the policies that develop to serve them.

Throughout this volume, authors have described the central role political culture plays in framing social policies at all levels of government.[3] Because our national political culture values independence, self-sufficiency, and individual achievement, these policies are quite constricted. But these majority cultural values are not universally held. In fact, there are competing sets of values, often enough found among disenfranchized subgroups of our population. Native American communities, throughout time and to this day, have valued interdependence, not independence. So it was, and is, within black communities since the days of slavery, and among newly arrived immigrant groups, before they become "assimilated." Most women, in most families, across the centuries, have valued interpersonal connections and mutual obligations—the support of human networks. This preference for communal, not individual, responsibility, and group, rather than individual, advancement, has existed throughout our history across peoples and gender.

What we are advocating, in essence, is that we listen to these alternative voices, both to extract lessons from the past and to build policies for the future. This is important not only because it is, simply, the right thing to do. Or because it is the strategic thing to do: insofar as women, persons of color, or of low income are overrepresented among social welfare recipients, policies crafted with their concerns and interests in mind have a better chance for success. We also believe that these alternative voices suggest a model for helping the United States make a successful transition into what is now called the post-modern period—an era of scarce resources, both natural and human—and therefore an era in which those who can collaborate, cooperate, and depend on one another will prevail most effectively.

We promote the use of race, class, and gender frameworks as analytic tools in this process. These lenses encourage us to break down policies into their component parts, and to disaggregate children, parents, and families, into meaningful subgroups, considering their needs, interests, and strengths separate from the mainstream. That is to say, it is not sufficient to ask the question, "Is this a good policy?" or "How well does it benefit children?" One must ask, "*which* piece of the legislation?" "with *which* children?" "under *which* living conditions?"

Similarly, one should not ask "What is good for families?" One needs to ask, "For which subgroups of families does the policy work? And furthermore, one needs to ask, "What benefits or harms individual family members as well as families as a whole?" For sometimes policies of great importance to certain members are largely irrelevant to others. For example, the absence of universal child care in this country does not affect men and women, mothers and fathers, equally. To begin, many children live in single-parent, mother-headed homes; these mothers, often strapped for money, must balance their desire for quality child care with the availability of affordable care.[4] They are compromised, or guilty, with either choice. And mothers in two-parent families more often stay home from work with sick children, or on snow days, or during vacations. To say that the lack of child care in this country affects young families is true but inexact. It does not point policy makers in the proper direction.

We have generated three broad sets of questions to be asked within these frameworks:

1. *The first pertains to the ways that a "social problem," to be addressed by a particular policy, is framed.* Social problems are socially defined. They represent some collective notion of what is a serious problem warranting public intervention. Rather than accepting problem definitions as givens, one should examine these problem statements critically. Oftentimes the way a problem is framed either *exaggerates* or *minimizes* the differences between subgroups and the majority.

   For example, there remains a public perception that single-parent, African-American women "take advantage" of the welfare system. They lack self-sufficiency, as the problem might be framed. But African-American families often care for their elderly family members at home, "underutilizing" nursing homes, while members of the "majority" culture quite easily lay that responsibility onto the public. And our policies support the majority's approach, discounting the virtues of African-American family behavior and highlighting what is likely a specious difference between the family self-sufficiency of poor African-American families and of others.

2. *The second set of questions pertains to the character of the policy and program.* It is generally believed that for child and family programs to be successful, they must be respectful—acknowledging and reflecting the attitudes, beliefs, and life circumstances of subgroup, as well as majority, members. In examining a policy or program critically, then, one must ascertain whether or not the service modality "fits" the prospective participants. For example, in providing AIDS education, a worthwhile venture, local school districts must consider whether children from diverse cultures are comfortable discussing sexual matters in coeducational classes.

    There are many other questions to include here. For example, are there differing participation rates across subgroups and if so, what accounts for them? Is there a bias to the policy, either as proposed, or as implemented? For example, Nelson compares benefit levels of men not working "outside the home" and receiving unemployment benefits, to those of women, also not working "outside the home," who are taking care of children and receiving Aid to Families with Dependent Children (AFDC).[5] Unemployment pays better, revealing a clear gender bias in the way society defines and values "work."[6]

3. *The third set of questions pertains to the potentially differential outcomes, intended or unintended, of policies and programs.* Here one might ask whether a policy's consequences are different for subgroups of people, based on their race, social class, or gender. When differences are established, do they appear intentional or unintentional? For example, in a study of the impact of no-fault divorce laws in California, which were enacted to replace what were considered to be demeaning and even sexist laws where the "fault" of one spouse or the other had to be proved, Weitzman found that the "unintended consequences" included a significant decline in women's financial security and economic status.[7] One also needs to question the assumptions that underlie definitions of success or impact. Through what process have outcome indicators been chosen, and do they reflect what subgroup members consider progress?

In using these sets of questions to tease out the racial, class, and gender-related components of child and family policies, it is also important to remember that these components intersect and interact with each other. A white middle-class woman who asserts her position in strident tones can be viewed as behaving "like a man," or in a more "lower-class" way.[8] African-American families differ by social class;[9] African-American women differ from African-American men.[10] Poor mothers in homeless shelters are often fleeing abusive home situations. Do programs frame their problems primarily as gender-related or as poverty-related, and how do services either address or ignore these problems? Because of the complicated, sometimes overlapping, sometimes divergent influences of these multiple identities, we turn next to a more differentiated examination of each individual characteristic.

RACE

Over 130 years after the Emancipation Proclamation, and 40 years after the advent of the Civil Rights movement, the issue of race is still very much with us. The worst urban riot of the twentieth century, which erupted in South Central Los Angeles in April, 1992, after the acquittal of four white police officers charged with beating an African-American motorist, was a potent reminder that race matters.[11]

Whether one is a member of a racial majority or minority, race profoundly affects the daily lives of children and families in America. This is manifest in various ways. Members of certain racial and/or ethnic groups may have a disproportionate share of a particular problem, and in many cases, the problem's definition is not their own; may be subject to discrimination, outright and intentional, or subtle and unintended; or may have developed particular strengths that could serve as models for many other groups.

The following are two examples of how an analysis by race can reveal the disproportionate impacts of problems on "minorities." Children of color, for instance, are more likely to be poor than white children. In 1989, fewer than 15% of white children were poor, compared with 36% of Hispanic and 44% of African-American children.[12] In an assessment of the status of African-Americans in the late 1980s, Moss and Reed concluded that although there had been certain significant advances over the preceding thirty years—notably in the number of elected officials—widespread discrimination in the areas of health care, housing, education, employment, and the criminal justice system still existed.[13] Race has been and continues to be one of the dominant factors in U.S. society.

Homelessness is another example. African-Americans are overrepresented among the ranks of homeless families.[14] Some of the causes of this are structural: African-Americans are disproportionately poor in the United States; cutbacks in federally subsidized housing have consequently had a disproportionate effect on African-Americans.[15] Some of the causes involve outright discrimination: banks have often red-lined neighborhoods that are poor and predominantly African-American;[16] landlords have refused to rent to African-Americans. While there is clearly concern about homeless families, that concern has not yet resulted in policies and programs, such as massive increases in funding for governmental programs to ensure that all families are safely and permanently housed.[17] It is possible that the absence of a more aggressive governmental response stems in part from the fact that homelessness is disproportionately an African-American problem.

Another question to be asked at this point is whether or not an agreed-upon problem affects different groups in different ways. For example, although infant mortality rates in the United States may have decreased slightly in recent years, the disparity between rates for African-Americans and for whites has increased.[18] A second example of the way in which race helps define a problem can be found in the study of AIDS education in Cambridge, which was one of the first communities in Massachusetts to provide it in the public schools.[19] As Griffith concludes, AIDS education was implemented in Cambridge through a fortunate combination of special circumstances: people from outside the school system who were willing to push for policies and then to do the bulk of the work of carrying them out, combined with a school administration that did not try to stop them. But the demographic diversity of Cambridge may also have played a role. Having a higher percentage of people of color than the average for the state, and given that the rate of HIV infection has so far been higher in communities of color than for the population as a whole, Cambridge also had a relatively high number of AIDS cases. Thus people in Cambridge concerned about public health were forced to be more aware of the problem, and to have more incentive to implement health-education programs as quickly as possible. In both these cases of AIDS education and policies for homeless families, race can be seen as a factor in the definition of a problem and its urgency.

"Minority" group behaviors are also sometimes seen as virtuous. Occasionally, strengths of so-called "minority" groups are not only broadly recognized, but even taken as models to emulate. One example is how some Cambodian families help their children with homework. Often, the entire family gathers around the kitchen or dining room table after supper, and everybody does their homework, parents and children alike. This family practice has been identified as a key to the rapid success in school of the children in recently arrived Cambodian immigrant families. Within the African-American community, a tradition of self-help, volunteerism, and community interdependence has been identified as key to the survival of families within an essentially hostile society.[20]

Finally, it is important to identify the sometimes unintended, differential consequences of child and family policies. The Family and Medical Leave Act (FMLA), signed into law by President Clinton in early 1993, applies only to firms with fifty or more employees, and employees who have been employed for at least one year. But African-Americans, Hispanic Americans, Native Americans, and Asian-Americans are both disproportionately employed in smaller firms with fewer than fifty employees, and disproportionately represented among those marginal workers who do not stay long with one employer. Thus employees from these racial groups are underrepresented among those workers covered by the Family and Medical Leave Act, and this legislation has an "unintended" racial consequence.

SOCIAL CLASS

One of the tricky aspects of identifying the impact of social class in the United States is that racial and social class factors are so frequently intermingled.[21] African-Americans, Hispanic Americans, and Native Americans are all disproportionately represented among the lower socioeconomic income groups. Nonetheless, to the extent possible, we should attempt to single out social class, and to examine ways in which it influences child and family policy.

Class analysis is important because it reinforces the understanding that people are members of social groups, as well as individuals. This may seem a simple and obvious point. But social policies in the United States have often carried the unspoken assumption that the plight of the "downtrodden" is the result of individual failure or personal misfortune, and can be alleviated by individual effort or acts of charity.[22] The nineteenth-century pauper was destitute through the error of his ways, not through the structural change wrought by the economic forces of nascent industrialization and urbanization; if only he would make the effort to mend his ways of sloth and intemperance, he could better his lot in life. The impoverished widow of the early twentieth century had suffered the misfortune of her husband's death and was worthy of the state's bestowal of a mother's pension. A more structural response of child care and adequate wages for women's work was rarely the solution of choice. This emphasis on the individual has often obscured the structural position of children and families from different social classes, and the ways in which class forces have shaped child and family policies.

"Class" can be used in a variety of ways. Class *position* refers to the place that a person or group occupies in a society's overall socioeconomic structure. Class *interests* come into play when people, either self-consciously or not, act in a way to maintain their own or their group's class position. Class *bias* refers to the way in which someone's class position or interests influence their attitudes or way of looking at the world.

Does class position have an effect on which people have the problem that policies are meant to address? Precisely because not all child and family policies in the United States are universal, some are specifically directed at people in certain socioeconomic classes, primarily the poor. In fact, this could be said of many social welfare policies in the United States—Aid to Families with Dependent Children, Medicaid, and school breakfast and lunch programs, to name just a few. Programs for the homeless definitely fall into this category. While this targeting certainly appears to make sense—families with secure homes do not seem to need any homeless policies—there is a fundamental drawback of targeting. Programs that are not for all people are the most vulnerable to cutbacks. In a society where caring for "other people's children" has not always been a priority, this is a risk.[23]

The Family and Medical Leave Act has also been criticized for not including families from the lowest socioeconomic groups who, like racial "minorities," are more likely to be employed in firms with fewer than fifty employees and whose marginal employment status causes them to move from one employer to another.[24] As Karr Kaitin points out, this criticism, as well as the criticism that it was only the more affluent families who would be able to afford to take advantage of an unpaid leave, has been levelled at the FMLA since it was first proposed in 1985.[25] But, as the case of Lillian Garland, a bank teller who was denied her job upon returning from the birth of her baby, illustrates, even lower-paid workers can benefit from the job security that the FMLA provides. Nonetheless, it seems plausible to argue that in practice, the FMLA will have the effect of excluding, not to say discriminating against, the lowest-paid and most marginal workers, and, therefore, those workers from the lowest socioeconomic strata.

It is interesting to note that the class position of two groups of people in the case studies underlay their very active mobilization to act on behalf of their class interests. In the case of the Baby Doe legislation, doctors actively organized, initially to prevent the regulations from being put into place at all, and having failed to accomplish that, to influence the scope and wording of the statute. While the doctors involved in this endeavor may have seen it simply as the "right thing to do," given their beliefs about the best process for medical decision making, it can also be seen as a clear example of doctors, members of the professional-managerial class, defending their control of their work and workplace.[26]

In the case of the long battle over the federal Family and Medical Leave Act, the Chamber of Commerce engaged in a very aggressive defense of what it construed to be the interests of the class of small businessmen and women. This campaign was successful in diluting the scope of the legislation when it was first introduced in 1985 (eighteen weeks of unpaid leave covering all firms with more than five employees), so that the legislation as passed in 1993 covered many fewer workers (twelve weeks of unpaid leave covering only firms with more than fifty employees).[27]

There has also been discrimination on the basis of social class within child and family policies. As Davidson outlines in her study of the care of dependent children, beginning with the establishment of almshouses in the nineteenth century, families were punished simply for being poor.[28] Orphanage care, particularly for children whose indigent parents were in fact still alive, the Westward Migrations which removed children from their families, and the abuses of the foster care system—all can be seen as examples of families being discriminated against because of their poverty.

Such outright discrimination has often been accompanied by, and even caused by, discrimination inherent in the class biases of some of the people designing and implementing certain policies. Considering poverty at least a personal failing if not a crime, middle-class social reformers and social workers of the late nineteenth and early twentieth centuries commonly defined poor families as deficient, and the care of their children as "neglect."[29] The Child Savers had little compunction about intervening in poor and working-class families to an extent that they would never have tolerated in their own, predominantly middle-class, families.

Inherent in this practice is a class-biased assumption that middle-class practices of raising and caring for children are the "correct" ones, and that some practices found among working-class or poor families are wrong. This issue has been joined within both the family support movement and homeless shelters. Just as providers have been suspected of attempting to impose their racially grounded values on clients, they have been charged with class-biased insensitivity in programs they provide for families.[30] A homeless family shelter worker in Little's study of municipal homeless policies stated: "I think family support is a classist notion."[31] The question of mandatory parent education classes is particularly thorny. Attention to the class biases and assumptions inherent in programs is important, for if programs do not speak to both the strengths and the self-identified needs of target groups, as well as their socially defined needs, those groups are unlikely to profit from the services.[32]

The impact of child and family policies can also vary by social class, and some of the consequences are not necessarily as they were intended. The Governor's Day Care Partnership Project in Massachusetts is an interesting case in point.[33] Designed to increase the supply of affordable child care, and to improve the quality of child care in part through increasing the salaries of low-paid child care teachers, the program enjoyed some initial success when it was first introduced in the mid-1980s. The most immediate beneficiaries were families with low incomes—through the expansion of child care subsidies—and child care workers whose salaries rose. When the recession of the late 1980s and early 1990s hit, state funding for child care in general, and these initiatives in particular, decreased at a violent rate. Hit especially hard were lower-income families using subsidized care. Some child care providers went out of business. Being low-income means that even when policies are helpful, one cannot feel secure in them.

GENDER

One could argue that child and family issues are by definition women's issues, and that most child and family policies have a more direct effect on women than they do on men, since women have been and are the primary caregivers in our society. They assume primary responsibility for raising children, and they also take care of other family members, for instance, aging parents. While many have warned of the dangers of defining child and family issues as women's issues,[34] it is hard to avoid.

Most of the policies examined by the case studies in this book are addressed primarily to women. People who helped to formulate the Family and Medical Leave Act saw it from the outset as legislation on behalf of women.[35] There was and is a good deal of debate among feminists about the advisability of supporting any legislation which speaks to the "different" needs of women.[36] Some people maintain that anything that carries with it even the whiff of "protectionism" can be used just as easily to keep women out as well as to protect them. But advocates of the Family and Medical Leave Act argued that, given the caregiving responsibilities that still rest in large part on women's shoulders, it is necessary to have policies that attempt to "level the playing field" for women in the labor force. Besides, since the FMLA does not mandate that women rather than men should take leave to care for a family member, it is not protectionist legislation. And early on, when the legislation was broadened to include medical as well as family leave, people were quite conscious that this would expand its support to people who would have no trouble in seeing medical leave as just as beneficial to men as to women.

The family support programs in Kentucky, Missouri, and Maryland examined by Bonnie Hausman were also more likely to have women as their clients than men. In some cases, such as the Parents as Teachers program in Missouri, this just happened because women were more likely to be able to use the program.[37] In others, such as the Friends of the Family programs for pregnant and parenting teens in Baltimore, the target population was teenage mothers. This focus on mothers, rather than on both parents or other family members, is both a strength and a weakness for the current crop of family support programs. On the one hand, it acknowledges who, indeed, is meeting day-to-day parenting responsibilities. On the other hand, this very assumption leads to particular program content and structure that does not encourage fathers to participate. In effect, there is a gender bias, born of experience.

It is also important to take into account the particular needs and differences of males and females, if indeed these differences are real. The PACE initiative in Kentucky is an interesting example of the ways in which gender shapes the nature of services. Apparently a number of the women who participated in the program and learned to read aroused the jealousy of their husbands, who felt that their wives were trying to better themselves to the detriment of their spouses. Staff in the PACE project responded by introducing "empowerment training" for the women so that they would be able to handle their husbands' objections. This was an example of the explicit recognition of the power imbalance between women and men, and of the attempt to redress that imbalance.

Gender differences are obscured however, when one looks at how domestic violence is framed. The common term, "spousal abuse," suggests that either spouse both commits and suffers the violence. As a recent journal article notes:

> By definition spousal abuse, more commonly of a woman, is a behavior pattern that occurs in physical, emotional, psychological and sexual forms. Its purpose is to control and maintain power by the abuser, usually a man. Women receive the greatest share of violence and battering, accounting for approximately 95% of all spousal violence victims.[38]

When wife battering is spoken of as "spousal abuse," it obscures real differences in its impact on women and men. Women overwhelmingly suffer it; men overwhelmingly commit it. The neutral term "spousal abuse," thus, can lead to wrongheaded interventions.

One of the reasons that some female-headed families are homeless is that the women are fleeing domestic violence.[39] It seems important for shelter staff and advocates to be alert and sensitive to this kind of situation. A woman who has summoned up the courage to leave an abusive situation is demonstrating a great degree of strength, and certainly should not be seen as someone who has trouble holding her family together—here, the issue of how the problem is defined pertains. Such a woman may be in little need of parenting education or child development courses. Instead, the best way to support her may be to help her establish a new, safe home, and to provide her with support and advocacy for making her way through the court system. Child and family policies that do not take into account many women's vulnerable position in society will often miss the mark.

It is also possible for the gender dimension of policies to have unintended consequences. In many shelters for homeless families, no males over the age of fourteen are allowed.[40] This rule was generally implemented to separate homeless families from the ranks of single homeless men, a significantly different population with its own specific needs. But such a policy can break families apart, separating fathers and older sons from the rest of the family, and making it all the harder to get domestic life reorganized.

The impact of race, class, and gender on the history and development of child and family policy in the United States is both complex and profound. The lessons drawn from the case studies in this book offer only a glimpse of the ways in which they need to be taken into account. Considering these factors in a central way will help make policies and programs better. It also will signal a shift in our appreciation of the rich diversity around us.

NOTES

1. Maintaining that "ethnicity is one of the most basic elements of our being," H. P. McAdoo argues that more attention must be paid to the distinct varieties of family cultural ethnicity that exist in the United States, particularly in light of our country's increasing demographic diversity. H. P. McAdoo (Ed.) (1993). *Family ethnicity: Strength in diversity*. Newbury Park, CA: Sage Publications, ix.

2. In *The way we never were: American families and the nostalgia trap* (New York: Basic Books, 1992), S. Coontz argues persuasively that there has long been more diversity in family composition than the ideological predominance of the self-sufficient breadwinner father/homemaker mother model would have us believe. See F. K. Goldscheider & L. J. Waite (1991). *New families, no families? The transformation of the American home*. Berkeley, CA: University of California Press, for another interesting perspective on this point.

3. See, for example, F. Jacobs (this volume), Child and family policy: Framing the issues; P. Little (this volume). Municipal policies for homeless families.

4. See L. Hudson & S. Vlodaver (this volume). A season in the sun: The Massachusetts Day Care Partnership Project.

5. B. Nelson (1990). The origins of the two-channel welfare state: Workmen's Compensation and Mother's Aid. In L. Gordon (Ed.), *Women, the state, and welfare*, 123–151, Madison, WI: University of Wisconsin Press.

6. See M. Davies (this volume). Who's minding the baby? Reproductive work, productive work, and family policy in the United States.

7. L. Weitzman (1985). *The divorce revolution: The unexpected social and economic consequences for women and children in America.* New York: Free Press.

8. Peggy Barrett (February 25, 1993). Talk at Tufts University, Medford, MA.

9. C. V. Willie (1991). *A new look at black families* (4th ed.). Dix Hills, NY: General Hall.

10. P. H. Collins (1991). *Black feminist thought: Knowledge, consciousness, and the politics of empowerment.* New York: Routledge.

11. See C. West (1993). *Race matters,* Boston: Beacon Press.

12. National Commission on Children (1991). *Beyond rhetoric: A new American agenda for children and families,* 24. Washington, D.C.: Government Printing Office.

13. E. Y. Moss & W. L. Reed (1990). Stratification and subordination: Change and continuity. In *Assessment of the status of African-Americans,* Vol. 1: Summary. Boston: William Monroe Trotter Institute, University of Massachusetts at Boston.

14. P. Little (this volume). Municipal policies for homeless families.

15. W. A. Leigh (Winter, 1989). Federal government policies and the "housing quotient" of black American families. *The Review of Black Political Economy, 17*(3), 25–42; R. G. Bratt, C. Hartman, & A. Meyerson (Eds.) (1986). *Critical perspectives on housing.* Philadelphia: Temple University Press. In this volume, see in particular Citizens Commission on Civil Rights, The federal government and equal housing opportunity: A continuing failure, 296–324; R. G. Bratt, Public housing: The controversy and contribution, 335–361; and C. Hartman, Housing policies under the Reagan administration, 362-376.

16. Citizens Commission on Civil Rights (1986), The federal government and equal housing opportunity; K. T. Jackson (1985). *Crabgrass frontier: The suburbanization of the United States.* New York: Oxford University Press.

17. There is even anecdotal evidence that homelessness is taken for granted: several professors at Boston-area universities in the early 1990s report that their students are surprised to learn that homelessness has not always been a problem in the United States. (F. Jacobs, A. MacEwan, S. Ostrander, personal communications.)

18. U.S. baby deaths hit new low in '90 (March 12, 1993). *Boston Globe.*

19. B. Griffith (this volume). AIDS education in the Cambridge public schools: An implementation study.

20. J. M. Martin & E. P. Martin (1985). *The helping tradition in the black family.* Silver Spring, MD: National Association of Social Workers; L. Gordon (September, 1991). Black and white visions of welfare: Women's welfare activism, 1890–1945. *Journal of American History, 78*(2), 559–590; P. Giddings (1984). Chap. 6: "To be a woman, sublime": The ideas of the National Black Women's Club Movement (to 1917). *When and where I enter: The impact of black women on race and sex in America.* New York: William Morrow.

21. W. Reed (Ed.) (1990). *Assessment of the status of African-Americans.* Boston: William Monroe Trotter Institute, University of Massachusetts at Boston; W. J. Wilson (1978). *The declining significance of race.* Chicago: University of Chicago Press.

22. M. B. Katz (1989). *The undeserving poor: From the war on poverty to the war on welfare.* New York: Pantheon; W. N. Grubb & M. Lazerson (1982). *Broken promises: How Americans fail their children.* New York: Basic Books.

23. Katz (1989), *The undeserving poor*; Grubb & Lazerson (1982), *Broken promises.*

24. D. M. Gordon, R. Edwards, & M. Reich (1982). *Segmented work, divided workers: The historical transformation of labor in the United States.* New York: Cambridge University Press.

25. Karr Kaitin (this volume), Congressional responses to families in the workplace:

The Family and Medical Leave Act of 1987–1988; A. Radigan (1988). *Concept and compromise: The evolution of family leave legislation in the U.S. Congress.* Washington, D.C.: Women's Research Educational Institute.

26. See M. Pott (this volume), Selective nontreatment of handicapped newborns: Implementation of the Baby Doe laws of 1984; P. Starr (1982). *The transformation of American medicine.* New York: Basic Books; G. E. Markowitz & D. Rosner (1979). Doctors in crisis: Medical education and medical reform during the Progressive Era, 1895–1915. In S. Reverby & D. Rosner (Eds.), *Health care in America: Essays in social history*, 185–205. Philadelphia: Temple University Press.

27. Family values at last (February 7, 1993). *Boston Globe*, 72; Radigan (1988), *Concept and compromise.*

28. C. Davidson (this volume). Dependent children and their families: A historical survey of United States policies; Katz (1989), *The undeserving poor*; M. B. Katz (1986). *In the shadow of the poorhouse: A social history of welfare in America.* New York: Basic Books.

29. L. Gordon (1988). *Heroes of their own lives: The politics and history of family violence.* New York: Viking Penguin.

30. B. P. Davidson & P. J. Jenkins (November, 1989). Class diversity in shelter life. *Social Work, 34*(6), 491–495

31. Little (this volume), Municipal policies for homeless families.

32. F. Jacobs, P. M. D. Little, & C. Almeida (1993). Supporting family life: A survey of homeless shelters. *Journal of Social Distress and the Homeless, 2*(4), 269–288; Davidson & Jenkins (November, 1989), Class diversity in shelter life.

33. L. Hudson & S. L. Vlodaver (this volume). A season in the sun: The Massachusetts Day Care Partnership Project.

34. M. F. Berry (1993). *The politics of parenthood: Child care, women's rights, and the myth of the good mother.* New York: Viking.

35. Karr Kaitin (this volume), Congressional responses to families in the workplace.

36. L. Vogel (1993). *Mothers on the job: Maternity policy in the U.S. workplace.* New Brunswick, NJ: Rutgers University Press; W. Sarvasy (Winter, 1992). Beyond the difference versus equality policy debate: Postsuffrage feminism, citizenship, and the quest for a feminist welfare state. *Signs: Journal of Women in Culture and Society, 17*(2), 329–362; J. Lewis & G. Astrom (Spring, 1992). Equality, difference, and state welfare: Labor market and family policies in Sweden. *Feminist Studies, 18*(1), 59–87; L. Vogel (Spring, 1990). Debating difference: Feminism, pregnancy, and the workplace. *Feminist Studies, 16*(1), 9–32; M. Minow (1990). *Making all the difference: Inclusion, exclusion, and American law.* Ithaca, NY: Cornell University Press.

37. B. Hausman (this volume), Policy entrepreneurship and the emergence of family support programs.

38. J. H. Kashani, E. D. Anasseril, A. C. Dandor, & W. R. Holcomb (March, 1992). Family violence: Impact on children. *Journal of the American Academy of Child and Adolescent Psychiatry, 31*(2), 181–189, 184.

39. M. Bograd (1988). Feminist perspectives on wife abuse: An introduction. In K. Yllo & M. Bograd (Eds.), *Feminist perspectives on wife abuse*, 11–26. Newbury Park, CA: Sage Publications.

40. Jacobs, Little, & Almeida (1993), Supporting family life.

11

On the Eve of a New Millennium

Francine H. Jacobs and Margery W. Davies

A friend described her niece's recent suburban high school commencement this way: "They looked like us—dressed down, long hair—and they talked like us—indignant about injustice, committed to activism. It was a 1960s graduation all over again!" This is a dramatically different scene than graduation at that same high school five years earlier, in 1988. At that commencement the students were dressed up and self-congratulatory; the conversation was about "making it" for oneself, not making it better for others. It was a 1980s graduation for sure.

This putative shift away from the single-minded pursuit of personal interests toward community service is one of the ideological cornerstones of the new Clinton administration.[1] As secretary of the Department of Health and Human Services, Donna Shalala, noted:

> Here's our vision: legions of Americans, in growing numbers every year, organizing immunization drives . . . teaching in public schools . . . counseling troubled kids . . . and sharing their enthusiasm for a better national future. We're investing in national service because there are huge needs in our communities. But that's not the only reason. Many young people are yearning to be part of something larger than themselves—some legacy for their generation. They want to serve. They want to learn. They want a social voice. They dream of a better future for all of us.[2]

In this concluding chapter, we attempt to discern the early outlines of that legacy. Using the five dimensions of policy activity presented by Jacobs earlier in this volume,[3] we identify trends in child and family policy over the 1980s and early 1990s. We note several of the structural and philosophical changes in the general culture, and most pointedly in assumptions about the form and function of the family, that are reflected in these policy trends. We conclude with considerations for future child and family policy.

PROGRESS IN THE POLICY DOMAIN

Taken as a whole, the United States can claim some progress since 1980 towards an expanded view of proper governmental actions on behalf of children and families. But this progress remains incremental, not dramatic, and it is not uniform across policy dimensions. We detail below the evidence for this assessment.

Are Policies Child-centered or Family-centered?

Over the decade, families have gained prominence in child policy deliberations, though in no way are they as visible as research and practice would suggest they be. The decade began with passage of a major piece of federal legislation, P.L. 96–272, the Child Welfare and Adoption Assistance Act of 1980, that acknowledged the critical role of families—even, in this case, the "failed" families of abused or neglected children—in promoting child development. The legislation proposed supporting and maintaining children in their families of origin as the primary strategy, reversing years of reliance on an out-of-home placement system that had, in fact, dissolved many of these high-risk families.[4] This former practice had denied the attachments of high-risk children to their families; P.L. 96–272 validated the family as a powerful, potentially growth-promoting entity. By mid-1993, virtually all state child welfare systems had progressed in developing at least some family-centered alternative interventions with high-risk families. In August, 1993, President Clinton signed the Omnibus Budget Reconciliation Act of 1993 (P.L. 103–66), which included almost one billion dollars, to be spent over five years, on family preservation and family support services.[5] State child welfare agencies must use the funds to strengthen families, including preventing child abuse and neglect, and thus "the unnecessary separation of children from their families"[6] through out-of-home placements. This capped entitlement program establishes a new federal funding stream for these services, and is considered by many a major step toward turning child welfare into a family-centered system.

Many other pieces of successful legislation, federal and state, attest to this trend towards family-centered policies. At the federal level, P.L. 99–457, the Amendments to the Education for All Handicapped Children's Act of 1986, and its successor, P.L. 102–119, provide states funds to serve handicapped infants and toddlers, and those at risk for handicap, in early intervention programs. Among these provisions is a requirement that programs develop an Individualized Family Service Plan (IFSP) for and with the family of each child enrolled, stating explicitly that the family is also a client of the educational system.[7]

The continuing success of Head Start, which has included a strong parent component since its inception in the mid-1960s, is visible by tracking its increased appropriations over the decade.[8] Most recently, the program received an additional $550 million in the FY 1994 federal budget,[9] with a promise of full funding to accommodate all eligible children by FY 1999.[10] The Comprehensive Child Development Act of 1987 extends Head Start legislation to provide comprehensive health, development, nutritional, and parent and family support services to poor families with children under age six. Its goal is to enhance children's development and future chances of academic success, and to this end, its demonstration projects are instructed to regard parents as legitimate recipients of these "child-oriented" services.

During the 1980s numerous state governments embraced family-centered programming, not only to further child development and achievement, but also to stabilize the family unit, improve family functioning, increase parental competence, enhance parental employment opportunities, prevent foster care and other out-of-home placements, and reduce adolescent pregnancy.[11] These programs fall under the rubric of family support and parent education, and while they are certainly not new—antecedents being the maternal associations of the nineteenth century, the settlement houses of the early twentieth, the self-help movements of recent decades and Project Head Start—they are experiencing substantial public recognition.[12]

In the late 1980s the Harvard Family Research Project identified five states with policy initiatives in this area (Connecticut, Kentucky, Maryland, Minnesota, and Missouri);[13] many more have since joined them.[14] The new federal monies, to be administered by state child welfare agencies, will expand state activity dramatically. Municipalities also have begun promoting family-oriented policies and programs through, for example, the establishment of child and family councils to review city activities for their impacts on family life, and the funding of family support services.[15] More local schools now offer parent education and family support programs to their students' families.[16] These initiatives are a promising indication that policies are developing to meet the needs of families as a whole, remaining at the same time mindful of the children within them.

Do Policies Support the Economic Functions of Families or their Caregiving Functions?

To what extent have child and family policies over the past decade provided economic support (in cash or in-kind), and to what extent have they provided support and instruction for caregiving and nurturing activities? To begin, the 1980s saw increased attention to economic support policies. The Earned Income Tax Credit, which lessens the tax burden or provides a refundable credit to low-income working families, was established on a modest level in 1975, but has been increased substantially since then. The recent Omnibus Budget Reconciliation Act of 1993 (P.L. 103–66) supports a substantial expansion to this program—$21 billion over the next five years.[17] The ever more widely used Dependent Care Tax Credit, a "large ticket" item which offsets child care and certain other dependent expenses, primarily benefits middle- and upper-income families. The Family Support Act of 1988 provides direct economic support of families through two mechanisms. One enforces noncustodial parents' child support contributions, and the other mandates states to provide job training and child care for parents on AFDC who are attempting to move from welfare to employment.[18]

The federal Family and Medical Leave Act, which finally became law in 1993, provides unpaid leave for some employees to care for a new baby or sick family member.[19] Although this act mandates only unpaid leave, it can be seen as a policy of economic support because it provides the assurance of job reinstatement.

Public support for caregiving and nurturing policies has also increased over the past ten to fifteen years, though less so than support for economic assistance. Many of the newly proposed or enacted programs have been viewed as innovative precisely because they have stressed the caregiving functions of families rather than their economic roles. Compelling testimony in favor of the Family and Medical Leave Act stressed that families need to reintegrate themselves after the arrival of a new child—time to learn how to be good caregivers.[20]

The wide array of publicly supported family support programs, which have appeared in state after state, include services such as parent education, parent support groups, and parent-child playgroups.[21] These family support programs assume that many families need more than "narrow" economic support to do a good job of caring for their members.[22] Whether they be home visits during which new parents are taught some basics of child care and development, community centers with programs for teenagers, or peer support groups where parents can discuss their common problems, family support programs focus on caregiving and nurturance.[23] Such programming has been advocated as well by the National Commission on Children.

Attention to the family's nurturing functions is also apparent in the federal Child Care and Development Block Grant's investment in improving state child care systems and broadening access to *high quality*, not simply *any*, child care. In addition to giving parents "peace of mind" about their children while they work, high quality programs support families in other ways. For example, they offer information on child development, opportunities for peer support, and advice on childrearing. And the Family Support Act's willingness to provide income support to certain two-parent unemployed families is itself an acknowledgement of the unemployed father's noneconomic contribution to family life.

State legislators and public agency personnel appeared more attuned to the noneconomic needs of families than had the federal government during the Reagan and Bush administrations (1980–1992). For example, in 1991, when Congress was unable to enact a federal parental leave bill, twenty-five states and the District of Columbia already had passed some form of job-protected maternity, parental, or family leave legislation.[24] A deepening of interest at the federal level, however, is now afoot. Although the Clinton presidential campaign focused primarily on the economic needs of families, the new administration appears interested in these caregiving functions as well. The recent establishment of a federal family preservation and family support services program within Title IV-B of the Social Security Act is one piece of convincing evidence.

An encouraging development of the 1980s was the recognition that the support of caregiving, as well as economic support, is crucial to families. A danger here, however, is that a focus on caregiving will obscure the economic needs of families.[25]

Are Policies Targeted or Universal?

With the recent exception of the Family and Medical Leave Act, there does not appear to have been much sustained progress, at least at the federal level, in the establishment of universal child and family policies. The Child Care and Development Block Grant, though a significant achievement, does not allow for universal access to early childhood education and child care programs. The United States still does not provide universal health care for pregnant women and children, and although the Clinton administration appears committed to that goal, it is yet unclear how receptive Congress will be. In fact, President Clinton modified an earlier proposal for universal access to childhood immunizations, apparently fearing that its universal nature would make passage in Congress too difficult.[26]

More activity in a positive direction has occurred at the state level. For example, by 1986, forty-six states offered universal access to public kindergartens. Between 1985 and 1986, the number of states offering prekindergarten programs for four-year-olds doubled, from fourteen to twenty-eight.[27] Other states, such as Minnesota and Missouri, provide parent-child activities and parent education in group and home settings on a nontargeted basis.[28] Eighteen states require school districts to offer some form of AIDS education at certain grade levels in all public schools.[29] A few states have introduced, or are considering, universal health care legislation. It may be that states—as more proximate, familiar governing units—are better able to convince their publics of the need for universal policies than is the impersonal federal government.

In contrast to actual policies, the National Commission on Children report and other recent policy pronouncements contain numerous recommendations universal in nature.[30] For example, the $1,000 refundable tax credit of the National Commission (to replace the less equitable Dependent Care Tax Credit) and the National Governors' Association goal that all American children start school ready to learn, require universal access to these benefits. Perhaps this new round of rhetoric will yield universal policies in the future, but for the moment, targeted programs and policies weigh more heavily in the balance.

Are Policies Treatment-oriented or Prevention-oriented?

If rhetoric is a prelude to action, then it appears momentum is gaining for adoption of preventive strategies to address issues of child and family well-being.

One of the major principles for action recommended by the National Commission on Children is that "preventing problems before they become crises is the most effective and cost-effective way to address the needs of troubled families and vulnerable children."[31] This principle suggests "secondary and tertiary prevention"—the nipping of problems "in the bud" or the forestalling of more serious consequences in troubled families. These services might include adolescent pregnancy prevention programs (to prevent repeat pregnancies and promote positive childrearing behaviors), or family preservation services in child protective cases (to stabilize families in crisis, preventing foster care and other alternative placements).

The 1980 federal Child Welfare and Adoption Assistance Act took a major step toward prevention by explicitly favoring approaches that attempt to preserve families over those that place children in alternative care arrangements. However, given established child protective systems, it has taken the better part of the 1980s to begin "shifting gears." Several national foundations have supported statewide efforts to overhaul these agencies,[32] and promising local and state program models have been identified and publicized.[33] A flurry of evaluation activity has surrounded these early family preservation efforts, and with the new federal monies, no doubt more will follow.[34]

Competition for health care dollars between public health services (such as community outreach to women not receiving prenatal care, routine home visits to first-time mothers) and "high-tech" hospital-based care continues.[35] Although much public rhetoric supports the implementation of less expensive, preventive strategies, actual expenditures for hospital care far exceed those for community health programs.[36] Moreover, emphasis on tertiary care has not resulted in gains in child health status. While national infant mortality rates dropped during the 1980s, much of the progress was achieved for children in the neonatal period (up to twenty-eight days) through "high-tech" means. An increase in postnatal rates (one month to one year) suggests an absence of essential preventive supports within communities to sustain these high-risk babies.[37] Health and developmental attrition often accompany these survivors.[38]

The availability of hospital-based care does not ensure positive health status. Boston, home to three medical schools and several world-class hospitals, had, in 1988, the third highest infant mortality rate among large U.S. cities, and one of the greatest disparities in rates between whites and blacks in the country.[39] Since the mid-1980s, city and state public health officials have collaborated with The Boston Foundation in supporting innovations in infant mortality prevention programs— another successful public-private partnership borne of necessity. But available funds have been insufficient for the task.[40] A promising development in 1991 was the receipt by Boston Health and Hospitals of a five-year multimillion dollar grant, under the federal Healthy Start program, to implement comprehensive, community-based strategies to address the problem of infant mortality. Another notable gesture toward prevention at the federal level is a new childhood immunization initiative, included in the FY 1994 budget.[41]

The preventive principle is also being applied throughout the educational system. The goal of preventing school failure has led to increased national attention to early childhood education,[42] with Project Head Start also a beneficiary of this prevention goal; there is strong support in Congress to increase its funding until all eligible children are served.[43] Drop-out prevention, adolescent pregnancy prevention, and suicide prevention programs are available in many schools. And public concern over the possible spread of AIDS has moved many state and local educational agencies into the prevention business.[44] Those who have followed debates about sex education in the public schools have been impressed by the rapidity with which schools have been willing to embrace this difficult issue. The endorsement of sex and AIDS prevention education, beginning as early as the third grade, by President Reagan's own surgeon general no doubt hastened this process.[45]

State-level family support and parent education initiatives are another promising indicator of policy shift. Most states that are currently investing substantial money in these efforts have highlighted a particular problem they seek to prevent: in Maryland, the focus has been on adolescent pregnancy and childbearing; in Kentucky, on intergenerational illiteracy;[46] and in Massachusetts, on child abuse prevention.[47] The strategic decision to market prevention by focusing on specific at-risk populations may be necessary to get a "toe in the door." But the crucial challenge for these policy entrepreneurs is to build public support for primary prevention efforts.

There have always been two languages for child and family programs—one preventive and one treatment-oriented. Though the prevention rhetoric has long been popular, public policy behavior has, until recently, favored treatment. Preventive policies that match the rhetoric are now on the increase.

Do Policies Reinforce Notions of the Private Family?

A reevaluation of the "privateness" of families and an investigation of the origin of this concept is emerging.[48] Almost 400 years ago, the English colonies of post-Columbian North America included agrarian societies where families were the center, both structurally and physically. Production as well as reproduction took place within the home. This economic organization did not distinguish between the *private* life of the family and the *public* life of the community. Rather, family life was in a sense public or at least community life, for families were the essential cells of communities.[49]

But in the nineteenth century, as industrialization arose and spread, families were less and less the "little commonwealths" of preindustrial times. Instead, the family became a haven from the world of work dominated by money and all the venal interests associated with it.[50] The departure of production from the household, accompanied by the redefinition of reproduction and caregiving as something other than work, gave rise to a conceptual dichotomy: the private world of the family versus the public world of work; women's work, centered on reproduction versus men's work, centered on production; family versus work; private versus public. This family and work duality, and the resultant privatization of families, has had a profound influence. Families were expected to manage on their own with neither direct support nor direct interference from the surrounding community. Over time, private life became viewed as a sanctuary protected from unwarranted intrusions by the public world and its agent, the government. These "sanctuaries," however, have not always been protected places for women or children; staggering recent statistics on wife battering and murder, and on child abuse, likely have historical resonance.[51]

Reconsideration of the private-public dichotomy began, in part, with the women's movement's tenet that "the personal is political." Much of recent feminist scholarship—by historians, philosophers, sociologists, and political scientists—offers critiques of the earlier conceptions of the relationship of private and public.[52] But feminist scholars are not alone in this interest in the issue. Growing concern over U.S. economic viability also has focused attention on the mix of public (governmental) and private (corporate as well as nonprofit) responsibility for families, and for the overall health of the country.[53]

The courts are providing a further lively forum for this discussion. As various cases have shown, endorsing public responsibility for children and families does not translate into abandoning private rights. For instance, providing education on the toxic effects of alcohol on fetal development, and mandating that liquor companies put warning labels on their bottles, does not necessarily mean that pregnant women who drink must be prosecuted—the issue is debatable.[54] Abridgements of individual rights, such as requiring motorcyclists to wear helmets, or children to be restrained in seat belts, occur instead when such regulation appears unequivocally in the public's interest. Current activity in state legislatures, lower courts, and even the U.S. Congress reveals that we are actively reevaluating the definitions of family membership and obligations,[55] and that we are increasing public involvement in the "private" family. The current U.S. Supreme Court, however, has essentially sidestepped this discussion by resorting to the nostalgic myth of the traditional, two-parent, patriarchical family as the basis for its opinions.[56]

Further evidence that the line between private and public is being renegotiated is reflected in policy prescriptions and policy itself. Community-based, private nonprofit agencies, with public funds, provide the main share of emergency aid for social problems such as hunger, homelessness, and domestic violence.[57] The developmental needs of disabled infants and children, once met within the family, are now the concern of the federal government.[58] But when it comes to whose right it is to make the ultimate decision about whether or not an extremely disabled infant should be kept alive, the story changes. Although the Reagan administration established the "Baby Doe" regulations to "protect" these infants, hospital personnel seem loathe to invoke them. Baby Doe decisions are thus, at present, still essentially private.[59]

To take another example, in the 1980s the business community repeatedly called for investment in the country's children and families through support of education.[60] But this corporate sense of responsibility for public welfare did not translate to comparable support of the federal Family and Medical Leave Act, even though researchers concluded that such legislation would not result in heavy administrative or financial burdens for most employers.[61] Here, instead, the overriding concern of businesses seems to be how to prevent the public polity from dictating mandated benefits to private firms. Of course, the corporate class is not monolithic: one segment of it may support policies that another does not. But all segments seem interested in maintaining control of how much responsibility for the public good corporations take on.

Public schools recently have assumed additional "family" responsibilities. Formerly health and sex education in the schools was restricted to personal hygiene and the biological facts of reproduction and physical child growth. But a heightened concern about child sexual abuse gave rise to a panoply of child abuse prevention curricula from preschool through high school. The sense of urgency about AIDS has provoked changes in the programs many public education systems feel compelled to offer.[62] Although the appropriate content of AIDS education in particular, and health and sexuality education in general, is still much contested, there appears to be growing public consensus that addressing these issues cannot be left to the discretion of private families.[63]

The earlier, more rigid, middle-class distinctions between private families and public life appear to be disintegrating. The boundaries between the two are becoming more porous. But this has long been true for poor families who were the object of social services.[64] The "child savers" of the late nineteenth century, for example, did not shrink from removing children from their urban immigrant homes and sending them to a more "salutary" life with farm families, often in the West.[65] Twentieth century social workers have policed the private lives of AFDC (Aid for Families with Dependent Children) recipients, looking for evidence of a man in the house.[66] Increasingly, however, the behavior of parents from all social classes is being scrutinized.[67] A renewed discussion about the advisability of making divorce laws more restrictive is a case in point.[68]

What Accounts for These Changes?

This shift in public behavior toward families has been propelled, or at least supported, by many structural and philosophical changes in the general culture, too numerous and complex to elaborate here. What follows, then, is a brief set of possible, partial explanations for the changes we observe:

"It just happens that way." In his treatise entitled *Cycles in American History*, Arthur Schlesinger, Jr., describes periodic "shift[s] in national involvement between public purpose and private interest," agreeing with his father that they are fairly predictable "swing[s] between conservatism and liberalism, between periods of

concern for the rights of the few and periods of concern for the wrongs of the many."[69] The complete cycle takes about thirty years: In the first fifteen years, the new political generation launches a successful challenge to its predecessor, and sets a political course. During the next fifteen years, it maintains its power, though toward the end of this period its influence wanes, making way for the next generation. Since elements of the "reform" tradition become integrated as accepted political truths, these shifts are dynamic—not from one stable point to another. Though the pattern is regular, one never quite returns to where one was.[70]

There is some fairly compelling historical evidence to support the notion of these thirty-year cycles, at least in the twentieth century. We moved away from the Progressive Era of the 1900s back to a similar era of the New Deal in the 1930s. The Great Society of the 1960s is now, perhaps, being followed by this new generation's call to public service and social concerns in the 1990s. A shift in this direction, then, was due to happen.

Threats to social peace. Middle-class families took quite a beating in the 1980s: their overall economic status fell, home ownership dropped, and an increasing number of family members lacked health insurance.[71] Changes in tax codes "taxed the middle class and poor more heavily and gave large tax cuts to the richest 1%."[72] A range of "lifestyle" social problems—cocaine and other drug use, adolescent pregnancy, sexual abuse and wife battering in families, HIV infection and AIDS, youth alienation—became more apparent in the middle class, and among white families, than ever before. These problems have long been associated with the "culture of poverty," and with caricatured depictions of poor people: they were believed the results of a lack of discipline or parental supervision, lax morals, and an emphasis on immediate gratification.[73] The "discovery" and the public discussion of these problems within middle class families threatened their self-confidence.[74]

The 1992 Clinton campaign spoke most directly to this growing uneasiness among the middle class, and many believe this was the key to his victory. When he spoke about children and families, he focused primarily on middle-class families' deteriorated economic circumstances. Most American families were raised on promises of the American dream: if you work hard, you should be able to own a home, afford health care, build up a nest egg, take family vacations.[75] Poor Americans have long known about the often tenuous connection between hard work and financial security. This sad knowledge has now passed on to the working and middle classes. Indeed, over half of poor families with children are headed by an adult who works at least part time for a portion of the year.[76] The ranks of the poor increasingly are filled with families in which substantial incomes have dropped precipitously through divorce, the desertion of fathers, the lack of affordable child care, or an unintended birth to an unmarried woman.[77]

The current challenges to social peace, then, appear less containable, and less ascribable to the poor; they wash across income groups, races, and communities. As a result, the public impulse for action seems that much more powerful.

Living in the post-modern era. According to observers across disciplines,[78] we recently have moved from modernity to the "post-modern era." At the core of modern thinking was the belief in social progress, in universal truths, and in regular patterns of development and change.[79] Post-modernity challenges those assumptions, proposing, for example, that truths are socially constructed, as are notions and evidence of progress. Further, the post-modern condition is one of limited resources—personal and environmental. This requires accommodation at all levels of human organization: individual, family, community, state, and nation. Post-modern virtues include more modest ambitions; thrift ("doing more for less"); permeable boundaries between entities; protection of resources; and collaboration.

Modern communication systems and the capacity to track dwindling and damaged resources also have set this period apart. The concepts of a "global village" and a world economy are now commonly accepted. We are not surprised to learn that pollution from Eastern Europe is contaminating the pristine Alaskan Arctic, or that American companies are increasingly choosing workers outside the United States, or that the United States, with 4.66% of the world's population, consumes 24.5% of the world's energy.[80] The horrors of ethnic intolerance are electronically transmitted daily across the world.

This thinking, with its emphasis on conservation,[81] cooperation, and interdependence, contradicts many traditional American values, especially those that extol individual rights and responsibilities.[82] It replaces self-sufficiency as the ultimate value with a sufficiency that is based in a larger community. In this context, interdependence, including a certain amount of dependence on the state for a return in labor and services, is more a virtue than a weakness.

With children an increasingly smaller percentage of the population,[83] the United States is confronting its own post-modern dilemma. As early as the year 2000, many employers will lack the labor force qualified to work in some sectors of our advanced economy; there will be a serious mismatch between the jobs available and the skills of the workers. In fact, even some *existing* jobs demand a better educated workforce than is being graduated from the nation's schools. Literacy and mathematics requirements have risen across jobs in response to the "up-skilling" of many positions, even those such as assembly line posts formerly held by semiliterate workers. Thus, rather than viewing children as a drain on public coffers, they may well be seen increasingly as a community resource—as the eventual leaders of our towns, cities, and country, as future workforce participants, and as contributors to the Social Security system we will be attempting to use.[84]

Child and family policy has begun to profit from this reframing. Investing in child care, for example, has been a relatively "easy sell," at least rhetorically. Quality early childhood programming has demonstrated numerous developmental benefits for children.[85] Child care also provides families the support they need to raise their children and remain in the labor force.[86] A recent report of The Boston Foundation Carol R. Goldberg Seminar on Child Care in Boston, a community child care planning effort, identifies child care as an *infrastructure* issue for the city.[87]

We generally apply this term to the brick and mortar elements of a city—roads, bridges, parks, public transportation. But it is clear that in order for Boston to thrive and to compete in the twenty-first century, public support of the *human* part of its infrastructure must be undertaken. At present, virtually all child care costs are borne by parents and by inadequately paid staff who, in essence, subsidize child care. This privatization of child care expenses does not serve us and is not the way we respond to other infrastructure demands. For example, those of us who do not own cars, or whose usual travel does not take us to Dorchester, do not resist supporting road work on Dorchester Avenue. We do not expect Dorchester residents and Dorchester Avenue travelers to pay for its upkeep. Road maintenance is a public good and is paid for accordingly. So it should be with child care.[88]

In keeping with other post-modern trends, the boundaries between poor and other communities have become increasingly porous. The gentrification of inner-city neighborhoods is an obvious example, as is the voluntary (and in some cases, mandatory) school busing arrangements between poor communities and their more affluent neighbors. Some wealthy communities have created affordable housing options for low- and moderate-income families. Institutions of higher education have increased efforts to recruit students from poor school districts. There is even some recent talk about making Head Start—the quintessential social welfare program—more economically integrated, shifting away from the strict means-test now applied to prospective enrollees.

Unique among industrialized nations, the United States has been resistant to acknowledging limitations in resources, both human and environmental. Cooperation, collaboration, and connectedness—hallmarks of post-modernity—sorely challenge our modern national political culture. It is possible, however, that as we experience contemporary life more fully, we will appreciate these values. Children and their families, our most precious national resource, may well be the primary beneficiaries.

THE BOTTOM LINE

Have we caught the pulse of a new day?[89] Did the 1991 National Commission on Children's report, for example, reflect and presage a sea change in America's approach to children and families? Perhaps. The collaborative product of members from across the political spectrum, it suggests that concern for families can be viewed as simply American, not politically progressive or conservative. It contains both a vision for the distant future, and specific policy recommendations for immediate implementation. It conveys a sense of compelling need.

On the other hand, the rhetoric of this report is not new; in fact it frames the issues in much the same way as did its predecessor White House Conferences on Children reports.[90] The 1909 White House Conference on the Care of Dependent Children drew an unflattering comparison between the paucity of support for families and children in the United States, and the relatively "abundant" support found "in every other modern nation."[91] The 1930 White House Conference on Child Health and Protection outlined the need for improvement in a wide range of areas that touched children's lives: education, health, and job training; the special concerns of the disabled; the need for understanding child growth and development. By 1970, the chairman of the White House Conference on Children and Youth could point to "a strong sense of urgency—a feeling that we must act *now* if our society is to flourish."[92]

The enduring question, then, is whether we appear to be moving beyond this rhetoric—from "kissing babies" to sharing in their care. On balance we find reasons for cautious optimism. There appears to have been modest movement toward family-centered, preventive policies that credit the nurturing and caregiving dimensions of family life. And we seem to have come closer to recognizing that the ability of private families to care for children is inextricably bound up with the public world where government plays such an important part. But this activity can be considered "progress" only if we also retain and strengthen the effective, more traditional policies that operate at the other end of the continuum—those that consider the child's individual needs, that offer necessary treatment to families and family members, and support families economically.

It would be unfortunate, and likely even dangerous, if the increasingly popular preventive, family-centered policy proposals were viewed wholly as replacements for our present approach. What if inexpensive family support programs were seen as legitimate substitutes for the intensive therapeutic interventions that some few families require? Or classes in home management and budgeting seen as the "cure" for family homelessness? Or, in the service of preserving the family unit, children were left in hopelessly dysfunctional homes? One of the central tasks in building child and family policies for the new millennium is resisting the urge to oversimplify, to look for quick, easy solutions to complex problems. For example, some advocates for preventive policies support them with the slogan "You can pay me now or pay me later," suggesting that prevention—early payment—will reduce later costs. The truth, however, is more complicated. For some families and children, the costs are not of the either/or variety, and there are no savings to be had: we will pay now *and* later. The larger question concerns the type of society in which we choose to live. As William Woodside, a corporate CEO and member of the National Commission on Children, remarked, "Are the investments in our children expensive? Compared to what?"[93]

Neither our past nor our evolving policies can be adequately assessed without considering issues of class, race, and gender, for while equity is a primary purpose of much social policy, such divisions make this egalitarian goal difficult to achieve.[94] There have been recent attempts to redress some of the worst imbalances of class structure in the United States. Increased funding for the Earned Income Credit, the Family Support Act of 1988, and the Child Care And Development Block Grant should help ameliorate the financial position of numbers of poor children and their families. Some of these policies, however, are only making up for the economic losses and program cutbacks sustained by families during the 1980s.

Families of color are overrepresented among the poor and are often more dramatically affected by many social ills, such as infant mortality.[95] While we are probably past the time when people are overtly excluded from social programs on the basis of race, as was the case with many of the state mothers' pensions programs at the beginning of this century,[96] insensitivity to cultural differences in the design of child and family programs can have a similar outcome—the underutilization or misapplication of services.[97]

Finally, gender analysis is critical, since many aspects of child, youth, and family policy concern women, and specifically the work of caring for children.[98] One reason that these social policies have been somewhat impoverished relative to others in the United States (compare, for example, Aid to Dependent Children to Social Security Insurance) is that they have had more bearing on the lives of women than men.[99] In fact, many of the problems that child and family policies are meant to address arise from gender inequality. Women are poorer than men, earning roughly sixty-nine cents to each dollar earned by men.[100] Female-headed families are therefore much more likely to be poor than are male-headed families, not to mention that they often have only one potential wage earner.[101] Many homeless families are female-headed, and often the woman is fleeing an abusive domestic situation.[102] Thus women's lesser power, both within society at large and within families, contributes to the need for government policies.

Building on the policy successes of the 1980s, resisting simple solutions, and maintaining awareness of the issues of class, race, and gender, are central considerations in crafting comprehensive child and family policies. The recent economic recession made it clear that the economy, left to itself, cannot support children and families. The imperative to move beyond rhetoric, a move that would signal the acceptance of child and family policy as a full-fledged adult in the policy world, is that much stronger. The positive models that have been developed during the 1980s should be continued and expanded; the National Commission on Children report provides a solid framework from which to start. President Clinton, the U.S. Congress, state and local policy makers, all have an opportunity to make these issues their own, and to move them to the foreground of the political landscape. Those of us who care about children and families must gather the political will to see that they do.

NOTES

1. The National Service Trust Act of 1993 is the centerpiece of these initiatives.

2. D. Shalala (April 25, 1993). Remarks at the inauguration of President John DiBiaggio of Tufts University. Medford, MA.

3. These dimensions include (1) child-centered vs. family-centered, (2) supportive of the economic functions of families rather than their caregiving functions, (3) targeted vs.

universal, (4) treatment-oriented vs. prevention-oriented, (5) committed to the private family rather than to a vision of shared public-private responsibility. See F. Jacobs (this volume). Child and family policy: Framing the issues.

4. C. Davidson (this volume). Dependent children and their families: A historical survey of United States policies.

5. U. S. House of Representatives (August 4, 1993). *Omnibus Budget Reconciliation Act of 1993.* Conference Report of the Committee on the Budget, House of Representatives (Report 103–213). Washington, D.C.: U. S. Government Printing Office.

6. Children's Defense Fund (1993). Summary of the protections for abused and neglected children in the Omnibus Budget Reconciliation Act of 1993. Washington, D.C.: Author, 1.

7. M. J. McGonigel, R. K. Kauffmann, & B. H. Johnson (1991). A family-centered process for the Individualized Family Service Plan. *Journal of Early Intervention, 15,* 46–56; M. W. Krauss & F. H. Jacobs (1990). Family assessment: Purposes and techniques. In S. J. Meisels & J. P. Shonkoff (Eds.), *Handbook of early childhood intervention,* 303–325, Cambridge: Cambridge University Press; P. Dokecki & C. A. Heflinger (1989). Strengthening families of young children with handicapping conditions: Mapping backward from the "street level." In J. J. Gallagher, R. L. Trohanis, & R. M. Clifford (Eds.), *Policy implementation & P.L. 99–457: Planning for young children with special needs,* 59–84, Baltimore: Paul H. Brookes. There also are concerns about including certain parents in a central way during the development of the IFSP. See, J. F. Goodman & S. A. Hover (April, 1992). The Individualized Family Service Plan: Unresolved problems. *Pyschology in the Schools, 29*(2), 140–151.

8. E. Zigler & S. Muenchow (1992). *Head Start: The inside story of America's most successful educational experiment.* New York: Basic Books.

9. Key 1993 Congressional actions (December, 1993). *CDF Reports,* (15), 1.

10. Clinton budget proposes key child investments (March, 1993). *CDF Reports, 14*(4), 15.

11. See Jacobs (this volume), Child and family policy, for a fuller discussion. For an interesting presentation of training and technical assistance needs to help move governmental entities and helping professions toward more family-centered practice, see, Family Impact Seminar (June 13, 1993). *Training and technical assistance to support family-centered, integrated services reform.* Washington, D.C.: Author.

12. E. F. Zigler & K. B. Black (1989). America's family support movement: Strengths and limitations. *American Journal of Orthopsychiatry, 59,* 6–19; S. L. Kagan, D. R. Powell, B. Weissbourd, & E. Zigler (Eds.) (1987). *America's family support programs.* New Haven: CT. There is a renewed interest in the settlement house as a family support center. See, for example, Revisiting the settlement idea (Fall, 1992). *The Boston Foundation Report,* 1–5.

13. B. Hausman (this volume). Policy entrepreneurship and the emergence of family support programs; H. B. Weiss (1989). State family support and education programs: Lessons from the pioneers. *American Journal of Orthopsychiatry, 59,* 32–48; H.B. Weiss, B. Hausman, & P. Seppanen (1988). *Pioneering states: Innovative family support and education programs.* Cambridge, MA: Harvard Family Research Project, Harvard Graduate School of Education.

14. See also National Association of State Boards of Education (1991). *Caring communities: Supporting young children and families.* The report of the National Task Force on School Readiness. Alexandria, VA: Author; H. B. Weiss, J. Simeone, & J. Heifetz (1989). *Innovative states: Emerging family support and education programs.* Cambridge, MA: Harvard Family Research Project, Harvard Graduate School of Education. The Council of Governors' Policy Advisors has developed a useful guide for states interested in developing

family support programming. See J. K. Chynoweth & B. R. Dyer (1991). *Strengthening families: A guide for state policymakers*, Washington, D.C.: Council of Governors' Policy Advisors.

15. C. Born (1989). *Our future and our only hope: A survey of city halls regarding children and families*. Washington, D.C.: National League of Cities; National League of Cities (1987). *Children, families & cities: Programs that work at the local level*. Washington, D.C.: Author.

16. B. D. Goodson, J. P. Swartz, & M. A. Millsap (1991). *Working with families: Promising programs to help parents support young children's learning*. Cambridge, MA: Abt Associates, Inc.; Building parent school partnerships (1989). *Family Resource Coalition Report, 8*(2), 1–27; J. Comer (1989). Poverty, family and the Black experience. In G. Miller (Ed.), *Giving children a chance: The case for more effective national policies*, 109–129. Washington, D.C.: The Center for National Policy Press.

17. Children win! Budget includes major gains for children and families. *CDF Reports, 14*(10), 1–2.

18. There is considerable skepticism about how well states will be able to accommodate this increase in the demand for child care. See, for example, K. O'Brien & C. Stevenson (July, 1993). Child care under the Family Support Act: Unfinished business. *Young Children, 48*(5), 54–57. And there are serious misgivings about the Family Support Act altogether. For a brief review of the central concerns, see R. A. Cloward & F. F. Piven (May 24, 1993). Punishing the poor, again: The fraud of workfare. *The Nation, 256*(20), 693–696.

19. The current Family and Medical Leave Act guarantees job security to some workers, for up to twelve weeks, for the birth or adoption of a child, or for a serious family illness. The unpaid leave is available only to those employees who work at least twenty-five hours a week in businesses with more than fifty employees. See K. Karr Kaitin (this volume). Congressional responses to families in the workplace: The Family and Medical Leave Act of 1987–1988.

20. See Karr Kaitin (this volume), Congressional responses to families in the workplace.

21. Hausman (this volume), Policy entrepreneurship and the emergence of family support programs; H. B. Weiss and F. H. Jacobs (1988). Family support and education programs: Challenges and opportunities. In H. B. Weiss & F. H. Jacobs (Eds.), *Evaluating family programs*, xix–xxix. Hawthorne, NY: Aldine de Gruyter.

22. For a discussion of family support services in homeless family shelters, and how cities decide what complement, if any, to provide, see P. Little (this volume). Municipal policies for homeless families.

23. C. Levine & I. Beck (1988). *Programs to strengthen families*. Chicago: Family Resource Coalition; S. L. Kagan, D. R. Powell, B. Weissbourd, & E. F. Zigler (1987). *America's family support programs*. New Haven, CT: Yale University Press; E. Zigler, H. Weiss, & L. Kagan (1984). *Programs to strengthen families: A resource guide*. Chicago: Family Resource Coalition.

24. M. Finn-Stevenson & E. Trzcinski (1991). Mandated leave: An analysis of federal and state legislation. *American Journal of Orthopsychiatry, 61*, 567–575.

25. For example, there is considerable discussion about the relative merits of economic-based vs. human service-based approaches to addressing the needs of young African-American fathers. While few dispute the virtues of encouraging these young men to be more involved in their children's care, many believe the emphasis first should be placed on job training and employment.

26. Clinton reported to cut back sharply on child vaccine plan (May 6, 1993). *Boston*

Globe, 9.

27. B. D. Day (1988). What's happening in early childhood programs across the United States? In C. Warger (Ed.), *A resource guide to public school early childhood programs*, 3–31. Alexandria, VA: Association for Supervision and Curriculum Development.

28. See Hausman (this volume), Policy entrepreneurship and the emergence of family support programs.

29. R. Griffith (this volume). AIDS education in the Cambridge public schools: An implementation study.

30. See, for example, National Commission on Children (1991), *Beyond rhetoric: A new American agenda for children and families*. Washington, D.C.: U.S. Government Printing Office; L. Sementilli-Dann (December, 1991). *The executive summary of the Family Supports Roundtable: A project of the Center for Policy Alternatives' Universal Family Agenda*. Washington, D.C.: Center for Policy Alternatives. Council of Chief State School Officers (1990). *Early childhood and family education*. Orlando, FL: Harcourt Brace Jovanovich; National Governors' Association (1990). *Educating America: Strategies for achieving the national education goals*. Washington, D.C.: Author.

31. National Commission on Children (1991), *Beyond rhetoric*, xx.

32. The work of the Annie E. Casey Foundation, Westport, CT, and the Edna McConnell Clark Foundation, New York City, NY, are particularly noteworthy here.

33. J. K. Whittaker, J. Kinney, E. M. Tracy, & C. Booth (Eds.) (1990). *Reaching high-risk families: Intensive family preservation in human services*. Hawthorne, NY: Aldine de Gruyter; Center for the Study of Social Policy (1988). *State family preservation programs: A description of six states' progress in developing services to keep families together*. Washington, D.C.: Author; L. B. Schorr (1988). *Within our reach: Breaking the cycle of disadvantage*. New York: Doubleday.

34. See, for example, W. V. Collier & R. H. Hill (June, 1993). *Family Ties Family Preservation Services Program: An evaluation report*. Unpublished report. New York, NY: Department of Juvenile Justice; J. R. Schuerman, T. L. Rzepnicki, J. H. Littell, & A. Chak (June, 1993). *Evaluation of the Illinois Family First Plaement Prevention Program: Final report*. Unpublished report. Chicago, IL: Chapin Hall for Children, University of Chicago; E. Kaye & J. Bell (May, 1993). *Final report: Evaluability assessment of family preservation programs*. Unpublished report. Arlington, VA: James Bell Associates; C. Bergquist, D. Szwejda, & G. Pope (March, 1993). *Evaluation of Michigan's Families First Program: Summary Report*. Unpublished report. Lansing, MI: University Associates; Center for the Study of Social Policy (May, 1991). *Keeping score: Locally directed evaluations*. Washington, D.C.: Author; L. Feldman (December, 1991). *Assessing the effectiveness of family preservation services in New Jersey within an ecological context*. Trenton, NJ: Department of Human Services; P. H. Rossi (1991), *Evaluating family preservation programs: A report to the Edna McConnell Clark Foundation*. Unpublished manuscript. Amherst, MA: University of Massachusetts, Social and Demographic Research Institute.

35. See, for example, N. Kane (1993). *Report on the financial resources of major hospitals in Boston*. Boston: Department of Health and Hospitals.

36. H. Karger & D. Stoesz (1990). *American social welfare policy: A structural approach*. New York: Longman.

37. A. L. Wilson & G. Neidich (1991). Infant mortality and public policy. *Social Policy Report*, 5(2), 1–21; S. Rosenbaum (1989). Recent developments in infant and child health: Health status, insurance coverage and trends in public health policy. In G. Miller (Ed.), *Giving children a chance*, 79–107.

38. Deborah Klein Walker, Assistant Commissioner, Bureau of Family and Community Health, Massachusetts Department of Public Health, personal communication, October 4, 1991.

39. D. Kong (February 8, 1991). City fears cut in U.S. aid to fight infant mortality. *Boston Globe*, 1, 13.

40. Personal communication, Jodi Hill.

41. Children win! Budget includes major gains for children and families (September, 1993).

42. P. M. Timpane & L. M. McNeill (1991). *Business impact on education and child development*. New York: Committee for Economic Development; National Governors' Association (1990), *Educating America.*

43. This proposed expansion is not without its notable critics. Zigler, Styfco, and Gilman worry that, "the push to move and move quickly may result in programs that are not carefully planned and do not provide the quality that is absolutely necessary to produce benefits." E. Zigler, S. J. Styfco, & E. Gilman (1993). The national Head Start program for disadvantaged preschoolers. In E. Zigler & S. J. Styfco (Eds.), *Head Start and beyond: A national plan for extended childhood intervention*, 1–41. New Haven, CT: Yale University Press, 27.

44. Griffith (this volume), AIDS education in the Cambridge public schools; D. K. Lohrmann (1988). AIDS education at the local level: The pragmatic issues. *Journal of School Health, 58*(8), 330–334; M. Quackenbush, M. Nelson, & K. Clark (Eds.) (1988). *The AIDS challenge: Prevention education for young children*. Santa Cruz, CA: Network Publications.

45. C. E. Koop (1986). *Surgeon General's report on Acquired Immune Deficiency Syndrome*. Washington, D.C.: U.S. Department of Health and Human Services.

46. Hausman (this volume), Policy entrepreneurship and the emergence of family support programs.

47. Special Committee on Family Support and the Child Welfare System (November, 1992). *From crisis to opportunity: Recommendations for promoting child and family well-being in Massachusetts*. Boston: Author; Massachusetts Children's Trust Fund (1988). *It's never too soon: A blueprint for preventing child abuse by strengthening Massachusetts families.* Unpublished manuscript.

48. M. Davies (this volume). Who's minding the baby? Reproductive work, productive work, and family policy in the United States; S. Coontz (1992). *The way we never were: American families and the nostalgia trap*. New York: Basic Books; S. Coontz (1988). *The social origins of private life: A history of American families, 1600–1900*. London: Verso.

49. J. Demos (1972). *A little commonwealth*. New York: Oxford University Press.

50. C. Lasch (1977). *Haven in a heartless world: The family besieged*. New York: Basic Books.

51. See G. T. Hotaling & M. A. Strauss, with A. Lincoln (1989). Intrafamily violence, crime and violence outside the family. In L. Ohlin & M. Tonry (Eds.), *Family violence*, 315–375. Chicago: University of Chicago Press; M. Bograd (1988). Feminist perspectives on wife abuse: An introduction. In K. Yllo & M. Bograd (Eds.), *Feminist perspectives on wife abuse*, 11–26. Newbury Park, CA: Sage Publications.

52. S. Ostrander (1989). Feminism, voluntarism, and the welfare state: Toward a feminist sociological theory of social welfare. *American Sociologist, 20*(1), 29–41; M. Abramowitz (1988). *Regulating the lives of women: Social welfare policy from colonial times to the present*. Boston: South End Press; S. Ostrander and S. Langton (Eds.) (1987). *Shifting the debate: Public/private sector relations in the modern welfare state*. New Brunswick, NJ:

Transaction Books; I. M. Young (1987). Impartiality and the civic public: Some implications of feminist critiques of moral and political theory. In S. Benhabib & D. Cornell (Eds.), *Feminism as critique*, 57–76. Minneapolis: University of Minnesota Press; C. Pateman (1983). Feminist critiques of the public/private dichotomy. In S. I. Bem & G. F. Gaus (Eds.), *Private and public in social life*, 281–303. New York: St. Martin's Press.

53. G. Loury (1988). Public and private responsibilities in the struggle against poverty. In W. Knowlton & R. Zeckhauser (Eds.), *American society: Public and private responsibilities*, 181–202. Cambridge, MA: Ballinger; R. Zeckhauser (1986). The muddled responsibilities of public and private America. In Knowlton & Zeckhauser (Eds.), *American society*, 45–77.

54. For an insightful discussion of this issue, see M. Dorris (1989). *The broken cord*. New York: HarperCollins.

55. The celebrated case of Gregory Kingsley, a 12-year-old boy who convinced the juvenile court to terminate his biological mother's rights, is a recent example. A. DePalma (September 26, 1992). Court grants boy wish to select his parents. *New York Times*, 1, 5; see also S. Mintz (1989). Regulating the American family. *Journal of Family History, 14*, 387–408.

56. J. O. Brown & P. T. Baumann (1990). Nostalgia as constitutional doctrine: Legalizing Norman Rockwell's America. *Vermont Law Review, 15*, 49–68.

57. M. Lipsky & S. R. Smith (March, 1989). When social problems are treated as emergencies. *Social Science Review, 63*(1), 5–25.

58. P.L. 99–457 and its successor, P.L. 102–119, direct states in their provision of early intervention programming for disabled infants, toddlers, and their families.

59. M. Pott (this volume). Selective nontreatment of handicapped newborns: Implementation of the Baby Doe laws of 1984.

60. See, for example, The Boston Foundation Carol R. Goldberg Seminar on Child Care in Boston (1992). *Embracing our future: A child care action agenda*. Boston: Author; P. M. Timpane & L. M. McNeill (1991). *Business impact on education and child development*. New York: Committee for Economic Development; Committee for Economic Development (1991). *The unfinished agenda: A new vision for child development and education*. New York: Author; Committee for Economic Development (1987). *Children in need: Investment strategies for the educationally disadvantaged*. New York: Author; Committee for Economic Development (1985). *Investing in our children: Business and the public schools*. New York: Author.

61. J. T. Bond, E. Galinsky, M. Lord, G. L. Staines, & K. R. Brown (1991). Beyond the parental leave debate: The impact of laws in four states. *Young children, 47*, 39–42.

62. Griffith (this volume), AIDS education in the Cambridge public schools.

63. Interestingly, there is a growing countermovement attack against providing AIDS education that is being fought in local communities. To some observers, this activity on the AIDS issue is part of a national strategy to promote a conservative agenda through control of local school committees. The struggle in Newton, MA, is exemplary. See R. Layne (June 29, 1993). Politics of sex education: National right-wing ties alleged as fight enters voting booth. *Newton TAB*, 1, 4, 10, 11. See also R. Sullivan (April 25, 1993). An army of the faithful. *New York Times Magazine*, 32-35, 40–44; S. Mydans (February 20, 1993). Political proving ground for the Christian Right. *New York Times*, 5.

64. L. Gordon (1988). *Heroes of their own lives: The politics and history of family violence*. New York: Penguin.

65. Davidson (this volume), Dependent children and their families; A. M. Platt (1977).

The child savers: The invention of delinquency. Chicago: University of Chicago Press.

66.   L. Gordon (1990). The new feminist scholarship on the welfare state. In L. Gordon (Ed.), *Women, the state, and welfare,* 9–35. Madison, WI: University of Wisconsin Press; C. Stack (1974). *All our kin: Strategies for survival in a black community.* New York: Harper & Row.

67.   B. D. Whitehead (April, 1993). Dan Quayle was right. *Atlantic Monthly,* 47–84; C. Lasch (October, 1992). Hillary Clinton: Child saver. *Harper's Magazine, 285*(1709), 74–82. According to developmental psychologist David Elkind, these permeable boundaries between the private family and the world outside it create some negative consequences for children. See, D. Elkind (in press). *The postmodern family.* Cambridge, MA: Harvard University Press.

68.   Family Research Council (April, 1992). The two-parent family: Policy ideas for strengthening marriage. *Family Policy, 5*(1), 1–8; Who owes what to whom? (February, 1991). *Harper's Magazine Forum,* 43–54.

69.   A. Schlesinger, Jr. (1986). *Cycles in American history.* Boston: Houghton Mifflin, 24.

70.   This belief in recursive cycles, rather than pendulum swings, also underlies cybernetic theory. See, for example, B. R. Kenney (1983). *The aesthetics of change,* New York: Guilford Press; G. Bateson (1972). *Steps to an ecology of mind.* New York: Ballantine Books.

71.   L. Mishel & D. M. Frankel (1991). *The state of working America, 1990–1991.* Armonk, NY: M. E. Sharpe. Census data from 1991 indicate that 85% of the medically uninsured in this country have jobs, or are children of parents who work. P. G. Gosselin (June 6, 1993). Who are the uninsured? *Boston Globe,* 76–77.

72.   Mishel & Frankel (1991), *The state of working America, 1990–1991,* 49.

73.   M. Katz (1989). *The undeserving poor: From the War on Poverty to the war on welfare.* New York: Pantheon.

74.   B. Ehrenreich (1989). *Fear of falling: The inner life of the middle class.* New York: Pantheon.

75.   Membership in the middle class virtually requires this belief, according to B. Bledstein: "The popular imagination has so closely identified being middle class with pursuing the so-called American dream that "middle class" has come to be equated with a good chance for advancement, an expanding income, education, good citizenship—indeed, with democracy." B. Bledstein (1987). The culture of professionalism. In R. N. Bellah, R. Madsen, W. M. Sullivan, A. Swidler, & S. M. Tipton (Eds.), *Individualism & commitment in American life: Readings on the themes of: Habits of the heart,* 286–296. New York: Harper & Row, 289. See also A. Bernstein, D. Woodruff, B. B. Buell, N. Peacock, & K. Thurston (August 19, 1991). What happened to the American dream? The under-30 generation may be losing the race for prosperity. *Business Week,* 80–83.

76.   National Commission on Children (1991), *Beyond rhetoric.*

77.   R. Sidel (1986). *Women and children last: The plight of poor women in affluent America.* New York: Viking; S. H. Preston (1984). Children and the elderly: Divergent paths of America's dependents. Presidential address to the Population Association of America. Minneapolis, MN.

78.   See, for example, Jacques Derrida in linguistics, philosophy, and literary criticism; Michel Foucault in psychology and philosophy; and Philip Johnson in architecture.

79.   D. Elkind (in press). *The postmodern family.* Cambridge, MA: Harvard University Press.

80.   The United States population figure is drawn from 1991 census data from U.S.

Bureau of the Census (1992). *Statistical abstract of the United States: 1992*. Washington, D.C.: U.S. Government Printing Office; The energy consumption figure is based on 1988 data from Statistical Office of the United Nations (1989). *Energy statistics yearbook*. New York: Author.

81. For a society to value conservation, it must be willing to take a "long view"—to see how an individual's daily actions affect a future that is collectively deemed worthy of protection. Environmentalists use the term "sustainability" to connote the practice of using fewer resources in order to preserve them for future generations to enjoy. J. K. Galbraith speaks of "short-run" and "long-run" investments, conservation activities being of the latter type, and details the United States' preference for "short-run inaction" as follows: "The cost of today's action falls or could fall on the favored community [the contented majority]; taxes could be increased. The benefits in the longer run may well be for others to enjoy." J. K. Galbraith (1992). *The culture of contentment*. Boston: Houghton Mifflin.

82. According to Bellah, et al. (1987), it is not so much that Americans yearn for a solitary life; rather, although they enjoy company, they prefer "the kind of belonging. . . which is freely chosen by individuals." These voluntary associations, or "lifestyle enclaves," differ markedly from communities. "A community in the strong sense is a group of people who are different yet interdependent, who are bound together by mutual responsibilities arising out of a common history, a history which they have not simply chosen to be a part of but which they are nonetheless responsible for carrying on." See Bellah et al. (1987). *Individualism & commitment in American life*, 246.

83. Population Reference Bureau (1992). *The challenge of change: What the 1992 census tells us about children*. Washington, D.C.: Center for the Study of Social Policy.

84. In 1935, when the Social Security Act was enacted, there were 16 workers "paying into" the Social Security system for every one elderly person receiving the benefit; today there are only three.

85. See, for example, C. D. Hayes, J. L. Palmer, & M. J. Zaslow (1990). The effects of day care. In C. D. Hayes, J. L. Palmer, & M. J. Zaslow (Eds.), *Who cares for America's children?*, 45 83. Washington, D.C.: National Academy Press.

86. See L. Hudson & S. L. Vlodaver (this volume). A season in the sun: The Massachusetts Day Care Partnership Project.

87. The Boston Foundation Carol R. Goldberg Seminar on Child Care in Boston (1992). *Embracing our future*.

88. F. Jacobs (April, 1992). Press conference statement on behalf of the Carol R. Goldberg Seminar on Child Care in Boston. Boston, MA.

89. We have paraphrased here the poem Maya Angelou composed for President Clinton's Inauguration. M. Angelou (January 20, 1993). On the pulse of morning. *New York Times*.

90. R. Beck (1973). The White House Conferences on Children: An historical perspective. *Harvard Educational Review, 43*, 653–668.

91. Beck (1973), The White House Conferences on Children, 655.

92. Beck (1973), The White House Conferences on Children, 662.

93. National Commission on Children (1991), *Beyond rhetoric*, 368.

94. See M. Davies & F. H. Jacobs (this volume). Considering race, class, and gender in child and family policy.

95. W. P. O'Hare, K. M. Pollard, T. L. Mann, & M. M. Kent (1991). African Americans in the 1990s. *Population Bulletin, 46*(1), 1–40.

96. B. J. Nelson (1990). The origins of the two-channel welfare state: Workmen's

Compensation and Mothers Aid. In L. Gordon (Ed.), *Women, the state, and welfare*, 123–151.

    97.   D. T. Slaughter (1988). Programs for racially and ethnically diverse American families: Some critical issues. In H. B. Weiss & F. H. Jacobs (Eds.), *Evaluating family programs*, 461–476.

    98.   For a detailed discussion, see M. Davies (this volume), Who's minding the baby?.

    99.   See L. Gordon (Ed.) (1990), *Women, the state, and welfare*.

    100.   U.S. Department of Commerce, Bureau of the Census (September, 1990). *Money, income and poverty status in the United States, 1989 (Series P–60, No. 168)*. Washington, D.C.: U.S. Government Printing Office.

    101.   S. Danziger & S. Danziger (Winter, 1993). Child poverty and public policy: Toward a comprehensive antipoverty agenda. *Daedalus, 122*(1), 57–84; D. Pearce (1990). Welfare is not for women: Why the war on poverty cannot conquer the feminization of poverty. In L. Gordon (Ed.), *Women, the state, and welfare*. 265–279; R. Sidel (1986), *Women and children last*.

    102.   N. Milburn & A. D'Ercole (1991). Homeless women: Moving toward a comprehensive model. *American Psychologist, 46*, 1161–1169.

Bibliography

We have compiled an introductory bibliography for child and family policy students. In general, we have confined our entries to books, not journal articles, and to more current sources. Readers should consult the endnotes of individual chapters for more extensive bibliographic information in specific areas of interest.

Abramovitz, M. (1988). *Regulating the lives of women: Social welfare policy from colonial times to the present*. Boston: South End Press.

Amott, T. L., and J. A. Matthaei. (1991). *Race, gender, and work: A multicultural economic history of women in the United States*. Boston: South End Press.

Anderson, E. A., and R. C. Hula, eds. (1991). *The reconstruction of family policy*. Westport, CT: Greenwood Press.

Berry, M. F. (1993). *The politics of parenthood: Child care, women's rights, and the myth of the good mother*. New York: Viking.

Blankenhorn, D., S. Bayme, and J. B. Elshtain, eds. (1990). *Rebuilding the nest*. Milwaukee: Family Service America.

Bremner, R. H., ed. (1970, 1971, 1974). *Children and youth in America: A documentary history* (Vol. 1: 1600–1865; Vol. 2: 1866–1932; Vol. 3: 1933–1973). Cambridge, MA: Harvard University Press.

Bronfenbrenner, U. (1979). *The ecology of human development: Experiments by nature and design*. Cambridge, MA: Harvard University Press.

Center for the Study of Social Policy. (1993). *Kids Count data book: State profiles of child well-being*. Greenwich, CT: The Annie E. Casey Foundation.

Cherlin, A. J., ed. (1988). *The changing American family and public policy*. Washington, DC: Urban Institute Press.

Children's Defense Fund. (1992). *The state of America's children 1992*. Washington, DC: Author.

Coontz, S. (1992). *The way we never were: American families and the nostalgia trap*. New York: Basic Books.

Costin, L., and C. A. Rapp. (1984). *Child welfare policies and practice*. New York: McGraw Hill.

Demos, J. (1986). *Past, present, and personal: The family and the life course in American history*. New York: Oxford University Press.

Edelman, M. W. (1987). *Families in peril: An agenda for social change.* Cambridge, MA: Harvard University Press.

Elkind, D. (In press). *The postmodern family.* Cambridge, MA: Harvard University Press.

Ellwood, D. T. (1988). *Poor support: Poverty in the American family.* New York: Basic Books.

Gallagher, J. J., R. L. Trohanis, and R. M. Clifford, eds. (1989). *Policy implementation & P.L. 99–457: Planning for young children with special needs.* Baltimore: Paul H. Brookes.

Garfinkel, I., and S. McLanahan. (1986). *Single mothers and their children: A new American dilemma.* Washington, DC: Urban Institute Press.

Giddings, P. (1984). *When and where I enter: The impact of black women on race and sex in America.* New York: William Morrow.

Glazer, N. (1988). *The limits of social policy.* Cambridge, MA: Harvard University Press.

Goldscheider, F. K., and L. J. Waite. (1991). *New families, no families? The transformation of the American home.* Berkeley, CA: University of California Press.

Goldstein, J., A. Freud, and A. J. Solnit. (1979). *Before the best interests of the child.* New York: Free Press.

Gordon, L. (1988). *Heroes of their own lives: The politics and history of family violence.* New York: Viking Penguin.

———, ed. (1990). *Women, the state, and welfare.* Madison, WI: University of Wisconsin Press.

Grubb, W. N., and M. Lazerson. (1982). *Broken promises: How Americans fail their children.* New York: Basic Books.

Gustaitis, R., and E. W. D. Young. (1986). *A time to be born, a time to die: Conflicts and ethics in an intensive care nursery.* Reading, MA: Addison Wesley.

Hayes, C. D., ed. (1982). *Making policies for children: A case study of the federal process.* Washington, DC: National Academy Press.

Hayes, C. D., J. L. Palmer, and M. J. Zaslow, eds. (1990). *Who cares for America's children? Child care policy for the 1990s.* Washington, DC: National Academy Press.

Hobbs, N., J. Perrin, and S. Ireys. (1986). *Chronically ill children and their families.* San Francisco: Jossey-Bass.

Hyde, J. S., and M. J. Essex, eds. (1991). *Parental leave and child care: Setting a research and policy agenda.* Philadelphia, PA: Temple University Press.

Institute of Medicine/National Academy of Sciences. (1989). *Mobilizing against AIDS.* Cambridge, MA: Harvard University Press.

Jencks, C. (1992). *Rethinking social policy: Race, poverty and the underclass.* Cambridge, MA: Harvard University Press.

Jewell, K. S. (1988). *Survival of the black family: The institutional impact of U.S. social policy.* New York: Praeger.

Jones, J. (1985). *Labor of love, labor of sorrow: Black women, work and the family, from slavery to the present.* New York: Basic Books.

Kagan, S., D. R. Powell, B. Weissbourd, and E. F. Zigler, eds. (1987). *America's family support programs.* New Haven, CT: Yale University Press.

Kamerman, S. B., and A. J. Kahn, eds. (1978). *Family policy: Government and families in fourteen countries.* New York: Columbia University Press.

———. (1987). *The responsive workplace: Employers and a changing labor force.* New York: Columbia University Press.

Kamerman, S. B., A. J. Kahn, and P. Kingston. (1983). *Maternity policies and working women.* New York: Columbia University Press.

Katz, M. B. (1986). *In the shadow of the poorhouse: A social history of welfare in America.* New York: Basic Books.

―――. (1989). *The undeserving poor: From the War on Poverty to the war on welfare.* New York: Pantheon.

Kessler-Harris, A. (1982). *Out to work: A history of wage-earning women in the United States.* New York: Oxford University Press.

Koop, C. E. (1986). *Surgeon General's report on Acquired Immune Deficiency Syndrome.* Washington, DC: U.S. Department of Health and Human Services.

Kotlowitz, A. (1991). *There are no children here: The story of two boys growing up in the other America.* New York: Anchor Books.

Kozol, J. (1988). *Rachel and her children.* New York: Fawcett Columbine.

Lasch, C. (1977). *Haven in a heartless world: The family besieged.* New York: Basic Books.

Liebow, E. (1993). *Tell them who I am.* New York: Free Press.

Lyon, J. (1985). *Playing God in the nursery.* New York: W.W. Norton.

Machiarola, F., and A. Gartner, eds. (1989). *Caring for America's children.* New York: Academy of Political Science.

Matthaei, J. A. (1982). *An economic history of women in America: Women's work, the sexual division of labor, and the development of capitalism.* New York: Schocken Books.

Meisels, S. J., and J. Shonkoff, eds. (1990). *Handbook of early childhood intervention.* Cambridge: Cambridge University Press.

Miller, G., ed. (1989). *Giving children a chance: The case for more effective national policies.* Washington, DC: The Center for National Policy Press.

Molnar, J., T. Klein, J. Knitzer, and B. Ortis-Torres. (1988). *Home is where the heart is: The crisis of homeless children and families in New York City.* New York: Bank Street College of Education.

Moroney, R. (1986). *Shared responsibility: Families and social policy.* Hawthorne, NY: Aldine de Gruyter.

Moynihan, D. P. (1987). *Family and nation.* San Diego: Harcourt Brace Jovanovich.

National Commission on Children. (1991). *Beyond rhetoric: A new American agenda for children and families.* Washington, DC: U.S. Government Printing Office.

Nelson, B. J. (1984). *Making an issue of child abuse.* Chicago: University of Chicago Press.

Ohlin, L., and M. Tonry, eds. (1989). *Family violence.* Chicago: University of Chicago Press.

Popenoe, D. (1988). *Disturbing the nest: Family change and decline in modern societies.* Hawthorne, NY: Aldine de Gruyter.

Platt, A. M. (1977). *The child savers: The invention of delinquency.* Chicago: University of Chicago Press.

Prothrow-Stith, D., and M. Weissman. (1991). *Deadly consequences.* New York: HarperCollins.

Reed, W., ed. (1990). *Assessment of the status of African-Americans.* Boston: William Monroe Trotter Institute, University of Massachusetts at Boston.

Schorr, L. (1988). *Within our reach: Breaking the cycle of disadvantage.* New York: Doubleday.

Schwartz, I. M., ed. (1992). *Juvenile justice and public policy.* New York: Lexington Books.

Sidel, R. (1986). *Women and children last: The plight of poor women in affluent America.* New York: Viking.

Steiner, G.Y. (1976). *The children's cause.* Washington, DC: Brookings Institution.

―――. (1981). *The futility of family policy.* Washington, DC: Brookings Institution.

Strober, M., and S. Dornbusch, eds. (1988). *Feminism, children, and the new families.* New York: Guilford Press.

Vogel, L. (1993). *Mothers on the job: Maternity policy in the U.S. workplace*. New Brunswick, NJ: Rutgers University Press.

Weiss, H. B., and F. H. Jacobs, eds. (1988). *Evaluating family programs*. Hawthorne, NY: Aldine de Gruyter.

Weitzman, L. (1985). *The divorce revolution: The unexpected social and economic consequences for women and children in America*. New York: Free Press.

West, C. (1993). *Race matters*. Boston: Beacon Press.

Whitebook, M., C. Howes, and D. Phillips. (1989). *Who cares? Child care teachers and the quality of care in America*. National Child Care Staffing Study. Oakland, CA: Child Care Employee Project.

Whittaker, J. K., J. Kinney, E. M. Tracy, and C. Booth, eds. (1990). *Reaching high-risk families: Intensive family preservation in human services*. New York: Aldine de Gruyter.

Willer, B., ed. (1990). *Reaching the full cost of quality in early childhood programs*. Washington, DC: National Association for the Education of Young Children.

Wilson, W. J. (1987). *The truly disadvantaged: The inner city, the underclass, and public policy*. Chicago: University of Chicago Press.

Wright, J. D. (1989). *Address unknown: The homeless in America*. Hawthorne, NY: Aldine de Gruyter.

Yllo, K., and M. Bograd, eds. (1988). *Feminist perspectives on wife abuse*. Newbury Park, CA: Sage Publications.

Zelizer, V. (1985). *Pricing the priceless child: The changing social value of children*. New York: Basic Books.

Zigler, E. F., and M. Frank, eds. (1988). *The parental leave crisis: Toward a national policy*. New Haven, CT: Yale University Press.

Zigler, E. F., S. L. Kagan, and E. Klugman, eds. (1983). *Children, families, and government: Perspectives on American social policy*. Cambridge: Cambridge University Press.

Zigler, E. F., and S. J. Styfco, eds. (1993). *Head Start and beyond: A national plan for extended childhood intervention*. New Haven, CT: Yale University Press.

Zimmerman, S. (1988). *Understanding family policy: Theoretical approaches*. Newbury Park, CA: Sage Publications.

———. (1992). *Family policies and family well-being: The role of political culture*. Newbury Park, CA: Sage Publications.

Index

Aaron and Lillie Straus Foundation, 129
Abortion, 188, 198
Act for Better Child Care (ABC–1987), 99, 100, 109, 255
Adoption, 75
Adoption Assistance and Child Welfare Act (1980), 77, 79
African-Americans: care system for, 79; community values of, 269; family values of, 266–67; homelessness among, 268; needs of, 292 n.25; in orphanages, 78
Agrarian economy, and industrialization, 44
AIDS: and family policy, 80, 81–82; prevention methods, 212, 218; reported cases of, 213
AIDS education programs: availability of, 207; components of, 214–17; considerations of, 267; elementary-school level of, 217; endorsement of, 283; factors critical to, 217–20; funding of, 235 n.105; implementation analysis of, 220–26; racial component of, 269; and sexuality education, 229–30; at state level, 281; success factors, 208–9. *See also* Cambridge, Massachusetts; Health education
Aid to Dependent Children (ADC), 67, 79
Aid to Families with Dependent Children (AFDC), 67, 75, 267; children under, 77; decreasing use of, 81; and foster

care, 79; inadequacy of, 57; real value of, 11, 23
Almshouses, 49, 80; conditions in, 69, 70; as family aid, 67–68
American Academy of Pediatrics, 184, 188
Annie E. Casey Foundation, 29 n.44
Apprenticeship, 66
Atlanta, Georgia: homeless policy in, 154–58, 169, 170; homeless population in, 172
Atlanta Task Force for the Homeless (ATFH), 154, 156, 157, 158, 166, 170

Baby Doe: medical decisions for, 179–80; public awareness of, 181–82; response to, 182–83, 184–85, 187, 188; similar cases to, 182
Baby Doe laws, 271, 284; best interests issue in, 194–96; and bureaucracy, 190–91; case study methodology, 180–81; compromises in, 184–85; court order for, 204 n.91; funding for, 191; impact of, 196–97, 198–99; implementation of, 186–96, 198; language of, 189–90; provisions of, 179–80, 185–86; and referrals, 191; value base for, 192–96; violation of, 186
Baby Jane Doe, as test case, 183–85
Bassuk, E. L., 152
Battered-child syndrome, 81

Contributors

Cherilyn E. Davidson, Ph.D., is currently a post-doctoral fellow in child psychotherapy at the Reiss-Davis Child Study Center in Los Angeles. In addition to the work presented here, her research foci include the intergenerational transmission of risk and resilience in high-risk families and its implications for intervention and policy formulation.

Margery W. Davies, Ph.D., is a Research Associate at the Center for Applied Child Development in the Eliot-Pearson Department of Child Study, and the administrator of the Community Health Program, both at Tufts University. She has done research for many years on women and work, with special attention recently to the work of caring for children. She is the author of *Woman's Place Is at the Typewriter: Office Work and Office Workers, 1870–1930* (1982).

Robert B. Griffith, M.A., currently attends Lesley College, where he is earning an M.A. in Elementary Education, and works with adult mental health clients as a residential counselor.

Bonnie Hausman, Ph.D., is Associate Director of The Better Homes Foundation, a research and grant-making organization devoted to developing effective program models for homeless families. Dr. Hausman was Senior Research Associate at the Harvard Family Research Project, where she completed this analysis of state-sponsored family support programs. Her most recent publication, in the *American Journal of Orthopsychiatry*, examines the issues of parenting and homelessness.

Lucy Hudson, M.A., has spent the last ten years in the field of child care, directing a multicultural child care center in Cambridge, Massachusetts, working at the Massachusetts Office for Children as the Child Care Affordability Project Director, and coordinating research for *Embracing Our Future*, a report issued by the Boston

Foundation on child care in the city of Boston. Most recently she has been the Project Director of the Massachusetts Trial Court Child Care Project, for which she wrote *CourtCare: Policy Guidelines and an Operating Plan for Child Care in the Courts*.

Francine H. Jacobs, Ed.D., is Associate Professor with a joint appointment in the Eliot-Pearson Department of Child Study and the Department of Urban and Environmental Policy at Tufts University. Her research and teaching interests are in child and family policy—child welfare, child care, family support—and in program evaluation, particularly of community-based organizations. She currently is on leave from Tufts at the Center for the Study of Social Policy, Washington, D.C., directing its National Child Welfare Research Center. Her 1988 volume, *Evaluating Family Programs*, was co-edited with Heather Weiss.

Katharine Karr Kaitin, M.S., has a background in political science and child study. Her research interests include the impact of workplace and social policies on the American family structure.

Priscilla M. D. Little, M.A., has a continuing interest in family policy issues, including those that affect homeless families.

Martha Pott, Ph.D., currently researches and writes about parent-child relationships and child and family policy. Previously, she worked for public and private agencies serving at-risk, disabled, and abused children and their families.

Susan Latts Vlodaver, M.A., is currently a policy analyst for the Commission on Reform and Efficiency at the State of Minnesota. Over the past few years, she has conducted research in the areas of public finance and family policy. Previously she was a head teacher in an early childhood program.

ISBN 0-86569-223-8

90000>

EAN

9 780865 692237

HARDCOVER BAR CODE